2 APR 77

THE ISRAELI ARMY

THE ISRAELI ARMY

EDWARD LUTTWAK AND DAN HOROWITZ

1817

HARPER & ROW PUBLISHERS
New York, Evanston, San Francisco, London

FIRST U.S. EDITION

Library of Congress Cataloging in Publication Data

Luttwak, Edward.
  The Israeli Army.
  Includes index.
  1. Israel—Armed Forces. I. Horowitz, Dan, joint author. II. Title.
UA853.I8L87 1975   355'.0095694   73-14270
ISBN 0-06-012723-6

75 76 77 78 79 10 9 8 7 6 5 4 3 2 1

Contents

Lists of Maps and Diagrams

List of Plates

Introduction

Written between 1968 and 1973, begun in the aftermath of a great victory and completed at a time of renewed war, this book is an attempt to explain the phenomenon of the Israeli Army.* There is much to explain. In the span of a single generation, a people that once had no soldiers has become a nation *of* soldiers, creating in the process an Army which, in 1973, sent into battle the third largest tank force and the sixth largest air force in the Western world. Unlike almost all other new armies, the Israeli Army did not grow out of colonial regiments nor did it receive its military expertise ready-made from foreign instructors as its neighbours have done and are still doing. Instead, through trial and error, through experimentation and debate, the Israelis have taught themselves virtually everything they know, from basic infantry skills to the intricacies of air combat. Sometimes very advanced and highly effective, sometimes merely different, and in some cases perhaps backward, the Army's doctrines, tactics and structures are all the original creations of the Israelis themselves, a nation of 650,000 in 1948 and even now fewer than three million. Among the lesser powers this is a unique achievement.

Though loosely chronological, this book is neither a history of the Israeli Army nor a history of Israel's wars. Its central focus is on the men and ideas that have shaped Israeli defence since the beginning. Men who first appear in these pages as young guerrillas in 1941 emerge as the leaders of the field battalions that fought in 1948; they reappear as brigade commanders in 1956 and as the generals of what had become a modern army in 1967. The man

* Throughout the text, *A*rmy capitalized stands for the armed forces as a whole, whose official title is Zvah Haganah LeIsrael, officially translated as Israel Defence Forces (I.D.F.); *a*rmy in lower case stands for the ground forces, as opposed to air and naval forces.

who led the crossing of the Suez Canal in 1973, fighting in the vanguard of his own division, is first introduced in these pages two decades earlier as the leader of a band of commandos.

Another kind of continuity is evident in the primacy of ideas over traditions. From the ideological controversies of the 1930s, when there was passionate debate over the exact limits of legitimate self-defence, to the controversies of the 1950s, when air force men and tank enthusiasts were contesting the predominance of the infantry, and in the strategic debates of the 1960s innovation and change were frequently opposed but not by the dead weight of ingrained tradition. The Israelis had no real military traditions of their own and neither did they import others' traditions as virtually all post-colonial armies have done. Created in the midst of war out of an underground militia, many of whose men had been trained 'in cellars with wooden pistols', the Israeli Army has evolved very rapidly under the relentless pressure of a bitter and protracted conflict. Instead of the quiet acceptance of doctrine and tradition, witnessed in the case of most other armies, the growth of the Israeli Army has been marked by a turmoil of innovation, controversy and debate. If the outcome of the 1973 War will be a further wave of radical reforms in doctrines, forces and tactics, this would merely conform to the pattern established since 1948: the imposition of formal military discipline after the War of Independence, the rise of the paratrooper school of combat in the fifties, the emergence of an autonomous all-fighter air force, the victory of the tank enthusiasts' approach to land warfare, and later the ill-fated acceptance of a static defence for the Sinai, were all drastic innovations accomplished amidst intense controversy and wide-ranging debate. In the last analysis, the formal authority of superior rank was indispensable to implement change but it never sufficed by itself to decide the issue.

Much of the book is concerned with these political, strategic and tactical debates whose results have shaped the growth of the Army.

From the dissolution of the elite Palmach striking forces of the War of Independence, whose tactics and morale were exemplary but whose politics were suspect, to the choice of successive Chiefs of Staff until the present day, party politics have consistently intruded in the workings of the Army and of the defence establishment as a whole. While among its neighbours the military frequently dominate civilian political life, in Israel it has always been the other way around. This unfortunate legacy of the days of the underground – and a direct reflection of the extreme politicization of Israeli life – is a further theme of this book, though the treatment of this complex subject is more episodic than systematic.

Of the many ironies of Israeli life, none is more significant than the sharp contrast between the near-pacifism of the founding fathers and the military preoccupations of modern Israel. Forced step by step into an ever-greater defensive effort to cope with a widening circle of enmity, beginning with the Palestinians and now including the entire Arab world forcefully supported by the Soviet Union, the Israelis have been transformed into a nation of soldiers. When fully mobilized, the Army includes within its ranks virtually all able-bodied men and many women. Army and society are thus reflections of one another, and this book is in a sense a study of Israeli society at war. Here too there is a paradox since Israel's exceedingly militarized society is not militaristic. The ethos of militarism – the glorification of war and the celebration of martial virtues – is absent from Israeli life as is its substance, the corporate political control of society by the military. As the events of 1973 showed, Israel could well have benefited from a touch of militarism; in the wake of the October war there was widespread gloom and pessimism among the Israelis even though their losses amounted to less than one-tenth of one per cent of the population (as opposed to one per cent in 1948), and even though it was Israeli troops that stood on the approaches to two Arab capitals and not the other way round. During the fighting, the anguished sensitivity to casualties shared by the public and the Army command alike acted as a powerful brake on the pace of military operations. After the war, with half the Syrian army destroyed and part of the Egyptian encircled, and with further net territorial gains on both fronts, Israeli despondency over the loss of fewer than three thousand killed and a desperate concern for a hundred or so prisoners held in Syria, undermined Israel's bargaining position in the initial round of post-war negotiations. However praiseworthy on humanitarian grounds, these counter-militaristic attitudes act as a further and self-imposed constraint on Israeli security policy, which is already severely hampered by the country's small size and its diplomatic isolation.

The book includes a detailed study of the strategy and tactics of the 1967 War, primarily because it was only then that the Army briefly emerged before receding again into the darkness of security restrictions. It also includes an analysis of the 1973 War which subjected many of the post-1967 concepts to the ultimate test of combat. In neither case has the attempt been made to write a definitive account of the fighting; in particular the Arab side is treated only incidentally.

The final chapter on the October war requires an explanatory note of its own. When the war began the text was otherwise completed; a further chapter was added to cover the lessons of the war but it was decided to leave the pre-1973 text unchanged. Since this is a book of analysis, and since the authors have views of their own, they did not hesitate to endorse one side or the other in the internal debates discussed in the text. As a result, in some cases, notably the 'armour debate', the authors will be found supporting tactics and methods that were invalidated in the October war. The record has not been altered but footnotes appended to the text refer the reader to relevant parts of the final chapter where the issues discussed earlier are re-examined in the light of the events of the October war and where, if needed, a *mea culpa* is duly registered.

Much of the documentation that would normally be used for a book of this kind was not available for publication. No detailed official histories have been published for any of Israel's wars, not even for the War of Independence whose secrets must by now be obsolete. The authors have therefore been forced to rely in large measure on personal sources, memoirs, journalistic accounts and data published outside Israel and beyond the reach of censorship. Needless to say such materials can only be used with great care and every effort has been made to correct political bias and sheer error. No particular claim of objectivity is made as far as the Arab-Israeli conflict is concerned; fortunately the rights and wrongs of the conflict have no bearing on the essential theme of this book which is the Army and its evolution.

Purists will find that the transliterations from Hebrew and Arabic used in the text are not always consistent; where the prescribed form would have been unintelligible to non-specialists, simpler and more readable versions have been given. Similarly, in some cases current rather than technically correct place names have been used, e.g., the Heitan defile is here described as the Mitla pass. Every attempt has been made to give correct unit and weapon designations but here too security restrictions sometimes made precision very difficult.

The same restrictions prevent the authors from acknowledging the help of many of their most valuable sources of information and advice. All must therefore be left equally anonymous.

1

Origins

The Army of Israel was established by decree on 26 May 1948, twelve days after the Declaration of Independence.[1] This was a formality. The creation of the Army had preceded and made possible the birth of the new State, whose allotted territory was invaded by the regular forces of five Arab states on the first day of its independence. By the time Israel's provisional Government issued Order No. 4 to give it a legal basis, a Jewish army had already been fighting for six months in the chaotic battles and bloody guerrilla raids that would decide the fate of Palestine. With the loss of 4,017 soldiers and two thousand civilians killed, almost one per cent of the population, the Jews ensured the survival of their State and enlarged its territory in thirteen months of sporadic warfare.[2] For the Israelis it is the 'War of Independence' or 'War of Liberation'; the Arabs still describe it as the 'Disaster of 1948'.

When the fighting began in December 1947, most of the men and women of the Jewish volunteer force, the Haganah, had received a total of fifty days of military training or less, and their heaviest weapons were eighty-four medium mortars. The Haganah did not have a single tank or combat aircraft. For six months the Jews and Arabs of Palestine fought a guerrilla war of ambushes and street battles which slowly spread from area to area as the British gradually evacuated Palestine. Although the Palestinians also had no heavy weapons, and fought in disorganized village bands, the Jews did not defeat them until the eve of the Arab invasions which began as soon as the British formally relinquished responsibility for Palestine on 15 May 1948. By then the Jews had built up their forces into nine light brigades in addition to the local defence groups of every Jewish town and village but they still had no artillery, armour or an air force. To contain the invasions, the Jews fought a series of desperate defensive battles in May and June 1948. The southern half of the country, the Negev desert, was cut off by the Egyptian advance that reached within thirty miles of Tel Aviv; the Old City of Jerusalem was lost to the Jordanians, and several outlying border villages were conquered by the Syrians and Lebanese.

But in the following six months the military balance was transformed. With weapons smuggled in from the scrapyards of Europe and America, with fighting units set up in weeks, days or in at least one case, literally overnight, with immigrant refugees and with volunteer veterans of the wartime Allied forces, but chiefly with self-taught soldiers and commanders born and bred in Palestine, the Jews had created a war-winning Army of twelve mobile brigades, supported by artillery, light armour and an air force; this was a notable achievement for a nation of 650,000 which received no foreign military aid, had no heavy industry or ready source of arms, and had no tradition of successful war since the days of David and Solomon. The brilliant and chaotic improvisations that forged the Israeli Army in the midst of war would not have been possible without decades of slow preparation.

The origins of the Army, like those of many other Israeli institutions, can be traced back to a wave of immigration from Russia and Poland which, between 1904 and the outbreak of the First World War, brought 30,000 Jews to Palestine, then part of the Ottoman Empire. The newcomers were not the first Jews to return to Zion. Orthodox Jews had been coming for centuries to pray and die in the traditional religious centres of Jerusalem, Safed and Tiberias; living on petty trade and charity collected in Europe, the Orthodox had slowly increased in numbers as communications with Europe improved. By the mid-nineteenth century they already constituted a majority of the population of Jerusalem. From the 1880s the first Zionists arrived in the country; unlike the Orthodox they tried to create a living community, and by the end of the century they had established farming villages in Galilee and the Plain of Sharon with the financial help of wealthy European Jews.

When the new wave of Zionists began to arrive after 1904, there were already fifty thousand Jews in Palestine but the newcomers had little in common with the Orthodox or with the first Zionist settlers. They were socialists, young men and women who had abandoned the strict religious observance typical of Eastern European Jews, and who were deeply influenced by the secret revolutionary movements of Tsarist Russia. Every shade of socialist ideology was represented among these Labour-Zionists, marxist and non-marxist, nationalist and internationalist, revolutionary and non-violent, but they all believed in the need to combine the physical reclamation of the Land of Israel with the social rehabilitation of the Jewish people.

Eastern European Jewry was not only persecuted and dependent, as were all the communities of the Diaspora, but also impoverished. The industrial revolution had disrupted the fossilized economy of the Jewish townships whose handicraft could no longer be sold and whose primitive transport and credit services were being displaced by railroads and modern banking houses. In Western Europe the Jews rose into the middle classes but in Eastern Europe only a minority did so. In their traditional caftans, full beards and side-locks, the majority of Eastern European Jews found no place in the intensely nationalistic middle classes of Russia and Poland. Instead they were herded into the new factories and industrial workshops or remained to live in increasing misery in the traditional townships; the most fortunate emigrated to Western Europe or America. Always endemic, violent anti-semitism erupted in mass pogroms, often encouraged by the Tsarist regime. The rising tide of exclusive nationalism that was to destroy the Austrian Empire, and which the Tsarist regime hoped to guide, had found in the Jews its most convenient target.

The Labour-Zionists had a diagnosis and a cure for the Jewish problem. In their view, the miserable condition of Eastern European Jewry was due to its lack of a solid working class based in a national homeland. Since, as they believed, the Land of Israel had become a wilderness of desert and swamp, the two requirements of their solution to the Jewish problem could be combined: the Jews would redeem the land by 'colonizing the desert'* and draining the swamps, forming a genuine working class of manual labourers in the process. When the newcomers discovered that Palestine was not an empty land, they came to believe that there was room enough for both Arabs and Jews.

The first Zionists employed Arab labourers to till the lands of their villages; only a minority did manual work. Although they were mostly the children of urban middle-class families, the new wave of Labour-Zionists saw manual work not only as a social necessity prescribed by their ideological beliefs but also as an ideal in itself. They had the zeal of true believers but no experience of farming or heavy labour of any kind; they were utterly unprepared for the harsh climate, the endemic malaria and the Asiatic squalor of Palestine. Within a few years a majority of the newcomers returned to Europe, migrated to America or died of sickness and malnutrition. Those who stayed and lived, a few thousand at most, became the founders of modern Israel. Forty years later, one of their number, David Ben Gurion, labourer, trade union organizer, party leader, community spokesman and finally Prime Minister, read the Declaration of Independence in a Tel Aviv museum on 15 May 1948. Others founded the collective settlements, the kibbutzim, the cooperative villages, the moshavim, the trade unions, and the trade union council, the Histadrut, which by the 1930s operated a network of health clinics, pension funds, industrial enterprises and commercial cooperatives, all run on socialist lines. Dreamers and ideologues, addicted to endless political debate and constantly preoccupied by the personal and party rivalries of Zionist micro-politics, the Labour-Zionists were also hard-working, indifferent to personal gain (though eager to accumulate personal power) and, above all, farsighted. Although successive waves of immigration brought a majority of non-Socialist Jews to the country after the 1920s, most of them refugees who came because of dire necessity and not because of ideals, the Labour-Zionists remained the motor and brain of the Jewish community, the Yishuv, guided its evolution into statehood, and controlled its destiny thereafter. It is only in the last decade that the veteran leaders of Ben Gurion's generation finally relinquished their key posts in the State, the Histadrut and the economy.

The Labour-Zionists began as penniless labourers in the orchards and vineyards of Ottoman Palestine and lived to see their dreams come true, but they failed in one crucial respect. From the beginning of their endeavour they came into conflict with the Arabs as neither the Orthodox nor the first non-socialist Zionists had done: the Labour-Zionists provoked a nationalist reaction among the Arabs that enveloped the Yishuv in hostility and denied peace to the new State. The young men and women who arrived from Russia full of ideology and hope were the very opposite of the *colons* of colonial Africa. Far from wanting to exploit Arab labour for low wages, they wanted to become manual labourers themselves; when the Labour-Zionists founded their kibbutzim, wage labour of any kind was barred as exploitative. Instead of the *colons*' racial contempt, the newcomers admired their Arab fellow-workers and tried to emulate their skill at farm work, their stamina and their simple tastes. But the pioneers' sense of social solidarity with the Arab masses did nothing to assuage the hostility of Arab labourers who lost their jobs when Labour-Zionists took their place on Jewish farms. They also aroused the hostility of Arab landlords and merchants by preaching socialism to the *fellahin* and trying to organize them into unions, and they scandalized all Arabs by their communal living and the immodest dress of their women. Later, the insistence of the Labour-Zionists on 'self-labour' had the unintended effect of displacing entire villages of Arab peasants whose absentee landlords sold their lands to collective farms, without making any provision for their dispossessed tenants. At first, the Labour-Zionists ignored the potential for conflict with the Arabs; later, they persuaded themselves that social progress and economic development would eradicate the causes of strife. In a socialist Palestine, Arabs and Jews could live side by side in a secular and egalitarian society where proletarian solidarity would outweigh nationalist sentiments. Finally, when Arab hostility erupted in riots in the 1920s, communal strife in the 1930s, and then open war in the 1940s, the Labour-Zionists came to believe that the restoration of Israel and the provision of shelter for persecuted Jews took precedence over Arab rights.

In the beginning, there was a strong pacifist strain in the Labour-Zionists' ideology. The harsh conditions of the Yishuv soon eroded this sentiment but even so the Labour-Zionists opposed the use of force by the Jewish community except for self-defence. As late as 1936 the movement was riven by sharp controversy over the exact limits of permissible self-defence, at a time when Arab guerrilla bands were attacking Jewish settlements all over Palestine. It was not until the summer of 1948 that the conquest and permanent occupation of Arab towns and villages became an accepted means of warfare; even today, undertones of pacifism persist though Israel has become a nation of part-time soldiers and the Army is the central institution of the State.

The transition was gradual, as was the intensification of the conflict. Each stage induced a change in attitudes towards the use of force, and a corresponding change in the nature and scope of Jewish military action. One of the first steps was the formation of a society of professional armed guards by a small group of young Labour-Zionists. There was no political conflict as yet but the Jews, like the Arabs, had to contend with the lawlessness of the Ottoman Empire in decadence.[3] Robberies, village land wars, blood feuds and Bedouin raids were commonplace in Palestine. Jewish farmers, like wealthier Arabs, hired Arab or Bedouin guards to protect their lives and property, but the Labour-Zionists insisted on self-reliance in defence as well as labour and in April 1909 they formed Hashomer ('The Watchman') whose members set out to protect Jewish villages.[4]

Combining the elitism of a secret society, on the pattern of the Russian revolutionary underground, with a romantic emulation of the traditional fighting skills of the Bedouins and Circassians, the young members of Hashomer learned to ride and shoot, wore Bedouin dress and did their best to shed their urban middle-class habits, copying the mannerisms of the desert warriors. Most Jewish farmers refused to employ the members of Hashomer, which remained very small, numbering less than one hundred at its peak.[5] Hashomer, nevertheless, created a legend and set a precedent of armed self-defence in the Labour-Zionist movement.

While the Turks still ruled Palestine the scope of Jewish immigration, land settlement and political organization was strictly limited; the Ottoman authorities had no intention of allowing the growth of a powerful Jewish community in Palestine. By the same token, Arab hostility and fear, and the nascent force of Arab nationalism, were subdued. The First World War changed the situation of the Yishuv for the worse; the Turks correctly suspected the Jews of collaborating with the British, whose forces were to invade Palestine in 1917; many Labour-Zionists left the country and others were deported and even the quiet non-political Zionists were harassed by the Turkish authorities.

Following the British conquest of Palestine in the winter of 1917, old and new settlers returned to the Yishuv (there was a Jewish battalion in General Allenby's army) which was now about to acquire a recognized political status. Under the terms of the Balfour Declaration, a formal promise issued by the British Foreign Secretary Lord Balfour on behalf of his government, the British were committed to assisting the Zionist movement in its endeavour to create a 'National Home' in Palestine. The product of genuine sympathy on the part of men such as Balfour and Churchill, of exaggerated notions of the influence of the Zionists in Europe and America, and of skilful propaganda and diplomacy by Zionist leaders in Britain, the Balfour Declaration nevertheless explicitly reserved the rights of the Arabs, and made no mention of political independence for the Jews, then or in the future. Further, until 1922* Palestine was ruled by a military government which did nothing to implement the Declaration. But Arab fear of a Jewish conquest by immigration and land-settlement under the aegis of British rule was understandably intense. In 1920 there were mob attacks against Orthodox Jews in the Old City of Jerusalem, isolated villages in Galilee came under siege. In 1921 and 1922 there were fresh outbreaks. Many among the British began to doubt the wisdom of the Declaration; the crescendo of Arab militancy and British appeasement that was to characterize the twenty-six years of British rule had begun.[6]

The Yishuv was unprepared for the new political threat. The small Hashomer no longer functioned and was in any case outmoded as an instrument for Jewish defence. Instead of forming small secret societies, the pioneers of the Labour-Zionist movement, high school students in Haifa and Tel Aviv, farmers in the villages, newly-arrived immigrants (including many First World War veterans), set up overt defence units manned by part-time volunteers in the towns and villages of the Yishuv.[7] At the end of

---

* The 'National Home' was formally inaugurated in 1922 when Palestine became a League of Nations Mandate administered by a British civilian administration under the authority of the Foreign Office. The first High Commissioner was Lord Samuel, a non-Zionist British Jew, who tried to conciliate the Arabs and who disappointed the Jews in their unrealistic hopes of British benevolence.

1920 delegates of the little parties and unions of the Labour-Zionist movement, each with a few hundred members or less, convened an all-party conference to form a trade union federation, the Histadrut,* as a roof organization for multi-party action; one of the first tasks assigned to the organizing committee was to merge the local defence groups into a country-wide militia, the Haganah.[8]

The growth of the Yishuv during the twenties was much slower than the Jews had hoped and the Arabs had feared; at the end of the post-war wave of immigration there were still only 120,000 Jews in Palestine. Arab fears were assuaged, attacks on Jews ceased and the Haganah became a moribund paper organization. Nevertheless, the Labour-Zionists consolidated their organizing endeavour even though their chronic factional and ideological disputes continued unabated.[9] The kibbutzim settled down to farm work and land reclamation, the cooperative villages, the moshavim, were becoming viable economic entities, and the Histadrut set up its first clinics and producer cooperatives. The experiments and expedients of the pre-war period now became functioning institutions, though they were still heavily dependent on donations from Zionists abroad. The gates of Zion were open but the Jews did not come. Only a minority of world Jewry belonged to the Zionist movement or actively supported its aims, and a still smaller proportion was affiliated to the rival parties in the socialist wing of the movement; religious Zionists, including the moderate Orthodox, formed their own political parties as did the secular non-socialists. All these small parties and factions were represented on the elected councils of the World Zionist Organization which raised funds, conducted propaganda and tried to enlist support for development and immigration. In the Yishuv, the W.Z.O. had an executive arm in the Jewish Agency, to which the British accorded a semi-official status; the Agency bought lands, financed kibbutzim, moshavim and non-party villages, supported schools and the Hebrew University, and generally acted as a community government. For a parliament the Yishuv had an elected National Council (Va'ad Leumi) in which all the micro-parties of Palestinian Jewry were represented.[10]

---

* The full name is *Histadrut Haklalit shel Haovdim Haivriim* (General Federation of Jewish Workers). It was founded on 9 December 1920.[8]

In 1929 the long peace of the twenties came to an end. The traditional leaders of the Arab community, the land-owning clans of Jerusalem, Nablus and Hebron, were forming alliances with landlords and village heads throughout Palestine in a competitive bid for power. Having blocked British-inspired attempts to form an Arab counterpart to the National Council of the Jews, and opposed the formation of modern political parties, the major clans were trying to extend their influence beyond their traditional spheres; they soon came into conflict with each other. The Husseini family, whose head was the politically astute Mufti of Jerusalem, a man originally appointed by the First High Commissioner, Lord Samuel, was in the van of this political struggle. In the circumstances it was inevitable that the clans should activate the Zionist issue; immigration had begun to increase, Arab lands were again being sold to Jews. Arab–Jewish relations had never recovered from the post-war disorders although at a personal and commercial level they could still be cordial, as they are to this day.

In the summer of 1929 Husseini agitators triggered a series of mob attacks against Orthodox Jews in Jerusalem which spread to other parts of the country; in Hebron sixty-five Orthodox families were massacred. The Yishuv was alarmed, disappointed at the British failure to protect Jewish lives, and utterly unprepared. The Haganah had received very little money from the Histadrut (its annual budget was under two thousand pounds sterling); there were few weapons and no organized training or leadership. Its local branches were run by a few volunteers who tried to keep up the membership rolls and assemble the infrequent meetings. Lacking the resources that were obviously needed, the Labour-Zionists agreed to hand over responsibility for the Haganah to the Jewish Agency. In the politically highly charged atmosphere of the Yishuv even the common defence could not be apolitical; the Haganah came under the supervision of a five-man committee with two Labour and two non-socialist party representatives and a neutral chairman.[11] With Agency funds, the Haganah bought weapons and recruited its first paid organizers, but the outbreak of 1929 was followed by seven years of tranquillity, and this scheme for all-party cooperation did not outlast the emergency. Following a controversy between socialists and non-socialists in the Jerusalem branch, the Haganah split in 1931.[12] For the next five years the non-socialists maintained a separate defence body of their own, the Irgun Zvai Leumi (National Military Organization).[13] The imposing title was later to acquire a sinister prestige of its own as the terrorist 'Irgun' of the 1940s, but the I.Z.L. was even less substantial than the Haganah of the Labour-Zionists, of which it was a poor copy (it was popularly known as the Haganah 'B'), with fewer members and weapons and even less training.

Until the 1930s Palestine was too poor and unattractive a place to draw the 'Jewish masses' that figured so prominently in Zionist plans; the marxist and anti-Zionist Bund enjoyed wider support among the millions of poor Eastern European Jews than any of the rival Zionist parties. But the rising tide of European anti-semitism worked in perverse symbiosis with Zionist hopes; immigration to the Yishuv increased rapidly and so did its population which reached 350,000 by 1935. The influx lent substance to Arab fears but also brought an unprecedented prosperity to Palestine;* the Arabs benefited too, and for some years full employment, high land prices and profitable trade undermined the nationalist opposition to immigration and the Yishuv.

The Labour-Zionists reacted to the challenge and opportunity of the new immigration of men and money by a characteristically pragmatic shift in policy. While the extreme left, marxist and revolutionary, continued to advocate the primacy of the class struggle and minimal cooperation with bourgeois elements in the Yishuv, the moderates followed Ben Gurion and his social-democratic Mapai party in broadening the appeal and programme of the movement 'from class to nation', in the words of the title of a tract published by Ben Gurion in 1933.[14] Like all the Zionist parties, the Mapai was constantly engaged in the bitter and futile verbal politics of the powerless, but its leadership also showed a capacity for the realistic and pragmatic politics of nation-building that was unique in the Yishuv. By the late thirties, the moderate Labour-Zionists established themselves as the leading party in the governing institutions of the Yishuv, the Agency and the National

* For the first time middle-class businessmen and manufacturers were coming to settle and many could still bring their capital with them; until 1938 the Nazis allowed departing Jews to take industrial machinery as well as consumer goods with them, in lieu of hard currency.

Council, and they have remained the leaders of the coalition governments that have ruled Israel ever since independence.

In 1936 the Mufti of Jerusalem and his Husseini clan succeeded in arousing a new wave of Arab opposition to Jewish immigration. The clans and village heads linked to the Husseinis launched an unprecedented campaign of guerrilla attacks against police stations, British officials, the Iraq–Palestine pipeline and, incidentally, Jewish settlements. Arab notables opposed to the Husseinis were of course the main targets. The purpose was to strengthen the clan, and pressure the British into stopping Jewish immigration.[15] The government's response, at first hesitant and largely ineffectual, damaged Jewish confidence in British rule; until then most of the Yishuv's leaders had been confident that its security could be entrusted to the British, and they believed that the Haganah was to serve only as a quick-reaction home guard. After the events of 1936 attitudes towards defence began to change.[16] By the following year, the Haganah was reunited and organized anew as a country-wide militia; one year after that it acquired its first standing forces, mobile Field Companies with one thousand trained and armed men that were available for service anywhere in Palestine.

The first step was the reunification of the Haganah, achieved in July 1937 after lengthy negotiations. Only one of the major parties stayed out; the rest were represented on a new National Command (Mifkadah Artzit) headed by two central coordinators, one Labour-Zionist and the other non-socialist.[17] The National Command controlled the local branches through regional headquarters but in fact it was at the local level that Haganah activities were focused. Each was animated by a small group of unpaid activists who supervised such training as there was ('in cellars, with wooden pistols') as well as the purchase and storage of arms. The Haganah was an illegal underground organization; the penalties for the possession of unregistered weapons were heavy and all activities had to be conducted in total secrecy and thus in local isolation. As a result, standards of training varied from place to place according to the enthusiasm and abilities of local activists. In the kibbutzim and the more isolated villages virtually all able-bodied men and women were in the Haganah; in the towns and cities its branches often existed only on paper.[18]

The radical right of the Zionist movement, the Revisionist party, had left the World Zionist Organization by the time of the July 1937 reunification. Under their charismatic leader, Ze'ev Jabotinsky, the Revisionists had adopted an authoritarian and ultra-nationalist platform and set out to challenge all other Zionist parties for the leadership of the Yishuv. Unwilling to defer to the Labour-Zionists, as other non-socialist parties were doing, the Revisionists retained the Irgun Zvai Leumi and made it over into a party militia of their own. Never a serious competitor of the Haganah, the I.Z.L. nevertheless posed a constant political challenge to its leaders. In 1948 this rivalry was to climax in a fire-fight on the Tel Aviv waterfront that threatened civil war, but in the beginning the challenge was largely ideological.

The policy laid down by the Labour-Zionists following the out-break of the 1936 Arab revolt with its riots, guerrilla attacks and acts of sabotage, was in sharp contrast to the aggressive stance of the I.Z.L.: force could be used to repel Arab attacks but the Haganah was not to retaliate against the Arab community at large.[19] Even after two decades of strife, the pacifist streak was still in evidence in the Labour-Zionist movement; its policy called for self-restraint and its slogan was *Tohar Haneshek*, or purity of arms. The weapons of the Haganah were to be kept 'pure' by limiting their use to self-defence, and Haganah men were not to indulge in reprisals against 'innocent Arabs', as the phrase went. Morally attractive and politically useful (through the favourable impression made on British public opinion), the 'self-restraint' policy was naturally opposed by many Haganah activists who felt that the mystical pacifism of the doctrine was outdated and tactically inept. In the heated controversy that ensued, the ethical issue was confused with a tactical question which had nothing to do with moral attitudes: should the Haganah continue to limit itself to passive defence, to man road-blocks in Jewish districts and guard the fields of the rural settlements, or should it also deploy mobile forces to seek out and ambush Arab bands?

The tradition of passive defence had already been breached. In the summer of 1936 Yitzhak Sadeh, a burly immigrant from Russia, one of the first officers commissioned in the Red Army, an outstanding leader of men and a believer in unconventional guerrilla tactics, had set up a small and unofficial mobile unit with young volunteers from the Jerusalem Haganah. The *Nodedet* ('Patrol'), trained and led by Sadeh, set out to track down and ambush the guerrilla bands based in the villages around Jerusalem instead of waiting passively for their attacks.[20] The *Nodedet* was only a brief experiment which the leaders of the Haganah did not choose to underwrite or extend, caught as they were in the midst of the 'self-restraint' controversy. But Sadeh was soon given another and far more significant opportunity to demonstrate his talents of leadership and organization. When the Arab revolt began, the British had only a few squadrons of R.A.F. armoured cars in Palestine. After an interval of hesitation and appeasement, a dim reverberation of the Foreign Office line in Europe, the British sent two divisions of troops to Palestine, and began to convert the Palestine police into a para-military force on the lines of the Ulster constabulary, the model of all the tough police forces created by Britain in the less secure colonies.

Even so, the British could not protect each and every farm, and were therefore forced to rely on Jews for some auxiliary police duties. A Jewish Settlement Police (J.S.P.) was raised, trained, armed and paid by the British to provide small guard units for isolated villages and kibbutzim; unpaid guards of various types were in addition given the right to carry arms.[21] Most of the J.S.P. and the guards, collectively known as *notrim*, were in fact members of the Haganah, which thus acquired a legal cover provided by the authorities themselves.

Since the *notrim* were authorized to carry weapons, they could train openly in the field; since the J.S.P. members among them were paid, they could serve on a full-time basis. The opportunity was there and after the usual convoluted ideological debates, and personal power struggles, it was taken: in 1937 the Haganah authorized Sadeh to draw on the *notrim* to form and train mobile forces out of the static and dispersed settlement guards. Sadeh picked the men and trained them in group action with the flair of an old hand. Known as Fosh from the abbreviation of the Hebrew equivalent of field companies, Sadeh's volunteer force was a thousand strong by 1938.[22] In July 1938, the Fosh were placed under the control of the National Command which could send Sadeh's men wherever they were needed in Palestine, instead of having to rely on the resources and goodwill of the local branches of the Haganah, with their parochial concerns and uneven leadership.

The centralized direction of the Fosh was paralleled by a change of command. In July 1938 the party representatives appointed a new chairman to the National Command, Yohanan Rattner, amateur strategist, professor of architecture and another ex-officer of the Russian Army, whose military ideas transcended by far the home-guard perspective of most of his predecessors, trade union politicians and party ideologists who were more interested in the political control of the Haganah than in its military capabilities.[23]

The revitalized Haganah was successfully preparing for a struggle with the Arabs but the Yishuv was about to come into conflict with the British, and Sadeh's one thousand riflemen counted for little against the armoured car regiments and infantry battalions of the British army. The Yishuv's fight against the British was therefore political in nature (propaganda abroad and civil disobedience at home) until after 1945 when the Haganah joined the I.Z.L. in launching a campaign of sabotage.

In the meantime, the Haganah resolved the 'self-restraint' controversy by reaffirming its ethics and detaching the unrelated tactical questions. The activists dropped their demand for selective reprisals and the defencists for their part agreed to accept the mobile and offensive tactics of the Fosh, whose formation marked the adoption of the new doctrine. But most of the Haganah's leaders were unaffected by the change or by Sadeh's ideas. In spite of his tactical ingenuity, his inspired leadership and his remarkable talent for picking the right men (his favourites were two teenagers, Yigal Allon and Moshe Dayan), Sadeh could not overcome the deeply ingrained defencist outlook that pervaded the Haganah, most of whose men still thought only in terms of towers and stockades, fence patrols for village lands and three- or four-man guard posts. Sadeh's campaign for a Jewish army of small guerrilla units ready to go out into the night to find and attack Arab guerrilla bands was lagging, until it was given a powerful and unexpected impulse by a captain of the British army posted to Palestine in 1938.

Orde Charles Wingate, a Protestant raised in the Bible-reading tradition of the Non-Conformist sects, became an ardent Zionist soon after his arrival. He saw the Yishuv in the guise of the Biblical children of Israel, and its task as the restoration of Zion. The Bible he believed in was that of Joshua and David rather than that of the gentler prophets, and he saw the Haganah as the heir of that tradition. Detached for duty with the Intelligence Corps, Wingate used the opportunity to come into contact with Sadeh and his superiors in the Haganah's National Command and in the Political committee of the Jewish Agency. His unkempt and eccentric appearance, his odd personal habits (he ate onions like fruit and usually carried a supply in his pockets) and, above all, his post in the Intelligence Corps did not inspire much confidence; the Haganah was an illegal organization and many of its men were traditionally secretive. (This is the one Russian revolutionary trait that survives in the Israeli Army to this day.)

Wingate was not easily discouraged. He persisted in making his approaches, and his Zionist fervour was soon accepted as sincere; within months of his arrival he was accepted in the highest councils of the Haganah, where he became known as *Hayedid* (The friend).[24] Sadeh welcomed him with open arms, introduced him to his men, and subsequently showed great generosity of spirit towards a man who came near to overshadowing his own influence among the young activists of the Yishuv.

In July 1938 Wingate led an improvised group of *notrim* and Haganah men from kibbutz Hanita in western Galilee on a successful raid against a band of Arab guerrillas, based in a near-by village. Shortly afterwards, he persuaded his British army superiors to allow him to raise a counter-guerrilla unit under his own command: the Special Night Squads (S.N.S.). A small mixed unit of British soldiers and Haganah men (under *notrim* cover), the S.N.S. cooperated with larger groups manned entirely by the Haganah on a clandestine basis.[25] As far as the British were concerned, the S.N.S. was a cheap way of protecting the Palestinian segment of the Iraq Petroleum Company pipeline from Arab sabotage; but for Wingate the S.N.S. was a Jewish army in embryo.[26] Wingate implemented the tactics originally advocated by Sadeh: night-fighting and commando-style raids for a strategy of active defence.[27] Under his leadership the S.N.S. carried out raids and ambushes against Arab bands all over Galilee and Wingate's superiors had every reason to be pleased with its performance in protecting the oil pipeline. Nevertheless, they eventually reacted to his outspoken pro-Zionist stance by posting him out of Palestine in 1939.*

By then Wingate's S.N.S. had demonstrated the fighting qualities of young Palestinian Jews and trained a few dozen of them as commando N.C.O.s skilled in small-unit leadership and night fighting. But Wingate's most important contribution was not so much the tactical training he gave to the Haganah as his influential backing for a more active and more aggressive strategy. As a professional officer of the British army, his views carried great weight with the political leaders in charge of the Haganah: men who lacked confidence in the Yishuv's own military men, like Sadeh himself, were willing to listen when Wingate advocated the same ideas.

In spite of its tacit cooperation with the British in the S.N.S. and the settlement police, the Haganah remained an illegal underground army. But the British made no real attempt to suppress the Haganah and there was little conflict between the two until 1939. In that year the British finally decided to solve their Palestine problem by adopting a pro-Arab policy, officially proclaimed in a government White Paper according to which Jewish immigration and land purchases were to be tightly regulated, while Palestine was to become self-governing. Since there were still many more Arabs than Jews in the country, the first plank of the policy was meant to ensure that Arabs would remain in the majority, while the second would deliver the fate of the Yishuv into Arab hands.[28] But it was the immediate effect of the new policy which triggered the most violent Jewish opposition. The fundamental goal of Zionism was to provide a homeland for the Jewish people, and it was a tragic irony that Jews were denied access to the 'National Home' at a time when Nazi persecution forced them to seek refuge wherever it could be found.

The White Paper was received by the leaders of the Yishuv as a declaration of war. For the first time the Haganah became a weapon directed against the British: its men organized illegal

---

* Wingate was killed in Burma in 1944 having reached the rank of Major-General and acquired world fame as the leader of the Chindit formations which fought against the Japanese in Burma.

immigration[29] and established new agricultural settlements* to secure the Yishuv's hold on the land.[30]

In April 1939 the Fosh was disbanded as a result of the British curtailment of the *notrim*, but by then the Haganah's political masters had accepted the need for well-trained field units, and a permanent mobile force known as Hish (after the Hebrew initials of *Hel Sadeh* or 'field corps') was set up in 1940.[31] Younger and better-armed Haganah men were assigned to these mobile units from their local branches so that they could train in group tactics. Unlike its predecessor, the Hish was not a full-time standing force, but its unpaid volunteers were supposed to be ready for mobilization at short notice; in reality, their weekend and summer-camp training was not enough for combat.†

Another step in the Haganah's development into a military force was the creation of a General Staff and G.H.Q. While the National Command remained a supervisory body for administrative regulation and political guidance, the General Staff was meant to be a genuine military command in charge of the deployment of Haganah forces. Paid staff officers and a Chief of Staff, Ya'acov Dori, were appointed to run the usual staff branches and a G.H.Q. was set up with offices in Tel Aviv.[33] In the Hish and the General staff, the Haganah acquired the structures of an army: men organized into field formations controlled by a central command. But the substance was still lacking: an adequate supply of weapons, men trained for sustained combat and a cadre of experienced officers who could lead them into battle.

The Haganah could train small groups of guerrillas in its kibbutz branches, but it was more difficult to assemble large bodies of men and have them manoeuvre in the open.[34] Further, the Haganah, unlike a national army, did not have a monopoly on organized

---

* By means of a technique known as a *Choma Humigdal*, which had originally been developed in 1937 for use against the Arabs. Watchtowers and a double-wall stockade (to be filled with stones) were prepared in prefabricated parts so that an entire settlement with all its basic utilities could be erected in a single day, ready to repel Arab attacks by nightfall.

† When the Hish was established, older men, with less training and even fewer weapons, were left to the local Haganah branches as a static home-guard force which came to be known as Him (*Hel Mishmar* or 'guard corps').[32]

military force. The elected leadership of the Yishuv, which controlled the Haganah, was not a sovereign government and had no way of imposing its authority over the rival para-military groups, the I.Z.L. and the small but very active Lehi.*[35]

The I.Z.L. only had a few hundred active members while the Lehi had no more than a few dozen, but both were aggressive terrorist organizations; the mobile tactics of the Fosh and S.N.S. had eroded the 'self-restraint' policy, but the Haganah continued to reject demands within its ranks for indiscriminate reprisals against the Arab community. This allowed the I.Z.L., and later the Lehi to compete with the Haganah for the support of the more activist elements within the Yishuv. Neither of its rivals could compete with the Haganah in military terms, but they challenged the authority of the Yishuv's leadership. The I.Z.L. and the Lehi by their very existence undermined its status as the sole representative of Palestine Jewry to the British government and the world at large. The terrorism of the I.Z.L. and the Lehi also gave the British a welcome opportunity to discredit the Yishuv as a whole.

During the course of the Second World War the conflict between the Haganah and the dissidents became steadily more acute. The Lehi and, from 1944 onwards, the I.Z.L. too, waged a campaign of sabotage and assassination against the British at a time when the majority leadership of the Yishuv had decreed full cooperation in the Allied war effort.[36] The Lehi had never agreed to cooperate – in fact its members had split from the I.Z.L. over this very issue – while the I.Z.L. cooperated in the war effort only until the Allied victory became certain. In January 1944, the leaders of the I.Z.L. launched a wave of terrorist attacks against British police and army installations.[37] The majority leadership of the Yishuv, the executives of the Jewish Agency and the National Council reacted forcefully against the I.Z.L.'s tactics which undermined their own political plans. Under the leadership of David Ben Gurion, chairman of the Political department of the Jewish Agency, and virtual Prime Minister of the Jewish shadow state, the Haganah was used as an internal security force in the struggle against the dissidents. I.Z.L.

* Lehi is an acronym of *Lohamei Herut Israel* (Fighters for the Freedom of Israel), known as the Stern gang to the British. The Lehi was formed in 1939 by a small group of I.Z.L. activists who split from the larger body in opposition to the I.Z.L. policy of cooperating in the British war effort.

activists were kidnapped, interrogated and, in some cases, handed over to the British by Haganah men chosen for their political reliability.[38] In spite of an energetic political campaign, public opinion in the Yishuv did not long tolerate the spectacle of Jews denouncing fellow Jews to the British, and the campaign soon stopped. But this breach of ethnic solidarity showed how far the Yishuv's leaders were willing to go to in order to control the dissidents.

As soon as the Second World War started, the leaders of the Zionist movement tried to persuade the British to form a Jewish army – or at least a Jewish division – to take part in the struggle against Nazi Germany. The Jews made little headway against the determined opposition of the Foreign Office. Many in the British government, whether pro-Arab or not, did not rate the military qualities of the Jews very highly, and feared the political consequences of sponsoring Jewish military units. Even so, there were no barriers to direct enlistment and some 27,000 of the Yishuv's men and women served in the British and Allied forces as volunteers.[39] The Haganah encouraged enlistment in the Allied armies in order to share in the fight against the Nazis but also to train the youth of the Yishuv in modern war; the Haganah was determined to make maximum use of this opportunity – even if compulsion had to be used in the case of some 'volunteers'.

With so many Palestinian Jews serving abroad, the ranks of the Haganah were depleted. This did not cause much anxiety at first; the Arab revolt had been defeated and Palestine was as secure as it had ever been. But in May 1941, Rommel's offensive in North Africa reached the gates of Egypt; suddenly the very survival of the Yishuv seemed to be threatened. On 15 May 1941, a new National Command was formed,* and the new leadership of the Haganah decided to raise a mobile force of full-time soldiers to be kept for the defence of the Yishuv, the Palmach.†[41]

The Palmach proved to be more than another transitory experiment. It became the training ground for many of the future leaders of the Israeli Army as well as the source of some of its most

---

* With four representatives of the 'bourgeois' parties and four of the Labour–Zionists under a neutral chairman, Moshe Sneh, who thus became *ex officio* the Haganah's Commander-in-Chief or *Rama* (*Rosh Mifkadah Artzit*). Ya'acov Dori remained the Chief of Staff.[40]

† From *Plugot Machatz* or 'striking companies'.

fundamental military doctrines. Once again, Yitzhak Sadeh was put in charge of the new force which he assembled around a core of former Fosh and S.N.S. men. By the summer of 1941, the first nine companies of the Palmach went into training under Sadeh's energetic leadership.

Like the S.N.S. before it, the Palmach was based on an unofficial arrangement with the British. Its first two companies of new recruits took part in the Allied invasion of Syria and Lebanon in August 1941, and in spite of their brief training performed very well as scouts and guides.* This was one of the last instances of military cooperation between the British and the Jews and both sides strictly limited their commitments: the Palmach was under Haganah command and fully independent of the British army. When, in the summer of 1942, the second wave of Rommel's offensive seemed on the verge of defeating the British forces in Egypt, the Palmach agreed to remain behind, as a guerrilla force, in the event of a British retreat from Palestine. A secret training camp was set up to train Palmach recruits with British and Haganah instructors; weapons and equipment were provided by the British who financed the scheme.[42]

British military aid to the Yishuv did not outlast the crisis in North Africa. When the Germans were defeated at El Alamein in November 1942, the British withdrew all support from the Palmach. But by then it was a force in being, with hundreds of men trained for commando and intelligence tasks, a cadre of trained officers and a distinctive *esprit de corps*; the one thing it lacked was a source of financial support.

The unofficial government of the Yishuv, the Jewish Agency, could have found the money to finance the Palmach, but it was paralysed by a major controversy over defence priorities. Some argued that Palestinian Jewry should continue to contribute all its military manpower to the Allied armies, while others insisted that some military forces were needed in Palestine itself under Jewish control. Partly owing to this controversy, no agreement could be reached on the financing of the Palmach, now threatened with disbandment. But in November 1942, the largest of the kibbutz federations, the left-wing Hakibbutz HaMeuchad came up

* Yigal Allon and Moshe Dayan were among them; Dayan lost an eye in the campaign.

with an original proposal: its kibbutzim offered to feed and house the Palmach in exchange for two weeks' farm work each month. This proposal was gladly accepted and the Palmach sent its boys and girls to the kibbutzim for alternate fortnights of work and military training.[43]

The Palmach has aptly been described as a 'youth movement in arms'. Days of training or hard work in the fields would often end with dancing and singing around the camp fire; boys and girls (few were over twenty) lived, worked and trained together in a summer-camp atmosphere evoked by the stories and songs still popular in Israel. Though living conditions were spartan and the work was hard, its morale was high. The Palmach was elitist; it attracted the sons and daughters of the pioneers who had founded the kibbutzim and moshavim and who were now part of the ruling elite of the Yishuv. But within itself it was egalitarian; officers had no material privileges and ranks were functional – attached to the task and not to the person. Although Sadeh himself was of the older generation of immigrant founding fathers, the Palmach was the first institution of the Yishuv to be taken over by the new generation born in the country. Symbolizing the transition, in 1945 the twenty-eight-year-old Yigal Allon was appointed commander of the Palmach in succession to Yitzhak Sadeh.

Palmach training methods owed little to its early contact with the British army. To make full use of the skill and morale of its members, the Palmach emphasized group cohesion and combat leadership at all levels.[44] In its training courses, even squad leaders were trained for independent command and not just as subordinate N.C.O.s. The Palmach could only compensate for its small size and lack of heavy weapons by reaching very high standards of individual skill and group morale; and these assets were to be put to good use by inventive tactics and morally compelling leadership.

The Palmach was a force of guerrilla infantry, but since it was also the only full-time force in the Haganah it was entrusted with the task of creating the Yishuv's first air and naval units. Under the cover of sporting clubs, training got under way with gliders, light aircraft and motorboats. Though not much could be achieved with such equipment the Palmach did produce the first locally trained airmen and sailors.[45]

The Allied victory came too late to save European Jewry. Less than one million survived in the areas which had been under German occupation and of these a majority were destitute refugees who no longer had homes to return to. Classified as Displaced Persons, the survivors of the concentration camps waited in transit camps; a few tried to seek a new life in Western Europe, but the majority saw Palestine as the only possible refuge.

In 1945 the Labour party came to power in Britain; more Zionist than the Zionists when out of office, the Labour leaders changed their minds once in power. After some hesitations, they decided to pursue the anti-Zionist White Paper policy inaugurated by the Conservatives in 1939.[46] Jewish immigration into Palestine was limited to a quota of 1,500 per month. As the Jews saw it, the British were intent on liquidating the 'National Home' for the sake of Anglo-Arab cooperation in the post-war era, from which great things were expected by the Foreign Office. The Jews, for their part, were no longer satisfied with the ambiguities of a 'National Home' and now demanded an independent state of their own.*

Thus, after more than two decades of British rule, the Jews and the British were set on a collision course. The Haganah attempted to run the British blockade with ships carrying illegal immigrants, and the British reacted with increasingly brutal searches, arrests and curfews. Tension increased further when the Haganah launched a campaign of sabotage; this culminated in the 'Night of the Bridges' on 17 June 1946, when ten out of the eleven road and rail bridges connecting Palestine with the near-by Arab countries were sabotaged by Palmach sappers.[48] The Haganah also began to collaborate with the I.Z.L. and Lehi,[49] which had long been waging a terrorist campaign against the British, though its leaders continued to reject attacks on people and used the Palmach only to sabotage installations. When it agreed to cooperate with the I.Z.L. and Lehi, the Haganah set certain conditions: no attacks against human life, and due warning in sabotage operations

* In 1942 the leadership of the Yishuv, headed by Ben Gurion, then chairman of the Political Department of the Jewish Agency, had decided to adopt the creation of an independent state as its political goal, in the so-called 'Biltmore Program'.[47]

to allow time for evacuation before the explosives were detonated. This arrangement did not last long. On 22 July 1946, a wing of the King David Hotel (which housed some government offices) was blown up in a joint Haganah–I.Z.L. operation – and ninety-five people died in the explosion. The Haganah accused the I.Z.L. of having failed to give adequate warning and refused all further collaboration. The I.Z.L. and Lehi continued to operate without coordination with the Haganah while the Haganah changed its tactics and avoided large scale sabotage operations. Its main effort was still focused on illegal immigration; Haganah men infiltrated Displaced Persons camps in Europe, organized the movement of D.P.s towards the ports of Italy and France, bought and equipped ships and attempted to run the British blockade. Most immigrant ships were intercepted by the Royal Navy, but the widely reported deportation of these victims of Nazism to detention camps in Cyprus earned the British a great deal of unpopularity in the West and especially in the United States – just when Britain urgently needed American economic aid.

Palestine had become an intractable problem for the British government: the United States was pressing for the immediate admission of 100,000 Jews while Britain's Arab client states demanded a total ban on immigration.[50] Even in purely military terms, the pressure of Jewish terrorism was a serious burden for the British. By 1946 less than 600,000 Jews were tying down almost 100,000 British soldiers and policemen – more than were required to garrison vast tracts of the Empire. Jewish terrorism was ruthless and effective, while British counter-terror tactics were inhibited by distaste for such warfare and the scrutiny of the international press. Finally, in February 1947 the British government requested the U.N. General Assembly to dispose of Palestine, and the Assembly appointed a committee of inquiry. While the U.N. committee was preparing its report, which eventually recommended the partition of Palestine, Jews and Arabs were marshalling their forces for war.[51]

In mid-1947 the Haganah consisted of 43,000 men and women, of which 32,000 belonged to the Him, the static 'Home Guard', ill-trained and poorly armed.[52] Actually, the size of its registered membership did not mean much, since in the well-organized kibbutzim and moshavim almost every able-bodied man and woman was available for defence duties. But in the towns Him membership was often purely nominal. Of the Haganah's mobile forces, the Hish 'field corps' was the larger by far with 8,000 part-time volunteer members who had received a few days' training each month as well as two weeks of field manoeuvres each year.[53] Though organized into battalions of several hundred men each, the Hish was only trained to fight by companies; the men had an average of less than fifty days of training behind them. A total of 27,000 men and women of the Yishuv had served in the Allied armies during the war, and they provided an important reserve of trained military manpower, much of which was eventually absorbed by the Hish.

The Haganah's only full-time force was still the Palmach. The morale and fighting skill of its 3,100 men and women (including 1,000 reservists) were superb, but after the first battles, in which it took the brunt of the fighting, the Palmach's main contribution to the Army of 1948 was perhaps the individual service of its members as officers for other, poorly trained forces. By 1947 half of the Palmach had received three full years of continuous training, while in the Hish the average was less than fifty days. Even Palmach squad commanders had on average more training than Hish officers. As a result, many Palmach men eventually served as officers and N.C.O.s in Hish units and the new brigades organized during the war. The main officer-training course of the Haganah, for platoon commanders, was common to both the Hish and the Palmach but not many of the part-time Hish had put in the three or more months of continuous service required to complete the course.[54] Yet another source of trained manpower for the Haganah was the Jewish Brigade Group of the British army, formed in 1944 as a belated and partial response to the Zionist demand for the creation of a Jewish army fighting under its own flag. The brigade had seen very little active service, since it was not fielded until the autumn of 1944, but its officers and N.C.O.s were well trained and familiar with the technical and support tasks required for sustained warfare. The Haganah still had neither armour nor artillery in mid-1947; as for air and naval forces, hampered as it was by its illegal status, the Haganah could do very little in the way of training or procurement. A clandestine underground army can camofluage its field exercises as botanical trips, but no 'cover' would hold for a military airfield and its combat aircraft.* The lack of air and naval forces was only one aspect of the crippling shortage of weapons which affected the whole of the Haganah. As late as December 1947, when the war had already started, according to an authoritative estimate it had a grand total of only 17,600 rifles (of many different types and calibres) and less than a thousand machine-guns.†[55] As for combat aircraft, tanks, field artillery or anti-tank weapons, the Haganah had none. Towards the end of 1947 both sides came to accept the fact that an armed struggle between the Jews and the Arabs of Palestine was imminent; it seemed increasingly probable that the conflict would become a full-scale war involving the regular forces of neighbouring Arab states. In response the Haganah G.H.Q. formed the Hish into field battalions and pressed for additional training in more realistic conditions.[56] Four regional H.Q.s were set up to cover the Yishuv's territory, but the Palmach retained its own country-wide H.Q.[57]

The Palmach was an integral part of the Haganah and subordinate to its G.H.Q., but its politics were distinctive and in opposition to those of the Haganah's leadership. Originally the arrangement whereby the Palmach was fed and housed by the kibbutzim of the Hakibbutz HaMeuchad federation had caused no political problems since the federation was associated with the Mapai party, the largest in the Yishuv, whose leaders dominated the Haganah. In 1944, however, Mapai split and most of the Hakibbutz HaMeuchad left to form a new party, the Achdut HaAvoda. Yigal Allon, who became the Commander of the Palmach in 1945, his deputy, and all but two of the senior commanders in the Palmach's H.Q., belonged to the Hakibbutz HaMeuchad, as did forty per cent of the rank and

---

* In mid-1947 the Haganah had nine light aircraft and about twenty-five trained pilots, some home-grown and some fighter and bomber pilots with wartime experience in the Allied air forces. Its naval unit, raised and trained by the Palmach, consisted of a small team of frogmen and a few armed motorboats.

† The secret workshops of the Haganah were producing hand-grenades as well as small quantities of simple mortars and submachine-guns, but no rifles or machine-guns. In the December 1947 inventory, there were 3,700 submachine-guns, 775 light, and 160 medium machine-guns (the *notrim* also had 75 antique Lewis guns), 670 small (two-inch) mortars, and 84 full-size (three-inch) infantry mortars.

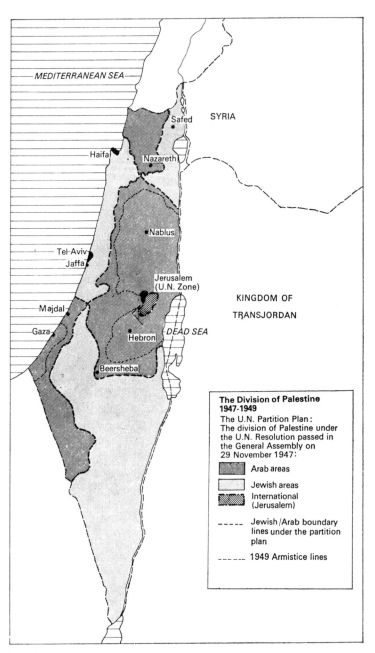

MEDITERRANEAN SEA

SYRIA

Safed

Haifa

Nazareth

Nablus

Tel-Aviv
Jaffa

Jerusalem
(U.N. Zone)

KINGDOM OF

TRANSJORDAN

Majdal

Gaza

DEAD SEA

Hebron

Beersheba

**The Division of Palestine
1947-1949**

The U.N. Partition Plan:
The division of Palestine under
the U.N. Resolution passed in
the General Assembly on
29 November 1947:

Arab areas

Jewish areas

International
(Jerusalem)

_ _ _ _ _   Jewish/Arab boundary
lines under the partition
plan

_ _ _ _ _ _   1949 Armistice lines

Map 1

file. As a result, the leaders of Mapai had no political authority over the Haganah's elite force, given the Palmach's close links with the Achdut HaAvoda party, Mapai's most direct political rival.*

If the situation was simpler in the case of the I.Z.L. and Lehi their conflict with the Mapai-dominated leadership of the Yishuv was also much sharper. The I.Z.L. and Lehi were trying to become self-contained as well as independent: both had their own printing presses and fund-raising networks. By the end of 1947 the I.Z.L. had about two thousand members though less than half this number were trained and equipped 'for street fighting and sabotage'; the Lehi was even smaller – at its peak it only had a few hundred members.[58]

When the U.N. General Assembly approved the partition of Palestine on 29 November 1947, the British government, which had voted against partition, decided to evacuate Palestine. A communal war of sniping, ambushes and terrorism broke out almost at once. On 1 February 1948, after two months of increasingly widespread fighting, the Jewish Agency and the Va'ad Leumi, the twin authorities of the Yishuv, issued a call for general mobilization. As the numerical strength of the Haganah increased with the inflow of new recruits, the process of militarization begun in November 1947 was taken a stage further: the battalions of the Hish, now larger and manned on a full-time basis, were formed into six brigades of 3–4,000 men each; the Palmach recalled its reservists, absorbed new recruits, and regrouped its forces into three brigades. In a final departure from the localist militia pattern, the Hish brigades were put under the control of the Haganah's G.H.Q. and could now be sent to fight anywhere in the country.[59] The war which was to decide the fate of Palestine had begun.

The Jews and Arabs of Palestine started to fight in December 1947 but their communal struggle did not become a conventional war with front lines and pitched battles until May 1948, when the British evacuation was completed and regular forces from the neighbouring Arab states invaded Palestine. Between December and May the country was gradually divided into Jewish and Arab enclaves as sniping and terrorism escalated into street fighting and

* Until the mobilization of February 1948, seventeen of the Palmach's twenty bases were located on kibbutzim which belonged to the Hakibbutz HaMeuchad federation.

guerrilla warfare. By the time the Arab armies intervened, the Jews had consolidated their hold on the coastal strip and eastern Galilee while the Palestinians held most of Judea, Samaria and western Galilee; Jerusalem was divided. Even in retrospect, the war of 1948 has few clear-cut points of reference. The fighting broke out at different dates in different places, and even the armistice agreements which brought the war to an end in 1949 were signed by four Arab states at different times. There is no clear date marking the beginning or the end of the war. Egypt, Jordan, Iraq, Lebanon and Syria intervened openly on May 14–15 1948, but regular contingents from these countries were fighting in Palestine even earlier, having infiltrated across the border while the country was still under nominal British rule.

The most ambiguous participant in the conflict was undoubtedly Great Britain. Officially, the British were neutral. Their declared intention was to maintain law and order until midnight on 15 May 1948, when the Mandate was to end, and renounce all responsibility thereafter. But their evacuation stretched over a period of months and, as each town, police fortress and army camp was evacuated, the British could often choose which side would take it over. This choice made a mockery of neutrality. If the British had a policy, it was to leave chaos in their wake. Not only was there no orderly transfer of power to any successor regime, but the very apparatus of government was allowed to collapse. Offices, files and installations were abandoned and local civil servants left to their own devices; the police, customs, tax collection and all other services of state were simply disbanded.[60] It now seems clear that the British aim was to create a political vacuum which would prevent the implementation of the U.N.'s partition resolution, but the results of this policy were quite different: there was no political vacuum as far as the Yishuv was concerned. The Jewish Agency and the Va'ad Leumi, together with their administrative services, already amounted to a state in all but name. As the British left each locality, the Jewish quasi-state simply took over some additional functions of government, especially law enforcement and defence.[61] The Arabs of Palestine, on the other hand, did experience a political and administrative breakdown; they were not organized into a self-governing community like the Yishuv and they had no elected leadership. Above all, none of the rival factions in Arab political life had developed an apparatus of government.[62] Chaos spread in the Arab areas of Palestine as British Mandatory rule was dismantled; in many places even such basic utilities as electricity and the telephone service ceased to function.

Despite the imminence of war, the British continued to forbid all military preparations, whether Jewish or Arab. This policy actually favoured the Arabs who could assemble men and weapons in the near-by Arab countries. The Haganah's secret weapon purchasing network (*Rekhes*) was very active in Europe and America but found it most difficult to smuggle weapons into the country, since the British continued to search all incoming shipping until the very end of the Mandate. The Arabs had no such problems; weapons could be brought into near-by Arab territory and carried across the increasingly unguarded land borders. In any event, immediately after 15 May 1948 Arab soldiers and Arab weapons could cross the borders of Palestine quite openly while most of the Haganah's weapons were still awaiting shipment. At the tactical level, too, the British presence tended to work in favour of the Arabs. Right up to the last phases of the evacuation, even quite small British contingents could often decide the outcome of local struggles by what they did or failed to do. Much was left to the discretion of junior officers; some were strictly neutral, a few were pro-Jewish, but the vast majority tended to be pro-Arab. Romantic notions about the Bedouins and Arabs, Jewish terrorism, and reverberations of Nazi anti-Semitism combined to induce pro-Arab feelings among the British that were to survive until 1956.

As Jews and Arabs mustered their forces in the spring of 1948, the Jews had the advantage of a centralized command in the Haganah's G.H.Q., while the Arabs of Palestine enjoyed the military support of several Arab states. Though neither very large nor particularly efficient, except for the Arab Legion, many of whose officers were British,* the armies of Egypt, Syria and

* The 7,400 men of the Arab Legion were trained and equipped to average British infantry standards. In May 1948 the Legion had 24 artillery pieces and 45 armoured cars. In a typically ambiguous arrangement the Arab Legion of the self-governing Kingdom of Transjordan served in Palestine *before* 15 May 1948 under British military command and *after* 15 May as an independent Arab army – though still with its full complement of British officers. Whatever its formal status, the Legion was inherently pro-Arab and

Lebanon were well equipped by local standards, and formidable enemies for the poorly armed Haganah. The British continued to supply weapons to the Egyptian army and the Arab Legion right up to the May invasions, and these supplies, together with the effects of the naval blockade, created a paradoxical situation during the first half of the war: the Jews who were technically the more advanced had only rifles, mortars and machine-guns, while the relatively backward Arabs had 152 field guns, 140–159 armoured cars, 20–40 tanks and 55–59 fighter aircraft (15 May figures).[64]

The Arabs also enjoyed a natural geographic advantage: the Jewish areas of Palestine, the coastal plain, western Galilee, north-east Palestine and the northern Negev were actually separate enclaves linked by vulnerable roads which crossed solidly Arab areas. A number of Jewish settlements were entirely surrounded, while Jerusalem, with one sixth of the Jewish population of Palestine, was cut off from the rest of the Yishuv by the strong Arab hold on the hills of Judea. In the early stages of the war much of the Jewish military effort was absorbed by attempts to clear and hold the main roads connecting different parts of the Yishuv, while the Arabs could stop Jewish communications with much smaller forces.[65] In the first stages of the war, the 'Battle for the Roads' (winter 1947 and spring of 1948), the Jews were forced to defend individual convoys rather than the roads themselves since the British effectively prevented the seizure of territory along the roads. The Haganah organized Jewish traffic into convoys protected by home-made armoured cars,* but this tactic proved very costly in casualties. Eventually it became totally inadequate, since convoys could not cope with the large road-blocks which the Arabs soon learned to build.[66] The task of defending the convoys was given to mixed Palmach and Hish units which assigned small escort groups to each convoy. Girl soldiers were essential for convoy duties since they could conceal hand-weapons under their

* Commercial vehicles which were armoured by means of two layers of thin steel plate with concrete poured in between. Wrecked 'Sandwiches', as they were called, are still dramatically displayed along the road to Jerusalem where convoys were frequently ambushed during the spring battles.

its military support to the local Arabs became overt even before it formally invaded Palestine on 15 May.[63]

clothes to get them past the (still gentlemanly) British troops manning the road blocks. Until the late spring of 1948 the British continued to disarm the convoys though they knew full well that they were liable to come under attack.

In April 1948, when the British evacuation was entering its last stages, the Jews finally went over to the attack. Operation *Nachshon*, in April 1948, was a first attempt at a large-scale offensive: Palmach and Hish troops were to launch coordinated attacks to secure communications with Jerusalem by seizing the natural strongpoints which dominate the road. *Nachshon* was part of the general war plan framed by the Haganah, Plan 'D', whose goals were:

> To gain control of all the area allotted to the Jewish State and defend its borders, and those of the blocs of Jewish settlements and such Jewish population as were outside those borders, against a regular or para-regular enemy operating from bases outside or inside the area of the Jewish State.[66]

This was a revolutionary departure for the Haganah. Plan 'D' called for the *permanent* seizure of Arab villages and the expulsion of their inhabitants; for a body which had always been defencist and whose leaders had so recently preached self-restraint as the best policy, this was a radical innovation and one difficult to absorb.

With the deployment of its first mobile battalions, the Haganah also experienced severe organizational strains, some purely technical, as in matters of supply and logistics, and some personal or even political. When the Haganah emerged into the open in the spring of 1948, a loose organized and voluntary underground army was subjected for the first time to military discipline. G.H.Q. was trying to impose its authority over the local and regional commands and some 'old Haganah hands' saw their powers drastically reduced, while others were displaced by younger men, some in their early twenties. For many Haganah officers the transition from underground to army thus involved a severe loss of status. Ya'acov Dori remained the Haganah Chief of Staff but it was thirty-year-old Yigal Yadin who was actually in charge of overall strategy as Chief of Operations; veterans like David Shaltiel, Regional Commander for Jerusalem, were overshadowed by men in their twenties such as Yosef Tabenkin, Commander of the

Palmach Harel Brigade. Mobile warfare on a country-wide scale also called for many organizational changes; in the past, supplies had been provided – and carried – by the men themselves, but proper logistic support for transport and supply was now obviously needed. What made these problems all the more difficult to resolve was that they coincided with the spring battles when the Jewish forces were fully engaged in the offensives of Plan 'D'.

Plan 'D' could not be implemented without capturing the many Arab villages astride the main roads linking Jewish areas. In many places, the Arab population fled of its own accord; in some instances they were expelled by local commanders though this does not seem to have been official Haganah policy.[67] The flight of the Arabs was unexpected but generally welcomed when it came.

The plan 'D' offensive also affected the 'mixed cities': Tiberias, Safed, Haifa and Jerusalem, in which both Jews and Arabs lived side by side. Street fighting on the borders between the Arab and Jewish quarters in these towns had broken out as early as December 1947 but it was not until the late spring of 1948 that local Haganah units went over to the offensive in order to establish a 'continuous and secure hold' over these areas. The first urban battle took place in Tiberias; after a brief fight the Arab lower town fell to the Haganah on 18 April 1948. The Arab quarters of Haifa, the third city of Palestine, with the country's only deep-water harbour, were captured four days later, after thirty-one hours of bitter street fighting. It is typical of the chaos of the 1948 War that large British forces were still entrenched in the port area while Jews and Arabs were fighting all around them. During this crucial phase of the war, British policy seemed entirely erratic to both Jews and Arabs. While in Galilee the British actively helped the Arabs, in Haifa the local British Commander, Maj.-Gen. Stockwell, simply announced that his troops were about to evacuate the residential areas of the town to fall back on the harbour and the British made no attempt to intervene in the fighting which broke out almost immediately. After the defeat of the Arabs in four days of house-to-house fighting, General Stockwell convened a meeting of Jewish and Arab leaders at which a surrender was negotiated.[68]

In Haifa and Tiberias the Jews were in the majority, but the next town to be fought over, Safed in Galilee, was predominantly

Arab; the local Jews were outnumbered and poorly organized. Palmach troops were sent to their aid and on 10 May 1948 a striking force supported by local Hish men seized the town and the natural strongpoints around it in a combined attack commanded by Yigal Allon. The Arab half of the twin cities of Tel Aviv and Jaffa held out against a series of somewhat desultory Jewish attacks but on 13 May, after I.Z.L. and Haganah attacks, the Jaffa notables decided to surrender. Most of the population fled to Gaza.

Jerusalem was the most important of the 'mixed' cities from the political point of view, and here the Jews came near to defeat. Jerusalem was surrounded by Arab towns and villages which formed an arc of dominant heights all round the city. Much of the Jewish population was orthodox and poorly organized while the local Arabs were better led than elsewhere. Moreover the Arab Legion with its armoured cars intervened more and more openly in the fighting which soon engulfed much of the city; the British still controlled a number of key points and on occasion interfered to assist one side or the other. During April and May 1948, when the guerrilla turned into positional warfare, the Jews succeeded in capturing several Arab districts, but the historic Jewish quarter of the Old City was cut off and besieged. Partly owing to indiscipline and poor coordination between the local Haganah, Palmach and I.Z.L. forces, the Jewish quarter fell to the Arab Legion on 20 May.[69]

While the Haganah was concentrating its mobile forces for the Plan 'D' offensive, few men and still fewer weapons were made available for the defence of the many isolated villages and settlements then coming under attack. It was Haganah policy that every settlement was to hold out to the last man: four villages and one kibbutz were evacuated none the less – with or without the consent of G.H.Q.; four fell to the Arabs after prolonged fighting, but the rest held out. By the first fortnight of May, the original goals of Plan 'D' had largely been achieved: Jewish territory in the northern Negev, the coastal plain and the valleys of Galilee now formed a continuous whole linked by secure roads but the Arabs still held the hilly centre of the country from Galilee through Samaria to Judea, including the dominating mountain ridges around Jerusalem.

On 15 May 1948, the reality of the Jewish State became official with the Declaration of Independence and the formation of a provisional government headed by the Mapai leader, David Ben Gurion, as Prime Minister and Minister of Defence. On the same day, the country was invaded by the regular forces of Egypt, Lebanon, Iraq and Syria. The Arab Legion of the Kingdom of Transjordan complete with its British officers stayed behind as an independent Arab force.* The fifteenth of May 1948 was a turning point in the struggle for Palestine. Until then the volunteer forces of the Haganah had been fighting Palestinian irregulars in the presence of the British. After 15 May the first sovereign Jewish state in Palestine since 70 A.D. was at war against five Arab armies which were invading the country from the north, east and south.

Following the general mobilization of February 1948, the battalions of the Hish had been reorganized into six territorial brigades (Alexandroni, Carmeli, Etzioni, Golani, Kiryati and Givati), which had some 18,820 men between them by 15 May. The Palmach was also expanding and its three somewhat smaller brigades (Yiftah, Harel and Hanegev) had about 6,000 men all told. Air Force, Artillery, Engineering and Military Police corps were formed and placed under the direct orders of G.H.Q., while 400 Haganah instructors were assembled into a Training branch.†

* Even before the formal transfer from British army command, Arab Legion armoured cars spearheaded the attacks of local Arabs against four kibbutzim (the 'Etzion bloc') south of Jerusalem. Totally isolated in the midst of solidly Arab territory, this Jewish enclave fell on 15 May after three days of fighting.[70]

† No fully consistent and comprehensive statistics have ever been published. According to Ben Gurion's diary,[71] on 15 May the Haganah forces consisted of a total of 29,677 men in all, distributed as follows:

Palmach (three brigades)	6,000	Training	398
Hish by brigades:			
Golani	4,095	Air Force	675
Carmeli	2,238	Artillery	650
Alexandroni	3,588	Engineers	150
Kiryati	2,504	Military Police	168
Givati	3,229	Transport units	1,097
Etzioni	3,166	New conscripts in training	1,719

(Other sources quote higher figures for Haganah forces – Ben Gurion makes no mention of the Him or of the supply services.)

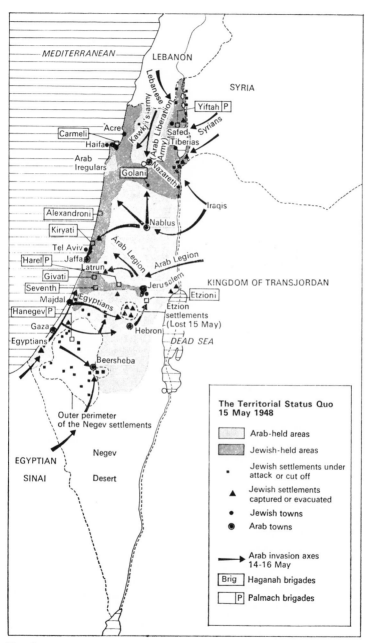

MEDITERRANEAN

LEBANON

SYRIA

Yiftah P

Carmeli
Acre
Haifa
Safed
Tiberias
Syrians

Arab
Irregulars
Golani
Nazareth

Iraqis

Alexandroni
Nablus

Kiryati

Tel Aviv
Harel P   Jaffa
Latrun
Givati
Seventh
Jerusalem   KINGDOM OF TRANSJORDAN
Majdal   Egyptians
Hanegev P   Etzioni
Etzion
settlements
Gaza   (Lost 15 May)
Egyptians   Hebron
DEAD SEA

Beersheba

Outer perimeter
of the Negev settlements

EGYPTIAN   Negev

SINAI   Desert

**The Territorial Status Quo
15 May 1948**

    Arab-held areas

    Jewish-held areas

▪   Jewish settlements under
    attack or cut off

▲   Jewish settlements
    captured or evacuated

●   Jewish towns

◉   Arab towns

⟶   Arab invasion axes
    14-16 May

Brig   Haganah brigades

P   Palmach brigades

Map 2

According to published estimates,[72] on 15 May the total inventory of Haganah weapons consisted of 22,000 rifles of various calibres, 1,550 machine-guns (light and medium), 11,000 (largely home-made) submachine-guns, 195 infantry mortars (three-inch calibre), 682 two-inch mortars, 86 P.I.A.T.* projectors and anti-tank rifles, and five (very old) 65mm field guns. A few tanks and the fighter aircraft still awaited shipment in Europe.

With the lifting of the British blockade, the Yishuv's forces were augmented by an inflow of weapons and manpower from abroad: Jews who had served in the Allied forces during the Second World War began to volunteer and eventually more than 2,000 were to serve in the Israeli Army. A large number of recruits including veterans of the Russian army came from British detention camps in Cyprus (where illegal immigrants had been held), but this source dried up when the British stopped the outflow of men of military age in response to a U.N. embargo. Except for their units in Jerusalem, I.Z.L. and Lehi forces were disbanded and these men too were inducted into the Army. Much of this new manpower went into the rear services, but three new brigades (7th, the 8th commanded by Yitzhak Sadeh, and Oded) were also formed during May and June 1948.[73] Although the Haganah G.H.Q. was nominally in charge of troop deployments, the Army's rapid growth during the summer of 1948 was largely the product of *ad hoc* improvisations. When the 8th Brigade was formed (on paper as an 'armoured brigade') under his command, Yitzhak Sadeh found himself in charge of (a) an infantry unit of ex-Lehi men, (b) a tank 'battalion'† manned by new immigrants and volunteer crews who knew no Hebrew, and (c) a battalion of 'jeep commandos' raised more or less independently by a former Palmach company commander, Moshe Dayan.‡

---

* P.I.A.T. stands for Projector Infantry Anti-Tank – a crude man-portable projecting device for armour-piercing explosive charges.

† Of the battalion's six companies only two were tank companies. One was equipped with ten H–35 French-built light tanks (with 37mm guns) and the other with two British Cromwell 'cruisers' (twenty-tonners) and a single Sherman M.4.

‡ Moshe Dayan formed the jeep battalion during the first truce (June–July 1948) and remained its commander until he was put in charge of the Jerusalem forces. Dayan had been one of two first company commanders trained by the Palmach (the other was Yigal Allon) but, after the 1941

On 26 May 1948, Israel's provisional government issued Order No. 4 which provided a legal framework for the military forces of the new State. Its first clause gave them an official name, Zvah Haganah LeIsrael,* soon to be popularly known as Zahal, and stated that it would include *all* land, air and naval forces.[74] (The official designation in English is Israel Defence Forces.) The second clause defined the procedures for general mobilization in times of emergency, and the third prescribed the form of the oath of allegiance to the State, its laws and authorized government. The fourth clause was of particular importance in the circumstances: it explicitly forbade the maintenance of any armed forces other than those of Zahal itself within the territory of the State.

The new, international war between Israel and the Arab states lasted sporadically until the armistice agreements of 1949. The war was waged in fits and starts, in a series of separate battles and short campaigns interrupted by truces imposed by the Great Powers at the U.N. Security Council.

The first U.N. truce went into effect on 11 June 1948, less than a month after the May invasions. In retrospect, this proved the most critical phase of the war for the Jews: their forces had been fully engaged in fighting the Palestinian irregulars even before the invasions and they had to meet the offensives of the regular Arab forces without any interval for rest and reorganization. Israel's trained military manpower was almost entirely committed† and the only immediate reinforcements were new immigrants from refugee camps in Europe and Cyprus – who were sometimes taken to the front after only a few days or even hours of training.‡

* The literal translation is 'Defence Army for Israel'; the official translation is 'Israel Defence Forces' abbreviated as I.D.F. in the text, Army is used with reference to the I.D.F. as a whole; in lower case (army) it refers to the ground forces only.

† The total population is estimated at 650,000 for 15 May 1948, of which approximately 85,000 were males in the fighting echelon age-group (18–32).

‡ In the first battle for Latrun (25 May 1948), a key position astride the Jerusalem road, more than four hundred new immigrant soldiers serving in

Syrian campaign, he left the Palmach. During the May invasions he commanded the forces holding the Jordan Valley kibbutzim against the Syrians where he distinguished himself by averting defeat when the demoralized settlers were on the verge of collapse.

Both sides tried to make maximum use of the U.N. truce (in violation of its conditions), but the Israelis were better placed to profit by the respite they had been given. Unlike the Arabs, whose lack of military coordination on the ground reflected bitter political rivalries between the five Arab governments involved, the Jewish military effort was increasingly centralized.*

The final unification of all Jewish military forces in Palestine was not achieved until the first truce, and even then not by agreement, but by force. Following the promulgation of Order No. 4, the leaders of the I.Z.L. had undertaken to dissolve the military wing of their organization and hand over their weapons to the Army. Except for those in Jerusalem (not yet legally part of the state territory) I.Z.L. and Lehi units duly joined the Army, but they did so *en bloc*, as distinct entities, often under their own officers. On 20 June 1948, the *Altalena*, a ship outfitted by I.Z.L. in France and loaded with arms and more than a hundred of its men, reached the coasts of Israel and triggered the final showdown. The I.Z.L. attempted to land men and weapons under its own auspices so that they could be sent to its units in Jerusalem and to I.Z.L. troops incorporated within the Army. Ben Gurion regarded the I.Z.L. as a dangerous source of dissidence and was determined to destroy it as a military organization. Following the failure of I.Z.L.–government negotiations, he ordered the Army to seize the ship and its contents upon landing, if needs be using force.[76]

The crisis culminated in a fire-fight on the Tel Aviv seafront. Civil war seemed to be in the offing; I.Z.L. men in the Army, including two complete battalions, deserted their front-line posts to come to the assistance of the *Altalena*. Desultory fighting continued until the ship was set on fire by a field gun firing from the shore. Fourteen I.Z.L. men and two soldiers were killed; the ship and its contents (including 5,000 rifles) were lost, but civil war was averted since the I.Z.L. leader, Menahem Begin, called off his men and gave up the struggle. Ben Gurion, who had refused all

* Apart from the Egyptian, Jordanian, Iraqi, Lebanese and Syrian armies, there was also the 'Arab Liberation Army', financed by the Arab League and commanded by a colourful soldier of fortune, Fawzi El-Kawkji.

the 7th Brigade were killed in a futile attempt to capture a police fortress held by the Arab Legion.[75]

compromise with the I.Z.L. in the face of two resignations from the provisional government, thus won a total victory over the I.Z.L.: the *Altalena* episode led to the final dissolution of its military wing. I.Z.L. units within the Army were disbanded and their men dispersed to other units while most ex-I.Z.L. officers were deprived of operational commands.

The final subordination of all military forces to a single national authority was symbolized by the oath of allegiance to the State and its government sworn by all Israeli soldiers on 29 June 1948. A day later, the last British soldiers holding the evacuation enclave at Haifa left the country.

Shortly after the beginning of the first truce, the commanders of the field brigades were summoned to Tel Aviv for a General Staff meeting with Ya'acov Dori, the Chief of Staff, and Yigal Yadin his number two,* as well as Ben Gurion and his deputy, Israel Galili. The record of the first month of all-out warfare was now reviewed and there were heated debates over administrative† and tactical problems, the most important of which was the question of operational command.

Given the small size of the country the Army G.H.Q. in Tel Aviv should have been able to control the brigades more effectively than had been the case. At the General Staff meeting brigade commanders claimed that valuable tactical opportunities had been missed because of poor coordination between different brigades fighting in the same sector. Neither the harassed brigade commanders nor the remote central G.H.Q. could cope with multi-brigade operations; most of the officers running the brigade staffs were totally inexperienced in large-scale warfare. They had barely come to grips with the problem of controlling their own battalions in combined brigade-wide operations. Nor did G.H.Q. fill the command gap. The obvious solution was to set up intermediate commands between G.H.Q. and the brigades in order to control all multi-brigade operations. Such commands could be based

* Yigal Yadin was 'Chief of Operations' and therefore the second in command since there was no deputy Chief of Staff. Owing to Dori's poor health and indifferent leadership, Yadin acted as *de facto* Chief of Staff for much of the war.

† No proper provisions for the maintenance of soldiers' families had been made and there were bitter complaints of hardship needlessly inflicted.

either on the area-H.Q. or on the task-force principle. After much debate it was decided at the June meeting to appoint *temporary* task-force commanders to control combat operations whenever more than one brigade was involved. A few months later, this makeshift arrangement was scrapped and stable Front Commands were set up instead. In the meantime, task-force commanders were made responsible for all day-to-day decisions, while objectives and forces were assigned to each separate operation by G.H.Q. in the framework of its overall strategy.

The most basic problem of the May–June fighting had nothing to do with command arrangements and could not be solved by organizational compromises. Regular Arab troops equipped with automatic weapons, artillery and some armour, were formidable enemies for the Israelis; in comparison to the Palestinians with their single-shot rifles, the fire-power of the Arab regulars was devastating. Crossing the borders of Palestine while the Haganah's mobile forces were still engaged in battle against local irregulars, the Arab invasion contingents found only the border settlements in the path. With no artillery and hardly any anti-tank weapons the settlers nevertheless fought in most places with stubborn determination, but the Egyptians advancing from the south, the Arab Legion from the east, the Syrians from the north-east and the Lebanese from the north, soon overran or bypassed the first line of border settlement

One Egyptian column moving up the coast reached to within twenty miles of Tel Aviv, and the second crossed the northern Negev and linked up with the Jordanians in Jerusalem. The Arab Legion had taken the Old City and the Etzion settlements south of Jerusalem; it now held the Latrun fortress astride the only road to Tel Aviv. The Syrians and Lebanese were stopped short by a series of local counter-attacks and neither was really prepared for an advance in depth, but the Arab Liberation Army, a force of mercenaries and volunteers financed by the Arab League, had entered central Galilee and threatened Jewish communications in the whole of north-east Palestine.

In spite of their successes, the Arab states, like Israel, welcomed the U.N. truce. The desperate resistance of the border settlements and the counter-attacks of small but determined Hish and Palmach units, had come as a rude shock to the Arabs. The Egyptians in particular had suffered heavy losses in their ill-prepared attacks against the kibbutzim in their path (especially at Yad Mordechai, where some of the settlers were survivors of the Warsaw Ghetto uprising). Both Jews and Arabs were utterly exhausted since their poorly trained troops were incapable of sustained warfare – and both hoped to gain a net advantage from a pause in the fighting. In retrospect, it is clear that the Israelis made the best use of the truce – which thus became the decisive turning point of the 1948 War. Mobilization was still increasing the Army's manpower and the Arab advantage in fire power was about to be reversed. The U.N. truce was supposed to include a freeze on all arms supplies, but this provision was openly violated by both sides.*

There was no effective inspection on the purchase and delivery of weapons from abroad and it was during the truce that the first tanks and field guns reached the Army. Israeli workshops, now no longer hampered by secrecy, were producing quantities of grenades and submachine-guns as well as simple mortars and crude anti-tank weapons. By the time the fighting resumed the shortage of infantry weapons was no longer as acute as it had been during the May battles. In heavy equipment the Army was still inferior to the Arabs, though this too changed within a few months. During the truce the Israelis had also gained another kind of advantage by building a detour on the road to Jerusalem (the 'Burma Road') south of the Latrun fortress, which was still held by the Arab Legion, so that communications were restored after a month-long siege.[78]

On 9 July 1948, the fighting started again and the Israeli Army seized the initiative in a series of swift offensives, never to lose it again. The most important of these offensives was operation Dani whose aim was to clear the Arab Legion from the centre of the country. In line with the new structure of command, the five brigades involved in Dani were controlled by a single task-force commander, Yigal Allon, whose subordinates included his mentor Yitzhak Sadeh, now commander of the 8th Brigade, and Moshe Dayan, in charge of Sadeh's 'jeep commando' battalion. By then

---

* On 15 June 1948, for example, Ben Gurion recorded the arrival of ten 75mm guns, ten light tanks with 37mm guns, nineteen 65mm guns and four 20mm automatic guns.[77] At the same time, Arab weapon inventories were being freely transferred to the forces in Palestine.

Allon had emerged as the Army's outstanding field commander in leading the Palmach forces which conquered Safed and defended upper Galilee. Allon confirmed his reputation in Dani: the two large Arab towns of Lod and Ramle were conquered and the coastal plain secured. But once again the Israelis failed to take the Latrun fortress, and the main highway to Jerusalem remained closed when the second truce came into effect on 19 July 1948, after ten days' fighting.

In the north, the Israelis launched operation Dekel against the irregulars of the Arab Liberation Army in central Galilee; after two days of fighting the entire area including Nazareth fell to the Israelis. The Egyptians were also forced on the defensive, though the Israelis, fully engaged on other fronts, did not mount a large-scale attack in the south as well. On the Syrian, Lebanese and Iraqi fronts in Galilee and Samaria, the fighting was inconclusive, but here too the Arabs failed to launch major attacks so that the Israelis were free to deploy their main effort against central Palestine and the Arab Legion in operation Dani. The lack of cooperation between the Arab armies in Palestine had now become apparent: the Arab Legion fought alone against numerically superior Israeli forces and received no help from other Arab forces.

When the second U.N. truce came into effect on 19 July, it was the Arabs who were undoubtedly the beneficiaries. The Israeli Army, now more than 60,000 strong, was ready to continue the offensives while the Arab armies were exhausted and demoralized. The Negev was still cut off by the Egyptians and much of northern Galilee was still held by the irregulars of the Arab Liberation Army. As far as the Israelis were concerned, the war was far from over. Although the second U.N. truce was not officially terminated until the armistice agreements brought the war to an end, the fighting was renewed several times, and each time the Israelis made additional gains.

By July 1948 the Jewish underground militia had grown into something resembling a modern army with field brigades, support units, a 'Sea Corps' and an 'Air Corps',* but its organization was still chaotic.

---

* In the unified multi-service structure the Air Force and Navy were designated as corps on a par with, e.g., the Artillery. In fact their autonomy was much wider.

There was a wasteful proliferation of detachments, units, corps and commands: scarce supplies and trained manpower were increasingly absorbed by staffs and rear services at the expense of the 'teeth' units. When the second truce came into effect, the General Staff attempted to impose some order on the haphazard if dynamic growth of the Army: it decreed that no more combat field formations were to be set up, so that any additional supplies, weapons and manpower could be channelled to the twelve existing brigades.* It also attempted to consolidate the loosely organized homeguards of the Him into new 'garrison brigades' responsible for static defence duties in their own home areas.

The competitive tendencies so typical of the Yishuv were much in evidence within the Army and especially in its service and support units. These hardly existed in May 1948 but by the onset of the second truce, just two months later, the Army had acquired no fewer than twenty-eight different support corps and service branches operating with a generous overlap in functions, and no coordination to speak of. The General Staff, which had already organized its own Operations, Manpower, Quartermaster and Training branches, now defined the jurisdictions of different rear-services and attempted to eliminate some of the worst instances of duplication.

The Army's command structure was also reorganized and four Front Commands (North, East, Centre and South) were set up to provide intermediate command echelons between the brigades and G.H.Q. The makeshift 'task-force' commands were scrapped but the new brigade-front-G.H.Q. structure still included an anomalous element, the separate Palmach Command headed by Yigal Allon. The three Palmach brigades had been fighting under the overall control of G.H.Q. on the same footing as all other combat units, but though they were part of the Army (as of the Haganah before it), Palmach units retained their distinctive features, which the existence of a separate Palmach Command helped to preserve. Since strategic direction was in the hands of G.H.Q., and tactical control was the responsibility of brigade and Front H.Q.s, the only functions left to the Palmach Command were administrative,

---

* The three Palmach brigades, Yiftah, Harel and Hanegev; the six former Hish brigades, Carmeli, Givati, Golani, Alexandroni, Kiryati and Etzioni; and the three 'new' brigades, the 7th, the armoured 8th, and *Oded* (the 9th).

mainly manpower and training – and these overlapped with the functions of the corresponding G.H.Q. branches. In other words, the separate Palmach structure was not efficient from the managerial point of view. But the real issue was political, and had very little to do with administrative arrangements.[79]

Most Palmach officers now belonged to the pro-Soviet left-wing Mapam party,* the main rival of the ruling Mapai, Ben Gurion's party.

This political problem had first arisen in 1944 but now that Ben Gurion was vested with state powers as Prime Minister and Minister of Defence he refused to tolerate the Palmach's separate organizational existence and distinctive politics. In October 1948, Ben Gurion, acting through the Army's Chief of Staff, Ya'akov Dori, ordered the dissolution of the Palmach Command – and thus triggered a major controversy which remained a live political issue for many years. The Mapam was only a small left-wing party, but the Palmach had won a great deal of prestige through the outstanding military successes of its members, and many Israelis outside Mapam rose to defend the Palmach's distinctive status. The order dissolving the Palmach Command was issued on 7 October 1948, but large-scale fighting broke out a week later and Ben Gurion's order was not implemented until November; in the meantime, Mapai and Mapam fought it out in a bitter political controversy.†

Throughout the controversy, Palmach men continued to serve

* In 1948 the Achdut HaAvoda merged with the marxist revolutionary HaAhomer HaAzair to form Mapam.

† The Mapam demanded that the issue be decided by the Histadrut's General Council, the supreme ruling body of the entire Labour movement (which included both the Mapan and Mapai). The Histadrut had been the strongest political force in the Yishuv, but with the creation of the State representative and executive bodies, it had lost some of its prominence. This was unfortunate for the Mapam which was far more strongly represented on the Histadrut's General Council than on its state counterpart, the provisional State Council. Ben Gurion insisted that the question of the Palmach Command was a national, and not a class question and that as such it should be decided by the representative body of the State, and not in the councils of the Labour movement. With the aid of Mapai's coalition allies, Ben Gurion won the procedural battle; Mapam's subsequent political defeat became inevitable, since Mapai was the largest party and it enjoyed the support of a majority coalition in the State Council.

as loyal national soldiers and there was no threat of overt dissidence. This was just as well since, apart from their own three brigades, Palmach officers were also in charge of several non-Palmach brigades and battalions. Moreover, in October 1948, Yigal Allon, the Palmach Commander, also commanded the key Southern Front and thus controlled a majority of the Army's striking forces. The prominence of Allon and other Palmach officers in the top command echelons resulted from their achievements in the May–June battles. Until then, many Israelis had regarded the Palmach as a guerrilla force unfit for sustained combat against regular forces, but by the summer of 1948 the Palmach had proved outstandingly successful in open warfare, and many of its officers were appointed to commands in the Army at large.

The Palmach controversy did not weaken the Jewish war effort. The Army continued to grow and, by October 1948, the number of men and women in uniform had doubled since May, reaching a total of more than eighty thousand. Moreover, the Army's manpower was now deployed far more efficiently. Instead of a disorderly flow to the nearest (or most acquisitive) unit, there was now a fairly efficient mobilization service with the rudiments of an induction procedure. Men and women were no longer sent to battle without some basic training at the newly established instruction camps. Soldiers were assigned to their units by the Manpower branch of the General Staff, and this put an end to the manpower free-for-all, though many imbalances remained.*

As a token of central regulation, the home-made ribbons and armbands worn by officers until then were replaced by standard insignia based on a table of ranks. The Chief of Staff alone carried the highest rank, *Rav Aluf* (a Biblical title), then equivalent to brigadier; other ancient titles were revived for the ranks of *Aluf* (colonel), *Sgan Aluf* (Lieut.-colonel), *Rav Seren* (major), *Seren* (captain), *Segen Rishon* (1st lieutenant) and *Segen* (lieutenant). Though regulation pips, ribbons and uniforms were also prescribed, the majority of Israeli soldiers continued to wear whatever clothes they liked – or could get – since there were not enough

---

* The Givati and Oded were both listed as brigades, but the former continued to be almost twice as large as the latter; overall, the distribution of scarce supplies and heavy weapons was still far from optimal.

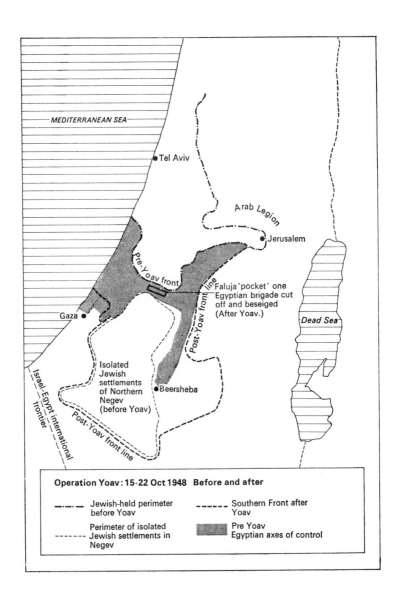

MEDITERRANEAN SEA

● Tel Aviv

Arab Legion

● Jerusalem

Pre-Yoav front

Faluja 'pocket' one
Egyptian brigade cut
off and beseiged
(After Yoav.)

Post-Yoav front line

Dead Sea

Gaza ●

Israel-Egypt international frontier

Isolated
Jewish
settlements
of Northern
Negev
(before Yoav)

● Beersheba

Post-Yoav front line

Operation Yoav: 15-22 Oct 1948 Before and after

—··—·— Jewish-held perimeter
before Yoav

------ Southern Front after
Yoav

------- Perimeter of isolated
Jewish settlements in
Negev

▨ Pre Yoav
Egyptian axes of control

Map 3

issue uniforms. No real attempt to enforce dress discipline was made and, in spite of the new ranks, relations between officers and men were still governed by the informality of a citizen army.

The U.N. embargo remained in force throughout the war and the supply of arms to both Arabs and Israelis was correspondingly restricted. In spite of a buyers' market, the abundant war surplus in Europe and America could not be imported without great difficulties. The thriving international black market in arms could not handle large and visible items such as tanks and aircraft, and, given its business ethics, it was difficult to ensure that any weapons obtained through this source would be battle-worthy. Nevertheless, between July 1948 and the end of the war the Israelis brought in several large shipments of rifles, machine-guns and ammunition, as well as hundreds of mortars, field guns and armoured vehicles (mainly light-armour troop carriers). Most of the weapons came from Communist Czechoslovakia; in the West they could only be obtained and flown to Israel by the most desperate expedients, as in the case of the British Beaufighter light bombers bought (legally) to make a war film which were flown to Israel as soon as the first take-off was filmed.

Then as now, the U.N. was ineffectual but the embargo decreed at its Security Council was eagerly enforced by the American State Department, the British Foreign Office and their powerful agencies in Europe. Severe shortages also affected the Arab armies whose stocks of pre-embargo equipment were running low. Neither side had any real difficulty in obtaining small arms and this made for a war of infantry battles.

Starting with operation Yoav in October 1948, the Israeli Army launched a series of major offensives with a far greater concentration of forces than ever before. Instead of the hurried preparations and scattered deployments of previous operations, the Israelis now assembled large, multi-brigade task forces and attacked on one front at a time. Air strikes began to be coordinated with the attacks of the ground forces, and even the poorly equipped and very small Navy took some part in the fighting. On 15 October 1948, the Egyptians provided the pretext the Israelis needed to break the truce by firing on a U.N.-authorized convoy; the offensive began almost immediately. Three infantry brigades (Givati, Yiftah and Hanegev) together with the 8th (Armoured), attacked on a front-wide scale under the overall command of Yigal Allon, now promoted to G.O.C. Southern Front. The main effort against the Egyptian front was assisted by a series of commando-raids against the Egyptian rear.[80] The Negev had been cut off ever since the Egyptian advance in May 1948 and the objective of operation Yoav was to break through and roll up the front thus clearing the Negev of Egyptian forces. While four brigades attacked on the ground, Israeli fighter-bombers attacked the air bases in Sinai. Not for the last time Egyptian aircraft were caught on the ground and the Israelis achieved superiority in the air. The Navy sent into action its frogmen who sunk the *Emir-Farouk*, flagship of the Egyptian navy, with man-guided torpedoes, the 'pigs' that the Italians had built during the Second World War. After six days of fighting, the U.N. reimposed the cease-fire and operation Yoav was brought to an end. The Egyptian army had not been surrounded and destroyed as the Israelis had planned, but the invasion salient along the coast towards Tel Aviv was driven back to its starting line just north of Gaza, while the second Egyptian invasion axis, which had frozen into a chain of strongholds astride the Negev roads, was breached, thus opening the main highway to the southern settlements. The only town in this desert area, Beersheba, was now in Israeli hands and, by driving a wedge across the east–west front, the Israelis had cut off an Egyptian brigade in the Faluja pocket.* Surrounded and besieged, the Egyptians repulsed every Israeli attempt to reduce the pocket until they were evacuated at the end of the war.

One week after Yoav, the Israelis launched their next major offensive at the opposite end of the country, in northern Galilee. Operation Hiram, spearheaded by the 7th Brigade, began on 31 October 1948 and was completed in less than three days: by then the whole of Galilee was occupied, and the Jews went on to take a strip of Lebanese territory (returned following the 1949 armistice). After this fresh defeat the Arab Liberation Army collapsed while the Lebanese army was driven across the border and out of the war.

The last of the offensives, operation Horev, was also the

---

* This Egyptian brigade was commanded by Col. (later Brig.) Taha Hussein, whose intelligence officer was Maj. (later Col.) Gamal Abdul Nasser.

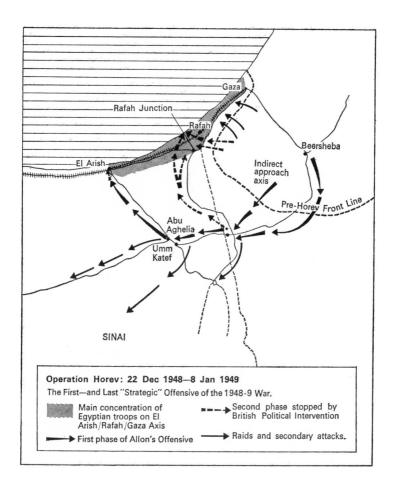

Operation Horev: 22 Dec 1948—8 Jan 1949

The First—and Last "Strategic" Offensive of the 1948-9 War.

Main concentration of Egyptian troops on El Arish/Rafah/Gaza Axis

First phase of Allon's Offensive

Second phase stopped by British Political Intervention

Raids and secondary attacks.

Gaza

Rafah Junction

Rafah

Beersheba

El Arish

Indirect approach axis

Pre-Horev Front Line

Abu Aghelia

Umm Katef

SINAI

Map 4

largest. The strategic aim was to destroy the Egyptian forces still in Palestine by a large-scale envelopment from the interior of the Negev to the Sinai coast at El Arish. Following their defeat in Yoav, the Egyptians had been pushed back to an L-shaped front whose hinge was at Rafah on the Mediterranean. Instead of a direct attack by way of Gaza, the Israelis planned an east–west swing from Beersheba to Rafah in order to cut the road and rail lines leading back to Egypt and thus surround the entire Egyptian army. Meanwhile, a series of raids deep into the interior of Sinai were to confuse the Egyptian command by threatening airfields and depots well behind the front. While the Alexandroni Brigade held the ring around the Egyptian brigade in Faluka, on 22 December 1948, the Golani, Harel and Hanegev together with the 8th (Armoured) Brigade launched the main offensive. The Israelis advanced across the Negev and moved into Sinai defeating the strongholds on their path. By the end of the first week Egyptian resistance was beginning to collapse; the way to Rafah and victory seemed open. Operation Horev had virtually achieved its objectives after two weeks of fighting when the Israeli government ordered an immediate withdrawal on 8 January 1949. The Israeli columns had already come within sight of the Mediterranean and the raiding parties were deep into Sinai, having reached Bir Hamma and Bir Haana, when a British ultimatum threatening military intervention (and an American warning), stopped the Israelis in their tracks.[81] The British had not yet recognized the government of Israel and there were enough British ground and air forces deployed in the Canal Zone to make the threat immediately credible.*

By the time operation Horev was suspended, on 7 January 1949, the Egyptians held only one small segment of Palestine, the coastal area which came to be called the Gaza Strip. The Egyptians had been saved by the British ultimatum but there was no doubt that their army had been thoroughly defeated. Its front had been breached, its lines of communication cut and, but for the ulti-

---

* The British ultimatum was based on the Anglo-Egyptian treaty of 1936, though the Egyptians had not asked for British help and had in fact already repudiated the treaty. The British government was later subjected to considerable domestic criticism for having issued an ultimatum in such circumstances.

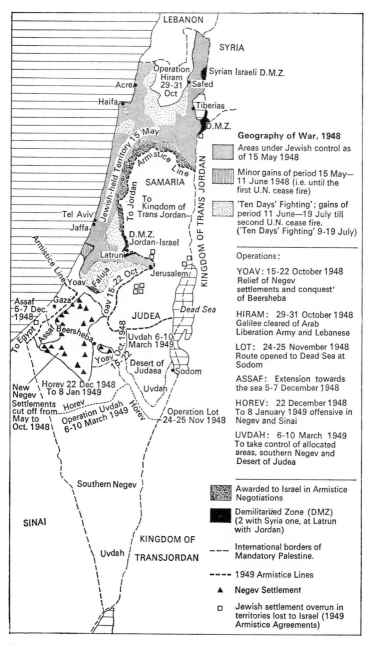

LEBANON

SYRIA

Operation
Hiram
29-31
Oct

Syrian Israeli D.M.Z.

Acre

Safed

Haifa

Tiberias

D.M.Z.

Geography of War, 1948

Areas under Jewish control as
of 15 May 1948

Minor gains of period 15 May–
11 June 1948 (i.e. until the
first U.N. cease fire)

'Ten Days' Fighting'; gains of
period 11 June—19 July till
second U.N. cease fire.
('Ten Days' Fighting' 9-19 July)

15 May

Armistice Line

SAMARIA

To Jordan

To
Kingdom of
Trans Jordan

Tel Aviv

Jaffa

D.M.Z.
Jordan-Israel

Armistice Line

Latrun

Yoav

Faluja

Jerusalem

Operations:

YOAV: 15-22 October 1948
Relief of Negev
settlements and conquest'
of Beersheba

Assaf
5-7 Dec.
1948

Gaza

Yoav 15-22 Oct

JUDEA

Dead Sea

HIRAM: 29-31 October 1948
Galilee cleared of Arab
Liberation Army and Lebanese

To Egypt

Assaf

Beersheba

Yoav 15-22 Oct 1948

Uvdah 6-10
March 1949

LOT: 24-25 November 1948
Route opened to Dead Sea at
Sodom

Desert of
Judaea

Sodom

ASSAF: Extension towards
the sea 5-7 December 1948

New
Negev

Horev 22 Dec 1948
To 8 Jan 1949

Uvdah

HOREV: 22 December 1948
To 8 January 1949 offensive in
Negev and Sinai

Settlements
cut off from
May to
Oct. 1948

Horev

Operation Uvdah
6-10 March 1949

Horev

Operation Lot
24-25 Nov 1948

UVDAH: 6-10 March 1949
To take control of allocated
areas, southern Negev and
Desert of Judea

Southern Negev

Awarded to Israel in Armistice
Negotiations

SINAI

KINGDOM OF

Uvdah

TRANSJORDAN

Demilitarized Zone (DMZ)
(2 with Syria one, at Latrun
with Jordan)

International borders of
Mandatory Palestine.

1949 Armistice Lines

▲ Negev Settlement

□ Jewish settlement overrun in
territories lost to Israel (1949
Armistice Agreements)

KINGDOM OF TRANS JORDAN

Map 5

matum, the surrender of all Egyptian forces in Palestine would only have been a matter of time.

The last operation of the war was Uvdah (or 'fact', i.e. *fait accompli*). Launched on 10 March 1949, Uvdah involved no serious fighting: three Israeli brigades were sent to take possession of the southern Negev down to the shores of the Red Sea – at a time when the armistice negotiations were already under way. The Arab Legion held some small outposts along the way, but these were pulled back without a battle. Both sides wanted to avoid fresh fighting. Except for the Egyptian hold on the Gaza Strip, only Abdullah's Kingdom of Transjordan had been able to retain a part of Palestine, the Arab-inhabited hills of Judea and Samaria, which his grandson, King Hussein, was to lose two decades later in the 1967 war.

The Arabs had tried and failed to conquer; utterly exhausted and facing Israeli forces they could no longer resist, Egypt, Jordan, Lebanon and Syria resorted to diplomacy. On 20 July 1949, the last of the four armistice agreements – between Israel and Syria – was signed on the Island of Rhodes.* The first Arab–Israeli war was over.

* The Arab states negotiated as they had fought, separately. Israel signed its armistice agreement with Egypt on 25 February 1949, with Lebanon on 23 March, with Jordan on 3 April, and with Syria on 20 July. Iraq, which had no common border with Israel, did not agree to an armistice and simply withdrew its forces without signing any agreement.

The Army of Independence

The Army which mounted the last offensives of 1948 scarcely resembled the Haganah of November 1947. There were more men who were better trained, there was much more equipment and a command structure; but the fundamental difference was that the guerrillas and home guards of the Haganah had become full-fledged soldiers in a national army. At the beginning of 1948, the Haganah operated in units no larger than companies with a hundred men or so, but less than one year later the Army deployed multi-brigade task forces with thousands of men. The Haganah High Command had been little more than a consultative body, while the Army's G.H.Q. had become the source of all strategic direction with a full complement of Intelligence, Logistic and Operational staffs. Haganah men had carried all their meagre supplies with them but, by the autumn of 1948, Army transport, supply and maintenance services could sustain large-scale offensives in depth. The Artillery, non-existent in April 1948, was now organized into a corps with 250 field guns and light cannon manned by trained gun-crews; an Armour Corps had also been formed, its tanks, half-track carriers and armoured cars serving with the mechanized forces of two brigades. The Air Force had been set up from scratch and within six months its fighter squadrons had defeated the Egyptians, who already had an air force when the Palmach was still experimenting with gliders.[1] Other changes, less visible but perhaps just as important, derived from the Army's status as the official force of a sovereign State. The Minister of Defence and the General Staff below him now had undisputed authority over all the armed forces, the I.Z.L. and Lehi no longer existed and the Palmach command had been abolished.

But the Israeli Army was by no means a sophisticated military force by world standards. Its equipment was poor, its officers inexperienced and of uneven quality, while its administration was still chaotic. Nevertheless, the basic structures proved sound. And if the Army's inner workings were different from those of traditional military forces, this was not necessarily a disadvantage. Indeed, Israeli military successes in 1948 and later years may have owed much to this difference, which derived from the very nature of the Yishuv. The fact that the Jews lacked military traditions at least allowed plenty of scope for original methods and new ideas. Not being experienced professionals, the Army's commanders tended to handle military problems in a manner which can best be described as 'intellectual' as opposed to authoritarian; this reflected the whole weight of Jewish tradition as well as the egalitarian social atmosphere of the Yishuv. Orders were commonly formulated after open debate in which rank often carried less weight than sound arguments, and could rarely be imposed by the sheer authority of superior rank.[2]

The Army of 1948 was too diverse to have a uniform method of command. In one brigade all decisions emanated from the top; in another, more leeway would be given to battalion commanders. But a theoretical doctrine of command did emerge in the course of the war, eventually becoming an accepted orthodoxy. Based on the principle of the 'maintenance of objective', this doctrine left the detail of tactics and methods to the discretion of unit commanders, so long as they achieved their objectives.[3] In the midst of battle, the subordinate commander at the head of his troops may see only a narrow segment of the fighting; his superiors at higher headquarters in the rear will have a far broader picture of the tactical situation, but one lacking in immediacy. In the flux of combat with its fleeting opportunities and sudden dangers, much depends on how quickly an army can respond – and this in turn depends on the *level* at which tactical decisions are made: the lower the echelon of decision, the nearer to the scene of battle and the faster the response. A decentralized method of command gradually became prevalent in the Army of 1948, increasing its flexibility.

The tendency to centralize command can derive from the reluctance of junior officers to shoulder responsibility as much as from their superiors' desire to dominate the conduct of the battle from the rear. The price of these common bureaucratic attitudes is that valuable tactical opportunities may be lost. Front-line commanders fail to act promptly because they want to be 'covered' by orders from above; while their superiors can only make decisions based on second-hand reports of the situation on the ground. The decentralized command system in the Israeli Army was a reflection of the mental outlook of its officers. Commanders, however junior, were willing to act on their own initiative. If this meant that there was no immediate restraint on field commanders who resorted to bold gambles in dangero. s situations, this was just as well in the specific context of the 1948 War. At the time of the May invasions, the Israelis were often under such severe pressure that the only solution was to adopt tactics outside the scope of sound military practice. Against an enemy whose superiority in fire-power was at first overwhelming, prudent (and therefore low-gain) tactics might simply have ensured defeat. The most successful Israeli commanders were those who saw that the underlying fragility of the Arab armies put a premium on boldness; the least successful were those who tried to copy conventional tactics.

The leading practitioner of the art of the calculated risk was Yigal Allon who experienced some of the most desperate fighting of the war while in charge of operation Yiftah in upper Galilee (6 May – 10 May). Safed, the key objective, was captured on 10 May after a series of daring attacks against Arab forces entrenched on commanding heights; Allon's tactics were bold but it was the strategic aspect of the operation that involved risk-taking of a high order. While Allon was concentrating his forces around Safed, the Jewish villages and kibbutzim in upper Galilee were under attack from Lebanese and irregular forces with vastly superior fire-power. Allon was responsible for the security of the area as a whole, but he chose to leave the settlements to fend for themselves so as to retain the initiative and launch the offensive against Safed. Throughout the four-day operation, Allon was under great pressure to divert some forces to defend the settlements, but he rejected their increasingly desperate appeals:

I did not agree under any condition to concede the initiative in the Safed area . . . I believed that consistent initiative on the part of our forces would in the end force the enemy to concede the initiative to us and go over to the defensive.[4]

When begged to send troops to Ramot Naphtali, one of the villages under attack, he refused and threatened to shoot the settlers if they abandoned the village. As it turned out all the settlements withstood the attacks, Safed fell to the Israelis and it was the Arabs who were forced to scatter their forces for defence, thus losing the ability to launch further attacks of their own.

After his success in Yiftah, Allon was appointed task-force Commander of operation Dani (9–19 July). The prime objectives of Dani were the Latrun fortress and large Arab towns of Lod and Ramle which dominated a section of the Jerusalem highway and the country's main airport. Both towns were fortified and defended by large numbers of Palestinian irregulars supported by Arab Legion detachments. Allon's immediate problem was tactical:

> Both towns were well fortified. Aerial photos showed a complete system of trenches and fortifications ... possibly this was the only locality in the country where the Arabs had established a comprehensive defence network.[5]

But as in the battle for Safed, it was the strategic setting which was really problematic: the two towns are on the edge of the hills of Samaria where Iraqi forces and Arab Legion mobile units were deployed. The plan for Dani called for a concentrated blow against Lod and Ramle; no forces could be kept in reserve to meet attacks from the flanks. Allon was aware of the risk of counter-attacks from Samaria, but felt that if adequate forces were held back to meet this eventuality, the forces left for the offensive would be too weak to succeed. As Allon wrote later:

> Such a course of action (an all-out attack) would bring about bloody battles whose outcome it was impossible to foresee. Penetration into thickly populated cities, without security for the mountain flanks, might lead to disaster.[6]

Allon took the risk, and operation Dani went ahead as planned. Lod and Ramle were both captured. The Jordanians only held on to Latrun because of the second U.N. cease-fire.

A famous episode of the Dani battles illustrates just how bold Israeli tactics sometimes were. When Lod was attacked, the tanks of the 8th Brigade were supposed to provide close fire-support to breach the fortifications of the perimeter. But when the tanks failed to arrive on time the commander of the brigade's jeep commando

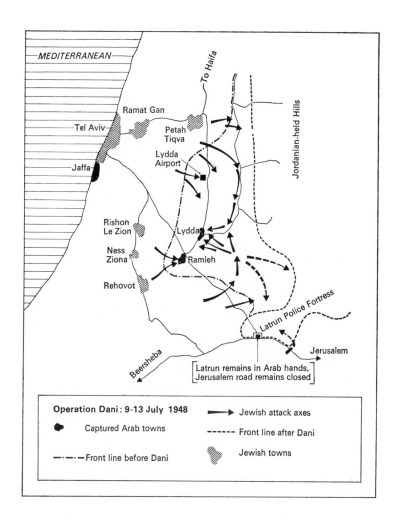

MEDITERRANEAN

To Haifa

Jordanian-held Hills

Ramat Gan

Tel Aviv

Petah
Tiqva

Lydda
Airport

Jaffa

Rishon
Le Zion

Lyddas

Ness
Ziona

Ramleh

Rehovot

Latrun Police Fortress

Beersheba

Jerusalem

Latrun remains in Arab hands,
Jerusalem road remains closed

Operation Dani: 9–13 July 1948

- Captured Arab towns
- Jewish attack axes
- Front line after Dani
- — · — · Front line before Dani
- Jewish towns

Map 6

battalion, Moshe Dayan, volunteered to attempt the breakthrough, even though his force lacked the armour and fire-power needed for the job. Dayan later described what happened:

The unit advanced in a column headed by an Arab Legion armoured car . . . captured in yesterday's operations. A gunner had somehow been found and a wireless operator . . . and immediately it was put to service in our ranks. When the column was about one kilometre from the city, it encountered heavy fire. The 'Terrible Tiger' [the captured vehicle] would halt from time to time, and return fire to the fortified positions, with the convoy continuing on its way.[7]

Dayan's jeep-mounted troops broke through the fortified perimeter around Lod, drove across the town at top speed and came out at the other side reaching Ramle. This raid shattered the defenders' morale, and both towns were captured in short order by a follow-up infantry attack.

After the second truce, Allon was appointed Commander of the key Southern Front and operation Yoav (15–22 October 1948) demonstrated his generalship in the strategic setting of a front-wide offensive. The goal of Yoav was to open a route to the Negev settlements that had been cut off since May by the west–east axis of the Egyptian invasion. The original G.H.Q. plan called for the capture of the village of Iraq el Manshie, one of the strongholds on which the Egyptian front was based. Located at the eastern end of the front, Iraq el Manshie was the chosen objective because it was thought to be weakly held, even though its capture would only open up an inferior and longer route to the Negev. As for the main highway leading to the south, this was dominated by the Huleikat junction, where Egyptian defences were much stronger. An attack on the village of Iraq el Manshie was duly launched on 16 October, after a preliminary air strike. This was the first Israeli attempt at a combined assault with armour and artillery and it was a failure. The Israelis were repulsed and suffered heavy casualties.

Immediately after the fight, Allon decided to switch the whole thrust of the attack westwards in order to seize the junction astride the main north–south highway and break through to the Negev.[8] This meant that much stronger defences than those of Iraq el Manshie had to be attacked, but Allon felt that a swift change of direction would catch the Egyptians by surprise, since they would scarcely expect the Israelis, who had just failed against a small stronghold, to attack a much stronger one. But Yadin and Allon's other superiors at General Headquarters disagreed; they felt that a direct attack against the strong Egyptian defences at the junction would lead to a costly defeat. Allon insisted and the others gave way, but only after he took full personal responsibility for the new plan. Once more, Allon was successful. The junction was captured and after a breakthrough at Huleikat, the highway to the Negev was opened.[9]

When the Israelis moved south through Huleikat, Allon once again exploited a fleeting tactical opportunity by mounting a surprise attack against Beersheba. Until the Israeli breakthrough, this township had been well in the rear of the Egyptian front and was weakly held, even though it controlled the Gaza–Hebron road, which was the only land link between the Egyptians and the Jordanians. Given time, the Egyptians would probably have tried to send major reinforcements to the town; Allon was determined to forestall them. He ordered an immediate attack with whatever forces could be assembled. At 4 a.m. on 21 October the Israelis reached Beersheba only thirty hours after the breakthrough: the sudden blow came as a total surprise to the defenders who had not even been told that the junction had fallen. Within five hours the town was in Israeli hands and, with it, the Gaza–Hebron road.

The kind of risk-taking initiative which Allon's generalship exemplified cannot be taught in staff colleges; it can only derive from the social and personal characteristics of the men who make up an army's officer corps. The men who led the Israeli Army of 1948 were the unselected product of hurried and sometimes haphazard promotions, but an elite of successful combat officers nevertheless emerged in the desperate fighting of May–June 1948. The tactical methods evolved in the summer battles of containment and the subsequent offensives were formative experiences for the Army. Their operational doctrine, which emerged gradually and never became explicit, was in some respects a reversal of 'sound' military practice. On the offensive, forces were not to be held back in reserve, nor detached to guard the flanks, since in order to accumulate a winning margin of numerical superiority, all available forces had to be thrown into the assault;[10] on the defensive,

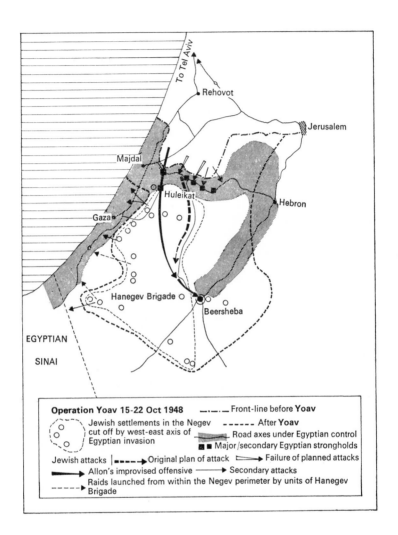

To Tel Aviv

Rehovot

Jerusalem

Majdal

Huleikat

Gaza

Hebron

Hanegev Brigade

Beersheba

EGYPTIAN

SINAI

Operation Yoav 15-22 Oct 1948 —.—.— Front-line before **Yoav**

Jewish settlements in the Negev - - - - - After **Yoav**
cut off by west-east axis of
Egyptian invasion Road axes under Egyptian control

■ ■ Major/secondary Egyptian strongholds

Jewish attacks ▮▬▬▶ Original plan of attack ▭▶ Failure of planned attacks

▬▬▶ Allon's improvised offensive ───▶ Secondary attacks

- - - - ▶ Raids launched from within the Negev perimeter by units of Hanegev
Brigade

Map 7

local home-guard forces were often left to fend for themselves while the mobile forces of the field brigades were concentrated for offensive tasks.

To sustain the severe pressures of the May–June battles, the officers of the Army of 1948 had to extract the utmost in fighting skill, morale and endurance from their poorly-trained soldiers, so as to offset the enemy's advantage in fire-power. The Palmach's methods had originally been worked out with this objective in mind. Instead of 'breaking' civilians in order to turn them into soldiers, Palmach training allowed maximum scope for personal initiative: in the words of its slogan, 'The smallest unit is the single man with his rifle.' Embodied in the method of the 'follow me' command order, it was Palmach doctrine that officers should 'pull' their men after them by being the first to advance instead of 'pushing' their men forward by direct orders. This meant that officers had to expose themselves to greater dangers than their men; then as now this doctrine exacted a high cost in blood. During operation Nachson (April 1948) a company of the Palmach's Harel Brigade was forced to withdraw from the hilltop village of Kastel near Jerusalem. Since the Arabs were about to reach the hilltop, the only way of saving at least part of the company was to leave a rear-guard to hold the summit while the others retreated down the slopes. Knowing that these men would almost certainly be cut off and killed, the company commander ordered his officers and N.C.O.s to form the rear guard. The words of his order have since been quoted in every Israeli officers' course:

'All privates will retreat, all commanders will cover their withdrawal.'

The company commander himself stayed behind and was killed together with the three platoon commanders and all but one of the nine section leaders.

In so far as Israeli soldiers had any combat experience before the war itself, this was mostly in guerrilla raids which put a premium on quick thinking and mobility. But the first defensive battles of May–June 1948 required disciplined endurance under fire. The Givati Brigade which countered the Egyptian advance towards Tel Aviv at the onset of the May invasion, showed how much could be achieved by sheer resilience and good leadership against an enemy vastly superior in fire-power. The Givati consisted of trained Hish

men and new recruits under the command of an outstanding
Palmach-trained officer, Shimon Avidan, who had already distinguished himself when in charge of operation Nachson one
month earlier. Most of the Givati officers were Hish-trained
and had no experience with defensive warfare against regular
troops supported by artillery. The Israelis nevertheless managed to
hold their ground in a series of small battles against the Egyptian
column whose drive northwards finally stopped at what is now
Ashdod. Since the Givati was the first Israeli brigade to fight
a full-scale battle against a regular army, its defensive victory set a
crucial precedent.[11]

For the Israelis, the main tactical problem during the May
invasion was Arab superiority in artillery and armour. The Arab
armies only had a few hundred guns and armoured cars between
them, but the Israelis at first had none. One answer was to use
guerrilla tactics to disrupt enemy deployments; they were put to the
test even before the May invasions. On 4 April 1948, the Arab
Liberation Army attacked the kibbutz of Mishmar Haemek with a
force of about 1,000 irregulars supported by seven field guns.
Artillery had never been used before by either Arabs or Jews and
the forces inside the kibbutz could not reply to the fire with conventional counter-battery tactics since they had no guns (their
heaviest weapon was a three-inch mortar). The founder of the
Palmach, Yitzhak Sadeh, was on the spot and he hit on the
solution: since the kibbutz had been a Haganah training camp
the Jews knew the terrain intimately, and they staged a series of
night attacks in guerrilla style to harass the Arab forces and
capture some villages in their rear. After ten days of skirmishing
the Arabs gave up the attempt to capture the kibbutz and withdrew into central Galilee. Sadeh himself later described the
fighting at Mishmar Haemek as an example of 'the superiority of
tactical flexibility and command initiative at all levels over a
numerically stronger enemy whose greater fire-power was deployed
in a routine and inflexible manner'.[12] This inflexibility, common to
all the Arab armies in 1948, is typical of colonial forces where, in
the absence of a sophisticated officer corps, combat methods are
based on rigid tactical rules.

Tactical inventiveness apart, the Israeli answer to Arab superiority in equipment was to acquire more and better weapons.

The Israelis had no precision machine tools with which to manu-facture heavy weapons or even simple rifles, but they did make submachine-guns, grenades and mortars. With the lifting of the British naval blockade on 15 May, imports of weapons and industrial equipment became easier and home production more sophisticated.

U.S.-built half-track carriers were turned into assault vehicles and, on at least one occasion, into tank destroyers. In September 1948, a month before operation Yoav, an Egyptian counter-attack on the stronghold of Khirbet Mahaz was spearheaded by Humber armoured cars, whose armour-plate the Israelis had no way of defeating. In a last-minute improvisation, a pair of 20mm anti-aircraft cannon were mounted on half-track carriers, thus con-triving a fighting vehicle which could match the armoured cars of the Egyptians. Two Humbers were destroyed and the Egyptian counter-attack was repulsed.[13]

The Israel of 1948 was neither rich nor technically sophisticated, but it was certainly a modern society. In education, outlook and social behaviour the Israelis approximated European standards, unlike the Arabs whose Western-educated elites were small. Accordingly, the Jewish war effort was characterized by a constant search for devices of the mind which could be brought to bear against a culturally backward enemy. Several of the commanders of the 1948 Army, including Yadin and Yitzhak Rabin,* have pointed out the similarity between Israeli practice and the theory of the 'indirect approach' evolved by the British military thinker, Sir Basil Liddell Hart.[14]

The 'indirect approach' is neither a strategy nor a tactic, but a general method of offensive warfare whose essence is the avoid-ance of frontal attacks on the enemy's forces. In a tactical sense, the 'indirect approach' implies that the offence should disrupt the enemy's defences rather than wear them down in a slogging battle of attrition. More generally, the concept of the 'indirect approach' covers all those strategies and tactics which are based on the 'line of least expectation'. If there is a highway from A to B which is strongly defended by the enemy, B should be

* In the War of Independence Rabin (Chief of Staff in 1967) commanded the *Harel* Brigade and later served as Allon's deputy at Southern Front headquarters.

approached by some other route, even though it may be a longer and more exposed one. In each case there is a price to be paid for not doing the expected thing, since risks have to be taken in doing the unconventional; but the assumption of this concept is that in war it pays to be unconventional.[15]

As Liddell Hart himself has put it:

Natural hazards, however formidable, are inherently less dangerous and less uncertain than fighting hazards. All conditions are more calculable, all obstacles more surmountable, than those of human resistance.[16]

The first, crucial stage of operation Horev (22 December–9 January 1948) was based on the 'indirect approach' in its most classic sense. Israeli mechanized columns advanced in a wide east–west envelopment and outflanked the Egyptians by driving along the bed of an ancient Roman road from Beersheba to Auja el Hafir. While the latter was not even marked on the map, there was also a good modern road to Auja, but this was held by strong Egyptian forces; by avoiding it, the Israelis cut off the Egyptian forces in eastern Sinai without having to fight grinding battles against the strongholds on the highway. It took a great deal of work to make this ancient route usable and sending mechanized columns along a narrow and very slow track involved considerable risk, but Yadin and Allon thought that terrain difficulties were a small price to pay for avoiding a frontal attack on the highway strongholds.

Another reason for the Israelis' preference for the 'indirect approach' in the 1948 War was the poor showing of Israeli troops in direct assaults against fortified positions. On the central front the Israelis made no fewer than five separate attempts to capture the police fortress at Latrun which controlled a segment of the highway to Jerusalem. All five attacks failed, more than seven hundred men were killed (as much as in the entire 1967 War), but the fortress remained in Jordanian hands.*

It was Ben Gurion himself, as Minister of Defence, who pressed for the repeated attacks on the Latrun fortress, against the advice of the senior officers at General Headquarters. While most

* The Israelis built a detour during the first truce, the 'Burma Road', and later a new segment of road, since Latrun remained in Jordanian hands until 1967 when it was captured without a shot being fired.

Israeli military historians have criticized Ben Gurion's insistence on repeated frontal attacks, at least one, the late Lieut.-Col. Israel Beer, argued that the Latrun battles had been worthwhile since they relieved Jordanian pressure against Jerusalem which was then under siege.*[17]

The pre-war Haganah had been trained and armed as light infantry to fight equally ill-equipped Palestinians and were expected to fight without supporting artillery or armoured vehicles. When the regular forces of the Arab states intervened in the war, the Israelis' lack of combat aircraft, artillery and armour threatened disaster. In the Yishuv there was neither the equipment nor the skills needed by such forces and if the Haganah's men could be hurriedly formed into infantry brigades, and even taught to use mortars and field guns, they could hardly become airmen, tank crews, or sailors overnight. Only a few Israelis had acquired these skills in the wartime Allied armies and the small group of Palmach airmen and sailors had only been trained to man light aircraft and simple motorboats. The Army did not have the time or the means to train men for such complex technical tasks. Nevertheless by July 1948 the Israelis set up an Air Force and a Navy, as well as a tank battalion; Jewish volunteers from abroad† provided much of the trained manpower of the Air Force and Navy, while immigrants who had served in the Soviet army manned most of the guns and tanks.‡

The volunteer pilots of 1948 were veterans of the American, British, Canadian and South African air forces, and their training

* Israel Beer was a leading military historian and commentator, but his prestige in the profession suffered a grievous blow, in 1961, when he was arrested and condemned for espionage on behalf of the Soviet Union.

† These were collectively known as *Mahal*; *Gahal*, the Hebrew acronym of 'overseas recruit', was applied to immigrants drafted into the Army directly upon their arrival from D.P. camps abroad.

‡ Ironically enough, the fighter pilots trained in the Allied air forces now found themselves flying the aircraft which had been the backbone of the German fighter wings, Messerschmitt BF. 109s, sold to Israel by the Communist government of Czechoslovakia. Although Israel was now a recognized sovereign state, no Western country agreed to sell her weapons. Czechoslovakia was the only legal government-to-government source of arms for the Israelis. For a brief period the Czechs also gave training facilities for Israeli paratroops and pilots.

and experience were far from uniform. The language barrier isolated them from the Israelis, and their relations with the few native-born pilots were not always smooth. Aharon Remez, a young Israeli fighter pilot trained in the R.C.A.F., headed the Air Force throughout the war and attempted to fashion his variegated aircraft and flight crews into an effective fighting force. He met with only limited success until the very end. Effective cooperation with the ground forces was the exception rather than the rule; independent, strategic operations, such as the bombing of Cairo in July 1948, were technically successful, but they had almost no impact on the conduct of the war.[18] The Air Force lacked a scale of priorities with which to choose between different combat missions, and neither did it have a tactical doctrine which fitted the needs of the ground forces. The few combat aircraft available at any one time were often used for poorly coordinated strikes in the enemy's rear at the expense of close support missions for the forces on the ground.

Nevertheless, the fact that Israel had an Air Force at all was of great military importance in itself. Within two weeks of the invasions, the first Israeli fighters were airborne, and on 29 May 1948 they flew their first combat mission. Four Messerschmitt BF. 109s, all there were, attacked the Egyptian column which was advancing along the coast; at that point, the Egyptians were less than twenty miles from Tel Aviv, and all that lay between them and the heart of the country was a sabotaged bridge and a battalion of exhausted troops from the Givati Brigade. The Egyptians suffered very few casualties from the air attack, but immediately afterwards they stopped to dig in; the spot was to mark the final limit of their advance which was never resumed. The Egyptians had not known that Israel had combat aircraft and their appearance on the battlefield came as a shocking surprise, as did the Israelis' first attempt at bombing in depth. The bombing of Cairo on 14 July 1948 by a single B-17 Flying Fortress which dropped two-and-a-half tons of bombs was in retaliation for a series of Egyptian bombing raids on Tel Aviv. The Israelis had managed to buy three B-17s in the United States through black market channels and the aircraft were flown to Czechoslovakia in order to load a cargo of bombs before flying on to Israel. At this point, the Air Force Command decided that, instead of taking the bombs as cargo, it was more efficient to fly via Cairo, dropping them en route. Only one B-17 reached the target and its attack apparently caused no damage of any kind, but the Egyptians did stop bombing Tel Aviv.

Following the Cairo raid, the Israelis staged bombing attacks against other Arab cities, including Amman and Damascus. Again, the tonnage of bombs dropped was small and the results negligible. Of far greater importance was the contest for air superiority over the battlefield. Neither side could intercept each other's aircraft since they had no proper radar coverage, but on the eve of operation Yoav the Israelis attacked Egyptian airpower at source: I.A.F. fighter bombers struck at bases in Sinai, catching many aircraft on the ground, and the Egyptian air force was knocked out of action. The Israelis retained air superiority for the rest of the war. By carrying out reconnaissance missions and preventing the enemy from doing so, by providing a reserve of flexible fire-power that could be switched quickly to any front, the Air Force contributed to the success of the forces on the ground, even though it often failed to give them direct support. The fighter pilots of the I.A.F. finished the war with a flourish: in January 1949, five R.A.F. fighters penetrated Israeli airspace on a reconnaissance mission and were promptly shot down. Anglo-Israeli relations were very tense and a retaliatory move was expected but the British government did not retaliate. British public opinion was incensed by the fact that the R.A.F. had been ordered to overfly a war zone for no compelling reason, and was in no mood to support a military reprisal against Israel. This incident did, however, play a part in bringing about the British ultimatum that brought operation Horev to an end on 9 January 1949.

With the Navy, matters were less satisfactory.[19] For much of the war, the fleet consisted of decrepit freighters armed with obsolete 65mm field guns on improvised mountings; landing craft and corvettes were also purchased, but did not arrive until the winter. Apart from the sinking of the *Emir Farouk*, and a useful blockade of Gaza port during operations Yoav and Horev, the Navy did not achieve very much. Commanded by an American Jewish volunteer, the Navy was marginal to a war in which naval power was insignificant on both sides.*

* Although with Israel dependent on seaborne supplies of food, fuel and arms, there would have been plenty of targets for Arab naval attacks. This

The Army's tank forces, or rather the single tank battalion of the 8th Brigade, were troubled by problems of structure and doctrine as much as by more prosaic shortcomings in training and equipment. The obvious need for technical expertise meant that the Israelis could not brush aside the standard operating procedures which foreign-trained tank crews brought with them. But attempts to imitate foreign methods almost invariably failed, owing to the equipment shortages* and the total lack of armour–infantry team training. Since there were no trained Israeli crews the tank battalion was manned by English-speaking volunteers and Russian-speaking immigrants who had served in the Soviet army. The battalion commander was an Israeli who spoke neither English nor Russian while his men spoke no Hebrew. Every order had to go through two interpreters and misunderstandings were frequent. In spite of chronic mechanical breakdowns, and the language problem, the tank battalion was employed in all the major operations from Dani onwards, though with meagre results. In later years, the Armour Corps was to establish a world-wide reputation, but the 1948 tank unit performed so poorly that right up to the Sinai Campaign Israeli armour was used only in support of the infantry.

If the 1948 Army remained essentially an infantry force, it was an increasingly motorized, and even mechanized infantry. The mechanized battalions, equipped with M.3 half-track carriers, armoured trucks and jeeps, performed very well right from the beginning.† The foot-mobility concepts of the Haganah were quickly and successfully adapted to mechanized warfare; and by the time the Israelis went over to the offensive, in Yoav and Horev, the mechanized battalions had become first-class combat units

* At first the 8th Brigade's tank unit consisted of one Sherman M.4, two Cromwell tanks brought by deserters from the British army, and ten H–35 light tanks of pre-war French origin.

† No fewer than three future Chiefs of Staff came out of the mechanized forces of 1948: Dayan, in charge of the 8th Brigade jeep commando, during operation Dani, Haim Laskov who led the 7th Brigade's mechanized battalion in the main Latrun battle, and in operation Hiram in October–November 1948, and Haim Bar Lev, who commanded the partially mechanized 9th battalion of the Palmach, in the Hanegev Brigade.

was not so in later Arab–Israeli wars, which were too short for effective blockade or interdiction strategies.

which spearheaded the advance of the motorized infantry with notable vigour. Their success was an example for the Army as a whole. It led to the belief that intellectual adaptability and originality were more important than specific expertise or formal military training, and that the home-grown officers of the Haganah (and especially those of the Palmach) could provide the creative military leadership which the Army needed to operate successfully in spite of its poor equipment.

The young men who shaped the growth of the Israeli Army and became its first officers were mostly born in the country rather than immigrants.* Many were the sons of the Socialist pioneers who had founded the trade unions, the kibbutzim and moshavim and built the political institutions of the Yishuv. Others came from the old-established families, which had settled the first Jewish villages in Palestine in the 1880s. While other institutions of the Yishuv remained under the leadership of the founding fathers, the Army did not. Under wartime pressures the veteran organizers of the Haganah were replaced by much younger men, who were more interested in problem-solving than in ideology, and who were also more self-confident since they were far better attuned to the environment of the country, and had no memories of Europe. Nevertheless the difference between the two generations did not impinge on fundamental issues since both fathers and sons belonged to the same small elite. It is striking to note just how many members of the new officer corps were the sons of parents who themselves belonged to the political elite of the Yishuv.† The Yishuv was an egalitarian society and the family connections between officer sons and politician fathers were not due to

* Jews born in Palestine and later Israel are popularly known as *sabra*(s) (*tsabar*) after a species of wild cactus or its fruit (prickly pear).

† These included Yadin, Dayan and three of the five who served at different times as brigade commanders in the Palmach (Yitzhak Rabin, whose mother, Rosa Cohen, was one of the early leaders of the Haganah; Yosef Tabenkin, son of the leader of the Achdut HaAvoda party; and Shmuel Cohen, son of the founder of the Histadrut's youth movement, Hanoar Haoved); the commander of the I.A.F. and three of his successors (Aharon Remez, son of a Yishuv politician and Israel's first Minister of Transport; Dan Tolkowsky, son of a Zionist leader, who became Israel's Ambassador to Switzerland; and Ezer Weizmann whose uncle, Chaim, was the head of the World Zionist Organization and first President of Israel).

nepotism.* The success of the sons of the elite in the Army derived from their peculiar background which had socialized them for leadership from childhood. A self-conscious elitism was part and parcel of the pioneering ideals of the Labour-Zionists and it carried over to their sons who were taught to seek leadership and not personal wealth.

The young officers of 1948 thus had many features in common with those pristine aristocracies (including military aristocracies) which base their claim to power or to a special social status on their service to the community. Needless to say, there was nothing aristocratic about their life-style; their behaviour was not conditioned by distinctive mannerisms or special tastes in consumption and, even by the standards of the Yishuv, their income was low. In so far as there was an etiquette in groups such as the Palmach, it was the avoidance of formal good manners or of any hint of conspicuous consumption. But the young officers did have some typically aristocratic features: a code of conduct peculiar to their own social group, and their self-image of born leaders responsible for the community as a whole.

The young men who became the brigade, battalion and company commanders of the Army of 1948, did not regard their service in the Haganah or the Army as a military career; they certainly did not think of themselves as professional soldiers belonging to a specifically military elite. Their circle of friends remained that of their original age group in the kibbutzim, moshavim or the city high schools, and these social links between Army officers and civilians were never broken, so that right from the beginning the Army became established as part of society and not as a body apart.

* Though party–political connections certainly did influence promotion.

3

After the Armistice: A New Army

When Israel demobilized most of the 80,000 wartime recruits in the summer of 1949, the Army of Independence virtually disintegrated. There was no peacetime military establishment to which to return, nor a cadre of pre-war professionals who would remain in uniform to pursue their careers. All that remained were some ex-British camps and airfields, a small stock of worn-out weapons and the first batch of post-war recruits. The officer corps, motor and brain of any army, had suffered the greatest disruption of all. So few officers agreed to remain in the peacetime army that combat units and command staffs became little more than empty boxes on organizational charts.

There had been fighting of one sort or another ever since the Arab revolt of 1936; Israelis had been through Arab terrorism, British repression, the Second World War and finally the 1948 War, in which one per cent of the Yishuv's population had been killed.* The country was war-weary, and this was perhaps the main reason for the mass resignations from the Army's officer corps.[1]

The young men who had led the Army of 1948 had never regarded themselves as professionals and had no desire for a life of peacetime soldiering. Many were eager to leave the Army in order to resume their education or to find jobs in the expanding civil service of the new State; others wanted to return to their kibbutzim and moshavim. For many officers, including some of the ablest field commanders of 1948, there was also another reason for leaving the Army.

Many Palmach officers belonged to the left-wing Mapam party,

* 4,017 soldiers and more than 2,000 civilians. There are no exact figures for the number of civilians killed while the definition of *military* casualties was often arbitrary.[2]

and political pressures led to their resignation from an Army which Ben Gurion and his Mapai party were now determined to control. The necessities of the war had forced Ben Gurion and Mapai to accept the promotion of Palmach officers to many important command positions, but as soon as the threat to national survival waned, political considerations again came to the fore. In January 1949, just after the battles of operation Horev, the first general elections were held; the social-democratic Mapai emerged as the largest party with 46 seats out of 120, but Mapam was the runner-up with 19 seats in the Knesset, Israel's Parliament.*[3]

The two parties were direct ideological rivals and in 1948–9 much of their rivalry focused on the Palmach. Mapam had made political capital out of its connection with the Palmach: its wartime Commander, Yigal Allon, was known to be a member, and he had commanded the victorious offensives of Horev just before the January elections. Allon was the outstanding figure of the war, but other Palmach officers such as Yosef Tabenkin, Yitzhak Rabin and Shmuel Cohen also enjoyed wide recognition, and it was well known that they belonged to the Mapam. Party membership was a serious matter in those days, since it implied personal commitment to a specific ideology; Army officers who were also members of Mapam would never have claimed that their politics were a purely private matter. On the contrary, many regarded their service in defence of the nation as an expression of their general political commitment. Nor did this apply just to officers: the training and indoctrination of all Palmach recruits was infused with the collectivistic ideology of left-wing Labour–Zionism, and its leaders repeatedly asserted that military training could not be divorced from social and political education. Indeed, they claimed that the Palmach embodied the pioneering values of political Zionism, and that it set an example for the rest of the Army and for Israeli society at large. In Allon's words:

The Palmach included all the pioneer youth movements, which combined their agricultural training for ultimate settlement [on the land] with their military training for special battle exploits; at the

* Neither then nor in any subsequent election did Mapai win an absolute majority in the Knesset; it has always had to rely on multi-party coalitions with the religious and centre parties to form the successive governments that have ruled Israel since 1949.

same time [they] did not segregate or isolate themselves from the rest of their units, but formed a nucleus for the entire force which included masses from the rural settlements, the colonies, the cities and the new immigrants. This was a blend that enabled the unit to remain military in character even during agricultural training, and agricultural in character [even] during military training.[4]

The elitist tone of this statement is not surprising, since the Palmach was dominated by the kibbutz element so prominent in the Yishuv's leadership. Another of Allon's arguments may appear somewhat incongruous, given the Mapam's revolutionary stance:

Anyone familiar with military practice will know how to evaluate unit tradition as a heartening factor in battle. Most of Zahal's units were lacking in tradition; the Palmach had behind it an organizational, social and professional tradition.

Ben Gurion had always denied the Palmach's claim to a distinctive 'pioneering' status: he explained his position in a famous letter to a wounded Palmach soldier who had appealed against the decision to dissolve the Palmach Command (in October 1948):

I do not believe that pioneering is the monopoly of the select few, a special privilege of a spiritual aristocracy. I am a great believer in the common folk, all Israel and every one in Israel, and if the seed of pioneering is sown in all army units, we shall be privileged to witness a blessed harvest. There is no need or justification for the setting apart or singling out of certain brigades as pioneering brigades or to consider all other brigades as non-pioneering ones.[5]

In view of the history of endless political controversy within the Haganah and the fresh memories of the bitter conflict with the I.Z.L. and Lehi, it is understandable that Ben Gurion was anxious to eliminate the Palmach's influence within the Army. Lacking state power, the politics of the majority leadership of the Yishuv had been a continuing search for a voluntary consensus, but Ben Gurion was now Prime Minister and Minister of Defence and subject only to the approval of the Cabinet and the Knesset, in both of which the Mapai and its coalition partners had a ruling majority. Vested with full state powers, Ben Gurion launched a relentless campaign against the Palmach.[6] Its three brigades (Harel, Yiftah and Hanegev) were among the first to be demobilized and, unlike some other brigades, these units were totally disbanded. Ben Gurion's policies discouraged Palmach men from staying in the officer corps and most of them resigned. For reasons of their own, the Mapam leaders were also advising them to leave. Two out of four front commanders, six of the twelve brigade commanders and many other ex-Palmach officers left the Army while Ben Gurion apparently used his ministerial powers to exclude Mapam members in the officer corps from major operational commands (i.e. the brigade and area commands). There can be no certainty about such matters, but this does seem to have been a consistent policy on Ben Gurion's part, since in the immediate post-war years senior officers with Mapam connections were largely confined to training and staff functions, and rarely given command of combat units.*

With the resignation of the senior officers linked to the Mapam the Army's higher echelons were filled with men trained in the wartime British army and with loyal members of Mapai. The Palmach men had been much more successful in war than either of these groups and yet it would probably be wrong to assume that Ben Gurion was deliberately sacrificing military efficiency for the sake of political reliability. It was Ben Gurion's personal belief that the Palmach methods were not suited to large-scale warfare against well-trained regular armies.[7] He wanted an army patterned on the British model, and he, therefore, wanted officers who had come from the British army. Political motives were more evident in Ben Gurion's cultivation of the handful of Palmach-trained senior officers who were members of his own Mapai party.† Even more blatant was the promotion of 'old Haganah hands' – whose political reliability was not matched by distinguished military achievement.

The man who became the principal architect of the post-war Army did not belong to any of these groups. A thirty-year-old

* In spite of the hostile political climate, several senior ex-Palmach officers did stay in the Army, including Yitzhak Rabin (Chief of Staff in 1967), Haim Bar Lev (Chief of Staff 1968–72), and other staff officers and company commanders, including David Elazar (Chief of Staff 1972), Amos Horev and Uzi Narkiss.

† Assaf Simchoni and Moshe Netzer who had served as battalion commanders in the Palmach and Moshe Dayan who had been one of the first two company commanders trained in the Palmach. (The other was his perennial rival Yigal Allon.)

Haganah-trained officer with no known political affiliations, Yigal Yadin was appointed Chief of Staff on 9 November 1949 in succession to Ya'acov Dori. During the 1948 War, Yadin had been head of the Operations branch of the General Staff, and Dori's deputy; his formal task had been the coordination of the four Front Commands, but because of Dori's ill-health and indifferent leadership Yadin had acted as *de facto* Chief of Staff for much of the war. Since there was (and is) no post of Commander-in-Chief in the Israeli system, this meant that Yadin was the executive head of the Army as well as the government's chief military adviser. A man of the new generation like Allon, Yadin was respected by the Palmach element as well as by the Haganah veterans and the British-trained officers. Ben Gurion had worked closely with him throughout the war and trusted his judgement; neither he nor anyone else was disturbed by Yadin's lack of formal military training.* By the time the new Chief of Staff was installed, the Army of Independence had ceased to exist. Yadin and his colleagues set about re-thinking Israel's military problems at the strategic level, while a planning group headed by Haim Laskov worked on organization and tactical planning.[8] The first group tackled the problem of matching Israel's limited resources with her vast defence needs, the second worked on the design of the Army's combat forces and their operational use.

The armistice of 1949 left Israel with more territory than was originally awarded by the U.N. General Assembly, but its total area was still only 7,993 square miles (the size of Wales or New Jersey) and the meandering armistice lines provided very little depth in any direction. The Jordanians held a broad two-pronged wedge of hilly territory west of the Jordan River (the so-called West Bank), which reduced the centre of the country to a narrow coastal strip, in places less than ten miles wide, and which surrounded Jerusalem on three sides. The country's major highways, linking Tel Aviv with Haifa and Jerusalem, and the only international airport at Lod, were within a few miles of the border, and also very vulnerable. In the south, the geographic situation was no better. While Egypt's main cities were hundreds of miles from the common border, Tel Aviv was only thirty-five miles from the Gaza

* Son of an eminent professor of archeology and himself an archeologist, in later years Yadin gained a world-wide reputation in his field.

Strip, the one part of Palestine which remained in Egyptian hands. The Negev desert, bordering on the Egyptian-held Sinai on one side and Jordan on the other, formed a triangle whose point at Elat on the Red Sea was only a few miles wide and whose base at the northern end of the Negev narrowed into a corridor twenty miles wide. In addition, there were few significant natural barriers in Israeli hands. Jordan and Syria held dominating heights all the way from Dan at the extreme north of the country down to Elat in the south, while Israel everywhere held the plains below. If the Arabs launched a surprise attack, they could cut the country's main lines of communication and reach its cities without having to advance more than a few miles across relatively easy terrain. It followed that Israel's defence had to be based on highly mobile forces kept permanently at a high state of readiness.

The fundamental problem that Yadin and his colleagues had to contend with was that, with a population of just over a million (in 1949–50), Israel could not maintain a standing conscript army of adequate size. The Army of Independence was almost 100,000 strong at its peak, but this had required the mobilization of almost all able-bodied males and many women too; it was clearly impossible to maintain such large forces on a permanent footing. Any solution to the manpower problem had to satisfy two conflicting requirements: the bulk of the country's population had to remain free to follow normal civilian pursuits, but trained, combat-ready forces comprising most of the male population had to be available at all times. Israel needed a militia of civilians trained and equipped for combat, capable of being mobilized at short notice.[9] But it is very difficult to maintain a part-time force up to standard. Many countries have militia forces and almost every army has reserves, but neither are expected to fight in mobile warfare at short notice. Israel's manpower could not provide more than 30,000 conscripts at any one time (1949–50), much less than was required to match the Arab armies; this meant that the Israelis had to go against all professional military opinion in relying on part-time soldiers to man *most* of their combat units. (U.S. National Guard troops are not expected to be combat-ready without undergoing prolonged refresher training.)

Yadin and the General Staff analysed two kinds of militia

forces, the Haganah's Hish, which had been a force of part-time soldiers organized into combat units; and the dual Swiss system of home-guard units for local defence and a pool of reservists for general military duties. The system they devised had elements of both and has formed the core structure of the Israeli Army ever since. The armed forces were built on a three-tier structure with a small professional cadre of officers and specialist N.C.O.s, a large number of conscripts, and a trained civilian reserve. Unlike their counterparts in other armies, Israeli reservists belong to specific combat units, support forces or staffs, some wholly manned by reservists and some not. Upon mobilization, reservists join their own operational units instead of simply forming a man-power pool from which the standing army can draw for reinforcements. What made the Israeli system unique was that the reserve forces were the most important part of the Army and not an appendage of its standing forces; in fact, the main peacetime role of the latter is to produce a steady flow of trained men for the Army's reserve units. Although the standing army of conscripts and professionals provided the only forces immediately available for combat, it was clear that the military strength of the country ultimately depended on the reserve formations. This enhanced their status and morale, thus solving the major problem of reserve forces everywhere, whose men are demoralized by a sense of futility – often aggravated by the contemptuous attitude of the regulars.

The standing army was small and could not be scattered around the borders without impairing its training for large-scale combat. It was therefore necessary to build some kind of local defence into the system that could contain an invasion while the reserve forces were being mobilized. The Haganah's home-guard system, the Him, was taken over more or less unchanged; men living in border settlements, too old or otherwise unfit for service in the field, as well as many women, were organized into local defence groups under their own leaders. Plans were made for refresher training, the issue and storage of arms and for coordination with any Army forces operating in the area.

In the event of an invasion, the local defence groups were to man the defence perimeters of their own settlements; since there was a systematic policy of establishing kibbutzim and moshavim near the borders, these local defence groups provided useful breakwaters against an invasion – except in the Negev, which was then virtually uninhabited. The second task of the local defence groups was to provide guards and patrols to protect their own settlements against infiltrators from across the border and this has proved to be far more important than their anti-invasion role. From the start there was a gap in the system of local defence: neither the reserve forces nor the standing army nor the local defence groups could guard all 500 miles of the borders on a continuous basis. In 1949–50 this did not matter very much but Israel's most immediate security problem during the fifties turned out to be border infiltration, whose ultimate consequences were momentous: the transformation of the Israeli Army and the 1956 Sinai Campaign.

The reserve system provided a solution for the manpower problem – but only if the reserve forces could actually perform as planned, serving as *first-line* combat units after little or no refresher training. And this was the principal concern of Laskov's planning group whose task was to design the structure of the combat formations. In their planning document, they defined the organization of the ground forces as follows:

In peacetime the Army will consist mainly of reserves relying on a professional command organization. The administrative and technical command apparatus of each basic formation [i.e. the brigades] will be responsible for the training and preparation of the formation for rapid mobilization and effective combat. In the immediate future the task will be to achieve two aims: (a) to organize reserve brigades on a regional basis, and (b) to prepare the command and administrative machinery and provide the professional cadre and technicians needed for each brigade.[10]

Laskov's team thought that the reserve brigades would need a core of career officers for their command echelon and specialist N.C.O.s for the more intricate technical tasks. Obviously the team had come to the conclusion that, even if civilians could be turned into soldiers at short notice, they could not be expected to carry out senior command functions or specialist tasks. In this, Laskov's planning group was proved wrong. When the system was established in its final form (1950–51), the reserve brigades were manned entirely by mobilized civilians. Since then reserve officers have served as battalion commanders and sometimes as brigade commanders too. In the 1967 War there was even a reservist divisional commander, Avraham Yoffe, in charge of the task-force which fought in the central sector of Sinai.

To serve as first-line troops Israeli reservists needed more training than is usually given to reserve or militia troops while officers had to acquire a level of military expertise comparable to that of career officers in other armies; this entailed a long period of conscription (which has varied from two to three years) and frequent refresher training thereafter. Under the Defence Service Law of 1949, male reservists can be recalled to their units for thirty-one days each year until the age of thirty-nine, and for fourteen days a year until the age of fifty-five. Over and above this, they can also be called for one day each month* while officers and N.C.O.s can be recalled for even longer annual periods.†[11] No other country asks so much from its citizens, and the ultimate logic of the reserve system has been described in words attributed to Yadin himself: 'Every civilian is a soldier on eleven months' annual leave.'

From the start, compulsory military service applied to women as well, so that at the age of eighteen all Israeli citizens (Arabs excluded) become eligible for military service. The period of conscription has been somewhat shorter for women, but they can serve for up to two years – more than men serve in most other countries. There are various exemptions including one for mothers who are exempt from both conscription and service in the reserves. In general, few women are recalled for reserve duty though all who have no children are still listed on the mobilization rolls. Another exception has caused considerable controversy in the post-1967 period: Orthodox girls (i.e. those who can prove strict and regular religious observance) may also request exemption, which is usually granted. This accommodates the objections of Orthodox parents who refuse to expose their daughters to the 'immodesty' of military service. Until 1967, the Army did not in any case conscript more than half of all eligible girls, but when conscription became more general owing to the manpower shortage, there were

* The *actual* length of the annual call-up has varied over the years according to military requirements, training schedules and budgetary limits.

† See Appendix 2 on the Defence Service Law of 1949 and subsequent amendments.

protests against the exemption granted to Orthodox girls. Various proposals for non-military compulsory service for religious girls were blocked by the National Religious party in the coalition Government, while attempts by the Army to investigate the exemption claims of marginal cases aroused fierce protests from their families. Since *Ultra*-Orthodox men do not serve in the Army either (although the normally Orthodox do) the most religious segment of the Jewish population is also the only one which does not serve in the Army.

The staffs and commands of the small standing Army have to administer the much larger reserve forces as well, and it is the women who do most of the administrative and clerical work. Other female tasks range from the folding of parachutes to staff work at fairly senior levels. Two kinds of duties were excluded right from the beginning: cooking, cleaning and other menial work, and combat duty; though women soldiers do receive weapon training, this is only intended for self-defence. In the War of Independence, the Palmach, I.Z.L. and Lehi did include girls in their fighting units, but few were actually involved in combat after the early stages of the war.*

As well as releasing a large number of men for combat duties, the presence of women in the Army had reduced the vulgarity and free-floating violence so frequent in all-male armies. Women are not stationed on separate bases (though male soldiers are barred from their sleeping quarters) and, wherever women serve, there is a Women's Corps officer responsible for the discipline of the girls in her charge. This is primarily intended to prevent the sexual exploitation of girl soldiers by their male superiors. The Army's 'sexual policy' – if there is one – is that sexual relations on base are strictly forbidden while the personal life of soldiers on leave is their own business.

With the creation of the reserve system and the introduction of conscription for both men and women, the Army acquired the basic structure it retains to this day. But Yadin and his colleagues formulated another policy which proved less enduring. Having decided to rebuild the Army, its workings as a social organism also had to be defined. Was the Army to be informal and more or less

---

* Women fighters played an important role in the 'Battle of the Roads' (April 1948) and some fought in Palmach detachments even later.

egalitarian like the Palmach in its heyday, or as regimented and hierarchical as the British army? Needless to say, the Palmach ideologists still wanted an egalitarian army governed by the 'internal' discipline of its members. They accepted the need for discipline but held that it should be less the formal (or 'external') discipline enforced by Army regulations than voluntary (or 'internal') discipline inspired by a collective sense of responsibility. In combat, Palmach officers had been taught to rely on 'internal' discipline inspired by the unit leader, rather than compulsion. As for parade-ground discipline in dress, saluting and drill, the Palmach school saw no need for any. In the pre-war Palmach there had been no badges of rank and the idea of comrades saluting each other would have seemed ridiculous.

Their opponents argued that these egalitarian doctrines did not fit the realities of the post-war Army. The volunteers of the Palmach, they pointed out, had come from the pioneering youth movements, where they had already developed a sense of social consciousness and strong feelings of group solidarity, but post-war conscripts were very different and included many new immigrants whose attitudes were quite different.

Mass immigration started in 1949 and continued until 1952, by which time the country's population had doubled.*

The conscript intake naturally reflected the composition of the country's general population so that almost half were new immigrants. Their families were living in tents, huts or abandoned Arab houses, and even the able-bodied among them were mostly working on relief projects, or surviving on small welfare grants. A majority of the new immigrants had come from European D.P. camps (and the concentration camps before that), or from backward Muslim societies. Many conscripts were physically debilitated and had little or no formal education; and their knowledge of Hebrew was usually very limited. It soon became obvious that the

---

* Immigration into Israel: 1948 : 118,993
                                    1949 : 239,576
                                    1950 : 170,249
                                    1951 : 175,095
                                    1952 : 24,369
The country's Jewish population increased from 716,678 in 1948, to 1,404,392 in 1951; of the latter, 353,220 were born in Israel, 289,565 were born in Asia, 98,576 in North Africa, and 663,031 in Europe.[12]

Army would have to conduct its basic training under conditions of formal discipline, or not at all.

Even among those Israelis who had no sympathy for the Palmach's ideology, many were opposed to the idea of 'external' discipline enforced by compulsion in a rigidly hierarchical army. If Yadin prevailed against the egalitarian grain of the Yishuv, it was because of Ben Gurion's consistent support. Apart from purely military considerations, Ben Gurion wanted a non-political and fully professional Army and this was, in his view, incompatible with the sort of volunteer spirit the Palmach had cultivated; the volunteer spirit implied social consciousness, and this in turn is usually associated with ideological belief and party affiliation. Willing as he was to promote loyal Mapai officers for political reasons, Ben Gurion did not want an Army pervaded by rival ideologies. Though Prime Minister as well as Minister of Defence, he was forced to campaign vigorously for his ideas since many Israelis equated hierarchy and discipline with militarism. In his words:

> In the Haganah there was no military discipline, and discipline is not acquired on the day a private joins the Army. Discipline demands tradition, example, law and order. The members of the Haganah were volunteers serving only a few hours a week or month, but it is impossible to have an army without discipline as it is impossible to have a State without a government and laws.[13]

The former leaders of the Palmach and their associates in the Mapam party knew that many Israelis were opposed to Ben Gurion's vision of a strictly disciplined British-style army on social grounds, but they argued their case primarily in terms of military effectiveness. Yigal Allon accepted the need for some degree of formal discipline but insisted on 'internal' discipline as well:

> The education for discipline should be oriented towards the activation of consciousness and good will. The more the fighter will identify with the mission of the army as a whole and the task of his unit in particular, the stronger and more sincere his discipline will be . . . The importance of the formal framework [of discipline] should not be dismissed, but woe to the army which has to rely on this exclusively.[14]

As he makes quite clear, the discipline he wanted was to be derived precisely from that kind of group consciousness that Ben Gurion opposed. Allon claimed that Israel could only overcome its permanent numerical inferiority if her Army developed the full potential of each soldier, and this, he argued, could only be achieved by stimulating the volunteer spirit and relying primarily on 'internal' discipline. It was typical of the debate and its protagonists that Ben Gurion invariably used the term 'soldier' (*hayal*) while his opponents preferred 'fighter' (*lohem*); the first implies a profession, the second only a function which may be temporary. Ben Gurion underestimated the difficulties of maintaining the Army's fighting morale, especially in his portrayal of a professional corps of career officers, which ignored the whole problem of generating high standards of combat leadership. The Palmach school, for its part, seemingly ignored the skill requirements of advanced weaponry. They failed to explain how it would be possible to maintain and operate weapons as complex as tanks and aircraft without relying on a system of standard procedures which soldiers followed as a matter of discipline.

Allon and the other spokesmen of the Palmach school were personally popular, but Ben Gurion was in a dominant political position and had the power to impose his views. Accordingly, during the next three years the new Army was built by Yadin on traditional lines after the British model. But the victory of the 'external' discipline school turned out to be temporary; in later years there was a partial reversal to the Palmach style, though stripped of its politics.

The most pressing problem of the new Army was a severe shortage of career officers in the junior ranks. Many battalion commanders and other middle-rank officers (including a number of ex-Palmach men) had stayed in uniform mainly because their relatively high rank was a powerful incentive to make the Army a career, especially since many were still in their twenties. It was in junior ranks that the shortage was crippling; salaries were low and it proved very difficult to attract able men.* One solution tried by Yadin fitted in neatly with the attempt to build a British-style army. Unable to increase the salaries of junior officers, he set out to raise their status by widening the social gap between officers and men. Officers' messes, the salute and strict dress discipline

---

* A career captain's salary in 1950–51 amounted to the current equivalent of £400–£500 ($1,100–1,400) per year.

were used in a deliberate attempt to increase the significance of rank. (The ranks themselves were taken over more or less intact from the Army of Independence.)*

The effects that Yadin was trying to engineer with his status incentives tended to be rather gradual; and in any case, he did not think that it would be possible to keep high-quality officers in the career by prestige alone. He tried to secure material incentives too. Salaries could not be increased at a time of publicized austerity but significant fringe benefits, such as housing loans and cars for higher rank officers, were given instead. Yadin also encouraged the rise of in-group feelings in the officer corps. Housing developments specifically intended for officers, such as the Tel Aviv suburb of Zahala, were launched under Army auspices; an Army radio station (Galei Zahal) was established, and the Army's weekly (*Ba-Mahane*) was revamped. The Army also sponsored military 'houses' attached to the prestigious Reali school in Haifa and the Gymnasia Herzlia in Tel Aviv. These were to combine a military orientation for the cadets with some of the best secondary teaching to be had in the country, and Yadin hoped that they would become a steady source of future career officers as well as select schools for officers' sons.

The military houses, the exclusive officers' suburbs and the new material incentives went against the egalitarian and anti-militaristic sentiments prevalent in Israel society, and Yadin was widely criticized for trying to create an officer caste.[15] It says much for Ben Gurion's power and Yadin's personal prestige that the attempt to construct a British-style officer corps went as far as it did. In the

---

* Uniform throughout the Army, including its air and naval forces, the table of ranks was patterned on the British model, with Biblical titles for each corresponding level: *Segen Mishne* (2nd lieutenant), *Segen* (lieutenant), *Seren* (captain), *Rav Seren* (major) and *Sgan Aluf* (lieut.-colonel); the wartime *Segen Rishon* (1st lieutenant) was abolished. The Navy and Air Force Commanders, the heads of General Staff branches and the Front (later Area) Commanders all carry the rank of *Aluf* which was equivalent to colonel until the introduction of two new ranks below *Aluf* increased its equivalence to brig.-general and later maj.-general. The Chief of Staff is the only serving officer with the highest rank, *Rav Aluf*, then parallel to brig.-general and now equivalent to lieut.-general. The first intermediate rank introduced after 1949, *Aluf Mishne* (between *Sgan Aluf* and *Aluf*), is equivalent to colonel (brigade commanders carry this rank). After the 1967 war, a second intermediate rank was added, *Tat Aluf* (brig.-general).

event, it was not political but social pressures that eroded Yadin's edifice. Galei Zahal soon became a radio station like any other (today it is noted mainly for its long hours of foreign 'pop' music). The military houses never grew into full-fledged military academies, and although Zahala does have many retired officers among its residents, it has become a suburb like any other.

Yadin's attempt to enhance the social status of the officer corps stopped short of its logical conclusion. He did not even try to set up a military academy. This would have been too great a departure from the egalitarian ethos of Israeli life, and to this day all officers are promoted from the ranks. Under the two-stream military academy system, officer candidates are trained separately from the rank and file which they are destined to command. In Israel there is only one stream: all conscripts join the Army on an equal footing. Not only is there no military academy system with all its connotations of social inequality, but even civilian academic qualifications are discounted. In most modern armies a secondary school diploma is essential for promotion to officer rank; a university degree normally earns automatic promotion. In the Israeli Army neither is the case. In reserve units it is fairly common for university graduates (and even professors) to serve as privates under the command of fellow-reservists with very little formal education.

Boys and girls are inducted into the Army at the age of eighteen after undergoing the usual medical, psychiatric, intelligence and aptitude tests employed by every modern army. Basic training is identical for all recruits who are fit for combat duty, including those who will eventually serve in the Air Force and Navy. The conditions are harsh and the training physically demanding; weaker conscripts are given a shorter and easier course which prepares them for non-combat tasks. This separation is essential since the Army will not reject conscripts unless their physical (and mental) standards are exceedingly low. Much the same as 'boot camp' in other armies, basic training also serves as a selection filter for future officers and N.C.O.s. Those who do well are earmarked for the 'squad commander' courses, though they normally serve briefly as privates in the field. It is characteristic of the one-stream system that squad commander courses, though fairly simple, are not mentally limited in the way that N.C.O. courses usually are; in the Israeli Army the course has to train future officers as well as N.C.O.s. There is not much parade-ground drill and therefore more time is left for weapons' and physical training. Instructors usually have recent combat experience and basic training is focused on normally practical combat skills rather than on textbook tactics.

Squad commanders serve for a few months in the field with the rank of corporal, even if they have already been selected for officer training. While other soldiers are sent to serve as privates or N.C.O.s throughout the Army – including the Air Force and Navy – potential officers proceed to their training course, whose content is most revealing of the distinctive features of the Israeli Army. Based on the platoon commanders' course of the Palmach and, therefore, a carrier of pre-1948 traditions, the officer training course is a most important unifying element for the Army; all potential officers undergo the same course, including those who have already been streamed into the Air Force and Navy.*

The officer course includes the usual range of military skills: fieldcraft, map-reading, weapon training and tactics; but it stresses what can best be described as social education, a feature symptomatic of its Palmach origins. Technical aspects of command are left to the courses run by each corps; the basic officer course emphasizes the cultivation of initiative to solve tactical (and human) problems, and of personal leadership to implement a solution. Both aspects of command are elicited rather than taught; the basic teaching tool is the practical exercise with the trainee himself in charge. Typically he is presented with a tactical problem, told that standard procedures may not be used and asked to improvise on the spot.

Since the approved style of combat leadership is based on personal example, problem-solving and 'leadership' interact: knowing that he will be able to 'pull' his men after him by being

---

* After basic training conscripts are assigned to the various combat and support branches (see p. 95 below) where they undergo corps training. The Air Force, Navy, Armour Corps, Artillery and the technical branches operate their own courses; officer candidates normally rejoin the infantry stream for the officer training course, regardless of the branch to which they have been posted, though there are exceptions, as in the case of Air Force pilots.

the first to advance, the officer can choose daring tactical solutions which he might otherwise have had to reject. When 'leadership' consists of ordering reluctant men to advance, bold tactics are out of the question, in battle if not in the training course, since the troops will not obey under fire. The combination of individual thought and leadership by personal example, sought in the course, was the ideal of the Palmach, and it remains the highest goal of the Army today.

While newly commissioned officers assigned to the infantry are posted straight to their units,* those who belong to the more technical branches are first sent to the specialized training courses run by the Air Force, Armour and other corps; only Navy officers and Air Force pilots are trained separately from the start.† Since the infantry nowadays receives only a small proportion of all newly trained officers, the course is losing its 'infantry' character and becoming a preparatory stage for the corps training of each branch. The undesirable alternative would be to replace the common army-wide basic and officer training courses with specialized corps training.‡

Newly commissioned officers normally reach the rank of *Segen* (lieutenant) during their period of conscription and then retain this rank when they pass over to reserve units upon returning to civilian life. As the Army becomes increasingly specialized, more and more reservists, whether officers or not, serve in support rather than in combat units. Nevertheless, the typical reserve officer is still a civilian who for one month a year becomes a platoon, company, battalion or even brigade commander, where his responsibilities dwarf those of his civilian existence. Every Israeli is familiar with the ordinary businessman, farmer or civil servant who has a second life as a battalion or brigade commander; after the 1967 War many discovered distinguished combat officers in their unnoticed neighbours or colleagues.

* With the rank of *Segen Mishne* (2nd lieutenant); promotion to *Segen* (lieutenant) is more or less automatic after one year, subject to a fitness report.

† Air Force pilots do not attend the common officer training course; they are commissioned when they complete their combat flight training.

‡ Since 1967 the trend has been towards divergence, though basic training is still common for all conscripts. Another post-1967 trend is the frequent elimination of the N.C.O. stage for future officers.

As for those officers who join the 'permanent' service after conscription, their subsequent career is marked by a series of increasingly selective training courses sandwiched between three- or four-year duty cycles. Standards have been high: officers who fail to be promoted do not long remain in the career; the thirty-year-old lieutenants and forty-year-old captains common in many other armies are rare indeed. Initially, the only advanced schooling received by officers, other than specialized training, was a battalion commanders' course, which was the gateway for promotion to the rank of Lieut.-Colonel and above. In the mid-fifties this was replaced by two separate courses: an elementary one for prospective company commanders (which is open to reservists as well) and a more advanced staff course known as Poum.* Focused on staff work and the problems of operational command, this course has become a requirement for promotion to senior ranks (colonel and above). An experimental university type 'War College' was abolished in 1967 after a few years' trial and Poum now includes an element of general military and non-military education. The Israeli Army thus has neither an officer academy such as Sandhurst or West Point nor an advanced school for senior officers such as the American War College or the French École de Guerre. Instead Israeli officers go to civilian universities to study civilian subjects of their choice; there they absorb civilian views along with a respect for academic minds.

While Yadin was constructing the enduring foundations of the Army's reserve system, planning, both tactical and operational, was being conducted by Laskov's group. Originally set up in 1949, while Ya'acov Dori was still Chief of Staff, Laskov's group set to work when the Army of Independence was being demobilized. Haim Laskov was in many ways ideally suited for the task. Trained in the British army, where he acquired a thorough knowledge of conventional tactics and organization, Laskov also brought to bear an original intellect which had assimilated the lessons of the 1948 War as well as the military ideas of the Palmach. His group was charged with devising from first principles a whole

---

* Poum is the Hebrew acronym for Command and Staff (*Pikud u Mate*). This course was introduced during Dayan's tenure as Chief of Staff (1954–7), and it is loosely patterned on the U.S. Army's Staff and Command College.[16]

new structure for the Army's combat formations and command echelons. Tactical and operational doctrines* were to be thought out afresh by Laskov's group, which was thus given *carte blanche* to define both the structure and methods of the Army; that this was done at all, is yet another sign of the open-minded outlook of the Army's leaders. Instead of preserving the fairly successful Army of Independence, new structures and new doctrines were to be formulated on the basis of rational thought.[17] While such a total reappraisal would not be surprising after a defeat, the Israelis were able to innovate even after victory, and this was the key to their future success. The new was not always better than the old, but the flow of fresh ideas at least prevented the ossification of the military mind, which is so often the ultimate penalty of victory and the cause of future defeat.

The first task of Laskov's group was to design the new combat formations for the ground forces, determine their size and composition, and select the basic unit of military operations. The battalion (800–1,000 men), typical of most 'colonial' armies,† the 10,000–15,000-man divisions of the major armies of the Second World War, and the 'light' brigades of the Army of Independence with 3–4,000 men and no organic support were all considered and rejected.

A somewhat unusual type of combat formation, the self-contained brigade, was chosen instead. Made up of three battalions and a contingent of service and support units, the self-contained (or 'independent') brigade had already been tried out by the major armies of the Second World War but only for special missions; operational plans were still cast in terms of divisions or corps. The Israelis were already abundantly familiar with the problems of deciding at which level tactical decisions were to be made. In

---

* Tactics and tactical doctrines can best be distinguished from 'operations' and operational doctrines by reference to the organizational context. The former apply to a specific type of combat force (as in 'infantry tactics') while the latter apply to military operations as a whole. In other words, a variety of tactical doctrines (each relevant to a given branch) may be combined in the execution of a single 'operation' planned according to a given operational doctrine.

† This is a matter of having officers capable of handling large groups of men efficiently. To this day, the Egyptian army has only a handful of brigade commanders who can control their 3,000–4,000 men effectively.

the first stages of the 1948 War, the key echelon had been the battalion. By the summer of 1948, battalions had become too small for effective operational planning, and they were combined into brigades, each with three or more battalions. At this point, the brigade headquarters became the focus of tactical planning, but the 1948 brigades were not self-contained; any armour, artillery, or other support was only assigned temporarily by G.H.Q., which also controlled the supply units. In other words, service and support units were placed under brigade command for specific operations rather than being *organic* to the brigades. This arrangement, for all its obvious faults, may have been the best way of distributing the few guns and tanks available, since they could be switched from brigade to brigade according to need. No such advantage was derived from G.H.Q. control of service units which were not in short supply. Laskov's group had based its operational doctrines on the swift offensive in depth, and having decided on the brigades it followed that the latter had to be self-contained in order to make sustained combat possible:

The field units in the ground forces will be reorganized in the form of reinforced brigades of infantry or armour, which will serve as the basic field units ready to operate as striking forces performing independent tasks.[18]

With three battalions and a headquarters company in the usual 'triangular' pattern,* the self-contained brigade was also intended to have its own organic armour, artillery and service units for supply and maintenance. Above all, it had to be capable of moving and fighting on its own, and this meant that brigade commanders and their staffs had to be trained to think and act independently. With its own supply train and heavy weapons, the self-contained brigade would have all the physical facilities needed for independent operations, but the validity of the concept ultimately depended on the ability of relatively junior officers to handle the brigades on their own, without relying on the instructions of their superiors at higher echelons. As the 1956 Sinai Campaign was to show, the

---

* The triangular structure is now more or less standard internationally: three squads (each of 8–12 men) plus a 2–3 man headquarters = platoon; three platoons plus a headquarters (and sometimes a heavy weapons' platoon) = company; three rifle companies plus a weapons' company and a headquarters unit = battalion, and so on.

availability of independently-minded brigade commanders was the least of the Army's problems; some were all too ready to wage war as if it was their own private affair.

It was not for many years that the Army acquired the equipment needed for the two types of brigades (infantry and armoured) envisaged by the planning group. In 1949–50 the Army only had a few dozen serviceable tanks,* hardly enough for a single armoured battalion, let alone the tank detachments which even the infantry brigades were to have under Laskov's scheme.

The tactics laid down in the group's planning document were to be: 'offensive in spirit, planning and organization . . .', even when the task was defensive. The self-contained brigades were to hold their ground not passively but 'as a base [from which] . . . to mount counter-attacks supported by the Air Force and paratroopers'.[19] Since the geography of the country made any other kind of defence almost impossible this far from original doctrine was more than a display of the 'offensive spirit' always so fashionable among the military of all nations. The borders were so long in relation to the size of the forces available to defend them that a linear defence was impractical, while an 'elastic' defence of deliberate retreats and counter-attacks was excluded by the lack of geographic depth; major cities were too close to the borders to permit the planned withdrawals of an elastic defence.

The planning group's defensive doctrine was never put to the test. In retrospect it is only the offensive doctrines which are of interest. At a time when the repeated failures of the one tank battalion of 1948 were still fresh in everyone's mind, Laskov's group did not hesitate to assign a key role in the ground battle to the armoured brigades. 'Armour', they wrote, 'is an offensive force which solves all its tactical problems by attacking.' Armoured brigades were to advance in column as self-contained combat teams; their task was to cut deep into the enemy's rear without trying to secure their flanks or supply lines by scattering their forces to hold ground. Acting as the spearheads of the ground forces, armoured columns were to attack the flanks and rear of the enemy while avoiding built-up areas and fortified positions.

* Authors' estimate is fifty Sherman M.4s in 1950.

The planning group followed the common practice of giving a list of priorities in the conduct of armoured warfare:

1. Speed
2. Surprise
3. Manoeuvrability
4. Concentration of forces
5. Shock effect.

As theory this sounded fine, but by the time the Army fought its first large-scale tank battles in 1967, the list had been reversed with 'shock' first and 'speed' perhaps last.*

That the shock effect of massed tanks operating as a 'mailed fist' was put last, again reflected the influence of the 'indirect approach', which emphasizes infiltration and surprise rather than frontal attacks.[20] Tank-to-tank battles were also to be avoided and it was laid down that strong concentrations of enemy armour were to be stopped by the anti-tank artillery whose task was to ambush and destroy enemy tanks. Here it was German practice rather than Liddell Hart's ideas that the Israelis were following, and here too the doctrine was eventually reversed; when the Army finally deployed its first well-equipped tank forces during the sixties, the enemy's armour became their prime target. Where the planning group did not go wrong was in seeing that armour could best be used to fight an independent† battle of deep penetration into the enemy's rear. Even this elementary principle was much too advanced for what was still an infantry-minded Army. As late as the 1956 Sinai Campaign,‡ Israeli armour was initially relegated to a secondary role in support of the infantry.

Manuals of tactical doctrine invariably include optimistic lists of inconsistent aims, but the priority given to 'fire', as opposed to 'movement', can sometimes tell us a great deal about an army and its thinking. Fire-power can be given priority only at the expense

---

* When the armoured forces were radically reorganized by General Tal in the mid-sixties. See below p. 186–92.

† Independent, that is, of the slow-moving infantry. The infantry may be mechanized or at least motorized but it will still be slower than the armoured forces whose better-protected vehicles can advance even in the presence of the enemy's fire.

‡ See p. 148–9 below for a discussion of the 1956 plans and the role of armour within them.

of movement, since heavy artillery barrages and accurate rifle fire are normally incompatible with rapid movement, and vice-versa. British manuals accurately reflect that army's firm belief in the value of 'aimed fire': they specify that as soon as the infantry comes into contact with the enemy, it 'will dismount' from its trucks or armoured carriers to take up positions from which it can fire accurately.[21] The German Panzer Grenadier* (or 'mechanized infantry') concept, later adopted by the Soviet army, reverses this order of priorities. According to this school of thought, accurate small arms fire is of little use on the modern battlefield since the enemy can rarely be seen. Forces should be trained to advance without pause, firing on the move whenever possible. Automatic fire from moving vehicles is far too inaccurate to do very much real damage, but it can still achieve a breakthrough by pinning down the defenders so that their fire becomes ineffective.

Laskov's planning group defined its own combination of fire and movement in a somewhat ambiguous manner:

Fire and movement are one. The winning side will be the one which can fire the maximum number of bullets at the enemy in the shortest possible time *in order to destroy him* ... This is why speed is necessary.[22] [our italics]

Although this formulation diverged from the Panzer Grenadier doctrine in calling for destructive, and not just suppressive, fire it seems clear that the planning group preferred this concept to the 'aimed fire' doctrine which Laskov had been taught in the British army. The Army of Independence provided no clear model in this respect. Its small arms were mostly German-designed† and thus meant mainly for suppressive fire, while many of its officers

* Literally 'armoured grenadier', this term was originally applied to infantry forces equipped with combat carriers and trained to fight on the move – usually in combination with tank units. In the last phases of the war the Germans extended this designation to ordinary infantry units not so trained or equipped.

† The composition of the Army's equipment changed during the course of the 1948 War and reflected market availabilities rather than Israeli preferences. In the first phases of the war, the British Bren was the most common (light) machine-gun but later on a far larger number of German MG. 34s arrived from Czechoslovakia. The Bren is the weapon of the 'aimed fire' school *par excellence*: its magazine holds only 30 rounds and the weapon is

favoured British-style 'aimed fire' tactics. The Palmach was, of course, movement-oriented. As head of the Training branch (1949–51), Laskov was able to implement the ideas of his planning group, which thus had a profound influence on the evolution of the ground forces.

Laskov's group gave top priority to the Air Force (whose primary task was to support the ground forces), and to the Intelligence Corps.* In Israel's case, the importance of advance intelligence on enemy intentions ('strategic warning'†) is magnified by the reserve structure of the Army which requires early warning for mobilization. While much else was being changed, the command pyramid of the Army of 1948 was taken over more or less intact, and few modifications have been made since then. The only original feature of this command structure is the *unified* General Staff which controls all branches of the defence forces including the Navy and Air Force. In most other countries each service has its own general staff and command headquarters, and even when there is a 'joint staff', it tends to be no more than a consultative body since each member acts as the representative of his own service. In Israel, the Air Force and Navy have never grown into full-fledged 'services', and when their officers serve in the G.H.Q. they do so more as individuals than as delegates of their respective corps. Since there is no Commander-in-Chief,‡ the Chief of Staff is the sole executive head of the entire multi-service Army. The Chief of the Operations branch (or, officially, the 'General Staff' branch) is his second-in-command, though a special post of Deputy Chief of Staff is sometimes created.

* The Army's Intelligence Corps is responsible for the collection of field intelligence (mapping, reconnaissance, P.O.W. interrogation, communications' intelligence etc.). More important, it is responsible for the collation and analysis of all intelligence data, some of which is collected covertly by a separate civilian service popularly known as the Mossad. The Intelligence Corps has no espionage or security functions (other than field security).

† As opposed to 'tactical warning' which refers to actual enemy preparations or troop movements.

‡ See below, p. 98.

best fired in short aimed bursts. The German machine-guns were belt-fed and meant for less accurate full-automatic fire (up to 1,100 rounds per minute cyclic).

The Chief of Staff is the presiding chairman of the General Staff, whose permanent members are the heads of the four Staff branches,* the commanders of the Air Force, Navy and Armour Corps, and the three Area Commanders for the Northern, Central and Southern Commands which replaced the four Front Commands of the Army of 1948.

The General Staff is linked to its political masters in the Cabinet through the Chief of Staff, who is responsible for all Army matters to the Minister of Defence. The Air Force and Navy are designated as 'corps', rather than services, and though they have many of the attributes of independent services, they lack the most important: direct access to the political level. The heads of the 'Sea Corps' and 'Air Corps' (to give them their official names) report to the Chief of Staff; there are no separate government departments in charge of service matters. The Air Force and Navy do have separate headquarters and, unlike the other corps (which are in fact inspectorates), they control their own forces in combat. On the ground the three Area Commands are responsible for all the troops deployed within their areas and for the supervision of the local defence units† along the borders. In wartime the Area Commands become operational headquarters for the combat forces assigned to their sector in the manner of divisional or corps H.Q.s, and their staffs change over from administrative to operational functions.

The four branches of the General Staff supervise a number of inspectorates and functional commands, the most important of which is the Armour Corps. Commanded by a general officer, the Armour Corps is responsible for all tank and mechanized infantry training and for the development of operating procedures and tactical doctrines.‡

The three other functional commands are the Training Command in charge of basic and combat training (i.e. all non-specialist

* The General Staff branch (abbreviated in Hebrew as *Agam*), the Manpower branch (*Akka*), the Quartermaster branch (*Aga*) and the Intelligence branch (*Amman*).

† See below, p. 105–6.

‡ Since the mid-fifties, the commander of the Armour Corps has held the rank of *Aluf*, like other members of the General Staff. In the Sinai Campaign and in the 1967 War the G.O.C. Armour served as a divisional task-force commander.

training), the Gadna, a para-military youth organization, and the Nahal, a military-agricultural corps, most of whose volunteer recruits join *en bloc* from the youth movements – which was originally set up as a non-political substitute for the Palmach.* The General Staff administers the Army through a network of inspectorates which are responsible for training, supervision and technical guidance. Each has a specialist staff of its own headed by a Chief Officer who reports to the General Staff.† As a result, the Chief of Staff ultimately controls every part of the Army through two different channels: a chain of command (area, divisional and brigade headquarters) and a chain of technical supervision which goes through the inspectorates supervised by one of the branches of the General Staff.‡ Only the Intelligence ('I') branch of the General Staff controls no specialized inspectorates; its head is responsible for the direct supervision of the Intelligence Corps which supplies 'I' officers to units throughout the Army. He also controls directly the central intelligence work performed by the 'I' branch itself. This system of dual control is common to every modern Army and its aim is to combine different types of technical expertise with a unified control structure. For example, a girl officer serving with an artillery unit deployed in the Northern Command reports to her superiors through the unit, formation and area headquarters in a chain of command which terminates with the General Staff and its chief; at the same time, she is subject to the technical super-

* Nahal is an acronym for 'fighting-pioneer youth'. Its recruits alternate periods of military training and combat duty with agricultural work. The Nahal operates farm settlements (in exposed border areas) which are eventually intended to become normal civilian settlements. See Appendix 1 for a discussion of the Nahal and its role.

† Under the general supervision of the 'General Staff' (i.e. Operations) branch come the Chief Armour Officer, the Chief Paratroop and Infantry Officer, the Chief Artillery Officer, and the Commander of the Civil Defence. The Quartermaster branch supervises the Chief Engineering Officer, the Chief Signal Officer, the Chief Supply and Transport Officer and the Chief of Ordnance; the Manpower branch supervises the Chief Military Advocate, the Chief Rabbi, the Director of the Women's Corps, the Chief Military Police Officer, the Chief Education Officer, and the Chief Medical Officer.

‡ Each branch of the General Staff is divided into specialized sub-divisions. The Operations branch, for example, has four divisions: Training, Operations, Local Defence, and Military Government.

Fig. 1

Organizational Structure of the General Staff

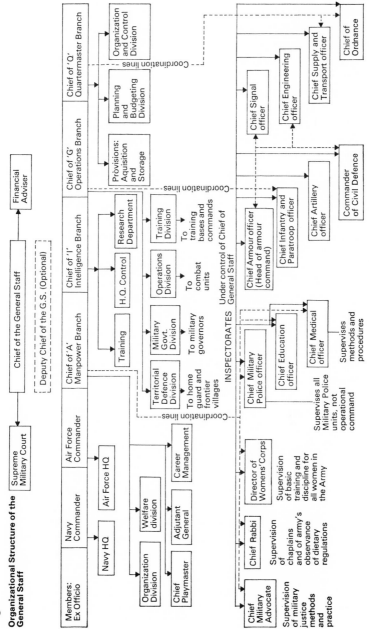

vision of the Artillery Corps whose Chief Officer reports to the 'General Staff' or Operations branch of the General Staff. In addition, her superior for all disciplinary matters is the local Women's Corps officer, who reports to the Director of the Corps, who in turn comes under the supervision of the Manpower branch of the General Staff.*

The Chief of Staff is the sole head of the Army and the only official link between the General Staff and the Cabinet, as represented by the Minister of Defence. In Israel's unwritten constitution there is no provision for the post of Supreme Commander or Commander-in-Chief; the Cabinet as a whole is vested with the ultimate authority of supreme command. In practice, such powers are delegated to the Minister of Defence who serves as the Army's sole political master and who is therefore responsible to the Cabinet and Knesset for all military matters. In addition, he is also in charge of the Ministry of Defence itself, a civilian body entirely distinct from the uniformed military. The Ministry is responsible for military research and development as well as the production or purchase of all equipment and supplies; it is also responsible for the financial planning and budgeting of the defence establishment as a whole.†

In theory, the division of labour between the Ministry and the Army is quite clear: the Ministry provides administrative and technical support, while the Army is responsible for 'professional' matters: organization, training, morale and, above all, the planning and conduct of military operations. But since the Minister of Defence is also the Army's supreme commander he has, at least in theory, the power to intervene in all Army affairs, including those which are purely professional. Not surprisingly, there have been several jurisdictional disputes over the years which have led to clashes between the Minister (or his deputy) and the Chief of Staff.‡

The years in which the new Army was being established were also the years of mass immigration whose immediate effect was a

* (Diagram)

† The Ministry does not control civilian Intelligence (Mossad) and the internal security service, the Sherut Bitachon Clali (Service of General Security), which are controlled directly by the Prime Minister's office.

‡ See p. 133–7 below.

drastic fall in the standard of living for all Israelis. In an effort to provide the essentials for all, the Government inaugurated a policy of severe austerity: food and clothing were strictly rationed and the small luxuries of everyday life disappeared from the shops; even the simplest domestic appliances were unobtainable, and private house-building was tightly regulated. If the internal economic situation was bleak, the balance of payments was an even more pressing problem. Much of the country's food, clothing and all but the simplest industrial products had to be imported while there was very little to export. Over the years 1949–51, the country's total exports (mainly fruit) could pay for only eleven per cent of imports, and the foreign exchange deficit amounted to more than 200 dollars per capita. The deficit was covered by low-interest loans and donations from the Jews of the Diaspora and the U.S. government, but at times this was not enough to pay for even the most essential imports, and the new State occasionally had to raise costly short-term loans from Swiss or American banks. As the economic crisis deepened in 1951, the defence budget was cut and cut again; the Army was given very little new military hardware, and still less in the way of creature comforts. With a budget of around $600 per man per year, the Army of 1952–3 was indeed poor.*

Defence expenditures	Million Israeli Pounds	Million U.S. Dollars (Current exchange rates)
1950	31·3	87·6
1951	54·1	151·5
1952	75·5	75·5
1953	82·0	63·8

Since the dollar figure is a closer approximation to the budget's buying power, it can be seen that the budget decreased very sharply from 1950 to 1953. (The 1951 figure does not mean very much, since the Israeli pound was by then grossly overvalued.) Assuming that at least 120,000 men served in the Army's regular and reserve forces, the 1952 budget amounted to $629 *per man per year*, which had to cover not only Army, but also Ministry expenditures.

Mortars and submachine-guns could be produced in Israel,

* Defence budget estimates and appropriations are classified (though certain annual figures have been released for individual years). The most reliable unofficial estimates are those compiled by N. Safran *et al.*, *From War to War*, Pegasus, New York, 1969, p. 157.[23]

Organizational Structure of Israeli Defence

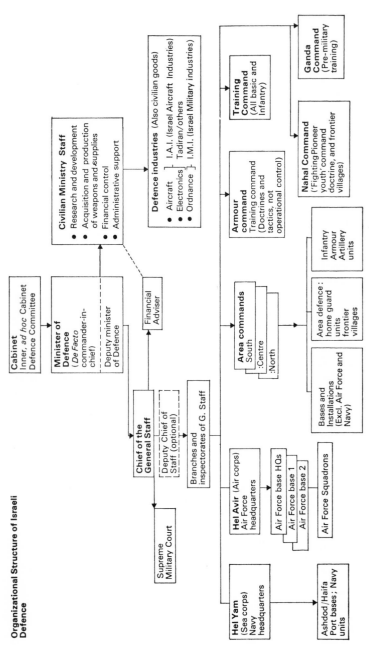

Fig. 2

officers' salaries could be paid by printing currency, but all imported materials were in short supply. Even some of the aircraft and vehicles which the Army already had were now out of action since there was no hard currency with which to buy spare parts. Living conditions in the Army were harsh; many soldiers lived in tents the year round and their food rations were always dull and sometimes inadequate. In their shabby, worn-out uniforms, conscripts drilled by command since many knew little or no Hebrew. Combat units were short of serviceable weapons and their training was poor owing to the inflow of illiterate immigrant-recruits trained by rote. All this could not but affect the Army's morale, especially since there was no immediate enemy threat to justify the hardships soldiers had to endure. Moreover, the mass departure of the senior officers of the Army of Independence had left few inspiring figures in top command positions.* It was widely known that the Army had lost some of its ablest leaders for political reasons, and this further depressed the morale of officers and men. Most senior command positions were filled by 'old Haganah hands', loyal members of Ben Gurion's Mapai party and by apolitical officers trained in the British army. None of these groups had distinguished itself in the war.†

Yigal Yadin did not long remain in command of the new Army which he had done so much to create. At one with Ben Gurion on many other issues, he clashed with his Minister over the budget. In 1951 when the country's economic situation became even more difficult as immigration reached its peak,‡ Ben Gurion was forced to press for further economies in the defence budget. Yadin was convinced that the budget was already dangerously inadequate and believed that further cuts would endanger national

---

* Yigal Allon, the outstanding field commander of the 1948 War, and another able front commander, Moshe Carmel (G.O.C. Northern Front), had left together with six brigade commanders (out of twelve): Shimon Avidan of Givati, Shmuel Cohen of Yiftah, Nahum Golan of Golani, Nahum Sarig of Hanegev, Yossef Tabenkin of Harel and the 'Old Man', Yitzhak Sadeh, the outstanding military mind of the Haganah, founder of the Palmach and Commander of the 8th Armoured Brigade.

† The outstanding (though not only) exceptions were Haim Laskov among the British-trained, and Dayan among the Mapai members.

‡ In 1952 there were only 24,396 registered immigrants as opposed to the annual average of 176,000 over the years 1948–51.[24]

security. One economy measure he resisted especially strongly: the release of career officers. Owing to the severe shortage of trained officers, it was Yadin's policy to retain in the Army all the wartime officers who wished to stay, including the less competent; Ben Gurion on the other hand wanted to weed out the officer corps while reducing the cost of officers' salaries.

Yadin repeatedly offered his resignation which Ben Gurion eventually accepted. Yadin's deputy, Mordechai Makleff, appointed Chief of Staff in December 1952, was a competent but rather unimaginative British-trained officer and apparently apolitical. His number two, Moshe Dayan,* was none of these things. Makleff carried out the ruthless budget cuts decreed by the government and forced the resignation of many officers, but like Yadin he came into conflict with the civilian staff of the Ministry of Defence including Ben Gurion's protégé, Shimon Peres. His tenure lasted for only one year.

In December 1952, the Israeli Army was established on the sound foundations of the reserve system, but its training and morale were at a low ebb. There are no official figures for the size and composition of the Army at this time, but it is known that the ground forces consisted almost entirely of infantry: there were probably two infantry brigades, one part-armoured brigade and one paratroop battalion† in the standing forces (i.e. manned by trained conscripts), and eight infantry brigades in the reserves. The troops were armed with bolt-action rifles and submachine-guns in almost equal proportion – a classic sign of poverty; and since there were both British ·303 and 7·92mm Mauser-pattern rifles (German Kar.98ks and Czech-made copies) their ammunition could not be standardized. The first Israeli-made Uzi submachine-guns‡ were just coming into service but many troops were still issued with the unreliable British Sten.

* Moshe Dayan, who served as Commander of Jerusalem in the last stages of the war, was appointed G.O.C. Southern Command (1949–51) and then G.O.C. Northern Command (1952). In December 1952 he was promoted Chief of the General Staff branch and as such Makleff's number two.

† See below, p. 111.

‡ The Uzi, a 9mm parabellum weapon, named after the then Major Uzi Gal, who designed it, has been produced and exported in very large numbers. It is very small (17·9 in. stock folded) and popular because of its

The most common machine-gun was probably the Czech-made 7·92 Beza (ZB.53), but there were also U.S.-made ·3 Vickers mediums. Mortars were produced in Israel, and were therefore available in adequate numbers, but the troops were short of anti-tank weapons, radios and transport. The Armour Corps had about fifty U.S.-built Sherman M.4 tanks* and some armoured cars as well as about 200 M.3 half-track carriers which equipped the mechanized units of the infantry.

These U.S.-built vehicles can carry twelve men and a pair of machine-guns and have been very popular with the Israelis ever since 1948; many more were bought – often as scrap – during the fifties and even later; they are still in use today. As for the rest of the ground forces, the Artillery had British 25-pounders and a few anti-tank guns while the Engineers, Ordnance and Supply Corps were short of vehicles and specialized equipment. All this indicates that the manpower strength of the ground forces (estimated at 30–35,000 conscripts, career officers and N.C.O.s, with 80,000 trained reservists) overstated the Army's actual combat potential which was sapped by equipment shortages as well as by poor training and low morale.

Since the state of the Arab armies was no better, the condition of the Israeli Army at this time presented no immediate threat, but neither did it offer much hope for significant improvement in the near future.

* Thirty-three tonners with 76·2mm guns bought in 1949 as scrap and partially rebuilt.

---

reliability. Weighing 8.9 lb. with a 25-round magazine it now equips all vehicle crews as well as much of the infantry.

4

Decline and Revival

When the 1949 armistice agreements were being negotiated, the U.N. mediator Ralph Bunche gradually persuaded the Arab delegates to deal directly with the Israelis by convening the supposedly separate talks in the same Rhodes Hotel and then in the same room. But his skilful stage-management did not affect the official stance of the Arab states. Even after negotiating and fraternizing with the Israelis, the Arab delegates insisted that they were dealing only with Mr Bunche and not with the delegates of Israel, whose diplomatic existence they did not recognize. Nevertheless, when the last of the four armistice agreements was signed with Syria on 20 July 1949, many Israelis believed that peace negotiations would eventually follow. It was some time before these hopes were disappointed, though the Arab regimes made it perfectly clear that they had no intention of inscribing their defeat in a treaty of peace, while Israel had no way of forcing them to do so. By the autumn of 1949 the Israeli Army was in dissolution, and in any case both Egypt and Jordan enjoyed the firm diplomatic support of the British government, which was still trying to build an Anglo-Arab military alliance. As a result the British did not necessarily favour peaceful relations between Israel and the Arabs.

Nor would the U.S. government have countenanced Israeli military pressure on Arab states that were already seen as potential allies in a Middle Eastern version of N.A.T.O. In the absence of external compulsion only domestic pressures could have induced the Arab states to come to terms with Israel, and there were none. Public opinion, manifest in street demonstrations if not at the polls, could not accept defeat at the hands of Jews, who were not foreign and imperial like the British or the French but a familiar and despised minority. The return of the Palestine refugees was no incentive either since their welfare had no more value as political currency than humanitarian considerations ever have in the presence of inflamed nationalist sentiment. The Arab regimes accordingly refused to open diplomatic or trade relations and forbade all transit to and from Israel so that her only links with the outside world were by sea and air. Limited movement across the Mandelbaum Gate between Jewish and Arab Jerusalem was permitted, but only for non-Jews.

What began as passive inaction eventually became deliberate policy: its aims were to isolate Israel and keep the option of war open for the future. A more immediate consequence of non-recognition was that the Arab states did not attempt to police the armistice lines so that Arab infiltrators could easily cross the 'green line', as the Israelis call it (after the green marking on military maps), to smuggle goods or steal crops in Israeli territory.

At first no more than a police matter, infiltration became a real threat when bands of armed marauders began to cross the border to rob and kill. It hardly mattered that this was not political terrorism but only commercial banditry: in 1951, no fewer than 137 Israelis were killed or wounded. Infiltration had now become a security problem, though it was still only 'current' security that was at stake, since there was no strategic threat to Israel's 'basic' security.[1] The distinction between current and basic security reflects a fundamental dilemma of Israeli military planning: current security in the border areas requires the deployment of large numbers of troops as border guards, lightly armed and trained for police duties; but basic security against large-scale attack requires field units with heavy weapons and battle training.[2] Neither the standing nor the reserve forces could be trained and equipped to carry out both tasks, nor was it practicable to divide the Army into guard units and field units since there was not enough manpower for both. There was and is a Border Police (Mishmar Hagvul) but this was only a few thousand strong. Equipped as light infantry with jeeps and trucks, the Border Police guarded the most sensitive parts of the armistice lines, but manpower limitations made it impossible to expand this professional force of long-service volunteers to the point where it could patrol the entire border.

Another partial solution was the Haganah Merchavit,* or Local

* Haganah Merchavit stands for 'regional defence' but it is actually a

Defence, which had been set up as part of the reserve system – on the lines of the Haganah's Him (Guard Corps). Like the latter, the Local Defence is manned by older (50–55) men and trained women living in villages near the border. The sentries and patrols of the Haganah Merchavit were meant to protect border settlements from infiltrators, but this was insufficient to cope with the problem.[3] For one thing, there was a wide gap between the performance of the Local Defence in villages inhabited by new immigrants and the well-organized forces of the average kibbutz, whose members were likely to include many experienced fighters. In any case Local Defence units were only responsible for their own village perimeters and not for the very wide gaps that sometimes existed between settlements along the border.

Unable to protect every mile of the meandering armistice lines, as from 1950 the Israelis adopted a more active strategy.[4] Reprisal raids against Arab police stations, army units and villages were seen as the only means of deterring Arab governments from allowing or encouraging attacks on Israeli territory. In later years, Israel's retaliatory policy was to cause severe diplomatic problems but in the beginning the problem was purely military. Incredible as it may sound in retrospect, there was apparently not a single battalion in the Army truly ready for combat, as was shown in a 1951 border clash with the Syrians.[5]

On 2 May 1951, a force of Syrian infantry entered the then demilitarized zone along the border and occupied Tel Mutilla, a small rocky hill just north of Lake Tiberias. The Army's Northern Command reacted immediately and sent an infantry unit* to dislodge the Syrians. Repeated Israeli attacks were inept and easily repulsed by the Syrians; more troops had to be sent into action and after four days' fighting the Syrians were finally evicted with the help of the Army's Druze battalion.†

* It was probably a reduced battalion of two or three companies. No official account is available for publication.

† After 1948 the Army formed a 'minorities unit' for Druze and other non-Jews who volunteered to its ranks. After 1956 the Druze community

system of local defence since it consists of separate units based on individual towns and villages. In less exposed parts of the country, over-age (50–55) or otherwise unfit men serve in the Haga, or Civil Defence, though there are also some armed detachments for guard duties.

By then twenty-seven Israelis had been killed. The duration of the battle and the heavy casualties were out of all proportion to the small size of the Syrian force holding the hill, and a clear sign that something was badly amiss with the infantry's training and morale. That Tel Mutilla was not an isolated incident was proved when the retaliatory policy was put into operation. The list of abortive reprisal raids is long: Wadi Fukin, Beit Sira, Beit Awa, Idna, Rantis, Beit Jalla and several others.

But it is the Falame raid which is still remembered as the most humiliating failure of all. In January 1953, an infantry battalion of the standing forces drawn from the Givati Brigade of 1948 fame was ordered to launch a night attack against the Jordanian village of Falame. Owing to its hilltop location, the village was not an easy target, but it was only defended by a dozen riflemen of the Jordanian National Guard with little training and no heavy weapons. The Israelis repeatedly lost their way in the dark and, when the advance unit finally reached the edge of the village, it was met by scattered rifle fire. Only six Israelis were hit, but the battalion commander, making no further attempt to push on with the raid, ordered a retreat back into Israeli territory. Three senior officers including Moshe Dayan, then Chief of Operations in the General Staff,* were waiting for the return of the battalion just across the armistice line to hear a report on the raid. Dayan wanted to discharge the commander on the spot, though it was known that other officers and other battalions would have fought no better.

Even the special night-fighting skills of the Army of Independence had apparently been lost and Israeli task forces frequently failed to find their objectives when engaged in night operations. In one incident, a platoon sent to blow up a well in the Gaza Strip lost its way and failed to locate its objective in the darkness. When morning came, the Israelis discovered that they had wandered in circles without even having crossed the armistice line. A squad commander left his men, hid behind a rock and killed himself by detonating a hand grenade.[6]

---

* Officially the Head of the General Staff branch (of the General Staff).

chose to serve in the Army on a compulsory basis as do all other Israeli citizens except Muslim and Christian Arabs.

While the retaliatory policy was undermined by the feebleness of the Army, infiltration increased and so did the death toll. In 1951 there were 137 casualties, mostly civilian; in 1952 there were 147, and in 1953, 180.[7] Most of the infiltrators came from the Jordanian-held West Bank,* their purpose was robbery and the killings incidental; as yet no terrorist organization masterminded their attacks in pursuit of political goals. Apart from the loss of life they inflicted the Arab infiltrators also demoralized a civilian population already enduring severe economic hardship. Food rationing and the chronic shortages of a crisis economy were all the harder to bear when it was realized that the longed-for Jewish state could not even protect its population from almost daily attacks. Dayan's immediate reaction to the Falame incident was an attempt to raise the Army's morale by order. At meetings of unit commanders he discussed the Falame episode and set the rule that no officer was to suspend an attack, on penalty of dismissal, unless his unit suffered a casualty rate in excess of fifty per cent. For an Army whose guiding principle was, and is, the reduction of casualties to the absolute minimum, Dayan's new rule was exceedingly harsh. Moreover, as Dayan himself should have realized, the Army's malaise could not be cured by speeches or regulations. Officers lacked confidence in their men, many of whom were poorly trained new immigrants, while the men were demoralized by their officers' visible reluctance to rely on them in battle. Each failure caused a further decline in self-confidence.

To deal with the immediate need, Col. Michael Shaham, the Jerusalem Brigade Commander, advocated the creation of a small force of skilled and dedicated fighters which could be counted upon to carry out the reprisal raids.[8] There was no such force in the Army, but among the junior officers who had resigned in 1949 there were just the sort of men that Shaham needed to form his special unit. And it had to be a *special* unit outside the formal structure of the Army, since the right kind of men would not volunteer for military service if it meant accepting the petty discipline of an Army now operating on traditional lines.

* Of the total casualties, 111 in 1951, 114 in 1952, and 117 in 1963 were caused by infiltrators based on Jordanian territory.

There were also political reasons for creating a special unit whose men did not wear Israeli uniforms or insignia. The U.S. and British governments were still trying to persuade Egypt and Jordan to join a regional alliance directed against the Soviet Union and could not be expected to tolerate Israeli reprisal raids against their potential allies. Then as now, Arab attacks against Israeli civilians were ignored by the great powers in the U.N. which took the view that such attacks were non-governmental. Israel reprisals, on the other hand, were overt military operations ordered by the government, and they invariably aroused U.S. diplomatic protests and sometimes British threats of intervention – since Britain was still linked to Jordan by a formal defence treaty. By forming the new unit outside the official structure of the Army, the diplomatic costs of reprisal operations would be lower since the Israeli government could always deny responsibility. The only alternative was to reply in kind by attacking Arab civilians at random, as the infiltrators were doing against Israeli civilians. Isolated actions of this type would certainly have evoked fewer diplomatic protests than organized attacks against Arab villages, police stations and military positions, but this alternative was never seriously considered.

In August 1953 the Chief of Staff, Mordechai Makleff, decided to go ahead with Shaham's plan – overruling Dayan who objected to the idea that the Army would have to rely on a special unit to do what every unit should have been able to do. To raise and lead the special unit, Makleff chose the man Shaham had suggested, a young student in the School of Oriental Studies at the Hebrew University, Ariel Sharon, who was then a civilian and a battalion commander in the reserves.*[9]

The men of 'Unit 101', as the special unit was called, were hand-picked by Sharon who travelled around the country looking

* When Sharon was still in the Army, serving as an intelligence officer with the Northern Command, Dayan, the G.O.C., once asked him to look into the possibility of capturing two Jordanian soldiers to be used as bargaining counters for two Israeli prisoners in the hands of the Arab Legion. Sharon gave a noncommittal reply. Taking another officer with him, he promptly drove to the Sheikh Hussein bridge on the Jordanian armistice line, captured two Legionnaires at pistol-point, and brought them back to Dayan. 'I asked him if it was possible,' Dayan said later, 'and he returned with two Arab Legion soldiers as if he had gone to pick fruits in the garden.'

for aggressive and intelligent fighters, mostly men who had served in the Army of Independence five years earlier.

Unit 101 never included more than forty men at any one time. It was in effect a private army; Sharon's men wore neither Army uniforms nor badges of rank and their weapons were not standard issue. All were good fighters, some were brilliant tacticians who later rose to high rank and one, Meir Har-Zion,* became a legendary figure in his own lifetime, 'the best soldier Israel ever had' according to Dayan. In fact Dayan's opposition to the 101 was transformed into enthusiastic advocacy by his personal contact with Har-Zion and his comrades.

During the few months of its existence, Unit 101 fought no major battles but its many small raids were invariably successful. Sharon and his men revived the dormant skills of the Army of Independence: silent infiltration across enemy territory, night fighting and superior field-craft.

The last of the unit's operations was also the largest and the most controversial. Following the killing of a woman and her two children in a village near Lod Airport, the Israelis launched a night attack against the Jordanian village of Khibye on 14 October 1953. Khibye was thought to be strongly defended and sixty-three men of the Army's paratroop battalion were sent into action as a covering force for the forty men of Unit 101. The Israelis fought their way into the village, rounded up the inhabitants and blew up forty-five houses. Not all the houses were cleared beforehand and more than forty villagers were buried under the rubble; others were killed during the assault for a total of sixty-six dead and seventy-five wounded in the course of the operation. The brutality of the raid led to sharp protests in Israel and abroad while the U.N. Security Council condemned Israel without making any reference to Arab attacks. The Israeli Cabinet was already divided on the wisdom of the retaliatory policy and Unit 101 was now threatened with disbandment. But instead of disbanding Sharon's unit, Dayan, who was about to be promoted to Chief of Staff, decided to merge

* Har-Zion was an exceptionally able scout and guerrilla fighter. When his own sister was murdered by Bedouin tribesmen while hiking with her boyfriend across Jordanian-controlled territory, from Ein Gedi to Jerusalem, Har-Zion crossed the border with a few friends and tracked down and killed four Bedouins of the tribe responsible for the murder.

it with the paratroop battalion. It mattered little that Sharon and his men had no parachute training; they could easily learn to jump, whereas until the Khibye raid the paratroops had never fought well. Dayan succeeded Mordechai Makleff as Chief of Staff on 7 December 1953, and one month later the merger went into effect. Sharon was appointed commander of the combined 101–paratroop battalion, a post that the more senior paratroop commander, Lt.-Col. Harari, had expected for himself. Instead, Harari was released from the Army and Dayan inaugurated his tenure as Chief of Staff with the first of many dismissals.

The history of the paratroop battalion exemplified the very problems that led to the creation of Unit 101. First formed in 1948 with a nucleus of fifty Haganah men who had received jump training in Czechoslovakia, the battalion also included a number of expert parachutists trained by the British for wartime intelligence missions. The battalion saw very little action during the war. As with most airborne troops during the Second World War, the paratroopers were kept in reserve to fulfil their own 'vertical envelopment' mission, but when the tactical opportunity arose no aircraft were available, and vice versa. When the Army was demobilized and most of its units disbanded or transferred to the reserves, the paratroop battalion was retained in the standing forces but many of its better men had left, and the quality of the unit deteriorated. If many of the conscripts of 1949 were poorly educated and demoralized, it seems that the volunteers who joined the paratroop battalion were worse. When instances of theft and black marketeering were traced to the paratroop base, the unit was reorganized under a new commander, Yehuda Harari, who weeded out some of the worst elements and began intensive training. In line with the Army's orientation at this time, the paratroopers were taught all the routines of soldiering in the British manner. Much attention was given to parade-ground drill, saluting and dress discipline. A regular course of jump training (with English-language drill instructions) soon turned the men into competent parachutists but, as it later turned out, it did nothing for the fighting ability of what was supposed to be the Army's elite combat unit. Even their commando training was conducted in a ritualized manner; the paratroopers could stage a knife-fighting demonstration for visiting V.I.P.s, but when sent into action to mount a reprisal raid they failed to press home the attack. It was not until they came under Sharon's command for the Khibye raid that the paratroopers fought well for the very first time.

When Sharon was put in charge of the combined 101–paratroop force, predictably designated 202, his main problem was to mould two very different groups of men into a cohesive combat unit. His own men from the 101 were nothing to look at on a parade ground; they wore whatever clothes they liked and never drilled or saluted. Operating as a loose band of fighters with no distinctions between officers and men, the 101 fought as a team linked by natural affinity and guided by Sharon's dashing leadership. The paratroopers, on the other hand, had been trained as disciplined parade-ground soldiers, and when Sharon took over the battalion most of their officers preferred to transfer to other units. One paratroop officer who did stay was Aharon Davidi,* as good a fighter as any in the 101, and he was appointed Sharon's deputy.

While the paratroopers were learning to scout and fight in small groups, Davidi taught Sharon's men how to administer a battalion, how to use heavy weapons in support, and all the other prosaic skills which had been ignored in the 101. The new paratroop battalion soon lost its spick-and-span appearance and acquired the casual and seemingly undisciplined look typical of the Israel Army under Dayan. More important, the men of the combined battalion soon attained the fighting standards of the much smaller 101; former paratroopers and 101 men were mixed in small groups and trained in realistic 'field exercises', which were actually guerrilla raids in enemy territory.[10]

The 202nd paratroop battalion demonstrated its newly found skills in a raid against the fortified Jordanian village of Nahalin on 28 March 1954. Operating as always at night, Sharon's men brushed aside the local National Guard and broke into the village; as in the Khibye raid their task was to blow up a number of houses in reprisal for acts of terrorism but this time there were no needless civilian casualites though nine Arabs were killed and twenty-eight wounded during the initial assault. The villagers were rounded up and disarmed and the houses carefully cleared of their inhabitants

---

* He rose to become Chief Officer of Infantry and Paratroops, serving in this post during the 1967 War.

before being demolished. After Nahalin there were eight* major
raids till the end of 1954; all were successful.

In Sharon's unit the General Staff had at last acquired a reliable
military instrument which could be trusted to carry out its combat
missions in full. Equally important, it also had a body of men who
could set standards for the rest of the Army. Just as the small Unit
101 had been used to reinvigorate the larger paratroop unit, Dayan
hoped to use the new paratroop battalion as a morale-builder and
tactical school for the mass of the infantry. That Sharon's battalion
was designated as a paratroop unit did not mean very much; parachute training was treated more or less as a sport, useful to develop
the unit's distinctive *esprit de corps* but of no great tactical significance.

The main tactical innovation introduced by the paratroop
battalion was a new technique for attacks against fortified positions. The conventional method still taught in Israeli training
courses was a step-by-step 'fire and movement' advance against
enemy trenches. Acting in turn as 'fire' and 'assault' teams,
troops were to advance towards the enemy lines by stages, each
team giving fire support for the other. Once inside the fortifications,
each line of trenches was to be assaulted in sequence while enemy
troops were pinned down by covering fire. Originally developed
during the First World War, and still a standard method, this
tactic relies on fire-power to reduce the physical defences (and
morale) of the enemy, while the element of surprise is sacrificed.
In July 1954 Sharon was wounded while leading a raid against an
Egyptian stronghold opposite the border kibbutz of Kissufim.
Like many others along the armistice line, this was a conventional
infantry stronghold consisting of concentric trench lines linked by
narrow communication trenches with barbed wire fences and mines
around the perimeter.

While lying in his hospital bed, Sharon worked out a new tactical
method to replace the old 'fire and movement' tactics learned from
the British.[11] Instead of relying on heavy covering fire, the men
were to approach the trench system without firing at all. Walking

---

* 7 April 1954 against Husan; 9 May at Khirbet Ilin; 27 May, Khirbet
Jimba; 28 June, Azzoun; 1 August near Jenin; 13 August at Sheikh Madh-
kur (all in Jordan); 3 April 1954 near Gaza; and 15 August, Bir es Saka (in
the Gaza Strip).

slowly and in absolute silence until fired upon, the men were then to run forward as rapidly as possible, firing on the move, while the barbed wire fences were breached by Bangalore torpedoes – long tubes filled with high explosives.

Once they reached the trench line, the men were to form small assault groups and, without pausing to clear the fire-trenches, they were to jump into the communication trenches, running and shooting all the way to the centre and out again. Sweeping one trench line after another, the assault teams were to keep moving until all the defenders were killed or captured. The essence of Sharon's tactic was the shock effect of relentless movement and surprise to confuse the enemy and break down his resistance. The method was peculiarly vulnerable to enemy counter-attacks during the actual assault. While the paratroopers were inside the stronghold, but not yet in full control, the arrival of enemy reinforcements could rally the defenders and this could easily disrupt a tactic which relied so heavily on morale effects. For this reason, Sharon prescribed that, prior to the assault, enemy strongholds were to be cut off by all-round blocking and ambush positions.

Since they invariably fought at night and were trained to fire on the move, the paratroopers were mostly armed with submachine-guns. In the Israeli-made Uzi they had a good weapon which has since been adopted by several foreign armies, but no sub-machine-gun is accurate beyond a hundred yards, and few men can be taught to hit even large targets at short range while firing from the hip. But at really close quarters, the rapid fire of sub-machine-guns is deadly and Sharon's men were taught to close in for hand-to-hand combat as soon as possible. Egyptian and Jordanian soldiers tend to fight poorly at close quarters; on the other hand they are often good riflemen, the Jordanian Legion-naires being especially good shots. By attacking at night, when no accurate long-range fire is possible, the paratroopers deprived the Arabs of this advantage while at the same time exploiting their aversion for fighting in the dark at close quarters. The special merit of Sharon's tactical methods lay not so much in the tech-niques themselves – which others had used long before – as in their particular suitability to the Arab–Israeli context.

Instead of using the dynamic leadership and *esprit de corps* of

Fig. 3

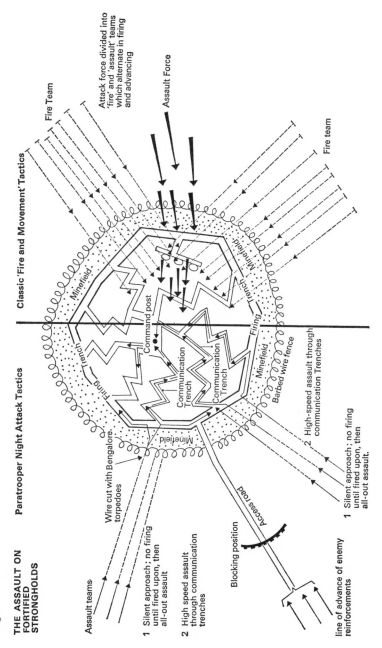

THE ASSAULT ON FORTIFIED STRONGHOLDS

Paratrooper Night Attack Tactics

Classic 'Fire and Movement' Tactics

Fire Team

Attack force divided into 'fire' and 'assault' teams which alternate in firing and advancing

Assault Force

Fire team

Minefield

Minefield

Trench

Firing Trench

Command post

Communication Trench

Communication Trench

Minefield

Firing Trench

Barbed wire fence

Minefield

Wire cut with Bengalore torpedoes

Assault teams.

1 Silent approach; no firing until fired upon, then all-out assault

2 High speed assault through communication trenches

1 Silent approach; no firing until fired upon, then all-out assault.

2 High-speed assault through communication Trenches

Blocking position

Access road

line of advance of enemy reinforcements

the paratroopers to enhance the value of conventional tactics, these assets were used to the full by adopting bold high-risk tactics which Israeli superiority in morale made possible.[12] In other words, Sharon's tactics were 'relational', rooted in the specific strengths and weaknesses of the adversaries. Egyptian and Jordanian soldiers were trained regulars who fought stubbornly and well so long as they were holding fortified positions according to plans prepared in advance. By relying on shock and surprise instead of more conventional tactics, Sharon exploited the enemy's inability to improvise amidst confusion.* Conversely, the high degree of mutual confidence within paratroops units was the key to Sharon's tactics for attacks on trench systems: the safety of each assault team was critically dependent on the relentless advance of every other team, since any loss of momentum would have exposed the attackers to deadly enfilading fire from trenches still in enemy hands. Any doubt among the men as to the will and ability of other groups to sustain the advance would have caused the assault to collapse.

Few of Sharon's original group of officers survived unscathed the reprisal operations of the mid-fifties, which re-established the 'follow me' style of leadership. Sharon himself and almost all his colleagues were wounded, some repeatedly, and many died. Among the survivors of this small group were three future generals, M. Gur, Y. Hoffi and R. Eytan. Even after the 1967 War, one full colonel (Arieh Regev), and two lieut.-colonels (Zvi Ofer and Moshe Stemple), of the original paratroop battalion were killed in action while personally leading small groups of soldiers in counter-guerrilla operations. The wisdom of allowing officers of General Staff calibre to fight and die in minor skirmishes has been repeatedly debated within the Army, but personal leadership in combat has remained the official doctrine on the grounds that the loss of much-valued individuals is compensated by the overall gain in morale and tactical skill. In any case, the follow-me ethos has such a strong hold on the mentality of Israeli officers that it has been very difficult to restrain even the most senior from taking the lead in combat.

Even after his appointment as Chief of Staff in December 1953, Moshe Dayan took a close personal interest in the paratroopers.

* As he was to do again in the October 1973 attack across the Suez Canal.

He was almost invariably present when they went into action and knew many of them personally. Important as their combat role undoubtedly was, for Dayan the paratroop battalion was still more valuable as an inspiring example for the Army as a whole. Dayan wanted officers who were fighting men rather than managers in uniform; he wanted training which stressed combat skills rather than parade-ground drills, and he wanted a maximum of 'teeth' units with an absolute minimum of 'tail' – and for all those things the paratroopers provided an exemplary model. To spread the 'paratroop spirit' in the Army as a whole, Dayan insisted that every officer, including himself, undergo jump training. He also enlarged the paratroop unit so that by 1956 it was of brigade size. The infantry brigades of the standing forces, and later reserve units as well, responded to the 'imitative pull' of the paratroopers, and even attempted to compete with them. In the November 1955 Sabha* operation, troops of the 1st Infantry Brigade, the Golani, went into action alongside the paratroopers, just as the 'old' paratroop battalion had fought together with the 101 in the Khibye raid. This was the first combat mission given to the ordinary infantry, since Sharon's men had monopolized combat missions ever since the 101 had been created, and the Golani came through with flying colours.

Dayan's tenure was marked by major organizational innovations and drastic changes in the internal allocation of the Army budget. Expenditure on creature comforts was reduced even further (reservists had to bring their own overcoats, the Army supplied none); budgets for construction, administration and all other non-combat activities were cut to the bone, and fewer officers were sent to courses at foreign military schools. The savings, especially in hard currency, were used to buy more and better weapons. To increase the proportion of 'teeth' to 'tail', Dayan stripped the Army of such ancillary services as bakeries, laundries and canteens, which were handed over to outside contractors or to the civilian staff Ministry of Defence. Dayan also displeased animal lovers by disbanding the army's cavalry and carrier-pigeon units. He also reformed officer training† and introduced systematic contingency planning for a wide range of possible operations. To

* See p. 139 below.
† See p. 88 above.

support operational planning Dayan formed special scouting detachments to collect topographic intelligence and, by 1956, the Israelis knew Sinai better than the Egyptians who had been stationed there for years. But Dayan's most important reform was undoubtedly his introduction of the two-careers scheme, where all officers have to retire in their forties to make way for younger men.*

Under Dayan's tenure the Army progressed from the humiliating failure at Falame to the successes of 1956, but it also came to reflect his own professional shortcomings. For all his sophistication, Dayan was infantry-minded; he understood the importance of motorizing and even mechanizing the infantry but until 1956 he failed to understand the use of tank forces. Like many others, he confused mere physical mobility with actual tactical mobility in the presence of enemy fire – and he therefore regarded the slow and heavy tank as a hindrance. This certainly retarded the growth of the Armour Corps.†[13] His eagerness to strengthen the 'teeth' units also led to a neglect of the technical and supporting branches. As a result, the Sinai Campaign was marked by frequent breakdowns in communications and logistics not all caused by poor equipment. Another shortcoming revealed by the campaign was of an altogether different nature: Dayan knew all about leadership and command but tended to underestimate the importance of control – and in 1956 his control of the offensive was so loose that two entire brigades acted in direct contravention of the plans of G.H.Q.‡ That both did more than was expected, and not less, shows how successful Dayan had been in his attempt to inspire the Army's offensive spirit, but this does not alter the fact that there were catastrophic breakdowns in the control of the fighting.

Whatever his limitations, there is no doubt that Dayan's reversal of the post–1949 trend towards the imitation of foreign armies was a major achievement. He revived many of the concepts of the Palmach – though stripped of their political undertones – and introduced so many innovations that the Army that was to fight in 1956 was much more his creation than Yadin's.

* See p. 182 below.
† See p. 148–9 below.
‡ See p. 160 below.

The Air Force 1949–56

At the beginning of the War of Independence, the Haganah Air Service (Sherut Aviri) had no combat aircraft and its nine light planes could offer no resistance to the fighter-bombers of the Egyptian and Iraqi air forces. By the end of 1948 the situation had been totally reversed. The clandestine purchasing network master-minded by Ben Gurion (Rekhes) had brought 205* aircraft into the country. Israeli fighter squadrons equipped with Spitfire Mk.9s and Messerschmitt 109s were in undisputed control of the air; a transport wing of DC-3s and C-46s was flying supply missions both at home and abroad – and there were even a few bombers, light Beaufighters and heavy B-17s. By then the Air Force (I.A.F.) was three thousand strong, it had a network of former British bases and an organized structure of command.

The rapid growth of the I.A.F. was an impressive achievement but its concrete military results were rather disappointing.[14] Having won superiority in the air, the I.A.F. failed to use its full potential to support the forces on the ground. Though formally a corps of the single-service Army† the I.A.F. tended to operate as an independent service. A majority of its bombing missions were interdiction strikes against targets deep in the enemy rear, or attacks against enemy cities – instead of close-support strikes coordinated with the forces on the ground. The I.A.F. had not worked out a set of priorities consistent with Israeli strategy on the ground, nor developed an operational doctrine suited to local conditions. This is not surprising since most of its pilots, command staff and technicians were foreign volunteers.

The I.A.F. had nevertheless made a major contribution to the victories of 1948 by gaining control of the air and there was a keen appreciation of the future potential of air power, even among those who were unimpressed by the I.A.F.'s record in the War of Independence. There were compelling reasons for assigning a high priority to the Air Force. For one thing, the Arabs would always

---

* Of 250 aircraft purchased in Europe and America, 205 reached Israel during the war. Five Spitfires were rebuilt locally from scrap left behind by the R.A.F.

† Its official title is Hel Avir or Air Corps.

enjoy numerical superiority in manpower and weapons of all types and Israeli military planning was therefore marked by a quest for qualitative superiority; manned aircraft were the most advanced of all weapons in those days where differences in equipment performance and human skill would matter the most.

The importance of air power was also enhanced by Israel's reliance on an offensive strategy. Air superiority, to cover the movement of forces on the ground, was especially important since the desert terrain affords very little natural cover; tactical air support and reconnaissance are also more important for mobile columns engaged in offensive operations than for static forces holding fortified positions. Another factor was the 'short-war' assumption: once war began, one or other of the Great Powers was bound to impose a ceasefire after a few days' fighting, and these narrow time limits put a premium on air power as the most rapid instrument of warfare.

There was thus a consensus within the Army on the importance of air power in the abstract, but its actual budgetary priority was still a matter of contention. The first Air Force Commander, Aharon Remez (1948–50), and the third, Haim Laskov (1951–3), both resigned after budgetary disputes within the General Staff.[15] What complicated these early debates was the lack of agreement on the shape of the I.A.F. Indeed, the most basic planning problem of the early post-war period was to decide what kind of air force was needed. In those days the 'balanced' air forces maintained by the Great Powers were equipped with a variety of different classes of aircraft: heavy, medium and light bombers, 'long-range escort' fighters, interceptor-fighters and fighter-bombers. The I.A.F. of 1948 resembled a miniature version of the 'balanced' model, since it had a few aircraft of each class, but this was more the chance outcome of wartime purchasing than the result of a systematic deployment policy.

During the War of Independence it had been so difficult for the Israelis to obtain combat aircraft that almost anything available on the market was bought. As an (anonymous) foreign expert quoted in Ben Gurion's *Diary* complained at the time: 'There is no method in aircraft purchases, there are small aircraft and there are "Flying Fortresses" [B-17s] but no medium bombers.'[16] This same expert drew up a plan for an establishment of three fighter squadrons (of fifteen aircraft each), one squadron of eighteen medium bombers and one squadron of eight heavy bombers as well as a transport wing of fifteen Dakotas and eight DC-6s. This 'balanced' structure was rejected on the grounds that very few aircraft of each type could be bought, but it was not until 1953 that a clear policy was framed. This was the concept of an all-fighter air force propounded by Dan Tolkowsky, the newly appointed Commander of the I.A.F.[17] Instead of having specialized aircraft for each separate task, the strategic bombing mission was abandoned, and all tactical missions were assigned to the same basic type of multi-purpose* fighter.

Under Tolkowsky the I.A.F. acquired its basic structure as an all-fighter force built to carry out two successive missions: first the fight for air superiority against enemy air power and then tactical strike and reconnaissance in support of land and naval operations. The decision in favour of sole reliance on multi-purpose fighters did not settle the airpower debate which merely shifted to a more narrow tactical question: how was air superiority to be achieved?

A majority on the General Staff held that superiority in the air could best be won by destroying enemy aircraft in the air, and called for a defensive strategy of interception for the *attrition* of enemy air power. Tolkowsky and his colleagues disagreed. They advocated an offensive strategy of air strikes against enemy aircraft on the ground.[18] The debate acquired a peculiar historical tint, since both sides tried to prove their case by using the Battle of Britain as an example. The airmen argued that the Germans lost the contest for air superiority because they switched their offensive from the airfields of the R.A.F. to the bombing of London too soon. Their opponents claimed that the great lesson of the Battle of Britain was that the Spitfires and Hurricanes of the R.A.F. had successfully worn down the Luftwaffe and that interception was a more reliable tactic than the all-out strike against enemy airfields. The airmen won this debate but it was only the air strike of 5 June 1967 that proved them right.

On strategic bombing there was no disagreement. To weaken

* The 'multi-purpose' design concept was not developed in the West until the sixties but it was always understood that any fighter with a respectable payload could perform a range of different tasks.

the enemy's war-making capabilities by striking at industrial targets was clearly irrelevant in the Middle East where wars are fought with imported weapons. Besides, the effects of strategic bombing 'if any' are slow to materialize since the impact of supply shortages on combat force is at best cumulative – and this did not fit the 'short-war' assumption. Having eliminated the heavy bomber role and disposed of the 'interception' theory (which called for specialized interceptor-fighters), the commanders of the I.A.F. built an air force based on fighter-bombers. As an inherently more versatile weapon, the fighter-bomber was particularly suited to Israeli needs since it could offset the weakness of lower-priority arms such as the Navy and the artillery.[19] As we have seen the I.A.F. is not a separate 'service' like most other air forces but a corps of the single-service Army; even so it has its own distinctive uniforms, maintains its own specialized services and has an operational headquarters. This semi-autonomous status was the result of a compromise between advocates of full integration (on a par with the Armour Corps) and early demands for independent status as a separate service. The I.A.F. does not induct its own conscripts, but receives men who have gone through the Army's basic training; nor does it operate its own supporting services (military police, general supplies, etc.). Above all, the I.A.F. is subject to the authority of the army Chief of Staff since there is no 'service minister' responsible for Air Force matters at the political level.*

When its first commander, Aharon Remez, resigned in 1950 in protest at the I.A.F.'s lack of autonomy and its limited budget, Yadin replaced him with a former infantry officer, Shlomo Shamir, who had earlier served as Navy Commander. The appointment of an infantry officer was a deliberate attempt by Yadin to emphasize the subordinate status of the Air Force in the face of demands for greater autonomy. Shamir served without distinction for only one year (1950–51); his successor, Haim Laskov, was also an army officer with no previous Air Force experience but, unlike his predecessor, Laskov soon found a common language with the airmen and himself came to advocate more independence for the I.A.F. During his tenure (1951–3), Laskov reorganized the Air Force

* In 1948 a deputy Minister was briefly placed in charge of the Air Force *and* Navy, but the post was soon abolished.

command structure, supervised a thoroughgoing analysis of the role of air power in Israeli strategy and developed the beginnings of a tactical doctrine.

In 1953 the Air Force once again came under the command of a pilot officer, Dan Tolkowsky. Under his leadership, the I.A.F. acquired many of the distinctive features it still retains today, though it was not until the tenure of Ezer Weizman, who succeeded Tolkowsky in 1958, that the Air Force which fought in 1967 acquired its final form. Tolkowsky and Weizman made technical perfectionism the dominant goal of the Air Force; as well as cultivating professionalism within the I.A.F. itself, they also inspired the establishment of civilian technical schools to train teenagers in the electronic and mechanical skills required by the Air Force. Their policy within the I.A.F. itself was marked by a relentless effort to maximize the quality of individual pilots* and to improve the speed and reliability of aircraft maintenance. In both cases, it was a matter of making the most out of a strictly limited number of combat aircraft – and in both cases it took years of relentless effort to achieve satisfactory results. For one thing, as pilot performance standards increased so did the failure rate, in spite of the introduction of scientific testing procedures which became increasingly stringent.[20] Realizing that the strength of an air force depends on the number of *serviceable* aircraft available at any one time, rather than on the total number of aircraft in inventory, every possible mechanical and psychological technique† was used to improve the work of the ground crews so as to reduce the time required for maintenance between sorties.

The reorganization of the I.A.F. under Tolkowsky coincided with the introduction of its first jet aircraft, British-built Meteors‡

---

* See p. 201 below for a brief discussion of pilot training procedures.

† See below p. 198.

‡ In 1953 four Meteor T.7s (trainer version) were bought from Great Britain and three from Belgium; in 1953–4 eleven Meteor F. MK.8s were bought from Great Britain. Seven F.MK.9s and six N.F.13s were bought at a later stage. The twin-jet Meteor was a first-generation jet. The basic fighter-version (F.MK.8) was a single-seater and had a top speed of 592 m.p.h. The N.F. (night-fighter) version was equipped with a large nose radar and had a top speed of 500 m.p.h. For Israel, the Meteor served primarily as a jet-conversion trainer; only fifteen were operational during the 1956 Sinai Campaign.

ordered during Laskov's tenure but delivered just after his successor's appointment. The Meteors bought in Belgium and the U.K. served alongside piston-engined fighters, Mosquitos and Mustang P-51s, which still made up the bulk of the I.A.F. Spitfires bought in Italy, Mustang P-51s from Sweden, and Mosquitos rebuilt from parts (250 air-frames were bought as scrap) made up the variegated collection of war-surplus aircraft in inventory. Jets were expensive and for political reasons difficult to buy. Tolkowsky, like Laskov before him, was involved in a running dispute with the General Staff over the budget allocated to the Air Force. Money was so tight that it restricted not only the purchase of new aircraft, but even that of spare parts for aircraft in inventory. Eventually the money to buy modern jets was found, and then the political troubles started.

After the failure of an attempt to purchase American Sabre F.86 jets, the Israelis turned to France. Neither Britain nor the U.S. wanted to antagonize the Arabs; but France had lost most of its influence in the Arab world and was therefore more likely to sell its aircraft to Israel. Negotiations covering the sale of a few Ouragan and Mystère fighters had already been finalized when the French cabinet of Mendès-France fell. The whole question had to be renegotiated with the new government in Paris; not for the last time, the Israelis had to contend with the peculiar instability of French politics. One thing did not change: the French Foreign Ministry, like the U.S. State Department and the British Foreign Office, always opposed arms sales to Israel. Nevertheless, this first round of negotiations was brought to a successful conclusion, after the French Foreign Ministry was circumvented by Israeli representatives in Paris who found staunch allies in the French forces and Ministry of Defence.[21]

At the beginning of 1955 the I.A.F. received its first French jets, twelve Dassault Ouragan single-seat fighters; twelve more were delivered at the end of that year.[22] A lightweight subsonic fighter comparable to the MiG-15, the Ouragan was of simple and reliable design, it made a very stable gun platform and could also carry a small bomb load.*

* The Ouragan is a single-seat, single-engine, low-wing fighter/fighter-bomber armed with four 20mm cannon. It can also carry up to two 250lb. bombs or rocket pods. Max. speed at sea level is 600 m.p.h.

A more modern aircraft, the Dassault Mystère IVA,* was already in production at the time and a first squadron of twenty-four Mystères was delivered to the I.A.F. in 1956. Though none of these aircraft was a genuine fighter-bomber with a substantial attack payload, the Ouragan and Mystère IV did have some bombing capability; the I.A.F. rejected another French aircraft, offered earlier, the Mystère II, because it was a pure interceptor.

On the eve of the Sinai Campaign of October 1956 the I.A.F. had three jet squadrons equipped with Meteors, Ouragans and Mystères but it still had to rely on its old piston-engine fighters, since out of 136 *operational* aircraft only fifty-three were jets.†

As against this the Egyptians already had an all-jet air force with forty-five MiG-15 (thirty operational), thirty Vampires (fifteen operational), thirty-two Meteors (twelve operational) and forty-nine Ilyushin-28 light bombers (twelve operational).[24]

As war became imminent, the commanders of the I.A.F. wanted to take the initiative with an all-out strike against Egyptian airfields. But Ben Gurion and Dayan refused to allow this. Unlike the airmen, they were aware of the Anglo-French invasion plan, to which the Israeli offensive was tied. According to the joint plan, the task of attacking the Egyptian air force was left to the British and the French while the I.A.F. was confined to the lesser role of supporting the Israeli offensive in Sinai. Political considerations aside, it seems that Ben Gurion doubted the effectiveness of the I.A.F.[25] He not only denied it a primary strike role against Egyptian air power, but also insisted that the French guarantee Israel's air defence; in a rare lapse from his usual good sense on military matters, Ben Gurion gravely overestimated the threat of the Egyptian bomber force. With a combined payload of less than fifty tons per strike, the twelve Ilyushins of the Egyptian Air force

* A swept-wing, single-seat fighter/fighter-bomber with one jet engine, armed with two 30mm cannon and 55 air-to-air rockets (obsolete feature); it can carry up to 1,000 kg. of mixed ordnance.

† According to Dayan's *Diary of the Sinai Campaign*, the operational inventory of the I.A.F. in October 1956 was as follows: jet fighters: 16 Mystères IVAs, 22 Ouragans and 15 Meteors; piston-engined fighters: 29 Mustang P.51Ds, 17 Harvards, 16 Mosquitos and 2 obsolete B.17Gs bombers; transport: 16 Dakotas and 3 Noratlas 2501s.[23]

then operational were no great threat, but Ben Gurion refused to
rely on the I.A.F. and obtained the deployment of French fighters
at Israeli airfields. As a result, in 1956 the role of the I.A.F. was
limited to close support of the ground forces, interdiction strikes
against enemy communications in the rear and battlefield air
cover. As we shall see, its performance exceeded all expectations
and paved the way for the 1967 war plan in which the I.A.F. was
given the central role.

The Armour Corps 1949–56

As part of the ground forces, the Armour Corps remained under the
detailed control of the General Staff, most of whose officers –
including Dayan – doubted the effectiveness of tank forces.
Their doubts were rooted in the experiences of 1948 when the
Army's one tank battalion fought poorly, while the fast-moving
mechanized infantry battalions equipped with half-tracks, jeeps
and armoured cars fought very well indeed. Since the Armour
Corps (*Hel Shirion*) was responsible for the mechanized infantry
as well as the tank units, the General Staff's preference for the
former seriously impeded the growth of the tank forces.

Dayan and his associates did not realize that the slow-moving
and heavily armoured battle tank is in reality more mobile than the
apparently faster vehicles of the mechanized infantry, because it
can advance against enemy fire. It is armour protection and not
just mechanical speed that makes for battlefield mobility. The
1948 tank battalion whose misfortunes dogged the Armour
Corps during the fifties was a battalion in name only. Instead of
three or more companies of ten–fifteen tanks each, it only had two
companies with thirteen tanks in all, ten French light tanks of
pre-war vintage, two British Cromwells and a single Sherman M.4,
the only modern tank of the lot.[26] Part of the 8th Brigade commanded by Yitzhak Sadeh, founder of the Palmach, was sent into
action in all three of the major operations of the war, but achieved
little in each case. It was far too small to generate the 'mailed fist'
shock effect which is the key to the strength of armoured forces,
while the tank crews, who had learned their trade in the wartime
Allied armies, could not adjust to the entirely different environment of the 1948 War.

When they found themselves advancing with a handful of tanks, with no infantry or artillery escort support, their instinctive reaction was to wait for non-existent reinforcements. In a situation where the most successful commanders were those who advanced at all costs and hoped for the best, the more prudent tactics of the tank men earned them little credit. But perhaps the most negative trait of the Armour Corps, in 1948 and till much later, was the chronic unreliability of its vehicles. Again and again operations had to be cancelled because of mechanical breakdowns. In the early fifties, Dayan heard the complaints of paratroopers who were often held up by the frequent breakdowns which plagued the half-tracks of the Armour Corps, and this record of unreliability made a greater impression on him than all the arguments of the tank enthusiasts.

In 1949, when the war was already over, the Israelis at last managed to buy enough Sherman tanks to equip a full battalion. A virtual embargo was still in effect and these tanks were bought as scrap. The U.S. army had 'de-weaponized' them by drilling a hole right through the gun-barrel of each tank. To provide some impressive-looking armour for the 1949 Independence Day parade, the holes were filled with paste and painted over. Later, Ordnance Corps technicians managed to repair the guns by fitting metal rings around the barrels.[27]

The Army now had tanks but still no trained crews, or instructors. Actually, the General Staff scarcely knew what to do with the tanks; there was no cadre of tank officers nor an operational doctrine for the use of armour, except for the theorizing of Laskov's group. The tank crews of 1948 had little to teach beyond simple maintenance, and were soon replaced by Israelis. Under the command of Shaul Yaffe, a former Palmach officer who had no real tank experience, the battlion set out to learn armoured warfare from scratch. Some American manuals were obtained and tactical do's and don'ts were at first learned from the pictures since none of the tank men knew enough English to read the text. Nobody in the Army had any knowledge of tank gunnery, but some artillery officers were familiar with anti-tank guns, and they trained the first gunners of the battalion.

Nothing was known about tank tactics or the use of armour in groups; the battalion at first adapted a rough and ready version of infantry 'fire and movement' tactics. A group of tanks (the 'assault team') would advance towards the enemy while a second group (the 'fire team') gave fire support from the flanks and rear. The first group would then in turn take up firing positions while the second took over the assault role.[28] The young officers of the embryonic Armour Corps* were eager to learn and full of enthusiasm; unable to benefit from the accumulated experience of other armies, the first generation of Israeli tank men learned by trial and error, and in endless debate. They drove their Shermans over, under and through every kind of obstacle to find out just what they could do; if a tank broke down in the process, its repair became an exercise in battlefield maintenance. Tactics were tried out, discussed, modified and tried again; new methods discovered in the process were added to a growing body of doctrine.

In a sense all this was very wasteful; what the Israelis learnt by painful experience could easily have been taught by a few skilled foreign instructors. But this slow process of trial and error did have a long-term advantage: insteady of copying what others had done, the Israelis worked out their own original tactical ideas, suited to local conditions.[29] At first the only peculiarity of the Israeli Armour Corps was that its tanks and half-tracks were few and antiquated. Later when the corps became larger than its counterparts in the British or French armies – and when circumstances had made it the most experienced tank force in the world – the habit of self-reliance in training and tactics became a most valuable asset.

In the beginning, however, there was only ignorance and lack of equipment. Few countries manufacture tanks and during the fifties none were willing to sell their products to Israel. While the armies of the major powers could obtain tailor-made equipment, and most smaller armies could at least buy what they wanted from a range of suppliers, the Israeli Army could do neither. The Tripartite Declaration of 1950 amounted to a virtual embargo on arms supplies to the Middle East.[30] Issued by Britain, France and the United States it opposed any forcible change in the 1949 armistice lines and called for limits on arms supplies to the Middle East. As long as the embargo applied to the Arabs as well, some sort of balance was maintained. But in 1955 the Soviet Union broke the

* The corps is basically an inspectorate responsible for training, doctrines and technical functions. It is *not* an operational command.

Western monopoly and supplied Egypt with more than five hundred armoured vehicles (including 230 T-34 tanks) and there was no corresponding supply for Israel. In 1955, in the first of a series of supply agreements, France did consent to sell tanks to Israel, but the two hundred AMX-13 light tanks and modified U.S.-built Shermans they provided were no match for the Soviet tanks received by Egypt.* By then Israel had already acquired more than a hundred Shermans sold as scrap by commercial sources but this first government-to-government supply agreement was a revelation to the Armour Corps. For the first time it received tanks in good condition, with a full stock of spare parts, repair kits and even transporters. This was just as well since the modernized Shermans did not arrive till the very eve of the Sinai Campaign. (The French *approved* the sale only three weeks before the fighting started.) The Israelis went to war in 1956 with 250 or so Shermans of all types and one hundred AMX-13s; neither tank was as good as the T-34s of the Egyptian army which were superior in armour protection, fire-power and mobility.

By 1956, the tank officers had acquired the technical skills and command expertise required by armour warfare; but all their enthusiasm and hard work failed to persuade Dayan to take the tank forces seriously.[31] Ben Gurion was won over; he authorized the budgets which allowed the corps to expand to seven battalions.† Haim Laskov, as usual far-sighted, gave his full support to the tank men within the General Staff (he was to serve as O.C. Armour Corps in 1956); but Dayan was still unconvinced, although the Armour Corps had given convincing proof of its capabilities

* The T-34 is a thirty-two tonner armed with an 85mm gun; the AMX-13 has a combat loaded weight of 14·8 tons, a high-velocity 75mm gun and thin armour; the Shermans (Super-Shermans) were M.4A3 E8s upgunned with a higher velocity French 75mm gun. The same gun was fitted in Israel to some Shermans already in stock.

† Assuming that there were 250 Shermans of all types (the 'short' 76·2mm gun version; the 'long' 76·2mm M.4A3 E8; and the 75mm French gun Super-Shermans) and one hundred AMX-13s, this force could equip either seven battalions of fifty tanks each or twenty 'squadrons' of fifteen tanks each. But some tanks are always out of order at any one time; some squadrons had more than 15 tanks and some battalions had less than 50. See below p. 151 n for the 1956 order of battle.

during the annual all-Army manoeuvres of 1952 and 1953. The first full-scale war game was held in 1952, during Yadin's tenure, with the 'blue' forces of Southern Command ranged against the 'green' forces of Central Command. By then, the tank battalion had been formed into a brigade together with two battalions of infantry riding half-tracks; it was part of the 'blue' forces.

Lieut.-Col. Uri Ben Ari, the most brilliant of the young officers in the Armour Corps and its moving spirit, was the brigade's deputy commander. Ben Ari had read descriptions of the Wehrmacht's Panzer tactics and, under the direction of Dayan, who was then C.O. at Southern Command, he proceeded to try them out for himself. Leading the brigade in a rapid advance of eighty miles, his tanks got behind the rear of the 'green' forces, cut their lines of communication and were on the verge of defeating them when the supervising staff intervened.[32] Yadin and the supervising officers had planned an orderly and deliberate infantry manoeuvre, and at Dayan's instigation Ben Ari had disrupted the war game with his spectacular envelopment of the 'green' forces. The tanks were neutralized by order: a circle was drawn on the map and the brigade was ordered to remain within it, motionless and inactive. Yigael Yadin, a very conventional infantry soldier, was harsh in his criticism of Dayan for having spoiled the war game. Dayan was unrepentant, so was Ben Ari and his brigade again used deep penetration tactics in the 1953 war game.

As in 1952 the tanks broke through the front and enveloped the 'green' forces. This time Yadin was no longer Chief of Staff,* the supervising officers did not intervene, and the 'blue' forces won thanks to Ben Ari's brigade. At one point during the game, the tanks swooped on a battalion of 'green' infantry which they caught in flat open ground. When the 'green' soldiers saw the tanks rushing towards them, they dropped their weapons and scattered in panic – even though they knew full well that this was only an exercise. Ben Gurion happened to be on the spot and was so impressed with the tanks that from then onwards he supported the tank enthusiasts in their continuing struggle with the General Staff and allocated funds for the purchase of tanks and carriers.

---

* Mordechai Makleff had replaced him in December 1952.

But he failed to persuade the General Staff to recognize the primacy of armour in its tactical planning.

There was still no agreement on how tanks were to be used in battle. The 'mobile infantry' school, consistently supported by Yadin and, until 1956, by Dayan, reflected the experience of the Haganah and the Army of Independence. Men like Dayan had no direct knowledge of the power of massed armour, while they were acutely conscious of the high cost of maintaining tank forces. They thought that tanks could best be used to support the motorized and mechanized infantry and refused to rely on tank forces to spearhead their advance.[33] The mechanized infantry, with its faster half-track carriers, could do this much better in their view. The massing of battle tanks in large all-armour units was thus seen as a sheer waste of expensive hardware.

A second school of thought acknowledged the scarcity of battle tanks but still advocated their concentration in all-armour units. Instead of distributing tanks in penny packets as support weapons for the infantry, they were to be used by the battalion as independent striking forces – though only for 'indirect approach' tactics in a cavalry-style exploitation of infantry break-throughs. Direct attacks against the enemy front were to be left to the infantry and artillery while battles with enemy armour were to be avoided. Instead, screens of anti-tank guns were to tackle enemy armour (as in the Anglo-German tank battles in North Africa). In this view, armoured forces could best be used to penetrate behind the enemy front, in the wake of the infantry, in order to cut supply lines and mount surprise attacks against the enemy's rear.

Most tank officers belonged to a third school of thought which made few concessions to the reality of equipment limitations and which advocated a leading role for armoured forces. Armoured brigades, spearheaded by their tank battalions, were to fight in self-sufficient combat teams of mechanized infantry, tanks and artillery to break through frontal defences, fan out in deep narrow thrusts and cut the enemy front into isolated pockets. The motorized infantry (and towed artillery) could then follow in the wake of the armoured combat teams to roll up the front and destroy the troops trapped by the armoured thrusts. This school of thought conceded that grinding tank-to-tank battles were to be avoided, but only if this could be done without slowing the advance of the armoured spearheads.[34]

Dayan and the General Staff continued to reject these tactics, opting instead for a blend of the first ('mobile infantry') and second ('exploitation') tank doctrines.[35] Accordingly, for the Sinai Campaign, the 350 or so tanks of the Armour Corps were not massed into three powerful armoured brigades. Instead, only Ben Ari's 7th Brigade had a full complement of two tank battalions; the remaining tanks were distributed by squadrons and battalions to four different brigades deployed in the south, and to the two Area Commands (North and Centre) which remained on the defensive.

Even Ben Ari's brigade, the only one equipped as an independent striking force, was given only a supporting role in the G.H.Q. plan. Nevertheless, as we shall see, the 7th Brigade gave a spectacular demonstration of Panzer tactics in the course of the campaign, though to do this it had to act against the orders of Dayan and the General Staff.

The Navy 1949–56

According to all the classic criteria – dependence on seaborne imports, length of coast-line and lack of land access – Israel is particularly vulnerable to naval attack and should accordingly maintain a powerful navy. And yet the Israeli Navy remained of negligible proportions until 1955; in that year two ex-British 'Z' class destroyers were added to some corvettes and patrol boats commissioned earlier. Even so, the Navy could do little more than guard the coasts and had little striking power. Apart from the 'short-war' assumption, which obviously undercut the importance of protecting the sea lanes, none of the warship types which Israel could conceivably buy suited her needs.

Until the introduction of missile-armed patrol boats in the 1960s the choice open to a small power navy was between cheap but ineffectual torpedo boats and costly ocean-going warships – and the latter are of little value if deployed in small numbers. Israel could afford dozens of jet fighters and hundreds of tanks but only a handful of destroyers or submarines. This meant that the Navy could not attain the minimum size needed to ensure that the number of warships operational at any one time was sufficient to provide the mutual support so essential in naval warfare. As the size of a fleet is reduced, there is a disproportionate loss of effectiveness; with only two destroyers available, only one can be operational at all times – and the effectiveness of a single destroyer is much less than fifty per cent of a two-destroyer flotilla. Only an impossibly generous budget could have brought the Navy to the 'critical mass' required for mutual support.

Small and somewhat remote from the rest of the Army, the 'Sea Corps', as the Navy is designated in Hebrew (Hel Yam), developed during the fifties on the lines of a separate service; it resembled a small slice of a great power navy. In 1956, the Navy had 5–6,000 men for a fleet of two destroyers, nine torpedo boats and two landing craft. To offset the Navy's inability to protect Israel's seaborne commerce, substantial stocks of essential supplies were maintained against the eventuality of a naval blockade. The General Staff and its political masters continued to believe that a prolonged blockade was unlikely and that not much naval power was therefore needed. In line with the 'short-war' assumption, it was assumed that sooner or later an Arab blockade would be lifted by the diplomatic intervention of the Great Powers, or by the defeat of the enemy on land. But weakness in any one dimension of military power always has its price; in the Israeli case, the price was that there was no way of dealing with even a small naval threat without all-out war on land.

Politics and the Defence Establishment

Ever since 1948, the Israeli defence establishment had been dominated by the personality of Ben Gurion who was both Prime Minister and Minister of Defence. But on 7 December 1953, Ben Gurion, tired of endless squabbles with his colleagues in the Cabinet, resigned from the government and retired to the kibbutz of Sde Boker deep in the Negev desert. His was an entirely voluntary resignation and the new Minister of Defence, Pinchas Lavon, was Ben Gurion's chosen successor. One day before resigning Ben Gurion had appointed Moshe Dayan as Chief of Staff in succession to Mordechai Makleff. But the new Prime Minister, Moshe Sharett, was the choice of the Mapai party rather than Ben Gurion. Sharett disagreed with the retaliatory policy, and Ben Gurion was counting on Lavon and Dayan to offset Sharett and thus maintain continuity in Israeli defence policy

Sharett advocated an altogether more conciliatory policy towards the neighbouring Arab states; he opposed Ben Gurion's strategy of reprisal raids and called for greater restraint in answering Arab attacks. Once in office Sharett repeatedly refused to authorize reprisal raids which Lavon and Dayan considered necessary, but he could not always resist their demands. The scope of Israeli retaliatory action was thus considerably reduced but several raids were nevertheless authorized by the Cabinet in spite of Sharett's anxieties about their long-term effects on Arab–Israeli relations.[36] Sharett also had a more immediate reason for opposing the retaliatory policy; he wanted to cultivate closer relations with the U.S. government, and the U.S. State Department protested vigorously at each reprisal raid. Sharett's attempt to set Israel on a new political course was undermined by the Arab failure to respond to his conciliatory policy. Ben Gurion's influence in the Mapai party was therefore unimpaired since Sharett's policies had yielded no visible results and Arab attacks continued.

Ben Gurion gave firm support to Lavon and Dayan and their activist policy, but he soon had to choose between the two men. Having inherited a post whose wide powers had derived from Ben Gurion's personal standing in the party and the country at large, Lavon attempted to maintain an undiminished jurisdiction based on the office and not its holder. Dayan was not only an ambitious professional soldier but also a highly political man with a background of party activity in the Mapai. He was unwilling to concede to Lavon what Yadin and Makleff had conceded to Ben Gurion, and a conflict between the Minister and the Chief of Staff became inevitable. Dayan held that the powers of the Minister of Defence should be limited to decisions of war and peace, and to financial control over the Army. In his view, professional and technical matters were the exclusive province of the Chief of Staff, who was to be the sole link between the uniformed military and their political masters. Lavon held that the Minister was empowered to direct the Army's activities in all spheres, organizational as well as technical. He saw the Chief of Staff as little more than an executive officer. In this he went beyond Ben Gurion's already very wide sphere since Ben Gurion was not interested in technical matters and left them to the Chief of Staff. It followed that Lavon claimed the right to intervene in Army matters at all levels, if need be by dealing with officers other than the Chief of Staff. This undercut the authority of the Chief of Staff since he could no longer claim to speak for the Army as a whole.

Though they were both 'activists', Lavon and Dayan also came into conflict over policy. Dayan supported the young and dynamic Director-General of the Ministry of Defence, Shimon Peres, in his attempts to obtain arms from France. A French-oriented foreign policy was consistent with activism *vis-à-vis* the Arabs, but Lavon opposed this policy (which Ben Gurion had initiated). There was also a clash of personalities between the two men: Lavon was a verbose politician of the older generation and something of an ideologue, while Dayan was of the new breed of more pragmatic, and in a way more sophisticated, native-born *sabras*. It was this multiple conflict of jurisdiction, policies and personalities which lay at the background of the so-called 'Lavon Affair'.[37]

The affair originated in a secret operation conducted by locally recruited volunteers in Egypt, which involved acts of sabotage against foreign embassies, cinemas and other public buildings. The aim was to undermine Western confidence in Nasser's regime and thus discourage attempts to enrol Egypt into the Western Alliance system. Mismanaged from the start, the operation failed, the Jewish volunteer agents were caught, and damage was done to the entirely distinct and far more professional Israeli intelligence network in Egypt, which lost one of its best men, sent to investigate the fiasco. As Minister of Defence, Lavon was ordinarily responsible for authorizing such operations but he claimed that in this instance the Chief of the Intelligence Corps, Benjamin Givly, had acted without his knowledge or consent. The latter, on the other hand, claimed that Lavon had himself ordered the operation, bypassing the Chief of Staff.

It was Lavon's practice of dealing directly with senior department heads, instead of channelling all his directives through the Chief of Staff, that lent plausibility to Givly's claim. Although Dayan had been abroad when the operation was launched, this did not alter the substance of the issue since there was an acting Chief of Staff, Yosef Avidar.

The dispute between Lavon and Givly became almost immediately a confrontation between the professionals of the Army and the Ministry of Defence, led by Dayan and Peres, and their nominal political master. As the dispute widened into a political crisis, factions formed around Lavon and Dayan in a struggle for power; nothing emerged in public, since military censorship prevented the publication of any information relating to the affair. Ben Gurion supported the anti-Lavonists and this decided the issue. In February 1955, after little more than a year in office Lavon resigned (when Sharrett refused to sanction his demand for the dismissal of Peres and Givly) and Ben Gurion became once again Minister of Defence. The authority of the government over the Army was thus re-established, but this did nothing to solve the policy conflict between Sharett – supported by a majority in the Cabinet – and the activists now led by Ben Gurion himself.

In Israeli politics it is the party machines which hold the reins of power, and Ben Gurion dominated Mapai, the largest party in the Knesset and senior partner in every coalition government since 1948. Sharett was supported by a majority of the Mapai and non-Mapai ministers in the coalition Cabinet, but lacked support in his own party. In November 1955 when Ben Gurion was nominated Prime Minister by the party leadership Sharett remained in office as Foreign Minister and continued to argue against military action mainly in order to safeguard Israeli interests with the U.S. government. But his influence was considerably reduced, and he was consistently overruled by Ben Gurion.

In the midst of Israel's internal crisis, in September 1955 Egypt and the Soviet Union released the explosive news of their arms supply agreement, the so-called Czech deal. The activists immediately demanded preventive war in order to defeat the Egyptian army before it absorbed the mass of new Russian material.[38] Sharett once again opposed military action but Ben Gurion now insisted that the displeasure of the Western Powers was less consequential than the military threat from Egypt.[39] It was not until July 1956 that Ben Gurion succeeded in persuading the rest of the Mapai leadership to go along with his views. Sharett was forced to resign, and Golda Meir became Foreign Minister in a Cabinet dominated by the activists. Four months later the Sinai Campaign began.

The Lavon Affair followed its own course through two commissions of inquiry, eventually erupting in a public scandal whose ultimate effect in 1963 was Ben Gurion's break with Mapai and his (final) resignation from the government. In spite of the weighty constitutional and political issues evoked in the course of the Affair, its outcome did nothing to clarify the demarcation of powers between the Minister and the Chief of Staff. Five years later, during the tenure of Dayan's successor, Haim Laskov (1958–60), there was once again a jurisdictional conflict between the Chief of Staff and the political leadership. This time it was not the Minister himself, Ben Gurion, but his newly appointed deputy Shimon Peres, now in the Knesset and a junior Minister, who came into conflict with the Chief of Staff. Peres, as Lavon before him, claimed the right to consult senior officers directly; Laskov, like Dayan before him, held that the Chief of Staff should be the sole representative of the uniformed military. Ben Gurion decided in favour of Peres, and the Chief of Staff resigned.

On the surface the Lavon–Dayan and Peres–Laskov controversies were not dissimilar, but politically the difference was deep: Lavon's position had been undermined by Sharett's refusal to support him while Peres could rely on the full backing of Ben Gurion; Peres in 1960 had many allies within the Ministry of Defence, where he had previously served as Director-General, while Lavon had no such power-base within the staff of the Ministry when the Affair began.

Institutional factors also affected the balance of influence between Army and Ministry. The prestige of the civilian side of defence, represented by the Ministry, had increased a great deal between the two crises. In 1954 little more than a bureaucratic appendage of the uniformed military, by 1960 the Ministry and its research, development and industrial affiliates had become of major importance within the defence establishment.

Even the Peres–Laskov clash did not set a final precedent. The relationship between the Army chiefs and their political masters is still determined more by the personal standing of the protagonists than by constitutional conventions.

5

The Sinai Campaign: Prelude and Aftermath

The Lavon Affair came at a time of steadily increasing tension in the Middle East. The tide of nationalist sentiment was perceptibly rising, and Nasser's new military regime in Egypt had apparently decided to extend its influence in the Arab world by activating the Palestine issue. Its first move was to sponsor Fedayeen* raids against Israel.

Until then a form of commercial banditry, armed infiltration now became an organized instrument of Egyptian policy.

A special unit of Egyptian military intelligence began to send raiders from Jordan and the Gaza Strip to attack Israeli civilians at random and other targets of opportunity.[1] The Israelis responded by increasing the scale of their reprisal raids. On 28 February 1955, shortly after Ben Gurion's return to power, the Israelis attacked an Egyptian army camp near Gaza city† in the first large-scale operation to be mounted by the paratroopers.[2] Following the Khiba raid, Israeli reprisals were no longer directed at Arab villages but against military targets, frontier strongholds, police fortresses and army camps. It was felt that, though more difficult, these raids would also have a greater political impact. Besides, attacks on Arab civilians evoked domestic opposition and damaged the army's morale.

After a series of smaller raids, on 1 September 1955, the Israelis raided another Egyptian military camp in the Gaza Strip, this time near the town of Khan Yunis.[4]

---

* Fedayeen (self-sacrificers) is an historic Arab term associated with struggles against unbelievers. Those so described by the Egyptians at the time were salaried volunteers, mainly recruited in the Gaza refugee camps.

† According to Nasser, this raid precipitated his decision to request arms supplies from the Soviet Union in the so-called 'Czech arms deal' of 1955. Recent research has cast doubt on this claim.[3]

The biggest operation of 1955 was not a reprisal raid but a dislodging attack against a force of Egyptian infantry which had occupied and fortified a stronghold at Sabha, a locality within the El Auja demilitarized zone.[5]

The Sabha operation of 2 November 1955, like virtually all the military operations conducted at this period, was tactically successful, and, for the first time Sharon's paratroopers were sent into action together with troops drawn from the Golani Infantry Brigade of the standing forces, as well as a Nahal unit. In all, there were fifteen major Israeli reprisal raids against military camps, police fortresses and outposts in Egypt, Jordan and Syria between February 1955 and the Sinai Campaign; the last and in some ways the most significant of these was an attack against the Jordanian police fortress near the border town of Qalqilya on the night of 10 October 1956 – less than three weeks before the campaign.

Following the well-practised* and by now stereotyped night tactics evolved by Sharon, the Israelis infiltrated a blocking force deep behind the target to cut the road linking Qalqilya with the interior. The paratroopers then launched their attack, supported by artillery fire and by the blinding glare of searchlights. The fortress was stormed and its defenders were overwhelmed in hand-to-hand fighting. At this point the raid should have ended as usual with the demolition of the fortress, but in fact the major part of the fighting was yet to come. A force of Jordanian motorized infantry had rushed to relieve the Qalqilya fortress. As usual, the blocking unit was in place to ambush the relief force, but this time the Jordanians were ready. They left their trucks on the narrow road, and encircled the fifty men of the blocking force which was soon in desperate straits.[6] The weapons and positions of the Israelis were best suited to the short firing ranges typical of night fighting.

The fifty Israelis cut off by the Jordanian relief force faced disaster unless they could be extricated before dawn: short of ammunition and trapped on a bare hilltop they would become easy targets for Jordanian riflemen as soon as the sun rose. Dayan was with the paratroopers near Qalqilya and he masterminded the

---

* In September 1956 Sharon's men stormed three Jordanian police fortresses (at Rahwa on 11 Sept., at Ghirandal on 13 Sept., and Husan on 26 Sept.) and raided an Egyptian outpost in Sinai on 12 Sept.

rescue operation on the spot. A column of paratroopers riding in half-track carriers was sent towards the fifty straight down the narrow road leading into the interior. There was no time for a more prudent advance on foot, and the carriers could not travel cross-country in the hills of Samaria. The column could easily have been trapped on the road, but the only alternative was to abandon the men of the blocking force – and this was unthinkable. The paratroopers were conditioned to run major risks to save even one man, let alone fifty; here the principle of minimizing casualties gave way before the demands of unit solidarity. To confuse the Jordanians and open an additional option, Dayan ordered two pairs of fighters to circle overhead. At the same time, 155mm howitzers gave long-range covering fire for the fifty paratroopers who did not have enough ammunition to keep the Jordanians at bay with their own weapons. The blocking force was finally extricated and disaster averted, but by then the raid and the rescue had cost the Israelis no fewer than twenty-seven killed and thirty wounded. (Arab losses were forty-eight killed and seventy-one wounded.)

The Qalqilya operation drew attention to all the shortcomings of the night reprisal raids: their benefits were at best uncertain while the casualty toll was high; Sharon's tactics had become repetitive and the enemy was beginning to anticipate Israeli moves; the narrow time limits, dusk to dawn, limited the scope of Israeli action and involved additional risks, such as those which materialized at Qalqilya. And such risks could lead in turn to unplanned and unwanted escalation if artillery and air power had to be called in to the rescue.

On 15 October 1956, five days after the Qalqilya raid, Dayan noted in his diary:

Neither at G.H.Q., nor in the Knesset committee, nor in the talks with the Prime Minister, was anything definite decided about the future; but it is clear to all of us that we have reached the end of the chapter of night reprisal actions.[7]

The next step was the Sinai Campaign. This was an altogether more radical attempt to solve the Fedayeen problem; the Israelis gave up a deterrence and set out to destroy the danger at source.[8] In 1956, as in 1967, the Israelis went on the offensive after Egypt had already proclaimed that 'a state of war' prevailed between the two countries. In both cases the Egyptians maintained the political initiative until Israel seized the tactical initiative and turned political defeat into a military victory. In both cases the war was triggered by an Egyptian blockade of the Straits of Tiran, but the Israelis were actually responding to a graver threat to their 'basic' security.

In 1956 there was, in addition, the 'current' threat of the Fedayeen raids which Sharon's paratroop reprisals had failed to deter. The reprisal operations were successful at the tactical level since the military objectives were almost invariably achieved while Israeli casualties amounted to a fraction of those suffered by the Egyptians. Nevertheless, Israel had failed to persuade Nasser's regime to suspend its campaign of terrorism. Until the Sinai Campaign the Egyptians stood firm: the regime had a high degree of tolerance for casualties amongst the rank-and-file, and its leaders saw no particular political advantage in abandoning the Fedayeen campaign. Even so, this need not have provoked the war but for the imminent possibility of a far more serious threat to Israel's basic security which arose from the Soviet–Egyptian arms' supply agreement. By Middle Eastern standards, the weapons delivered by the Russians were advanced, and the quantities unprecedented. As of October 1956, 330 tanks and assault guns (T-34/85s and Su-100s), 200 armoured carriers (BTR-152s), 500 mortars, guns and howitzers, and 170 combat aircraft (MiG-15s and Il-28s) reached Egypt together with two Skory-class destroyers and a dozen torpedo boats.*

Israel had no comparable source of armaments and its accumulated stock of military hardware was outmatched by this one Russo-Egyptian supply agreement. The Egyptians needed time to absorb the mass of new Soviet equipment but Nasser's political strategy failed to ensure this: the blockade of the straits of Tiran and the related announcement that Egypt considered herself to be at war with Israel already came in September 1955. By 22 October 1955, Dayan noted in his *Diary* that Ben Gurion, then Minister of Defence but not yet Prime Minister, had asked him to prepare for military action against Egypt. Ten days later, on 2 November 1955, Ben Gurion became Prime Minister in place of Sharett. For a

* A number of submarines included in the original agreement were delivered later.

whole year the Cabinet hesitated, and Ben Gurion himself was too undecided to force its hand, but on 29 October 1956 the Israeli Army went to war for the second time in less than seven years.

The classic objectives of war are the destruction of the enemy's forces and the occupation of his national territory, but according to the 1956 strategic directive framed by Dayan, the Israelis had no intention of doing either. No march on Cairo was even contemplated and, instead of force-destruction, the stated goal of Dayan's plan was subtle to the point of ambiguity: 'To confound the organisation of the Egyptian forces in Sinai and bring about their collapse.' To destroy well-armed forces entrenched in fortified positions, hard battles must be fought and many casualties sustained, even if the enemy is as feeble and poorly led as the Egyptians turned out to be. But the Israelis were not prepared to pay that price. Dayan was determined to avoid costly battles of attrition, especially since he saw little advantage in killing the enemy's soldiers:

> We should try and capture what we can of the enemy's weapons and equipment but we have no interest in killing a maximum number of his troops. Even if Egypt suffered thousands of casualties, she could replace them fairly quickly.[10]

Dayan envisaged a campaign of large-scale raids orchestrated into a front-wide offensive; it was obvious that the Egyptians could not be dislodged from their strongholds by mere raids, but Dayan believed that the Egyptians could be out-manoeuvred into yielding their fortifications: 'We should seize the crossroads and key military positions which will give us control of the area and force their surrender.'[11] In other words, Egyptian fortified perimeters would not be attacked directly since Dayan thought that the entire deployment would collapse once the Israelis penetrated deep into Sinai and cut the enemy's lines of communication.

Dayan's plan for a fast-moving campaign fitted in with Israel's political objectives and the tight constraints on her feedom of action. To defeat the Egyptian army and open the Straits of Tiran to Israeli shipping, speed was of the essence since the United States or the Soviet Union might step in at any time to impose a cease-fire. As for the exact timing of the Israeli campaign, this was largely determined by Anglo-French military plans for seizing the Canal

Zone. Relations between France and Israel were very close, while Anglo-Israeli relations were cool.* The degree of military co-ordination between Israel and her partners was limited: Israel was to pin down the Egyptian army and provide a plausible excuse for Anglo-French intervention in exchange for post-war diplomatic support and for wartime military aid: air cover over Israel's cities and some shipments of military hardware from France.[12]

At 4.59 p.m. on the afternoon of 29 October 1956, the Israelis began their offensive by dropping 395 paratroopers at the Parker Memorial near the Mitla Pass,† in western Sinai. At that time, the Egyptian forces in the Peninsula consisted of six brigades deployed in northern Sinai and the Gaza Strip, two reinforced battalions at Sharm el Sheikh and several small garrisons and patrol units in central Sinai. Most Egyptian units were under strength but well equipped.‡ In addition an Egyptian armoured brigade assigned to the defence of Sinai was deployed near the Canal together with two divisions of infantry. As against this, the Israelis deployed a total of nine brigades and a detached battalion; only one brigade was fully armoured (Ben Ari's 7th Brigade) and two were mechanized. Counting the forces of both sides by brigades and battalions, the Israelis enjoyed only a small margin of numerical superiority over the Egyptians. But in fact, most Israel units were at full strength while their Egyptian counterparts were not – and most Israeli units were reinforced with artillery batteries, tank squadrons and engineer units. The Egyptians had the major advantage of being on the defensive; they could fight behind their fortifications, while the Israelis had the far more demanding task of advancing and attacking in the open. To do this, force-ratios of

---

* Britain was a close ally of the Nuri-es-Said regime in Iraq, and was actually linked to Jordan by a defence treaty. In October 1956, just *two weeks* before the joint Anglo-French-Israeli offensive against Egypt was launched, Britain came close to issuing an ultimatum against Israel, over the Qalqilya raid of 15 October 1956. Of greater consequence was a British political manoeuvre of 1955 which was intended to deprive Israel of the Negev.

† Marked as the Heitan defile on international maps.

‡ As an indication of just how well the Egyptians were equipped, it is interesting to note that the Israelis eventually captured or destroyed 120 tanks and self-propelled guns, more than 200 artillery pieces and large quantities of small arms and ammunition.[13]

two or three attackers to one defender are often quoted as being necessary, though it is doubtful whether such ratios apply in mobile warfare, where one side or the other can often build up an overwhelming numerical superiority at each successive point of contact, regardless of the overall ratio of forces. As we shall see, Dayan's plan did *not* attempt to coordinate the advance of different task-forces in order to concentrate them on a single objective – and this is one of the unusual aspects of his strategy in the campaign.

The first Israeli objective in point of time was to pose a military threat to the Suez Canal so as to pave the way for the Anglo-French invasion – whose ostensible goal was to protect the Canal for international navigation. This was duly achieved with the air drop near the Mitla Pass, which leads directly to the Suez Canal. According to the joint plan, the Anglo-French forces were to start bombing Egyptian airfields twelve hours after issuing an ultimatum to both Israel and Egypt ordering both to withdraw their forces from the Canal. The main Israeli offensive was to start only after the Anglo-French air attack had already destroyed the Egyptian air force, and this meant that the 395 paratroops deep in enemy territory at the far end of Sinai could not be reached by the general advance of the Israeli forces for four or five days. The risk was far too great and the link-up had somehow to be achieved *before* the Egyptian front collapsed. This task was given to the rest of Sharon's 202nd paratroop brigade which was mounted on trucks and half-track carriers, and reinforced with artillery and a squadron of light AMX tanks. Sharon's men had to make an independent advance of 125 miles inside Egyptian territory from Kuntilla to Mitla, while Egyptian forces were still intact and in place on both sides of the route. In the event, Sharon's forces covered 190 route miles in twenty-eight hours, fighting several small engagements on the way: at 10.30 p.m. on 30 October the advance guard of his column reached the battalion parachuted the previous afternoon.

The main effort of the Israeli campaign consisted of two separate offensives on the major trans-Sinai routes, the Rafah-El Arish–Kantara road running along the coast of northern Sinai, and the central axis from the Abu Agheila crossroads to the Canal at Ismailiya. A two-brigade task force was deployed against

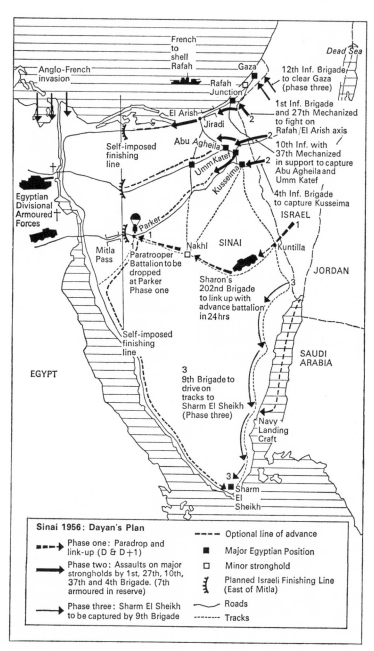

French
to
shell
Rafah

Anglo-French
invasion

Gaza

Rafah
Junction

12th Inf. Brigade
to clear Gaza
(phase three)

El Arish

Jiradi

1st Inf. Brigade
and 27th Mechanized
to fight on
Rafah/El Arish axis

2

Abu Agheila

Self-imposed
finishing
line

Umm Katef

Kusseima

10th Inf. with
37th Mechanized
in support to capture
Abu Agheila and
Umm Katef

2

4th Inf. Brigade
to capture Kusseima

Dead Sea

ISRAEL

Egyptian
Divisional
Armoured
Forces

Parker

1

1

Mitla
Pass

Paratrooper
Battalion to be
dropped
at Parker
Phase one

Nakhl

SINAI

Kuntilla

1

Sharon's
202nd Brigade
to link up with
advance battalion
in 24 hrs

JORDAN

3

Self-imposed
finishing
line

EGYPT

3
9th Brigade to
drive on
tracks to
Sharm El Sheikh
(Phase three)

SAUDI
ARABIA

Navy
Landing
Craft

3

Sharm
El
Sheikh

Sinai 1956: Dayan's Plan

- - - - ▶ Phase one: Paradrop and
link-up (D & D+1)

━━━▶ Phase two: Assaults on major
strongholds by 1st, 27th, 10th,
37th and 4th Brigade. (7th
armoured in reserve)

━━▶ Phase three: Sharm El Sheikh
to be captured by 9th Brigade

- - - - Optional line of advance

■ Major Egyptian Position

□ Minor stronghold

⌇ Planned Israeli Finishing Line
(East of Mitla)

⌒ Roads

- - - - - - Tracks

Map 8

the northern axis while a four-brigade division force was to attack in the centre. Each force was to fight independently, advancing in the general direction of the Canal. The Gaza Strip, also treated as a separate objective, was assigned to a reinforced infantry brigade which was to clear the area of Egyptian troops and seize the towns. Sharm el Sheikh, at the remote southern end of the peninsula, was the ultimate objective but it was only to be attacked after the Egyptians had been defeated in the rest of Sinai. Yet another independent task force of brigade size was to reach Sharm el Sheikh by advancing straight down the roadless coast of eastern Sinai.

A conventional offensive would have started with the seizure of the nearest objective, Gaza, and continued with the main offensive against Rafah in the north, and Abu Agheila in the centre, the two major crossroads leading westwards to the Canal. Instead, the Gaza Strip was left till last and the crossroads were attacked first while Sharon's column was to move still farther to the west. Seeking the line of 'least expectation', the plan reversed the logical order of objectives in order to deceive the Egyptians as to the scope and direction of the Israeli offensive. To do this, the plan sacrificed proper advance preparations for the sake of surprise on a front-wide scale. Three weeks before the start of the campaign, Dayan noted in his *Diary*:

> We are torn between our desire to postpone the call-up almost to the last moment before the opening of the campaign, and our need to give the units time to get organized, do maintenance on their tanks, carry out advance patrols, and make the numerous other preparations necessary for battle.[14]

It was suggested to Dayan that the infantry brigade assigned to the Southern Command for the campaign should be mobilized four days before 'D-Day', with an additional four days' preparation for armoured units, but he rejected these requests categorically. In the event, the armoured brigades were only called up on D-3, while the infantry was given only forty-eight hours. Plainly this was not enough. Civilians were in fact mobilized and sent into battle with only a few *hours* of actual preparation, since travel to jump-off positions and mobilization hold-ups took up most of the two days available.

The Sinai Campaign has been described elsewhere in considerable detail; here it is enough to say that the dimensions of Israel's victory were obvious while some of the Army's shortcomings were not. A peninsula three times as large as Israel itself was conquered and the equivalent of two Egyptian divisions routed in less than eight days of fighting, and for fewer than 170 Israelis killed.[15] This was an extraordinary achievement, but the Army's leadership was not deluded by victory; it was acutely aware of the tactical errors and organizational shortcomings revealed by the campaign. Almost as soon as the fighting was over, the post-mortem debates started, and soon developed into a wide-ranging critique of doctrines and methods which led in turn to sweeping reforms.

Some problems had emerged even before the fighting actually started, as in the case of the all-important mobilization system. The number of civilian trucks and jeeps which actually reached the Army after the vehicle call-up was issued turned out to be much smaller than had been expected (13,013), partly because of faults in the mobilization procedure itself (drivers were called up separately from their vehicles and many failed to deliver their trucks to Army depots before reporting for duty), and partly because of inadequate inspection which failed to remove broken-down vehicles from the mobilization lists. Many were barely roadworthy while others lacked repair kits and essential spare parts. The gravity of this maintenance problem was highlighted by the experience of Sharon's mechanized column; it brushed aside Egyptian resistance at successive strongholds on the way to the Mitla Pass, but

... the outstanding [problem] was [the] shortage of suitable vehicles for movement across desert. The brigade had first been promised 153 6×6 trucks. Twenty-four hours before H-hour they were notified that they would be receiving ninety. When they went into action it was with only forty-six. *And in the entire column there was not a single spanner to fit the wheel nuts of the vehicles with front-wheel drive, so that any truck with a punctured tyre had to be abandoned.*[16] [Our italics.]

To some extent this state of affairs merely reflected the Army's (and the country's) poverty, but nothing can explain the absence of a single spanner in the whole column except gross inefficiency on the part of the transport and brigade staffs. With communications, too, there were serious problems. Contact between the far-flung Israeli forces frequently broke down and entire brigades were sometimes cut off from rear H.Q.s. Coordination between Air Force and ground radio-links was defective and at least in one case this had fatal consequences when I.A.F. fighters strafed and bombed an Israeli column on the ground. The supply system was also defective, and in this case problems could be traced to the Army's low standards in basic management more than the lack of resources.

But the main issue in the post-war debates was tactical rather than technical. The debate between the 'mobile infantry' school, led by Dayan, and the tank officers, led by Haim Laskov (O.C. Armour Corps) and Assaf Simchoni (O.C. Southern Command), was still unresolved when the campaign was being planned; the fundamental disagreement between the two groups was to have a major impact on the conduct of the campaign.

In the first version of the G.H.Q. plan for the campaign, Ben Ari's 7th Brigade, the only armoured brigade of the standing forces, was not even given a combat role. It was to stage a feint against Jordan while serving as a frontal reserve to protect the rear of the Southern Command. Considering that the 7th had the best tanks and the best crews of the Armour Corps while its commander was regarded as the leading 'tank specialist' in the Army, this could only mean that Dayan still failed to take the armoured forces seriously. The tank officers, led by Laskov and Assaf Simchoni, argued against the plan and managed to persuade Dayan to give it a combat task. After much debate, a new version of the plan was produced and the 7th was duly given a combat role in the central axis, but Dayan still insisted that the brigade should only go into action *after* the infantry had breached the main Egyptian defences at the Umm Katef/Abu Agheila crossroads. Having conceded this much, Dayan then made the absurd demand that tanks be carried on transporters, instead of riding into battle on their own tracks. In other words, the tanks were only to be used as support weapons for the infantry, instead of acting as an independent force. When the General Staff debated the new version of his plan, Dayan explained why he was reluctant to rely on Ben Ari's tank battalions:

We shall move some tanks forward on transporters only as a demonstration of strength [but] we should not hamper the rapid advance [of the motorized and mechanized infantry] by using tanks.[17]

The largely symbolic role given to the tank forces did not satisfy the tank officers who thought, in Laskov's words, that 'armour is the decisive weapon of the land forces and should be operated in concentration'. They wanted the tanks to spearhead the advance of the motorized columns of infantry and artillery rather than to follow in their wake.

Dayan and Laskov debated the issue once again at a September meeting of the General Staff attended by Ben Gurion who was there as the judge. This time the debate was cast in organizational terms; Dayan argued that, since tanks were to be used as support weapons for the infantry, they should not be massed into battalions but kept in a reserve pool from which single tank squadrons could be supplied to infantry units according to need. 'The typical formation', Dayan said, 'should be an infantry battalion plus a company of armour plus artillery support.'[17] Accordingly the tank battalions of the Armour Corps were to be administrative units rather than fighting forces, servicing a pool of support weapons instead of being organic combat formations in their own right. Haim Laskov, a very able all-rounder who had done well as Commander of the Air Force and was now O.C. Armour Corps, was in total disagreement with Dayan. He opposed the fragmentation of the tank battalions into single squadrons. To do this, he argued, would undermine the particular strengths of the tank forces, since they would then be too dispersed to engage concentrations of enemy armour, and this would in turn mean that the tanks could only advance at the pace of the infantry. Laskov wanted the tanks to be massed in a few but powerful all-armour units which could fight independently to breach the enemy's fortified defences, and then wage battles of penetration deep into the enemy's rear.

It was not until after the Sinai Campaign that Dayan and his followers in the General Staff were finally persuaded of the value of tank forces in the land battle. But once Dayan changed his mind he did so without reservations. A rapid expansion now began of the Armour Corps while the Ministry launched a major purchasing effort to acquire more and better tanks. It was not for several years that the political barriers were overcome, but if it took that long to obtain the hardware from abroad there was no delay in building up the command echelons of the Armour Corps. Dayan acted with his customary dynamism:

> [The Army] began transferring senior officers from the infantry to armour, the first being Col. Israel Tal. When the [Sinai] Campaign was over the Chief of Staff, Maj.-Gen. Moshe Dayan, asked Tal, who was then commander of Zahal's Officers Cadet School, when he would be ready to transfer to the Armour Corps as deputy commander.
> Tal: In two to three weeks?
> Dayan: No, no, I meant what time today?[18]

Although Dayan's pre-campaign position on the use of armour reflected his long-standing belief in the 'mobile infantry' approach, it also derived from a serious underestimation of the resilience of Egyptian troops. His overall view of the campaign – characterized by his critics as the 'collapse theory' – is given in a key passage of his *Diary*:

> Our task is to bring about as quickly as possible the collapse of the enemy forces and to achieve complete control of the Sinai Peninsula. Our units . . . must press forward and not stop to clean up isolated enemy positions. *There is no need to fear that Egyptian units who will be bypassed will launch a counter-attack or cut our supply lines.* We should avoid analogies whereby Egyptian units would be expected to behave as European armies would in similar circumstances.[19] [Our italics.]

Generals Laskov and Zorea in a critical review article claimed that the 'isolated enemy positions' did not just collapse – they had to be attacked by strong Israeli forces, including tank units.[20] They pointed out that the main Egyptian fortified perimeters at Rafah and Umm Katef/Abu Agheila had only fallen after determined *tank* attacks, and that the infantry had failed to breach Egyptian defences without the support of tank units and artillery. The only exceptions were those strongholds which had been evacuated after the Egyptian High Command issued orders for a general withdrawal.

The link between the 'collapse' theory and the pre-campaign debate on tank warfare was each side's expectation as to the likely behaviour of Egyptian armour. Dayan was sure that Egyptian armour, whose task was to counter-attack the Israelis while the latter were still engaged against the first line of Egyptian defences, would not in fact move out of its bases near the Canal; it followed that the Israelis could advance across Sinai with fast mechanized columns without needing tanks with which to fight Egyptian armour. Others were less confident. They held that it was imprudent to ignore Egyptian armour, and felt that the Israeli columns manoeuvring around the fortified perimeters should be protected by strong tank forces. In the event, once the main Israeli offensives began, the Egyptians *did* send an armoured brigade into Sinai but this sally failed to develop into a real counter-attack as Dayan had correctly predicted. On the other hand, it was not 'fast motorized columns' that led the Israeli offensive but tank forces; two armoured brigades, the 7th and the 27th, decided the outcome of the offensive on the central and northern axes respectively.

The 27th Brigade, made up of mixed teams of tanks, infantry and artillery,* under the command of a future Chief of Staff, Haim Bar Lev, fought according to plan on the Rafah-El Arish axis taking El Arish after a breakthrough across the Rafah and Jiradi defences.

After all the pre-campaign debates Uri Ben Ari's 7th Brigade, the only one with a full complement of two tank battalions, followed neither the original nor the modified campaign plan. In fact it acted in direct contradiction to the orders of G.H.Q. – but won a spectacular victory in the process across the entire central axis. According to the *modified* campaign plan, the 7th was to advance to the western reaches of Sinai along the central axis, but only after the infantry had opened the way by defeating the Egyptian defences astride the Umm Katef/Abu Agheila crossroads. The front commander, Assaf Simchoni (O.C. Southern Command), decided to disobey Dayan's orders and allowed Uri

* The 27th Brigade was in fact a mechanized unit, since its tank forces were quite small. It consisted of one battalion of motorized infantry, two armoured combat teams (A.C.T.) of battalion size and two squadrons of Shermans with the long 75mm gun. The first A.C.T. had a squadron (15–20 tanks) of AMX–13 tanks, a company of mechanized infantry riding half-track carriers, a troop (9 guns?) of AMX–105mm self-propelled howitzers, a reconnaissance detachment and a section of engineers; the second A.C.T had a squadron of Sherman tanks and the same complement with the addition of a tank-recovery detachment. As against this, the 7th Brigade was organized on standard tank brigade lines with some additional infantry; it consisted of one battalion of Sherman tanks, one battalion of AMX–13s (about 100 tanks in all) and one battalion of motorized infantry supported by one artillery battery.

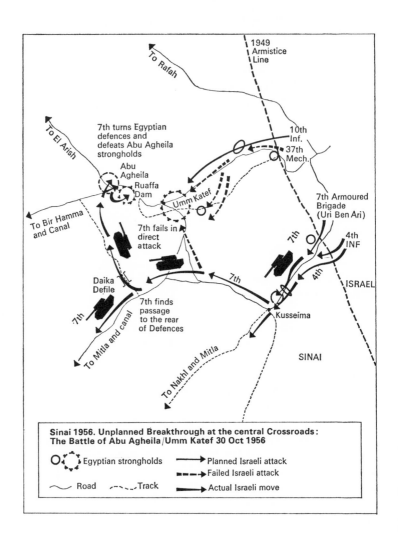

To Rafah

1949
Armistice
Line

To El Arish

7th turns Egyptian
defences and
defeats Abu Agheila
strongholds

Abu
Agheila

Ruaffa
Dam

Umm Katef

10th
Inf.

37th
Mech.

7th Armoured
Brigade
(Uri Ben Ari)

4th
INF

To Bir Hamma
and Canal

7th fails in
direct
attack

7th

7th

4th

ISRAEL

Daika
Defile

7th finds
passage
to the rear
of Defences

7th

Kusseima

To Mitla and canal

To Nakhl and Mitla

SINAI

To Mitla and Mitla

**Sinai 1956. Unplanned Breakthrough at the central Crossroads:
The Battle of Abu Agheila/Umm Katef 30 Oct 1956**

○ ⟨ ⟩ Egyptian strongholds   → Planned Israeli attack

                                                ---▶ Failed Israeli attack

〰 Road   ⌁ Track   ▶ Actual Israeli move

Map 9

Ben Ari to take his brigade into action a full twenty-four hours ahead of schedule – and before the infantry had taken the cross-road defences. By attacking on D+1 (30 October) and advancing deep into Sinai during the next day, the 7th Brigade ruined Dayan's deception plan (which called for a two-day delay between Sharon's advance and the main offensives). As against this, Ben Ari's forces achieved a spectacular victory. His tank units infiltrated to the rear of the Egyptian positions at Abu Agheila and, after some hard fighting, defeated the Egyptian fortifications which the infantry was failing to breach at Umm Katef, at the other end of the same perimeter. Without pausing to regroup, the 7th Brigade then moved west, sending out combat teams which took control of most of central Sinai in a single day of non-stop advance (D+2). Thus the outstanding success of 1956 was the result of a classic armoured attack – in direct contradiction to Dayan's orders, and all the plans of G.H.Q.

The Air Force, like the premier brigade of the Armour Corps, was denied an opportunity to implement its own strategy. And unlike the latter it could hardly violate the directives of G.H.Q. Instead of an all-out attack on enemy airfields to destroy the Egyptian air force on the ground, the I.A.F. was given only defensive and ground support tasks; it was only to attack enemy airfields if the Egyptians were the first to escalate by attacking targets in Israel proper. Since Ben Gurion had insisted that the French take over the air defence role by providing interceptor squadrons to protect Israeli cities, the I.A.F. was limited to battlefield missions: air defence over Sinai, interdiction bombing and close support for the forces on the ground. The I.A.F. therefore concentrated all its operational fighter bombers (fifty-three jet, sixty-two piston) on these tasks. Confined to their fixed defences and a few narrow roads in an open desert devoid of natural cover, the Egyptians suffered heavily from Israeli air attacks, especially at Sharm el Sheikh, where the Air Force acted in direct support of the ground forces.*

---

* An Egyptian officer of the Sharm el Sheikh garrison, Lieut.-Col. Neguib, has been quoted as saying that the Egyptians lost their battle on the ground even before the Israelis reached their perimeter. 'I learned about close air support during my schooldays (sic) in England, or so I thought until I stood at Sharm el Sheikh.'[2]

Most I.A.F. strikes were 'interdiction' attacks against targets in the rear; Egyptian convoys came under constant fire as they moved eastwards to reinforce the front and then again as they fled westwards once the general withdrawal had begun. The sight of burnt-out Egyptian vehicles along the roads of Sinai did much to educate the more infantry-minded among the Israeli officer corps in the uses of tactical air power. Dayan himself had no blind spot for air power, but the Air Force did not make the best use of its interdiction capabilities – and this was probably due to the directives it received from G.H.Q.

Instead of attacking Egyptian forces from west to east – so as to act as the anvil for the hammer of the advancing ground forces – the I.A.F. attacked east to west. This meant that the Egyptians were harried westwards towards the Canal and safety, instead of being stopped by west-to-east air attacks, so as to allow Israeli forces on the ground to catch up with their retreat. This tactical error probably derived from the strategic goals laid down by Dayan. ('To confound the organization of the Egyptian forces in Sinai and bring about their collapse . . .')[22] Had the strategic goal been less subtle and oblique, the I.A.F. would have had no great difficulty in following standard air-ground tactics to destroy the Egyptian forces in Sinai. This would not necessarily have meant the killing of individual Egyptian soldiers but the destruction of equipment and the total disintegration of unit cohesion – as indeed happened in 1967.

The Egyptian air force showed no great eagerness to meet Israeli fighters in air combat during the first phase of the campaign. On 29 October, while sixteen Dakotas were flying the paratroopers to their drop-zone, I.A.F. Mystères patrolled the length of the Canal, flying well within sight of Egyptian airfields. No attempt was made to intercept them. But when the Egyptians finally realized that the Israelis were launching a front-wide offensive rather than a raid, their air force became more active – until the Anglo-French bombing offensive put an end to the contest. During this short interval, there were air battles over Sinai, and repeated Egyptian air attacks against the Israel paratroopers whose positions were only forty kilometres from the Canal airfields. Twelve Egyptian jets were shot down by the I.A.F., which lost only a single Piper Cub spotter plane in air combat. (The I.A.F. also lost several aircraft to Egyptian anti-aircraft gunners who fought with remarkable skill and courage.) Although the I.A.F. failed to provide total air cover (the paratroopers suffered casualties from Egyptian air attacks), its performance in air-to-air combat augured well for the future. There were also some spectacular exploits in pure Israeli style: propeller-driven Mustangs cut Egyptian telephone lines with their wings (when special cutting hooks failed), and ultra-light Piper Cubs rescued pilots shot down behind enemy lines, in at least one instance landing and taking off in full view of near-by enemy troops. More prosaic but also of considerable importance was the I.A.F.'s transport mission: its sixteen Dakotas and three Nords delivered the paratroopers and then supplied Sharon's brigade as it advanced towards them. Misdirected I.A.F. attacks against Israeli troops on the ground caused several casualties but as Dayan noted in his *Diary*, the I.A.F. was not to blame:

> In accordance with my orders, formations continue to operate even when there is a breakdown in communications . . . In addition, when our troops capture equipment, particularly vehicles which are service-able, they hasten to use them without bothering to repaint them and mark them with our army signs.[23]

In a campaign marked by the romantic-heroic style which Dayan did much to inspire, the I.A.F. had already emerged as a well-controlled and precise instrument of warfare, though it was not until 1967 that it had an opportunity to make full use of its capabilities.

Between the strategic and tactical there is an intermediate level of military planning and action, the operational. And it is at this level that most of the post-Sinai debates and the changes that flowed from them occurred. Changes in tactics and techniques were mostly of minor importance while at the strategic level none of the fundamentals was really affected: the offensive-only strategy, the 'short-war' assumption and the concept of the reserve system, together with all they implied in the way of strategic and logistic planning, emerged intact from the post-Sinai reappraisals.

In so far as the campaign tested the basic assumptions and the concept of the reserve system, together with all that implied in the way of strategic and logistic planning, they emerged intact from the post-Sinai reappraisals.

In so far as the campaign tested the basic assumptions of Israeli strategy, it was the performance of the reserve troops that represented the most important test by far. In 1948, the Israelis had fought with a wartime army mobilized 'for the duration'; in both world wars many armies had relied on reserve troops, but in almost every case reservists called to the colours were given weeks or months of refresher training before being sent into battle. No army had relied for the majority of its troops on men who were sent into combat one or two days after their recall. The Israelis did so in 1956 in the face of tight political constraints, but not without intense anxieties as to the outcome.

Dayan's anxiety was understandable. There were even doubts about the conscripts of the standing forces. The deliberate use of Sharon's paratroopers to evoke a competitive response from the ordinary infantry could have backfired. In the pre-1956 reprisal raids, the paratroopers were sent into action time after time while the conscript infantry was held back. The infantry might have felt that competition was pointless and the gap unbridgeable. The performance of reserve brigades was an even bigger question mark. For one thing, reservists were of course rather older than the conscripts, there were men up to the age of forty (and beyond) even in first-line combat units. The main burden of the attacks against the Egyptian fortified perimeters at Abu Agheila/Umm Katef and at Kusseima, fell on three reserve brigades: the 10th Infantry, the 4th Infantry and the 37th Mechanized; the particularly exacting march to Sharm el Sheikh was also assigned to a reserve brigade (the 9th Infantry) commanded by Col. (later Gen.) Avraham Yoffe.*

Since these brigades were only mobilized on D+2, they had virtually no pre-combat refresher training; their most recent training period was their last annual call up. Most of the reserve troops of 1956 had served as conscripts before the Army was regenerated under the impulse of Dayan's leadership. As a result, officers and men had acquired their military experience during the War of Independence or in the early fifties, and much of their training was obsolete.

---

* He claimed that age was no handicap. Yoffe had been quoted as saying that men in their thirties have greater endurance than younger men.[25]

The Sinai Campaign showed that fears about the combat performance of the conscript troops were groundless; they were more than a match for the enemy and the 1st Infantry (Golani) Brigade, the 7th Armoured Brigade and other conscript units fought very well indeed. As for the reservists, their performance was very uneven; some reserve brigades were distinctly better than others and at least one failed to show fight.

Of the seven reserve brigades that took part in the campaign, two, the 10th Infantry and the 37th Mechanized, failed to attain their objectives; their officers proved deficient in combat spirit and lacked elementary tactical skills. The commander of the 10th Brigade was actually replaced in the midst of the battle for the Umm Katef strongholds; the commander of the 37th, on the other hand, was killed in action while personally leading a daring but ineffectual attack with his mechanized infantry battalion – which went into action without awaiting the arrival of the brigade's tank unit. Three reserve brigades and their officers also did very well indeed: the 9th Infantry under Yoffe carried out the spectacular cross-country advance to Sharm el Sheikh; the 27th Armoured under Haim Bar Lev (Chief of Staff 1968–72) fought a hard battle with great tactical skill at Rafah and at the Jiradi fortifications on the road to El Arish; and the 4th Infantry also was successful in its assault on the Kusseima stronghold.

With irresolute commanders, units made up of hastily mobilized civilians with minimal standards of discipline can easily degenerate into a sluggish mass incapable of advancing against enemy fire. One brigade, the 10th, suffered such a paralysis of will, but a majority of the reserve troops exceeded the expectations of the General Staff.

With Sharon's 202nd Brigade no morale problems had been expected and none occurred. Instead, there was a problem of control: the brigade advanced too far and needlessly fought a bloody battle for a position it had been ordered *not* to capture. After the battalion air drop on 29 October, and the brigade link-up on the following night, the paratroopers were supposed to remain inactive until the final stage of the campaign, when the brigade was to advance down the western coast of Sinai to Sharm el Sheikh. There was no need to cross the Mitla Pass to do so; the Pass was defended by an Egyptian force of unknown strength while the Israelis could use a route to the coast which bypassed the Mitla and the Canal zone.*

When Sharon's column reached the air-dropped battalion at the Parker Memorial east of the Mitla Pass on the night of 30 October, Dayan specifically ordered the paratroopers *not* to advance westwards into the Pass. Unable to obtain Dayan's consent for an advance, the following day Sharon and his officers asked for, and received, permission to send out a reconnaissance patrol. At noon on 31 October, the Israelis set out. Instead of a few jeeps on the road and flanking foot patrols on the crest, the brigade had sent a battalion-sized combat team whose half-track carriers, trucks and tanks drove straight down the road and into the Pass. When the first paratroopers had reached the far side, and the rest were still in the defile, five heavily armed Egyptian infantry companies holding skilfully concealed firing positions on the steep slopes of the Pass opened fire with anti-tank weapons, mortars and machine-guns. As their vehicles went up in flames one after the other, the paratroopers tried and failed to fire back; they were pinned down without any cover and could not even locate the enemy's firing positions. Some paratroopers

mounted [on] the ridge and began to fight on it. When they reached the top of the ridge, the enemy opened strong fire with medium and light weapons from the . . . ridge opposite, and from the caves. The unit was equipped in general with submachine-guns [and] did not have weapons capable of returning the enemy fire . . . Two further attempts . . . to get onto the ridge failed . . . [with] heavy casualties. At this junction, the reinforcements sent by the brigade commander arrived, and they helped the unit in rescuing the wounded . . . [then] four enemy Meteor aircraft appeared and attacked the heavy mortar positions and the reinforcements, inflicting casualties on both.

At dusk, the paratroopers tried to mount a concerted counter-attack from both ends of the Pass. Part of the combat team had reached the other end of the Pass before Egyptian fire blocked all movement; these men climbed the ridge and then scrambled down to attack the Egyptian positions on the slopes. At the same time,

* Which was in any case out of bounds according to the ten-mile limit of the Anglo-French ultimatum.

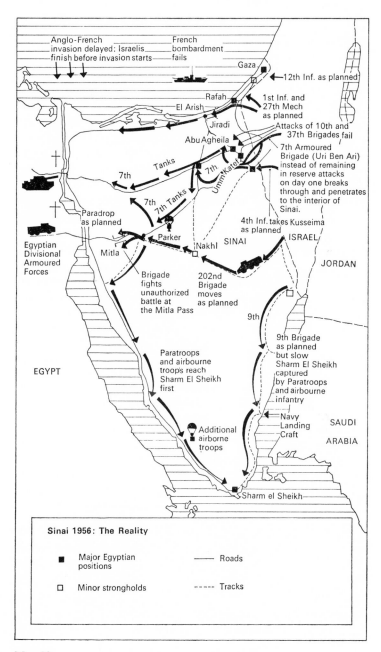

Anglo-French invasion delayed: Israelis finish before invasion starts

French bombardment fails

Gaza

12th Inf. as planned

Rafah

1st Inf. and 27th Mech as planned

El Arish

Jiradi

Attacks of 10th and 37th Brigades fail

Abu Agheila

7th Armoured Brigade (Uri Ben Ari) instead of remaining in reserve attacks on day one breaks through and penetrates to the interior of Sinai.

Tanks

7th

7th

Umm'Kateť

7th

7th Tanks

4th Inf. takes Kusseima as planned

Paradrop as planned

Parker

Nakhl

SINAI

ISRAEL

JORDAN

Egyptian Divisional Armoured Forces

Mitla

Brigade fights unauthorized battle at the Mitla Pass

202nd Brigade moves as planned

9th

9th Brigade as planned but slow Sharm El Sheikh captured by Paratroops and airbourne infantry

EGYPT

Paratroops and airbourne troops reach Sharm El Sheikh first

Navy Landing Craft

SAUDI

ARABIA

Additional airbourne troops

Sharm el Sheikh

Sinai 1956: The Reality

■   Major Egyptian positions

──── Roads

□   Minor strongholds

----- Tracks

Map 10

two companies of reinforcement from the brigade's main force attacked from the eastern end of the Pass. After fierce and prolonged hand-to-hand fighting Egyptian resistance finally collapsed. Thirty-eight paratroopers were killed and a hundred and twenty wounded during the ambush and the subsequent battle, including the casualties inflicted by the Egyptian aircraft (Israeli fighters were patrolling near by but could not be called in to assist because of a communications breakdown). After the battle the paratroopers returned to the Parker area; they did not occupy the Pass nor did they drive through it when the brigade was eventually ordered to advance towards Sharm el Sheikh.

At the Mitla Pass, as in the case of Ben Ari's armour, troops were sent into action against specific orders from above. A brigade commander, Sharon, and, even more serious, a front commander, Assaf Simchoni (C.O. Southern Command, who ordered the 7th Brigade into action), had disobeyed the Chief of Staff, and ignored the plans of G.H.Q. Nevertheless, Dayan took no disciplinary action. He apparently saw this kind of 'positive' indiscipline as a consequence of the high morale and fighting spirit which he had striven so hard to inspire. His attitude was made clear by his final comment on the unauthorized advance of the 7th Brigade: 'better to be engaged in restraining the noble stallion than in prodding the reluctant mule!' Not all his colleagues approved of Dayan's lenient attitude. Generals Laskov and Zorea pointed out that command consists of control as well as leadership; taking up Dayan's metaphor they wrote:

> When every commander knows that the Chief of Staff prefers 'noble stallions' it is obvious that the 'stallions' will not only run forward but also kick from time to time, as happened in the Kusseima/ Abu Agheila sector [i.e. the 7th Brigade] and in the case of the use of a reinforced battalion as a 'patrol unit' in the Mitla.[26]

Dayan's style of command was exceedingly informal. He frequently bypassed regular chains of command and stressed leadership at the expense of central control. He left the supervision of staff work to others, and in fact refused to stay at G.H.Q. During the campaign Dayan seems to have spent most of his time with the front-line, instead of remaining behind to coordinate their operations. He drove and flew all over Sinai with, or preferably without, his personal staff, often escorted only by his driver and a single staff aide. On one occasion he drove in the wake of the paratroopers advancing towards Sharm el Sheikh in a convoy of two (civilian) vans and a single command car while hundreds of armed Egyptians were retreating in the opposite direction along the same and as yet unsecured road. Seeking as always the thrill of battle Dayan wanted to catch up with the paratroopers and, if possible, to lead them into action against Sharm el Sheikh. After a 'managerial' discussion at G.H.Q. Dayan noted in his *Diary*:

> Where, oh where, are the good old days of the simple wars when as the hour of battle approached, the commander got on his white horse, someone blew the trumpet, and off he charged towards the enemy![27]

In 1956, the brigades operated as virtually independent forces under the loose control of divisional headquarters* while the control of the Area Command (responsible for the entire front) and the G.H.Q. in Tel Aviv was looser still. Without having to follow detailed plans prepared in advance or being subject to a continuous flow of orders from above, the brigade commanders and their staffs were free to make their own tactical decisions. As Yitzhak Rabin has written, the brigades were given a set of initial guidelines which defined only 'objectives, targets and time-tables ... demarcation lines between different units [and] the general method of conducting the battle'.[28] Higher headquarters at the divisional, area and G.H.Q. level could always intervene to coordinate the moves of different formations, but in practice their function was limited to making sure that the units in the field adhered to the 'objectives, targets and time-tables'.

The opposite practice of centralizing command at higher levels is more common among the armies of the world. Indeed the standard method of command is still a hierarchical two-way system: in its most classic form, the commander receives messages from the units in the field and makes the tactical decisions which are then passed down the chain of command until they finally reach

---

* There was a divisional headquarters for the northern axis (for the 1st and 27th Brigades) and one for the central axis (for the 10th and 37th brigades).

the junior officers who actually implement the orders. Many armies still tend to operate in this way despite much preaching of the virtues of low-level initiative. Effective in set-piece battles where the Commander-in-Chief can survey the battlefield from a suitable hilltop, this method of command is wholly unsuited to mobile warfare.

To make the right decision the commander must know the location of the forces of both sides, their physical condition and the nature of the terrain around them; he needs also information on the morale of his own troops and those of the enemy. When forces are advancing or retreating no more than a few miles a day, there is time to collect and analyse data. This is impossible in the fluid setting of mobile warfare where tactical intelligence becomes obsolete very quickly.

When mechanized forces fight and manoeuvre across vast battlefields tactical opportunities are fleeting and dangers sudden; the command response must therefore be equally prompt. In the absence of 'real-time' intelligence from a comprehensive battery of sensors suspended over the battlefield, the command function must be left to the men on the spot if the delay between perception and response is to be minimized. The Israelis were by no means the first to realize the crucial importance of decentralized command for mobile warfare, but they can be credited with having evolved the first explicit method of command based directly on its needs.

Only one side of the method was fully developed at the time of the Sinai Campaign. Field commanders were given freedom of action to respond to the sudden contingencies of battle, but no provision was made for an equally rapid coordination of the different formations in the field. However decentralized the method of command, some form of high-level control is still essential: divisional and frontal H.Q.s must be able to guide the operations of front-line units in the light of their broader picture of the tactical situation. The forces in the field must also be controllable at the G.H.Q. level in order to exploit strategic opportunities – or avert strategic dangers – which lie beyond the horizon of field commanders. Besides, the tight political constraints which have always limited Israeli military operations require firm G.H.Q. control: an objective may be tactically attainable while being out of bounds for political reasons.

In 1956, the problem of control was evaded and not solved. Self-contained brigades were ordered to advance along a given axis all the way from the Israeli border to the finishing line, and no real provision was made to coordinate their operations. 'We can base our operation on forces which are not interdependent,' Dayan wrote. 'We shall organize separate forces for each of the main military objectives, and it will be the task of each force to go there in one continuous battle.'[29] This solved the problem of coordination very elegantly by avoiding all need for it, but it also sacrificed the advantages of concentrating different task-forces for concerted attacks. In fact, during the campaign, Dayan focused his attention on each tactical problem in isolation and, with one major exception,* the brigades advancing along the different axes of Sinai did not depend on each other for mutual support. As for overall strategic control, this was exercised by Dayan in person. Dayan would fly, drive or otherwise contact the brigade, divisional or area headquarters and issue his orders on the spot. Frequently out of touch with G.H.Q. in the rear, Dayan improvised as he went from place to place, sometimes in radio contact with Tel Aviv and sometimes not. In the absence of systematic control by a central staff, it is not surprising that G.H.Q. plans were sometimes ignored.

It was only years after the campaign that the Army's decentralized method of command was balanced by the refinement of a control counterweight, which we shall call 'optional control'.[30] With this the power of immediate decisions is still left with the units in the field, but higher echelons can step in to take control of the battle whenever the situation seems to warrant a 'broad picture' response. Although great stress is put on fast and accurate reporting, the information picture of headquarters in the rear can never be as timely as that of lower echelons; but it is less fragmented. Except when their superiors choose to exercise their optional control, unit commanders are still expected to act independently; they have to report back continuously but do not have to wait for orders before making their command decisions – as in the classic two-way system. When the new method was tested in the 1967 War, optional control worked very well indeed. By then,

---

* Sharm el Sheikh was captured by the concerted assault of the Paratroop Brigade and the 9th Infantry coming from opposite directions.

the Army had changed out of all recognition: once again, successful war had been followed by radical reappraisal and extensive innovation.

The Army's transformation in the post-Sinai decade was the product of new ideas and new weapons, but little could have been achieved without the victory of 1956. The visible gains were limited to the stationing of U.N. troops in Sinai and the Gaza Strip. Their posts and patrols on the Egyptian side of the border were meant to ensure Israeli navigation and overflight rights across the Straits of Tiran, and to prevent the renewal of Fedayeen attacks. Little more than symbolic in itself, the U.N. presence anchored these Egyptian concessions which stood until May 1967. As against this, the 1956 victory did not lead to Arab–Israeli negotiations, let alone recognition or peace, nor did it secure Israeli transit rights across the Suez Canal. Nevertheless, the small concrete gains won by Israel were sufficient to free the Army from many current security tasks and to relieve the siege atmosphere which had prevailed in the country until then. Far more important were the intangible gains. The campaign gave stature to Israel, showed her to be a determined and reliable partner and demonstrated her military strength. Regarded until then as little more than a transitory anomaly in an all-Arab region, Israel now became a recognized power within it. This had an important bearing on the subsequent development of the Army since it facilitated Israel's efforts to buy arms. Most important, perhaps, was the renewed confidence inspired by the victory. The post-independence period had been marked by poverty and growing insecurity, many veteran settlers were disillusioned and many newcomers disappointed. 1956 was thus an important psychological turning point.

From War to War: 1956-67

Between the Sinai Campaign and the war of June 1967 Israel enjoyed a decade of relative tranquillity. The Egyptian armistice line was almost entirely quiet and there were few incidents on the Jordanian front until 1965; on the Syrian armistice line fighting broke out repeatedly but the clashes remained localized until 1964.* Not that the underlying tensions were abating; on the contrary, Arab ideological attitudes were hardening and the tone of official statements was steadily becoming more warlike. By the early sixties both sides knew that there would be a third round, though war never quite seemed imminent, even when the conflict became manifest once again in the struggle over the distribution of the Jordan waters.[1]

In 1964 Israel was on the point of completing the construction of the 'National Water Carrier', a country-wide irrigation network fed from the waters of the Jordan river; the Arab regimes wanted to obstruct the project, with the Ba'ath leadership in Syria the most active. Its first move was an attempt to pressure Egypt into direct action in support of a Syrian attack against the waterworks. President Nasser refused to underwrite the Syrian plan and convened a meeting of all Arab heads of state to plan common action, or at least to provide a plausible excuse for inaction.

Nasser's statements at the time indicated that he had no illusions about the outcome of another war with Israel, but he still felt obliged to match the verbal activism of his political rivals in the Arab world – primarily the same Syrian leaders who were asking for Egypt's military support. In his speeches, Nasser spelled

* But in 1960 an Israeli retaliatory raid at Tawarfik threatened to escalate into a general war when Egypt sent forces into Sinai and Israel responded by mobilizing two brigades; both sides reversed their moves after three months.

out a systematic strategy for the destruction of Israel. As against the more or less disingenuous demands of the Syrians for immediate war, Nasser listed the necessary conditions for a final solution: Arab political unity and a suitable moment in international politics in which Israel would be isolated from her patrons and left only with her own intrinsic strength; the sufficient condition was the growth of Arab military power until it reached the level required to defeat an isolated Israel.[2] In the meantime, Nasser steered a series of Arab summit meetings towards an agreed strategy for the denial of the Jordan waters to Israel: Lebanon, Jordan and Syria were to divert the headwaters of the river with the financial help of other Arab states which pledged their support in the event of an Israeli reaction but gave no precise guarantees.

The most visible manifestation of these political trends was an arms race, sustained by increasingly generous Soviet supplies, which accelerated sharply after 1962. Egypt's defence spending increased from $290 million in 1960–61 to about double this figure in five years. Since Soviet equipment was very cheap and sold on long-term credit, the force build-up was even greater than the budget figures would suggest: the number of battle tanks increased from 700 in 1960 to more than 1,200 by June 1967 while the number of jet fighters increased from 165 to 350. Egypt also acquired thirty strategic bombers, modern Tu-16s with a payload of up to ten tons each.[3]*

The average number of Egyptians in uniform (all three services) increased from 130,000 in 1960 to 270,000 by 1967, of which more than 180,000 were regulars. The Yemen War added to the burden on Egyptian resources and, as the build-up continued, military expenditures absorbed an increasing share of Egypt's total G.N.P., from six per cent in 1960 to more than thirteen per cent by 1966, an exceedingly high figure for any country, let alone one as desperately poor as Egypt.[5] The growth in the military forces of Jordan and Syria was also very rapid: the Syrians increased their tank strength from 350 in 1960 to 550 in 1967, while the number of jet fighters in the Syrian air force went up from 50 to 120; the

---

* On conservative assumptions about fuel etc., the total payload per strike of the Egyptian air force increased from 170 tons in 1960 to 360 by 1967 (for Egypt–Israel combat ranges).[4] Apart from the Tu-16s, Egypt also had over 40 Il-28 light bombers and some Su-7 ground-attack aircraft.

Jordanians added 25,000 men to their forces (reaching a total of 55,000 by 1967), tripled their tank strength (to 300 tanks) and virtually doubled their small air force.[6]

In spite of these ominous developments, it still seemed that the 'third round' lay in the distant future; in fact during the sixties Israeli defence planners seem to have worked on the assumption that there would not be a general war before the end of the decade. From 1962 the Egyptians began to move forces to the Yemen and by the mid-sixties they were involved in a full-scale war; it seemed certain that, with 50,000 troops in the Yemen, the Egyptians would not go to war against Israel.

Since the borders were quiet during the sixties the Israeli Army could devote its efforts to 'basic' security preparations without having to divert its manpower and resources to cope with day-to-day problems. This was fortunate from the managerial point of view but it meant that the Army could not test its forces in battle nor try out its tactical doctrines. If during the fifties the pressure of 'current' security needs hampered the Army's long-term development, during the sixties it was the lack of up-to-date combat experience that worried many officers.

This anxiety was connected to the wider question of whether the balance of military power was moving in favour of the Arabs. All agreed that the determining factor was the pace of social and economic development in the Arab world: how soon – if at all – would it reduce Israel's advantage in the quality of her manpower, to the point where it would no longer outweigh Arab superiority in numbers? At that time many Israelis were inclined to accept Arab claims of social and economic progress; they were impressed by the growing number of the formally educated throughout the Arab world and by Egypt's industrial development, dramatized by the Aswan Dam.[7]

Some defence officials held out the threat of an imminent Arab superiority in non-nuclear military power, generated by both numbers and a qualitative improvement in Arab military manpower. Others argued that the large number of diplomas issued by Arab universities, the production of heavily subsidized industrial goods and the development of papiermâche Egyptian jet-fighters and rockets were only futile attempts to bypass basic cultural problems that could only be solved by fundamental reforms in

Arab society – reforms that no Arab government had even begun to consider. According to this school of thought, the development of Egypt and other Arab countries into effective modernized societies was a matter of generations and not of years.[8]

The debate was never fully resolved and Israel's defence planning was based on a compromise. The civilian Ministry of Defence invested considerable resources in the research and development of new weapons while the Army continued to deploy its forces on the assumption that if war came it would be fought without nuclear weapons.[9]

The debate on long-term defence needs was paralleled by a debate of more immediate significance. By the end of the fifties, both Israel and Egypt were in the process of acquiring sophisticated weapons including transonic fighters and modern battle tanks; by the early sixties the fighters were full supersonics while surface-to-air missiles and radar warning plus interceptor control systems were being introduced. The crucial question was whether the superior quality of Israeli manpower had become irrelevant in an age of automatic weapon systems. Some claimed that such things as missile systems were so automated that the morale and even the technical aptitude of their crews would count for little; so long as routine procedures were followed, these systems would work anyway. Others argued that, while men would have to do less manually, the tasks left to the human crew were becoming increasingly complex so that the introduction of more sophisticated weapons would enhance the importance of the human factor and not reduce it – or not at any rate until *fully* automatic systems were introduced.* A jet fighter equipped with electronic fire-control releases its weapons as soon as a target acquired by its radar comes within range, but it is still the pilot who has to manoeuvre the aircraft and make all the tactical decisions. His role is more limited than with the previous generation of fighters, but it is also more exacting: supersonic speeds require split-second decisions while extreme accuracy is needed for the manual portions of flight and weapon control.

The debate on long-term trends continued until the 1967 War,

---

* This condition virtually materialized by the time of the 1973 War. The weapons were still not fully automatic but very nearly so, e.g., the 'Sagger' anti-tank and Ṣam-7 anti-air missiles.

and optimists and pessimists struck a rough balance in official estimates of the military threat. The supreme test of war showed that the average quality of Egyptian officers was lower than even the most sanguine Israelis had hoped; the much advertised social and economic progress of Nasser's Egypt had no observable impact on the skill and morale of her soldiers. Finally, the human factor had not become irrelevant; on the contrary, it decided the outcome of the war. It is entirely fitting that Israeli officers and defence officials should have erred on the side of caution. Prudent defence planners could not ignore the physical growth of Egyptian and other Arab military forces, nor could they discount concrete facts on the basis of sociological speculations (as they in fact did by October 1973).

Between 1956 and 1967 the Army grew rapidly in size and effectiveness; conservative estimates of the Arab threat* provided the incentive, the rapid progress of Israeli society, the means.

The success of Israeli society during the sixties was visible in terms of rapid social and economic progress: between 1948 and 1960 the pre-independence settlers (650,000 in May 1948) had successfully absorbed no fewer than 900,000 newcomers and the economy was no longer derelict as in the post-war period. In 1951 (peak immigration year), export earnings covered only 11·3 per cent of the import bill, the rest coming from U.S. government grants, Jewish donations and loans; in that year the deficit on the balance of trade amounted to $225 *per capita*. By 1960, 42·6 per cent of the import bill was covered by visible exports and in 1967, 70 per cent so that the *per capita* deficit decreased to $134 in 1960 and $82 in 1967. (Total export earnings increased from $44·8 million in 1951 to $216·6 million in 960 and $554·5 million in 1967.)

The continuing inflow of capital from abroad, the dynamic if not very efficient management of a high-pressure economy, and sheer hard work had produced results: while the population trebled between 1948 and 1967, the gross national product grew even faster,

---

* There is no such thing as a 'realistic' threat estimate; apart from the factual unknowns and the uncertainties of war there are the cost variables: how great a risk is to be accepted, how many casualties sustained in order to defeat a given threat? In practice an 'overestimate' may simply reflect a low tolerance for casualties.

at an annual rate of more than ten per cent. In spite of a steady increase in defence expenditures, and the large slice taken up by investment, living standards increased rapidly. Within a decade, many Israelis experienced a heady transition from unemployment and relief work to full employment, from tented camps and wooden huts to modern blocks of flats, and from strict rationing to relative abundance. Economic development enabled the country to sustain steadily increasing defence expenditures which reached $400 million in the last fiscal year before the June War (1966–7). When a comparison is made with Egypt, Israel's economic success is apparent: in 1951 the Egyptian G.N.P. was three to four times as large as the Israeli but by 1966–7 the ratio had fallen to 1·6 – while Egypt's population was twelve times as large.[10] Since the competitive build-up of forces between Arabs and Israelis placed an increasing burden on the economies of both sides, Israel's economic development became a crucial variable in the balance of power.*

The dynamics of an arms race are notoriously difficult to disentangle, but it seems that Egypt was the pace-setter after the intervention in the Yemen. The Egyptians did not rely on other Arab states to augment their strength *vis-à-vis* Israel, while the Israelis tried to achieve parity as against all Arab forces combined. As both sides attempted to reach mutually exclusive positions the outcome was a classic, accelerating, arms race. A contributing factor was the ready availability of weapons from the Soviet Union for the Egyptians and from France for the Israelis. Relations between the French military and arms authorities and their Israeli counterparts became very close after 1956. Though Israel had to pay the full commercial price for each item, the French were willing to supply whatever Israel wanted to buy, and this was primarily aircraft: Super-Mystère fighters in 1959–60 (these were the first supersonic aircraft of the I.A.F.), Vautour II light bombers and, from 1963 onwards, Mirage IIIs, 'first-line' Mach 2 fighters roughly comparable to the Soviet MiG-21s then being supplied to Egypt.

Working through a network of unofficial contacts, the Israelis had also developed another special relationship with West Ger-

* With a plateau in the aftermath of the Sinai Campaign Israeli defence expenditures rose sharply:
Million U.S. $ 1958: 155; 1960:209; 1962:183; 1964:310; 1966:459.

many. Although the Germans could not supply jet fighters, they did provide U.S.-built surplus helicopters, Patton battle tanks, modern anti-aircraft guns and ancillary equipment. This relationship was so delicate that it had to be terminated following leaks in the world press but while it lasted the arrangement provided Israel with substantial supplies of weapons – which, unlike the French, were almost entirely free.[11] After 1956, Britain also consented to sell arms to Israel, primarily Centurion tanks of which at least 250 were purchased by 1967.[12] Only the United States held out against selling weapons to Israel (though it allowed Germany to do so) until the mid-sixties, when a number of Hawk anti-aircraft missile batteries were supplied; somewhat later, two squadrons of Skyhawk A-4 attack aircraft were promised* following the shipment of Soviet Tu-16 bombers to Egypt.[13]

As the arms race continued, Israel's technical and educational superiority gave her a major advantage in absorbing increasingly advanced weapons. The Egyptians appear to have accepted any Soviet weapon they could get, whether or not it suited their particular needs, and they accepted Soviet tactical ideas together with the hardware. Since the Soviet army did not believe in self-propelled artillery, the Egyptians were equipped with shield-and-carriage towed artillery, though this is ill-suited to mobile warfare in the open desert. The Soviet air force trained its pilots to fight in group formations with missile-armed interceptor fighters (i.e. primarily anti-bomber tactics), and here too the Egyptians accepted Soviet concepts uncritically. In fact the Egyptians were already fully extended in trying to maintain the new weapons they were receiving and could not even begin to modify them; they were having great difficulties in training crews who could operate the equipment and had no time for tactical innovations of their own. The Israelis, on the other hand, purchased weapons selectively, analysed their performance critically and insisted on modifications to suit local conditions and Israeli tactics.

In a process resembling physical digestion, imported tanks (all second-hand) were taken apart and rebuilt with local modifications (i.e. anti-sand air filters); aircraft could not yet be modified locally and so the French manufacturer was asked to modify his fighters according to Israeli specifications. At no time were the

* These were not delivered until after the 1967 War.

Israelis swamped by complicated technologies they could not understand.

The foundations of Israeli strategy did not change in the post-1956 period of tactical and operational innovation.[14] The net effect of the 'short-war' assumption was still to magnify the importance of a pre-emptive attack since it was thought that neither side would have enough time to recover from the effects of a powerful opening blow. Another and more specific incentive for striking first was the possibility of achieving superiority in the air by means of an all-out attack at the beginning of a war.[15] Air superiority is even more crucial in the Middle East than elsewhere since the desert terrain affords little or no natural cover against attack from the air.

Taken together, the 'short-war' assumption, the offensive orientation and the first-strike requirement dictated the structure of the Israeli Army, which was reshaped during the sixties around fast-moving armoured forces on the ground and a strong Air Force.

Haim Laskov, who succeeded Moshe Dayan as Chief of Staff in 1958, was just the man to guide the development of the Army along these lines. His writings form the most comprehensive statement of Israeli military doctrine;[16] he was Chief of Staff at a time of transition when new ideas could be readily absorbed by the Army. His tenure (1958–60) was too short* to allow Laskov to implement his ideas, but these were very influential in the seven years prior to the 1967 War.

A former Air Force Commander (1951–3) and O.C. Armour Corps (1956), Laskov had been a prominent advocate of mobile warfare based on the tank/jet-fighter combination. His ideas went far beyond a commonplace striving for tactical mobility: Laskov, his colleagues and successors grasped the deeper implications of mobility, and set out to shape the Army's organization, doctrines, and method of command around the sometimes subtle requirements of mobile warfare.[17]

Laskov had an important influence on the evolution of the method of command we have named 'optional control'. In this, middle-rank officers in charge of battalions and brigades are given

---

* Laskov resigned following a controversy with the deputy Minister of Defence. See p. 137 above.

full powers to make tactical decisions in the course of the battle, while their seniors at the divisional, area and G.H.Q. level can still intervene to guide the moves of units in the field.

Optional control requires self-reliant officers who are willing, and able, to shoulder responsibility without waiting for orders from their seniors. Another requirement, and one even more important with optional control than with more centralized systems, is accurate reporting. The stream of battle reports sent back by the commanders in the field must be truthful, even if the truth is unpleasant. Optional control is not suited to junior officers who are not willing to act on their own and insist on being 'covered' by written orders from above. And with officers who cannot be trusted to report accurately on the course of the battle, who try to conceal their failures or exaggerate enemy strengths, it breaks down disastrously. When reporting is inaccurate, field units are caught in a vicious circle; having supplied false information to their superiors, they can no longer trust orders received from above, which may have been formed on the basis of reports as false as their own.

At its best, optional control allows an army to respond quickly to the dangers and opportunities of battle, fighting and manoeuvring under the impulse of command decisions coming from several different levels at once. A more centralized method of command would certainly make for a more orderly conduct of the battle, but only at the expense of the relentless drive and fast reactions which optional control can generate. Of course, with many headquarters intervening simultaneously, optional control can also generate confusion. As many observers have pointed out, the Israeli Army in battle is often suspended between dynamism and utter chaos.

Perhaps the main virtue of optional control is that the 'fog of war' is not only taken into account but actually treated as a protagonist of the battle. Israeli officers are taught that neat battle plans will invariably break down, that the enemy will behave unpredictably and that one's own forces will never fight quite as planned; they are taught to *accept* all this. Instead of trying to overcome confusion by pausing to regroup after each breakdown, Israeli officers are trained to keep their forces fighting and moving in the right direction. By acting in full force, advancing without hesitations, they are 'to impose their will on the confusion of battle and determine its outcome'.[18] The training exercises of brigade and battalion commanders are designed with this objective in mind: they are asked to prepare a plan for an attack on a given objective and, when ready to present it, they are told that the situation had changed radically and that new orders have to be issued immediately. By combining the principle of the 'maintenance of objective' with optional control, the Israeli method of command is intended to give maximum flexibility in all respects – except for the objectives themselves. Working backwards from the fixed points of their assigned objectives, commanders can achieve them as they see fit, but they cannot ask for reinforcements nor defer their tasks.

Since field commanders can make their own plans as they go along, the Israeli method of command is incompatible with detailed blow-by-blow advance planning. There is still plenty of scope for other kinds of planning: strategic planning to define lines of advance and unit objectives, and 'convenience' tactical planning. In other words, detailed tactical plans may be made available but they are not binding. As the Israelis discovered in 1956, the Egyptians went in for a quite different kind of planning, detailed, comprehensive and quite rigid:

> The Egyptian army is accustomed to planning in advance all the details of its defensive array, down to the personal 'fox hole'. The impression we got in Sinai was that planning on paper . . . embraced each machine-gun and rocket launcher position in the defensive deployment.

This observer went on to comment:

> How is it possible to plan in detail a defensive array . . . without knowing at all what the attacking force will be and from which direction they will attack?[19]

As against this, one of the standard slogans of the Israeli Army is that plans are 'merely a basis for changes'.

A system is only as flexible as the most rigid of its parts and there would have been little point in freeing units in the field from the constraints of central control and advance planning without providing them with an equally flexible supply system. Mechanized forces equipped with rapid fire weapons use vast quantities of fuel and ammunition; as they fight and manoeuvre, supply lines must follow. Combat and supply units are necessarily far apart from each other in the presence of the enemy, and any logistic system will break down unless tanks and troop carriers can rendezvous with supply vehicles before they run out of fuel or ammunition. When tactical moves are planned in advance, supply arrangements present no particular problem, but with fluid and loosely co-ordinated forces moving in accordance with improvised plans or no plans at all, the logistic problem becomes critical. How can it be decided beforehand what supplies will be needed, where and when, if combat units are not following a detailed plan? The simple, conventional solution is the 'pulling' system, where combat units ask for re-supply, arrange a convenient meeting point and wait until the supply convoys reach them. Inevitably, this slows down the pace of advance.

When Laskov and his successors were re-thinking the Army's approach to mechanized warfare during the sixties, the head of the Logistics branch of the General Staff, Matityahn Peled, introduced a new logistic system which fitted in neatly with the needs of mobile forces. Originally devised by the U.S. army, this was a 'pushing' system, where fuel, ammunition and other supplies are continually sent forward along the lines of advance without waiting for requests and without holding up the advance. Under this system, Area Command depots would send forward as many supplies as the divisional logistic units could cope with; divisional supply units would in turn form smaller convoys which would be 'pushed' forward to the brigades, again acting on the principle that the flow of supplies should only be restricted by the storage and vehicle capacity of logistic units. Finally, supplies would travel in yet smaller convoys towards the combat units, and if necessary would go looking for them. Ideally, this system needs no 'pulling' and no central direction: as soon as a fighting unit pauses during an advance, it will be reached by a supply convoy ready to hand over as much fuel and ammunition as its tanks, troop carriers and trucks can hold.

Yet another requirement of flexibility is a fluid force structure. To fight and manoeuvre in the most flexible manner, units and sub-units have to concentrate, spread out and combine again in accordance with the changing requirements of the battle. In the

Army force structure, which dated back to 1948 and was fairly conventional in form,* the main unit of planning and command was the brigade. During the War of Independence the brigade was also the highest command echelon below the Front Commands; there were no divisions or corps, let alone 'armies' and army groups. By 1956, a higher field echelon was introduced, the *ugdah*. Like the traditional division, the *ugdah* consists of two or more brigades, but unlike the division or the brigade, the *ugdah* was merely a command framework for tailor-made task forces and had no organic forces. It consisted of little more than a command staff to which any desired combinations of brigades, battalions and supporting units could be attached. In the planning stage, this allowed the Army to shape the force structure according to the task at hand, the various units, large and small, being placed under the control of the *ugdah* whose commander was provided with a staff of operations, quartermaster and intelligence officers as well as air liaison and other specialist units.

In 1956 the *ugdah* system was semi-experimental and did not work too well,† but its advantages were obvious even then: for one thing an *ugdah* could cater for any combination of armour, infantry, artillery, airborne troops and service units instead of being a rigid structure such as the conventional division. The traditional division includes several kinds of supporting forces and service units; if tailor-made combat teams are carved out of it, these small, highly specialized units must often be left aside since it is difficult to put all of them into the combat teams. With the *ugdah* system, on the other hand, the problem did not arise; combat and service units were self-contained, independent organisms and their commanders were trained to work smoothly within the loose *ugdah* framework.

If Laskov was the initiator of many of the Army's new concepts, he was not the man who put them into practice. His tenure was

* Squads of ten men combine in threes to form platoons; three platoons plus a support unit make up a company, and in the same triangular pattern, companies form battalions, and battalions, brigades. In practice the number of sub-units and the men in them varied but the average size of an infantry brigade was about 3,500 men while armoured brigades were somewhat smaller.

† The commander of the Central *ugdah* was dismissed by Dayan following the failure of the brigades under his control to take the Abu Agheila/ Umm Katef crossroads.

cut short,* and at the beginning of 1961 he was succeeded by an undistinguished nuts and bolts man, Zvi Zur. The aircraft and battle tanks which figured so prominently in the June War were acquired during Zur's tenure; the operation and maintenance of Centurion and Patton battle tanks, Mirage fighters and Hawk anti-aircraft missiles required above all technical and managerial skills, and it was Zur who supervised the absorption of the Army's new equipment.

The first Chief of Staff to come out of the Palmach, Yitzhak Rabin, took over at the end of 1963. Significantly, it was only after Ben Gurion's final resignation as Prime Minister and Minister of Defence that a former Palmach man was appointed to the Army's highest post, though reportedly with Ben Gurion's consent. Ben Gurion's successor, Levi Eshkol, belonged to the same Mapai party, but, like most of his colleagues, he no longer shared Ben Gurion's long-standing suspicion of those officers who had a Palmach background†.

Rabin inherited from Laskov and Zur the basic framework of an Army built around a jet-fighter Air Force and mechanized units on the ground; if the Army's capabilities were thus magnified, the mass of new equipment was of unprecedented complexity and made new demands on the technical and managerial skills of officers and men. Under Rabin's leadership the Army upgraded the support services such as Ordnance and Logistics, introduced new management techniques (with the extensive use of computers) and attempts were also made to streamline administration. But the principal task of the Chief of Staff is to build the combat forces, and with the Armour Corps and I.A.F. in capable hands, Rabin,

* See p. 137 above.

† According to a story which circulated years later, an incident dating back to 1949 hindered Rabin's career while Ben Gurion remained in office. A rally of former Palmach members was held in the Tel Aviv sports stadium in 1949 and Rabin, as a prominent ex-Palmach man and Army officer, was expected to attend. Ben Gurion was then locked in a political battle with the Palmach's associates in the Mapam party, and he did not want a senior army officer to attend the rally; he therefore requested a meeting with Rabin, fixing a time which coincided with the rally, in order to prevent his attendance while giving him a good excuse for missing the rally. But Rabin did not cooperate. He went all the same, and was given a disciplinary reprimand. This incident is said to have contributed to Ben Gurion's opposition to Rabin's appointment as Chief of Staff.[20]

like Zur before him, devoted special efforts to the dethroned queen of the battlefield, the infantry.

With the expansion of the tank forces and the continued ascendancy of the paratroopers, the ordinary infantry trained in the Golani Brigade of the standing forces suffered from a skimming effect: dashing young men volunteered for the I.A.F. or the paratroops and others were drafted to the Armour Corps, while the Golani had to make do with the rest. The problem became more acute with the expansion of the paratroops after 1956. Organized into a battalion before the campaign, Sharon's 202nd Brigade was still an irregular unit. In a deliberate attempt to extend the high standards of the original paratroops to a larger force, after 1956 Sharon's unit became a regular brigade of the standing forces and as conscripts passed through its ranks, additional paratroop brigades were formed in the reserves.

Inevitably, the ordinary infantry trained in the Golani was adversely affected and the manpower intake of the reserve infantry brigades was now largely made up of those conscripts who neither volunteered for the paratroops nor had the educational standards required by the technical branches. At the same time, the elitist young men who had been content to serve with the original paratroops were not satisfied with the larger and less exclusive force formed after 1956. Under Rabin's tenure, the Army went a long way towards solving these problems. The Golani was systematically upgraded by assigning to it particularly good officers, many of them paratroopers. They set to work to raise the riflemen of the Golani to the standards of the paratroops and, by 1967, with the improvement of the Golani and the dilution of the paratroops, the two became almost interchangeable. As for retaining elite fighters in the ground forces, this was accomplished by sending them to the small and very selective 'reconnaissance' detachments which operated as independent units directly under the Area Commands and G.H.Q. Highly trained and frequently used for special (i.e. intelligence) missions, the semi-secret detachments became centres of tactical innovation and general dare-devilry as Sharon's paratroops had been before them.

Rabin's drive for technical and managerial improvement was evident in the less glamorous branches such as the Ordnance Corps. In 1956, when Sharon's paratroop column drove across the desert, it lost half of its vehicles to simple mechanical break-downs. A decade later, in June 1967, Sharon was once again leading a force in the Sinai, a much larger *ugdah*. This time his units were not only serviced by mobile repair shops but also supplied with mobile showers and electric hair-cutters. If Napoleonic armies 'marched on their stomachs', modern mechanized armies depend on the quality of their maintenance, repair and recovery services, and the differences between 1956 and 1967 was striking: instead of chronic breakdowns, much of the Army's now far more complex equipment was still in running order after six days of non-stop fighting.

While Rabin and his colleagues deserve much of the credit, there is no doubt that the Army's improved technical standards reflected the general growth of Israel's industrial base during the economic boom of the late fifties and sixties. Apart from the growth of civilian industry,* the Ministry of Defence built up a network of state-owned military industries. Its aviation group (Israel Aircraft Industries) produced Fouga-Magister jet trainers under French licence, supplied maintenance and repair services and carried out its own R. & D. work (in 1969 I.A.I. unveiled the Gabriel surface-to-surface missile, the first weapon of this type to become operational in the West). Except for the most complex back-to-the-factory repair work, by the mid-sixties I.A.I. was carrying out airframe, avionics and engine work for both civilian and military aircraft. Ta'as (Israel Military Industries) was responsible for land weapons and produced a wide range of military equipment of original design, including 52mm, 81mm and 120mm mortars and the widely exported Uzi submachine-gun. Ta'as also produced several weapons under licence, including the standard Army rifle, the 7·62mm FN, as well as much of the ammunition used by the Army.

Neither Ta'as nor the rest of Israel's industry could produce heavy equipment such as tanks or field artillery, but the Ordnance Corps did the next best thing: heavy equipment, chiefly tanks and

---

* Direct indices are not reliable (owing to the drastic devaluations of the Israeli Pound). Electricity sales to industry increased from 464 million kWh. in 1950 to 3,968 million kWh. in 1967; while the number of employees in industry (excluding construction) increased from 86,300 in 1955 to 159,500 in 1967.

half-track carriers, imported second-hand or as scrap, were reconditioned and drastically re-built to produce serviceable weapons.
U.S.-built Sherman M.4 tanks of wartime vintage were taken
apart and rebuilt with the addition of locally made running gear,
105mm guns* and new engines. (Other Shermans were modified
into self-propelled guns and fitted with the French 155mm howitzer.) Shimon Peres, as Director-General and later deputy Minister
(1959–65), was the driving force behind the Ministry's industrial
activities. In particular, he was instrumental in the creation of I.A.I.
and of Tadiran (Israel Electronic Industries). From small beginnings this group became a major force in Israeli industry and by
1967 it produced much of the Army's radio and electronic equipment as well as T.V. sets and other appliances for the civilian
market.

With the absorption of the mass immigration of 1949–52 and
the socio-economic progress of Israeli society, the quality of the
Army's manpower could not but improve too. Conscripts were
fitter and better educated and the training they received was also
improved since their instructors were the products of the post-
1956 Army. The nuts and bolts of the reserve system remained unchanged. Reservists could be mobilized by mail for the annual
recall as well as for tests and refresher courses, and by radio for
emergencies. A third means combined the speed of the emergency
procedure with secrecy – and this was the method used in 1967.
Unit commanders and their deputies are called by messengers or
on telephone; the deputies in turn call their subordinates and so on
down the chain of command until all the men are called to their
base. Once there, each soldier is registered and given his kit from
personal and unit stores kept ready by the service troops of the
standing forces. In most cases, the reserve brigades are ready for
deployment in less than twenty-four hours – even without using
the emergency radio procedure. Many reservists no longer serve
in the brigades but in administrative, command and service slots
within the regular Army structure and as they reach their posts,
skeleton command staffs and support services are fleshed out:
electricians to the Signal Corps, mechanics to Ordnance, drivers to
Supply, political scientists to the Intelligence Corps, doctors to

* A French-made medium-velocity (800 m/s) gun. The Sherman's 30-ton
chassis is too light to take a high-velocity 105mm gun.

the Medical units and so on. (In 1973, for the first time, an almost full-scale mobilization was carried out under extreme emergency conditions and while much else was going wrong the system worked without a hitch.)

In border areas, over-age reservists, both men and women, continued to serve in the Local Defence (Haganah Merchavit); in Jerusalem, semi-surrounded as it was by Jordanian territory, a large proportion of all reservists is retained in the Jerusalem Brigade, a large multi-battalion formation which serves as a self-contained defence force responsible for the entire area. In Jerusalem, as elsewhere, most younger reservists belong to the combat forces proper; upon mobilization they report to their brigades, artillery regiments or motorized supply units in the ground forces, or to the Air Force and Navy.

The tendency to reduce the length of the annual recall had been reversed after 1956, while training became more intensive. The average quality of reserve officers sharply improved during the sixties as the men who received their training in the Army of Independence and during the early fifties were replaced by graduates of the post-Dayan officer courses (or retrained at these courses). In 1956 many reserve officers lacked such basic skills as desert navigation, while their tactical thinking was still coloured by the rudimentary methods of 1948. During the sixties reserve officers mastered far more exacting techniques (e.g. air-ground cooperation) and absorbed the fairly sophisticated concepts taught in the new officer courses.

Rabin's special achievement as Chief of Staff was to preserve the raw fighting spirit inspired by the paratroopers, while introducing modern management and planning methods; the officer corps became more professional but it did not become desk-bound or bureaucratic. Two things made this possible: job rotation and the practice of early retirement for all officers.

The most obvious feature of the Israeli officer corps was, and still is, its youth. No longer so young as in 1948, when Yigal Allon was the principal Front Commander at thirty-one and several brigade commanders were still in their twenties, the Israeli career officer corps is still very young by world standards. Twenty-year-old lieutenants in charge of platoons, captain-rank company commanders in their mid-twenties, and battalion commanders (majors and lieut.-colonels) in their mid-thirties are typical. In 1967, most brigade commanders were in their late thirties, while no general officer, including the Chief of Staff and Area Commanders, was over fifty.* (By 1973 average ages had increased in some cases but senior officers were still under fifty.)

There is no formal rule laying down a fixed retirement age but in one of his major innovations Dayan introduced the principle that career officers should retire at half-pay while they are still young enough to begin a new civilian career, in other words between forty and fifty. In any case, except for specialists, most officers who do not reach high rank leave the Army while still in their thirties. Whenever a competent officer retires, the Army loses valuable knowledge, costly and difficult to replace. But a constantly renewed officer corps is more likely to promote new ideas and original methods than an older and more static group of men. The principle of early retirement is thus a radical answer to an old dilemma: experience versus innovation. It is not so much that new men bring original thinking with them, but that the Army's collective capacity to absorb rapid change without disruption derives from the open-mindedness of its young officer corps.

As for the source of new ideas, it is mostly the senior officers who promote change – the very group that elsewhere often tends to oppose innovation. Most Israeli officers are exposed to higher education *during* their military career: instead of studying at universities or academies before they begin their career, prospective senior officers are usually given paid leave to study at universities in the middle of their service (often in addition to attendance at military courses abroad). Since all but a handful of officers will eventually need educational qualifications for their second, civilian, careers this is something of a fringe benefit – but it also means that the Army's senior officers are often men who have both plenty of military experience and a fresh mind.†

* Average age for colonels in the U.S., British and Soviet armies.

† All career officers, of whatever rank, are assisted by the Army to complete their secondary education; middle rank and particularly promising junior officers are given paid leave to study for a university degree in the middle of their career. In a 1970 radio interview, the Army's Chief Education Officer, Col. I. Arad, stated that 25% of all career officers have a university degree or the equivalent, 42% have a full secondary education and 31% a partial secondary education.[21]

Except for specialists, who rarely reach the highest ranks, as officers climb the promotion ladder they are posted from combat units to staff jobs, from support to command posts and back again. Rotation, like early retirement, is a radical answer to a familiar problem: specialized knowledge and group integration. If an officer is retained throughout his career in a particular job or branch, he is likely to become an expert at his work but he will not know very much about the role of his own particular branch in the workings of the Army as a whole. He is also less likely to promote innovation.* The preference for integration is ultimately based on the belief that officers must be fighting-men rather than bureaucrats or technicians.

The phenomenon of the staff officer who has never been under fire or the supply officer who has never served in a field unit is very rare in the Israeli Army. Not that rotation is intended to produce a military version of the 'well-rounded' gentleman: as they move from one job to another, officers have to absorb a great deal of new specialized training. During the post-1956 expansion of the Armour Corps, many infantry officers were transferred to the corps – not for the sake of rotation but because of the mechanization of the ground forces. Whatever their rank, officers posted to armour had to undergo a full programme of command training, rank by rank, from crew leaders to company and then battalion commander, in addition to the separate trade courses for drivers, gunners, loaders and radio operators. There is little or no rotation from one corps to another – except when structural changes lead to the expansion of one branch at the expense of another – but rotation between staff, training and command is the rule. Tours of duty last four or five years with training courses, higher education or attendance at foreign military colleges sandwiched in between.

Early retirement, mid-career education (often in the humanities) and job rotation have all contributed to the making of an alert and innovative officer corps, but more important than any of these has been the Army's ability to attract many of the most talented

* In more rigid structures, rotation has the opposite effect. Where innovation is difficult, rotation merely discourages would-be innovators who have no real incentive to fight bureaucratic battles on behalf of reforms that others will soon inherit. In the U.S. forces, innovation is usually associated with *long* tenure.

Israelis to its career service. In fact one of the hidden costs of Israel's national defence is that much of the country's creative and managerial talent is absorbed by the Army and lost to productive civilian pursuits. In most developed countries, it is the more conservative who go in for a military career, seeking the psychological job security of a stable and perhaps old-fashioned institution. In Israeli business concerns and government departments it is notoriously difficult to fire anybody; both offer much more in the way of job and psychological security than the Army, where those who do not make the grade are rarely retained. As against this, career advancement can be very swift and does not depend on seniority. Moreover, the prestige of the Army has allowed many senior officers to enter desirable upper-echelons jobs upon retirement.* Thus, career incentives in the Israeli Army are the direct opposite of those of most other armies – and not surprisingly, they have attracted a very different type of man. The Army was the first major Israeli institution to offer rapid promotion to young men at a time when most high-level positions were still monopolized by the first generation of founding fathers. (Until quite recently, most senior Israeli civil servants, politicians, and heads of state enterprises were in their sixties while the Army offered its most senior positions to men in their forties.)

For all its virtues, the career officer corps is not representative of Israeli society as a whole. There are no social or ethnic barriers to advancement but cultural and educational standards are very uneven in Israeli society, and the Army makes no allowance for the disadvantaged. There is equality of admission but certainly no equality of opportunity. Most Israelis are either immigrants or children of immigrants; some were highly educated, others had no formal education at all; some came from the most advanced societies of the world, others from the traditional Oriental communities of North Africa and the Middle East. Of the 1,240,000 immigrants who arrived in Israel between 1948 and 1967, about

* In 1972 three retired generals (Dayan, Bar Lev and Allon) served in the Cabinet; one (Makleff) headed the Citrus Marketing Board responsible for the country's main export; another was Ambassador to Washington (Rabin). In that same year, the heads of the largest industrial holding company, the largest investment bank, the national port authority, and other key institutions, were all retired generals.

half came from countries in Africa and Asia and the balance mainly from Europe. Even in the second generation, among the children of these immigrants, gross differences in educational standards and social outlook persist.

The Army is a most powerful pressure cooker, but prospective officers are selected from new recruits who have not yet been conditioned by the long and arduous years of conscript service. The lower educational level of Oriental Jews is not a real obstacle to entry in the officer corps (a secondary education diploma is *not* one of the requirements), but the Army does require an aptitude for leadership and for motivation – and these qualities are seen in terms of the pioneering and national ideals conspicuous amongst the sons (and daughters) of pre-1948 'veteran' settlers. Except for the junior ranks, career officers are mostly the *sabra* sons and grandsons of the Yishuv, rather than newcomers or the children of post-independence immigrants. Moreover, the officer corps also includes a disproportionate number (25–30 per cent) of men born and raised on kibbutzim and the old-established moshavim, though such settlements account for only eight per cent of the country's total population. Kibbutz and moshav children are brought up in small and cohesive groups where status competition is intense – and expressed in service to the community. Since the Army is the main outlet for these powerful competitive pressures, kibbutz and moshav youth are strongly motivated to make the grade by serving as officers or by volunteering for high-prestige units such as the reconnaissance detachments, the frogman-commandos and Air Force flight crews.*

No figures are available but it is known that only a fraction of all career officers are immigrants from the Middle East and North

* A recent study examined the careers of three groups of recruits: one kibbutz-born, one partly kibbutz-educated, and the rest. No less than 30% of the kibbutz-born served in one of the high-prestige volunteer units, while only 16% of the kibbutz-educated and 6% of the rest did so; 61% of the kibbutz-born passed the Army's aptitude tests for officer selection, as compared to 40% in the other two categories. The researcher who conducted the study came to the conclusion that the higher performance of kibbutz children was due to the 'personality variables' derived from the communal way of life on the kibbutzim.[22] Only 3–4% of all new recruits come from the kibbutzim; most Israeli officers come from the town and city population that accounts for 81% of the country's total.

Africa, or children of such immigrants. The Army is so important in the country's consciousness and social life that the under-representation of Oriental Jews in its higher ranks could cause intense resentment – but so far this has not happened. With few exceptions, most Israelis seem to believe that promotion in the Army is based on merit alone. Complaints of deliberate discrimin-ation* are very rare indeed and the Army is often singled out as the one major institution free of any trace of discrimination – though perhaps nowhere else is the predominance of elite elements so apparent.[23]

The Armour Corps

The final outcome of the armour debates of the fifties was the decisive victory of the 'tank school', following the Sinai Cam-paign. Dayan and his followers in the 'mobile infantry' school were thoroughly converted, and the tank battalions of the Armour Corps were recognized as the key weapon of the ground forces.[24] Under the successive leadership of Uri Ben Ari, whose tenure was brief,† Haim Bar Lev and David Elazar (Chief of Staff 1972), the Armour Corps expanded rapidly between 1956 and 1964. High-grade officers from the infantry were transferred to the corps and modern battle tanks were purchased, Centurions from Britain and Patton M.48s from West Germany.

One of the first officers transferred from the infantry was Col. (later Maj.-Gen.) Israel Tal. A man noted for his mechanical talents, Tal was given leave in 1961 for a three-year period of study. Unlike most senior officers, who study economics or similar subjects with an eye to their subsequent civilian careers, Tal studied philosophy and political science at the Hebrew University in Jerusalem. Upon his return to the corps in Novem-ber 1964, Tal was appointed its commanding officer. Like Uri

* As for the natural preference of officers for men of a background similar to their own, most Israelis are innocent enough to take such things for granted – though this does not include the Army's Manpower branch whose researchers are forever searching for more objective testing tech-niques.

† He was forced to resign from the Army by Ben Gurion who had dis-covered that Ben Ari had shielded a subordinate involved in a black market violation.

Ben Ari and his immediate predecessors, Tal believed that battle tanks were best used in concentration, massed into solid wedges ready to fight as the spearheads of the ground forces. But during his years of service and study, Tal's ideas had moved far beyond this basic principle, which by then was universally accepted. He evolved an original approach to the use of armour and some of his ideas were diametrically opposed to the conventional wisdom of armour officers in Israel and abroad.

Ever since the Second World War, armour experts everywhere have never tired of preaching the need for close cooperation between battle tanks, the mechanized infantry in its carriers, and the artillery. They argue that battle tanks would be very vulnerable to bazookas, recoilless rifles and especially anti-tank missiles, unless they are escorted at all times by infantry forces. Combined armour–infantry tactics are based on the premise that mechanized infantry troops riding in armoured carriers will protect the tanks, while the latter will in turn defend the infantry from enemy tanks. Following the experiences of the Second World War, this sensible tactical doctrine acquired the force of a widely accepted orthodoxy. Since the Armour Corps was, and is, responsible for the mechanized infantry as well as for the tank forces, followers of the armour–infantry school argued that the corps should strengthen the mechanized infantry and devote greater efforts to teamwork training for armour–infantry cooperation. Unfortunately, the Israeli Army's armoured carriers were old and poorly protected half-tracks dating back to the Second World War vintage (U.S. M.3s). Infantry riding in these carriers could never hope to keep up with tanks in the thick of battle, and those who called for more armour–infantry cooperation also wanted to purchase modern armoured carriers for the infantry. They realized that this would mean that fewer tanks could be bought.

Tal disagreed with the solid consensus of international expertise and flatly rejected the validity of the armour–infantry doctrine in *Israeli conditions*. He argued that massed formations of battle tanks moving across the open spaces of the Sinai desert needed no mechanized infantry to protect them. In his view heavily armoured battle tanks had little to fear from most anti-tank weapons since the lack of natural cover would make it very difficult for the enemy to use short-range weapons such as bazookas and recoilless rifles.

The older but effective anti-tank gun was a more serious threat: the Egyptians had adopted Soviet anti-tank methods, where large numbers of anti-tank guns are deployed in fortified pak-fronts and their crews are trained to fire in salvoes against a single tank at a time. Tal's answer to this threat was to rely on a high standard of tank gunnery. If Israeli tank gunners could be trained to shoot accurately at long ranges, they would force the enemy to fire their anti-tank guns too soon, thus giving away their positions while the range was still too long for their shells to penetrate thick tank armour. (As became quite clear in 1973, Tal's concept – which the authors had endorsed – failed to take into account the anti-tank missile which can destroy tanks at long range from concealed positions.)

In open areas such as Sinai, the main threats to the battle tank were minefields and anti-tank guns. Armour–infantry cooperation, aimed at the enemy's infantry and its *short-range* weapons, was no doubt very useful in the wooded plains of Europe but not in Sinai. Tal refused to sanction the demand for modern armoured carriers and devoted the resources of the corps to the tank battalions of the armoured brigades. His impressive knowledge and persuasive arguments carried the day, but not all his colleagues accepted this radical departure from accepted doctrine.[25] (See chapter 10 for a post- 1973 re-appraisal of Tal's 'all-tank' concept.)

Like other tank enthusiasts, Tal emphasized mobility as the prime quality of the armoured phalanx. At first sight this fitted in with the consensus of expert opinion abroad which called for the design of lighter and faster tanks, not so heavily armoured nor so slow as the Pattons and Centurions then available in the West. The Russians, the West Germans and later the French deployed a new generation of battle tanks with powerful guns but relatively light armour. At thirty-five tons or so, their tanks were almost twenty tons lighter than the Pattons or Centurions and therefore faster and more agile. It was argued that with the introduction of anti-tank missiles and the spread of lightweight tank-killers in the hands of the infantry, heavy armour was obsolete. According to this school of thought, a more agile and lighter tank was needed with no more armour than is required to stop small or medium-calibre weapons. The German Leopard, the French AMX-30 and the Russian T-54/T-55 were all designed on these lines. Only the British and the U.S. army still favoured heavily armoured tanks.

Most Israeli officers were attracted by the fast-tank concepts current in Europe. But Tal regarded the 'fast' tank as the product of a simple-minded confusion between tactical mobility on the battlefield, i.e. *movement in the presence of the enemy's fire,* and mere physical speed. A Centurion whose top road speed is only 20 m.p.h. is certainly slower than the new French tank, the AMX-30, which can travel at 50 m.p.h. on roads; but on the battlefield, Tal pointed out, Centurions can advance against heavy fire, while AMX-30s cannot. Tal wanted the Armour Corps to have heavily armoured tanks that could absorb a great deal of enemy fire before being stopped, and he remained unimpressed by the higher road speed of the 'fast' tanks. Once again, Tal prevailed over expert opinion, though not all of his colleagues were convinced by his reasoning. (And here he was proved to be right in both the 1967 and 1973 wars.)

Brilliant theoretician though he was, Tal's expertise in tank warfare was based on his detailed practical knowledge of weapons and tactics. Like other officers transferred from the infantry, Tal had gone through all the armour training courses for command as well as the trade courses for gunners, loaders, drivers, fitters and radio operators. Already a full colonel, Tal worked as a mechanic in the tank repair sheds so as to become familiar with every aspect of maintenance and repair for the five different tanks then serving with the corps.*

With this background, Tal was acutely conscious of the need for high technical standards in crew training, accurate gunnery and reliable maintenance. His two predecessors, Haim Bar Lev and David Elazar, had built a cadre of dedicated tank officers but the training of the conscripts and reservists still left much to be desired. Battle tanks such as the Centurion and Patton are complicated and also fragile; gears will break, engines seize and radiators melt unless carefully handled. Unlike motor cars their design makes no allowances for rough handling. Tank operation and

---

* When O.C. Armour Corps, Tal once served as a tank gunner (under the command of one of his subordinates) in a fire-fight with Syrian tanks: Tal destroyed a Syrian tank but his own tank was also damaged in the encounter.

maintenance require fairly advanced mechanical skills. In many armies tank crewmen are long-service professionals, but in Israel tank crews are conscripts, or worse, reservists who usually serve only one month in each year.

When more or less unskilled men have complex machines in their charge, they tend to let things ride; maintenance will be superficial and they will patch up rather than repair. This works well enough with private cars, but to keep tanks functioning on the battlefields their crews must know how to maintain their machines from the ground up, since specialists are not on call in the midst of battle. As Tal struggled with his training problem, he came to the conclusion that conscripts and reservists could never be taught to *understand* all the different mechanical and electrical technologies embodied in their tanks.

His solution was specialization, and the imposition of operating routines performed under strict disciplinary control. Since recruits could not be taught mechanical engineering, hydraulics and electronics, Tal resolved to have them follow detailed working procedures – even if they did not understand what they were doing. In an Army that called for versatility and originality in all its members, and which rejected narrow specialization, resistance to Tal's ideas was inevitable. As for the demand that orders had to be obeyed, even when they were not understood, this caused intense opposition both inside and outside the Army. Tal saw a connection between the Army's informality and easy camaraderie and the specific technical problems of his corps, and instead of accepting the lack of discipline as an inevitable fact of life, he campaigned to introduce formal discipline in dress, saluting and drill in the Armour Corps.

The stream of new orders, regulations and disciplinary controls emanating from Armour Corps headquarters soon transformed the armoured brigades subject to its control. While casual dress and informal discipline remained the approved style among the infantry and paratroopers, the conscripts and reservists of the armoured brigades became conspicuous in their regulation dress, from the correctly worn black hat down to the prescribed type of boots. As Tal had predicted, technical discipline went hand in hand with formal, 'external' discipline. Instead of improvised 'fixing', tanks were strictly maintained; instead of rule-of-thumb methods, equipments were operated according to the precise instructions laid down by corps headquarters. Assisted by a growing band of like-minded officers, Tal introduced many innovations alongside his discipline campaign: more technical courses were given to officers and men, and a strict inspection system was introduced for every item of equipment; this included a detailed maintenance log-book for every tank. When the reservists were mobilized in 1967, they found their tanks in unit sheds in perfect running order and ready for action; personal, troop and company equipment was neatly stored and well maintaind.

The battles of 1967 showed that Tal's insistence on technical proficiency did not erode the command initiative of armour officers. (But in 1973 this was not always so.) Those units that went to war with reconditioned Shermans* and poorly protected light AMX-13s managed to hold their own against anti-tank defences and the better Russian tanks of the Arabs. The Centurions and Pattons, massed into battalions, swept all before them and advanced rapidly on all fronts, thus proving conclusively that their 'old-fashioned' heavy armour was the key to genuine battlefield mobility.

Two years after the June War, Tal was criticized by a military commentator† for having neglected the mechanized infantry: with the best officers and men assigned to the tank battalions, the infantry element of the corps‡ had to make do with the rest. It was also pointed out that the mechanized infantry was short of anti-tank weapons, while its thirty-year-old half-track carriers were totally inadequate for the modern battlefield.

---

* At 34–36 tons combat weight, the basic Sherman chassis is too light to take a high-velocity gun of large calibre, such as the 105mm L.7 A.1 mounted on the Centurion (which weighs about 52 tons). Israeli Shermans were modernized with new diesel engines and running gear and fitted with a French-built medium-velocity (800m/s) 105mm gun firing hollow-charge shells. In 1967 some old Super-Shermans were still fitted with 75mm high velocity guns.

† See pp. 295–6 below.

‡ Built on the usual 'triangular' pattern, each tank brigade has two battalions of tanks for one of mechanized infantry; mechanized infantry brigades had one tank battalion and two of infantry. Some of the latter were fielded in 1967 but this type of formation was virtually abandoned in later years.

As a serving officer, Tal could make no direct reply to his critics, but his position was known: if tank forces are properly used as an armoured phalanx, they do not require high-grade mechanized forces to ride into battle with them, but only to mop up *after* them. It followed that the mechanized infantry could safely be given a lower priority, thus preserving scarce human and material resources for the tank forces. As we shall see, the experiences of 1967 were not conclusive in this respect, and the war was followed by yet another round of reappraisal and discussion (and still more so after 1973).

The Air Force 1956–67

During the sixties the Air Force continued to enjoy a clear priority in the allocation of money and manpower; it had the pick of the country's youth in its all-volunteer force and received a major share of the hard currency in the procurement budget. As a result, the I.A.F. managed to achieve something which no other branch of the Army could do: it kept up with the Egyptians in the quality – if not the quantity – of its equipment. By the time the Egyptian air force obtained Russian MiG-15s, 'first-generation' subsonic jet fighters, the I.A.F. had received comparable French-built Ouragans; by the time of the Sinai Campaign, the I.A.F. had the improved Mystère IVA, good enough to cope with the next Russian fighter supplied to Egypt, the MiG-17. After 1959 the contest became transonic: the Russians gave MiG-19s to the Egyptians while the Israelis deployed the Super-Mystère, their first fighter to fly faster than the speed of sound, if only for short dashes, at high altitude.

When Dan Tolkowsky became Commander of the Air Force in 1954 he had to struggle against the purchasing policy imposed on the Air Force. The ground forces were equipped with reconditioned weapons, bought second-hand or even as scrap, and the same make-do philosophy had been applied to the I.A.F. Between 1950 and 1954 no fewer than 250 Mosquito fighter bombers were bought as scrap to rebuild a much smaller number of air-worthy aircraft. Only *sixteen* were still operational in 1956. Tolkowsky had an uphill struggle in persuading his colleagues of the General Staff that buying the latest available jet fighters, and all the supporting gear that goes with them, was more *economical* than trying to make do with inferior equipment: on the ground, good tank crews could defeat bad ones even if their tanks were inferior, but no pilot could bridge the gap between a modern jet fighter and a piston-engined relic of the Second World War. As for the policy of using what little money there was for weapons, neglecting maintenance equipment and support facilities, this may have been a good idea for the ground forces, but in the air war a small number of advanced aircraft maintained in top condition would always prevail over a larger number of inferior or badly maintained aircraft.

Such arguments had to contend with equally persuasive budgetary realities: the 1954 defence budget was only sixty-five million dollars, while a single squadron of jet fighters cost ten million* (enough for 400 reconditioned Shermans or 100,000 rifles). Nevertheless Tolkowsky eventually prevailed and by the time Ezer Weizman took over as I.A.F. Commander, in 1958, the battle was won.

Brash, aggressive and youthful (he was then in his thirties), Weizman was very different from Tolkowsky, an elegant and far more sedate figure; both had been R.A.F. fighter pilots but it was Tolkowsky who had the manner of an aristocratic Englishman. Weizman, nephew of the first President of Israel and Dayan's brother-in-law, nevertheless liked to give the impression that he was 'one of the boys', rather like the Palmach commanders who headed brigades but affected the clothes and manners of the left-wing youth leaders they had been.

The two things Weizman and Tolkowsky had in common were far more important than any mannerisms: they were both good fighter-pilots, excellent organizers and very able leaders of men; both had a deep understanding of the technological aspects of airpower – and both had great confidence in the future of the I.A.F. In pursuit of technical excellence, Weizman continued to refine Tolkowsky's training policies for aircraft mechanics, electronic engineers, fitters and craftsmen. As the technology became more complicated, more of the work was performed by professionals serving on (post-conscription) contracts. With its resources becoming more abundant after 1956, the I.A.F. could obtain

* The squadron IOC cost is a rough estimate for 24 Ouragans, plus spares and type ancillaries.

sophisticated maintenance equipment and a radar ground-control system. Still spartan by others' standards, I.A.F. bases were made almost luxurious in comparison to the transit-camp atmosphere of army bases (I.A.F. conscripts slept under solid roofs, the ground troops often in tents).

During Weizman's tenure, the I.A.F. deployed its first helicopter squadrons equipped with S-58s, American-built sixteen-seaters obtained second-hand from West Germany;* later, a small number of Alouette IIs were bought in France. The I.A.F. had old DC-3 Dakotas for its transport wing and used Piper Cubs as spotter and liaison aircraft: its high-quality philosophy applied only to combat aircraft. The Israelis continued to believe that strategic bombing was not worth the cost and, though the Egyptians added full-fledged medium bombers (Tu-16s) to their air force, the I.A.F. made no effort to acquire such big-payload machines. It did buy twenty Vautour II (and four Vautour IIN) light bombers, but planned to use them as long-range strike aircraft against distant Arab airfields and not for strategic bombing against cities.

Weizman, like Tolkowsky before him, made the quality of individual pilots his first preoccupation. Serving on multi-year contracts, the fighter-pilots were filtered out of the mass of volunteers by gruelling selection tests and training stages.[26] Originally trained on light aircraft and then on Fouga-Magister jets,† I.A.F. fighter-pilots flew many more than the ten hours per week of their Egyptian counterparts – and trained under conditions of stringent discipline.

The small group of first-line pilots entrusted with the seventy-two‡ Mirage IIIC Mach 2 fighters delivered by the French from 1963 onwards was the most exclusive elite of the Army. Each pilot could make a perceptible difference to Israel's defence – and he knew it. Unlike the Mystères, hurriedly introduced in 1956 before

* 24 were acquired in 1960; two earlier model S-55s were also acquired by the I.A.F.

† French two-seat trainers, some of which were assembled in Israel by I.A.F. As an economy measure, the Fougas were convertible for close-support missions armed with machine-guns and anti-tank rockets. Reserve pilots – some from the Israeli air line El Al – were assigned to combat duties in the Fougas. Lacking an ejection seat and too slow to evade A.A. fire or enemy fighters, the Fougas were dangerous aircraft to fly.

‡ Does not include trainer version (Mirage IIIB) or replacement aircraft.

their pilots and ground crews were ready, and unlike the interim Super-Mystères, of which only twenty-four were bought, the Mirage squadrons were gradually built up in a carefully planned deployment: training schedules were matched to the pace of deliveries, maintenance gear was ready and spares stocked while the 'ground environment' of radar, control and communications was mated to the avionics of the new aircraft. The Mirage was a Mach 2 fighter like the MiG-21 supplied to Egypt by the Russians; both aircraft were genuine supersonics that could fly at twice the speed of sound for short 'dashes' but unlike the MiG-21, a pure interceptor with superior climbing abilities, short range and no payload to speak of, the heavier Mirage could also be used as a fighter-bomber (though with only a small weaponload).

The Israelis had little choice in selecting their new generation of Mach 2 fighters, since only four Western countries produced such aircraft: Britain (the Lightning), Sweden (the S-35 Draken), the United States (F-104, F-105, F-106 and F-4); and France with the Mirage – and only the last would sell to Israel. Unable to choose their airframe, the Israelis could at least determine its contents: frills were eliminated and the weapon configuration radically altered. What started off as little more than a platform for air-to-air and air-to-ground missiles was converted at the Israelis' request into a cannon-firing fighter that could *also* use missiles, as well as drop bombs and launch rockets.

With its low wing-loading (good for altitude and range) and fair acceleration (crucial for dogfights), the Mirage was a good aircraft to fly; if its electronics equipment was inferior to its U.S. counterparts and needlessly difficult to maintain, the I.A.F. could always take care of the problem with some modifications and a great deal of hard work. Very little could be done about a far more basic shortcoming of this aircraft: originally designed as a high-altitude interceptor (hence the optional rocket engine for rapid climb), the Mirage had been adopted for the 'strike' role as well (i.e. low-level penetration followed by precision bombing). But the weight of bombs and rockets it could carry was very limited, scarcely more than 2,000 lb. over Israel–Egypt ranges – and what the I.A.F. needed above all was a large strike payload since its optimal strategy was to destroy enemy airpower at source by attacking aircraft on the ground in a single, disabling strike.[27]

Having converted the 'Battle of Britain' enthusiasts in the General Staff, who had advocated a defensive strategy in the debates of the early fifties, the I.A.F. worked out a detailed battle plan for the destruction of Egyptian and other Arab air forces at the beginning of any future war. To do this, however, hundreds of tons of bombs, rockets and cannon shells had to be delivered, accurately, against hundreds of enemy aircraft on dozens of airfields, some fairly remote. An additional tonnage of weapons was also needed to take care of enemy air defences. Moreover, unless the attack came in a single, devastating, knock-out, blow enemy fighters would take to the air, wreaking havoc against incoming fighter-bombers loaded down with weapons and fuel. In other words, to launch a disabling strike against enemy airpower, the I.A.F. needed a large combined weaponload per sortie: either many fighter-bombers each with a small weapon capacity or a fair number of heavyweight fighters. What the I.A.F. actually had was a small force of small-payload aircraft.

In a calculation familiar to every amateur strategist, the problem that faced the I.A.F. looked something like this:

Combined Tonnage Requirements (*notional*)

Number of individual targets times* the payload of weapons required for each = total weight of bombs, rockets, missiles and cannon shells required to destroy enemy runways, aircraft and radar units*	say, 1,000 tons
Allowance for E.C.M. payload and for inaccuracy due to A.A. fire and its evasion (30%)	add　300 tons
Allowance for operational errors (i.e. target misidentified, aircraft off-course, aircraft with wrong weaponload on target, aircraft on target already destroyed, etc.) (20%)	add　260 tons
Allowance for aircraft lost (before successful strike) or aborting mission (10%)	add　156 tons

* Assumes optimum allocation of weapons and Electronic Countermeasures (E.C.M.) to targets, and standard accuracies.

Allowance for aircraft in maintenance and
repair at H-hour on D-day (10%)   add   172 tons

Total force-wide weaponload required (over
stated ranges) for disarming one-wave attack   1,888 tons

It was obvious that, even if all its combat aircraft were committed to battle with the maximum possible weaponload, the
I.A.F. was simply too small to do the job. The tonnage could be
made up by flying more than one sortie per aircraft, but it would
take time to refuel and re-arm the aircraft and brief the pilots on
their next set of targets. And any gap between the waves of attacking aircraft would allow the enemy to 'scramble' its remaining
fighters. Weizman and his colleagues had to fight against these
arithmetical facts of life. Unable to buy a force of fighter-bombers*
with adequate payloads, they set out to squeeze every ounce of
useful payload out of their existing force of slow Ouragans (less
than 500 lb. per sortie), Mystères (1,000 lb.), Super-Mystères
(2,000 lb.), Mirages (2,000 lb.) and Vautours (4,000 lb.)†

Having calculated that more payload was likely to be lost by
attempting to evade the enemy's anti-aircraft fire than through the
aircraft losses it could cause, pilots were taught to approach the
target slowly and carefully for accurate delivery, paying no attention to fire from the ground. Thus the allowance for aiming errors
due to A.A. fire was cut. The payload loss due to operational
errors was reduced by improving target intelligence; the I.A.F.
intelligence unit and the Intelligence Corps staff kept the enemy
under continuous surveillance so that a constantly updated map of
all priority targets could be maintained. Operational control, to
direct aircraft against priority targets, was brought to a fine
art to ensure that the right aircraft would be sent with the right
weaponload over the target whose priority was highest at that
moment in time.

  The allowance for aircraft in maintenance at any one time was
already low, but ground crews were trained and motivated to do

---

* The U.S. promised 48 Skyhawk A-4 light attack aircraft (with good
payloads) in 1966 but they were not delivered until after the 1967 War;
50 Mirage 5 attack aircraft (with more than twice the Mirage IIIC payload)
were ordered from France but never delivered.

† Rough estimates over Israel–Egypt ranges.

better until the 'down-time' loss became smaller still. In a country where poor workmanship is the rule rather than the exception, and where industrial workers are only half as efficient as their Western counterparts, the standards achieved by I.A.F. technicians and repairmen were remarkable, and the product of a massive organizational effort: among other things it meant devising morale boosters for the unglamorous ground crews, and organizing technical courses in many civilian schools so as to prepare youngsters who would eventually serve in the I.A.F.

Even so, the I.A.F. still lacked the minimum payload needed to destroy even the highest priority targets in a single strike. Each aircraft would therefore have to fly more than one sortie. By spacing the attack in waves the enemy might be prevented from scrambling his interceptors so long as all fighter airfields could be kept under continuous attack. This meant that the I.A.F. had to reduce the time needed for 'turn-around' (return flight, landing, refuelling, re-arming, de-briefing and target briefing) until it corresponded to the length of the waves in the battle plan. By 1967 this too was achieved.

There was one hurdle that the I.A.F. could not overcome: it could hope to destroy the Egyptian air force in a matter of hours – if everything went according to plan – but not if it also kept back a reasonable number of fighters to defend the skies over Israeli cities. Aircraft fitted out as fighter-bombers for a conveyor-belt attack could not perform as interceptors too – and it was interceptors that would be needed if the enemy managed to launch his aircraft first.

In 1956, Ben Gurion had demanded an air defence guarantee from the French; he feared Egyptian bombing attacks against Israeli cities – even though the Egyptians only had a dozen light bombers actually operational.[28] By the mid-sixties, the Egyptians had acquired a real bomber force, including thirty Tu-16 medium bombers – and yet Ben Gurion's successor, Levi Eshkol, and the General Staff, were forced to rely on the I.A.F. and its high-risk strategy. In 1956 Ben Gurion had shown timidity, or perhaps a statesmanlike prudence. In 1967 the ominous threat from the Russo–Arab alliance, and the passivity of the West, forced Israel to accept a very dangerous gamble: less than one squadron of I.A.F. fighters was kept in reserve and all others were committed to an all-out strike which could have failed.

Although its basic strategy was offensive, the I.A.F. could not neglect normal air defence tasks: surveillance, identification of incoming aircraft – and interception; the latter meant mostly air-to-air combat* which remained the focus of Air Force training and the source of its ethos. Ever since Dan Tolkowsky's tenure, the Israelis had been evolving a home-grown combat doctrine of their own; as in the case of Tal and the Armour Corps, the tactical ideas of the I.A.F. were in flat contradiction to the consensus of expert opinion abroad. Among modern air forces, the I.A.F. was virtually unique in not accepting the fashionable 'missile theory' of air combat. With the introduction of homing (radar and infra-red) missiles, most aviation experts agreed that guns were obsolete for air-to-air combat owing to the high speed of modern jet fighters, which allowed little or no time to see and hit the target when both hunter and quarry were manoeuvring at speed. The Mirage IIIC, like its American and British counterparts, was originally developed with no guns at all; its air-combat weaponry was to be a single air-to-air missile. Even for air-to-ground strikes its main weapon was meant to be a missile (the A.S.30).

Ezer Weizman and his colleagues in the I.A.F. were almost alone in insisting that aircraft guns were not only essential for ground strikes but also still very efficient in air combat – and of course, infinitely cheaper. In the course of its many realistic exercises, the I.A.F. had established that even supersonic fighters would not engage each other at supersonic speeds, since human pilots could not see their targets and guide their aircraft against them at very high speeds. This implied that most air duels would still be dogfights fought out at short ranges, and not remote-control engagements with each side firing its one or two missiles from several miles away. The Israelis therefore insisted that their Mirages should be equipped with a pair of 30mm guns as well as missile gear. It was not easy for the young commanders of a very small air force such as the I.A.F. to stick to their own ideas in opposition to the weight of expert opinion. The French insisted that dogfights and guns were hopelessly out of date. They were not only Israel's sole suppliers of aircraft but also genuinely sympathetic – and they

* Though Hawk anti-aircraft missiles were also deployed.

tried very hard to persuade the Israelis to listen to reason and accept the missile theory.*

Their belief in the continued value of aircraft guns was tied to another unfashionable opinion held by the commanders of the I.A.F. Modern air forces† no longer trained their pilots to fight primarily in old-fashioned air duels. The new fighter tactics were based on formations of missile-armed fighters stacked in a vertical phalanx, and it was thought that speed mattered more than agility since any manoeuvring would be done by the missile. Israeli tactics were entirely different: fighter-pilots were taught missile tactics, but their training stressed classic dogfighting at slow speeds and close firing ranges. The standard formation was a pair of fighters acting in tandem. It was not until 1967 that the I.A.F. was vindicated.

In the meantime, its tactical concepts did wonders for the morale of I.A.F. pilots who were taught individual combat in the manner of 'medieval knights' (in the phrase current among them), instead of soulless and – as it turned out – ineffectual push-button warfare.[29] I.A.F. fighter-pilots were convinced that their own success or failure would have a decisive impact on the outcome of a war. High morale is not easy to sustain during years of endless training, and the sense of personal responsibility of the fighter-pilots was thus an especially valuable asset, and one that derived primarily from the I.A.F.'s small size. To be a Mirage pilot out of a force of seventy odd necessarily meant more than to be a pilot in an air force with thousands of fighters – where what any single man or squadron does, or fails to do, can have little impact on the outcome of a war.

* Ezer Weizman has left a touching description of what the experience was like:

'I once spent a whole day with them [French aviation experts] in Paris. They were trying to persuade me that we should have a more sophisticated piece of equipment – and of course a more complicated and more expensive one. I wanted something simpler. But then I was seized by doubts. All these experts with a world reputation were saying 'A' and I, a callow young man from Israel, was saying 'B'. I went back to my hotel but I could not sleep all night. In the morning I went back and said: 'Gentlemen, I insist on "B".'

† The only significant exception was the carrier air force of the U.S. Navy which trained its C.A.P. fighters to fight in pairs.

The pilot training programme developed by the I.A.F. is sophisticated and rather original. The full course lasts for twenty months, divided into five phases; potential pilots are quickly taught to fly Piper light aircraft in the first stage of training, though the nine hours on Pipers are regarded more as a practical selection test than an actual teaching course.[30] I.A.F. training methods differ from those of most other air forces since trainee pilots are given a comprehensive (and superficial) education in mathematics, physics, meteorology, aeronautics, electronics, navigation and weaponry in the second stage. This as against the university (or academy) education required elsewhere; the I.A.F. gets its recruits straight from school and they learn their applied science in the first stage of training. This is considered preferable to the 'black box' method used by other air forces in which aircrew operate equipment whose inner workings they are not required to understand.

As well as book learning, the second stage stresses physical training and endurance. Potential pilots are sent to take the para-troop jump course, and go on long marches. Demands on the physical resistance of recruits are extreme, and a large percentage of trainees drop out at this stage. General and acrobatic flying are taught in stage three; after having found it easy to fly in stage one, with no demands made on them and very simple aircraft, trainees now have to learn precision flying with jet trainers. Again the failure rate is high. By the fourth stage, training concentrates on basic day and night flying and a final selection of potential combat pilots is made. Pilots are trained for combat in stage five, while serving in a training squadron which eventually becomes a fully operational regular after prolonged air-to-air and air-to-ground exercises in eighty-three flight periods.

In the U.S., three-quarters of all pilot trainees complete the flight course, in Egypt and France more than half do so, but in Israel the failure rate is of the order of ninety per cent in spite of sophisticated preliminary testing. The results of this extreme selectivity were demonstrated in the June War: in actual air combat (i.e. dogfights) the score was sixty to three; as for the precision of ground attacks, press photographs of scores of Egyptian air-craft, each destroyed with a few cannonshells, tell their own story.

Army and Society

By the mid-sixties, the Armour Corps with its rigid discipline, the Air Force with its technological preoccupation and the paratroopers with their straightforward fighting spirit had developed in divergent paths. Both in the individual appearance of the men and in the social climate that prevailed within their units, it was almost as if paratroopers, armour troopers and airmen were members of different armies. Guided by the personal vision of men like Sharon, Tal and Weizman each corps had followed its own line of evolution, and had grown apart in the process. The Chiefs of Staff of the sixties, Laskov (1958–60), Zur ('60–'63) and Rabin ('63–'67) did not neglect the lesser branches; the Artillery, Engineers and other support corps* had also kept up with the modernization of the Army, becoming steadily more specialized. Only the Navy was marking time. Having at last found a remedy for the problem of scale in its totally new missile-firing boats, it had to wait for their delivery until after the 1967 War.

As the main combat branches grew more specialized, the Army lost the uniformity it once had. In Yadin's time the Army had been essentially an infantry force with small air, naval and armour adjuncts but by the mid-sixties the latter had become the major fighting forces while the infantry was relegated to the background. Yadin had tried to stimulate the growth of a distinctive Army-wide *esprit de corps* but by the sixties the different branches had become so diverse as social groups that the Army could only derive its cohesion from the solidarity of common citizenship. This would have been a weak foundation on which to build in Yadin's time. Israeli society with its immigrant masses was then very fragmented, but by the time Rabin became Chief of Staff in 1963, the post-1948 immigrants had become Israelis and the Army had acquired a natural base of solidarity without having to create one artificially.

Resting on the cohesion of Israeli society as a whole, the Army

---

* Under the Quartermaster branch (A.G.A.): General Service, Supply and Transport, Ordnance, Engineer and Signal Corps; under the Manpower branch: the Judge Advocate branch, The Rabbinate, Women's, Military Police, Education and Medical Corps; G.S. Commands: Military Intelligence and the Nahal. (See Appendix I below.)

could hardly become a 'segregated' social group with its own out-look and values; nor could its career officers become a caste apart, as some had hoped and others feared. (Even attempts to form officers' clubs had failed; except for the occasional lecture, the clubs stood empty.) Given this, the reserve system could not mili-tarize civilian society; instead it was the other way round and it was military life that was pervaded by civilian influences. With reservists serving at every level of command and in every branch of the Army, with regulars anticipating a civilian career after retirement in middle age, an exclusively military sub-society did not develop.

In the reserve formations, the atmosphere remained resolutely civilian in the midst of all the trappings of military life. As the same group of men came together for their annual stint of reserve duty year after year, a kind of relaxed *esprit de corps* often de-veloped among them. Orders were given and obeyed in the spirit of men who had a job to do and meant to do it, but the hierarchy of rank was of small importance, especially since it often cut across sharp differences in age and social status. Cases of university professors who serve under the command of their students, or clerks who carry higher ranks than their bosses, are commonplace and so no longer attract attention. Reserve officers are proud of their rank status *vis-à-vis* their families and friends, but among their fellow-reservists it usually gives them little or no status advantage.

This is not to say that the reserve system has no impact on civilian society. The professor acquires respect for his student, the boss for his high-ranking clerk. Reservists living and working together in uncomfortable and sometimes dangerous conditions tend to develop a group solidarity of their own; every Israeli has his friends 'from the reserves' with whom he might not otherwise have any kind of social contact. Sleeping in bare huts or tents, eat-ing dull Army food, often going without a shower for days, reser-vists of widely different social backgrounds meet on an equal footing; Israel is still a society with fewer class differences than most, and the reserve system has contributed to keeping it that way.

Another consequence of the reserve system is that military expertise is not confined to the professional military. With a population still under three million, Israel has been compared to the city-states of classical Greece. In one respect the comparison is particularly apt. As studies have shown, Israelis have a strong feeling of participation in the affairs of the state in the specific sense that a high proportion of the population believe that its own individual action makes a perceptible difference to the nation's public life. Ironically, it is only the best informed, and especially the academics, who feel, as people do in the larger societies of the West, that whatever they may do as individuals will fail to influence society at large. This feeling of participation, and the related interest in detailed information about affairs of state, is particularly evident with respect to military matters. While press censorship is so strict that even an otherwise alert and critical press can publish little more than official releases on most military questions (unless the news has previously been published abroad), information circulates quite freely in informal channels.

A small society like Israel is not simply a large society writ small but *qualitatively* different; one difference is in the way that information flows from person to person. Since friends made at successive stages in life, high school, university, army service or profession do not simply 'drop out of sight' as they do in the spatially more extended, and socially fragmented, societies of the West, the average Israeli, as statistical studies have shown, has a wider and professionally more varied circle of friends than his counterpart in the United States, Britain or France. At the elite level, academics, businessmen, civil servants and Army officers tend to belong to the same intermingled social groups rather than watertight professional circles. At the Friday-evening gatherings that are a fixed point in Israeli social life, military matters are discussed over coffee and cakes with professional expertise, and with little regard for security restrictions. (While cases of espionage by agents-in-place have occurred, normal, innocent leakages are rare since few Israelis will speak freely to strangers and certainly not to foreign diplomats, journalists or visitors.)

The country has lived with war and censorship since 1948; in the absence of these personal channels of information, Israelis would remain ignorant of military issues that are of urgent concern to all in a society where every family has its soldiers, and where a crisis can affect the survival of all.

When fully mobilized, the Army is a nation-in-arms in the most literal sense: virtually every able-bodied male and many women too are enrolled in either the conscript or reserve forces. In its Israeli setting, the concept actually has a double meaning: the Army is not only a mass citizen force, but also the principal agent in the transformation of variegated immigrant groups into a nation. Many immigrants learn Hebrew and the ways of the country during their army service but, more fundamentally, the Army is the major unifying agent in a country where distinct immigrant groups have very few common customs and values. The religious and the agnostic, the Western and the Eastern, kibbutznik and the slum-dweller have a common framework in the Army whose importance, and whose demands, they all have to recognize.

Even if Israel faced no immediate military threat, the Army would still be of central importance in the nation's consciousness since it embodies the revolutionary change that has transformed the Jewish people from persecuted minority to self-reliant nation in a single generation. The significance of the Jewish past in the Israeli present is not confined to memories of persecution. Traditional Jewish political attitudes are, for example, manifest in the instinctive rejection of the ethos of militarism by a people which is now more militarized than virtually any other in the world. The core of militarism as an ideology is the belief that war is a positive phenomenon in itself rather than a necessary evil of statecraft. Whether it takes a personal form, in stressing the intrinsic value of death in the pursuit of national or religious aggrandizement (as with the Spanish Falangists or in Islam), or a sociological form as with the Nazi belief that war is an indispensable crucible of racial superiority, the militaristic ethos provides an incentive to go to war. That militarism in any form has few adherents in Israel is best shown by the prevailing attitude to the casualties of war. Instead of the glorification typical of militaristic beliefs, there is only a deep sense of anguish which in a provincial society of extended families carries far and wide. Even after twenty years of readiness for war, the Prime Minister is informed immediately of every single casualty, day or night. President Nasser himself is reported to have said that a country where the photograph and biography of every dead soldier is published on the front page of the daily press would never be able to sustain his 'War of Attrition', the Egyptian artillery offensive of 1969–70.

In the Army, the influence of anti-militaristic attitudes is apparent in the absence of the resplendent uniforms and martial posturings that are so common in countries at war. Israeli officers do not even have dress uniforms, only combat khaki. More important, from the General Staff downwards, the level of tolerance for the casualties of war is very low; a small number of deaths have been known to trigger a reconsideration of basic strategy, as when the I.A.F. was ordered to launch the air offensive of 1969 which involved major diplomatic costs – in order to reduce front-line deaths on the Suez Canal caused by Egyptian artillery barrages.

Morally sound though they may be, such attitudes are a military handicap. If the perceptible concern for the life of every private soldier does wonders for their morale, it also restricts the scope of military operations. Soldiers know that they will not be exposed to risks unless there are compelling reasons of national security for doing so; they also know that, if wounded, they will not be abandoned and that every effort will be made to rescue them; this, and the knowledge that they are fighting for the survival of their own families, can generate a formidable fighting spirit. On the other hand, when the Cabinet and the General Staff examine the range of military options in any given situation, major political gains may be sacrificed for the sake of avoiding a handful of additional casualties.

Military operations may evoke strong press criticism even when eminently successful, if the human cost is thought to be too high: the Karameh raid of March 1968, in which twenty-eight Israelis were killed (as against 150 Fatah men) was widely criticized in the daily press as far too costly. A 1969 raid mounted by frogmen-commandos against Green Island in the Gulf of Suez achieved a major tactical objective,* but six of the frogmen were killed and some press commentators argued that the cost of the raid outweighed its undoubted strategic benefits (the destruction of the southern hinge of the Egyptian radar network).

Most of the soldiers and officials who make operational decisions share these attitudes. The reported comment of the Minister

* See p. 319 below.

of Defence, Moshe Dayan, on the Green Island raid was characteristically bitter and poetic:

> All night we stood on the shores of the Red Sea waiting for their return. At sunrise, they came out of the water bearing the *prize* of victory on their backs. [the bodies of the dead][32]

As for the enemy's casualties, attitudes have changed a great deal since the days when the leaders of the Haganah preached that weapons were to be used strictly in self-defence and that 'innocent Arabs' should not be hurt during the conduct of operations. Nevertheless, high ethical restraints remain evident: captured terrorists are imprisoned but not executed; allegations of torture are widely disbelieved by all neutral parties and have never been pressed with any conviction by the Arabs themselves. In the 1967 War, tens of thousands of fleeing Egyptians in Sinai were allowed to return to Egypt unmolested; no serious attempt was made to kill Egyptian soldiers once their combat formations had collapsed. In the 1973 War, this extreme sensitivity to casualties was clearly the major cause of the failure to achieve a complete victory over the Egyptian army. For the fear of losing an additional few hundred dead, the Israelis sacrificed a military victory of major proportions.

A tragic incident that occurred during the Sinai Campaign (though far from the front) raised for the Israelis in an acute form a basic ethical issue that affects all armies. Forty-three farmworkers from the Israeli Arab village of Kafr Kassem were shot by men of the Border Police for having violated the curfew proclaimed at the onset of the campaign. When the officers and soldiers* involved were tried in a military court, the soldiers denied responsibility claiming that they were acting under orders. The court disallowed this defence, holding that a soldier is duty-bound to disobey any 'manifestly unlawful' order; the soldiers were sentenced to prison terms of up to fifteen years, as was the officer in charge, a major.

In his verdict the presiding Army judge pointed out that the regional commander, a Col. Shadmi, should also have been tried. The Colonel was duly brought to trial but it was ascertained that

---

* Border Police are considered as soldiers from the juridical point of view.

he had given no order to execute curfew-breakers. At the briefing attended by the convicted Major he had answered a question on how curfew-breakers were to be punished with a vague aside, *Allah Yarchamu*, an Arab idiom equivalent to 'God will receive his soul'. Col. Shadmi was found guilty of negligence for having used ambiguous language in giving a military order, and fined one agora (i.e. the smallest coin of the realm).

The Kafr Kassem trial resulted in an important legal precedent: a soldier has a positive duty to interfere with the execution of a 'manifestly unlawful' order. The verdict referred to, and extended, Article 125 of the Israeli Code of Military Law of 1955 which laid down the principle that a soldier is guilty of no disobedience if it is manifest that an order given to him is unlawful. In interpreting the term 'manifest' the judges of the military court maintained that the unlawfulness of an order reveals itself through the deeds it commands, which 'strike the eye and move the heart . . . if the eye is not blind and the heart is not numb and corrupt'.[33]

7

War: 1967

In the spring of 1967, the danger of war seemed remote. The strongest power on the Arab side, Nasser's Egypt, was already at war in the distant Yemen; Jordan and Lebanon were ruled by realistic and moderate regimes acutely aware of their military weakness. In Israel, Ben Gurion had finally resigned from the Government in 1963, and his successor as Prime Minister and Minister of Defence, Levi Eshkol, was disposed towards conciliation. Only Syria remained in an acutely militant phase; Syrian troops entrenched on the dominating heights of the Golan frequently shelled Israeli farm villages on the plains below (thirty incidents in 1964) and, from 1965 onwards, Syrian military intelligence sponsored the Fatah guerrillas who crossed the armistice lines to plant mines and attack civilians in border areas. Nevertheless, Syrian calls for an immediate war against Israel were not taken seriously by either Arabs or Jews.

Misgoverned by transient regimes of rival officer cliques, Syria had lost all credibility as a military power. In February 1966 the seventeenth coup since independence brought to power a stridently militant left-wing junta that soon established very close ties with Moscow. The new leadership stepped up war propaganda but continued to keep border incidents and Fatah activities at a low threshold of violence, in order to avert massive Israeli retaliation. For the same reason, Fatah guerrillas operated mainly from Jordanian and Lebanese soil though trained, paid and controlled from Damascus. Their attacks were only pinpricks, but Israeli civilians were being killed and public opinion demanded a response. Reluctant to inflame the conflict and deterred by loud Soviet support for the new men in Damascus, the Eshkol government hesitated to retaliate against Syria. On 13 November 1966, the Israeli Army finally went into action but, instead of punishing Syria, the reprisal was inflicted on Jordan, on whose territory Fatah guerrillas operated against the will of the Jordanian government.[1]

Israeli troops riding in half-track carriers and supported by a detachment of light tanks crossed the armistice line in broad daylight, entered the township of Samua and demolished forty houses. Very different from the paratroop night attacks of the fifties, the Samua raid was marked by the detailed planning and precise execution that Chief of Staff Rabin had striven to perfect. The soldiers were calm and deliberate, they identified the houses marked for destruction, carefully cleared out each building and set their demolition charges. In the meantime, Arab-speaking soldiers with loudspeakers led the inhabitants to a safe assembly area without using violence. Everything was going according to plan when a battalion of Jordanian infantry riding on trucks drove straight into the fire of a group of Israeli AMX light tanks guarding the approaches to Samua. The tanks opened fire, their shells tore into the crowded trucks and fifteen Jordanian soldiers were killed before the convoy retreated. The Israelis made no attempt to pursue or destroy the Jordanian force, but the damage was done: the raid was to have been bloodless. More important, by failing to attack the real culprits, the Israelis encouraged the Syrians to believe that, so long as they had the might of Russia behind them, they could attack Israel with impunity.

Bolstered by a new defence treaty with Egypt, the Syrians continued their campaign of trans-border shelling and terrorism by proxy. Harried by accusations of timidity and inaction, the Eshkol government was forced to respond. On 7 April 1967 when the Syrians once again opened fire on the border villages in upper Galilee, Israeli fighter-bombers went into action against their guns entrenched on the Golan foothills. Escalation was immediate. The Syrians sent MiG-21 fighters to intercept the fighter-bombers, but Israeli Mirages pursued and shot down six MiG-21s. From the panic of the unpopular rulers in Damascus, to a fabricated invasion scare and the publicized movement of Egyptian troops into Sinai, the drift to war was relentless.*

In their strategic planning, the Israelis had long since decided

---

* The May crisis that led to the June 1967 War has been described and interpreted in a number of scholarly accounts.[2]

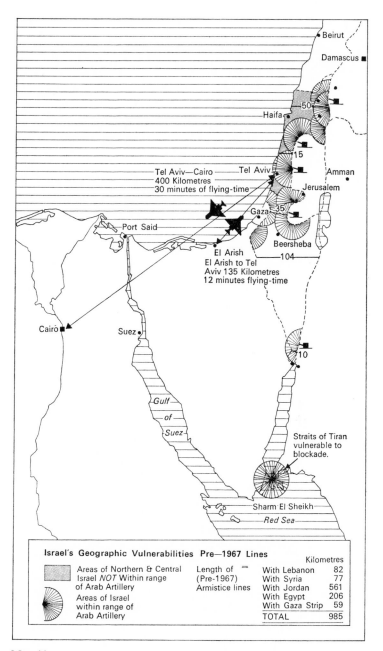

Beirut
Damascus ■

Haifa —50

—15

Tel Aviv—Cairo
400 Kilometres
30 minutes of flying-time

Tel Aviv ■
Amman

Jerusalem

Gaza —35

Port Said

Beersheba

El Arish
—104

El Arish to Tel
Aviv 135 Kilometres
12 minutes flying-time

Cairo ■
Suez ●

—10

Gulf
of
Suez

Straits of Tiran
vulnerable to
blockade.

Sharm El Sheikh
Red Sea

Israel's Geographic Vulnerabilities Pre—1967 Lines

		Kilometres
Areas of Northern & Central Israel *NOT* Within range of Arab Artillery	Length of ═ (Pre-1967) Armistice lines	With Lebanon 82
		With Syria 77
Areas of Israel within range of Arab Artillery		With Jordan 561
		With Egypt 206
		With Gaza Strip 59
		TOTAL 985

Map 11

their enemy was Egypt. The possibility of having to fight simultaneously on the Jordanian and Syrian fronts was also taken into consideration, but a three-front war was thought unlikely.

On all three fronts, the balance of forces and the geographic setting made it impossible for the Israelis to follow a defensive strategy if the enemy was intent on all-out war. As between Israel and Egypt there was a basic assymetry in the structure of forces: the Egyptians could deploy at any time their large army of long-term regulars on the Israeli border and keep it there indefinitely; the Israelis could only counter their deployment by mobilizing reserve formations, and reservists could not be kept in uniform for very long. In the event of a competitive build-up of forces, Egypt could therefore stay on the defensive while Israel would have to attack unless the crisis was defused diplomatically.

On the Jordanian front, an offensive strategy was imposed by geographic considerations alone. With a penetration of only ten miles Jordanian forces could cut the long coastal strip north of Tel Aviv. Between the border and the sea the terrain is flat, and the armistice line left Israel with no fall-back depth to speak of. Without advancing at all, Jordanian artillery could shell Jerusalem, the suburbs of Tel Aviv, at least two important airfields and the country's main highways. If the Jordanians shelled any of these targets, Israeli planners assumed that an offensive would be required to dislodge the guns, even if there was no real danger of a Jordanian invasion. Under the terms of the 1949 armistice agreements, a small enclave on Mount Scopus in east Jerusalem was left in Israeli hands; garrisoned by a small force rotated monthly under U.N. escort to guard the empty buildings of the Hebrew University, the enclave was surrounded by Jordanian territory and was thus very vulnerable. In the event of a Jordanian attack, Israeli plans called for a localized breakthrough across north Jerusalem to link Mount Scopus with the rest of Jewish Jerusalem.

Syria, like Jordan, presented no real threat to Israel's 'basic' security, but the Israelis were forced to plan offensively owing to the topography of the border. The Syrians held the high ground, the Golan Heights, directly above Israeli towns and villages in the Hula Valley and around the Sea of Galilee and they had built a chain of strongholds and artillery fire-bases on the Heights. The Israelis expected that in the event of a general war the Syrians would use their artillery to the full, even if not risking an advance. The only answer was to launch an offensive to seize the border ridge.

The Israelis did not expect war in 1967, and when war came it caught the Army in the midst of several major re-equipment programmes.[3] But there are no delivery time-lags in the sphere of intelligence and tactics, and here the Israelis were well prepared. Egyptian tactics had been subjected to close scrutiny, and the ground forces were ready with their counter-tactics. Through the influence of Russian equipment and training, the Egyptians had absorbed Russian tactics and methods. The Israelis were naturally anxious to learn as much as possible about Russian tactics but the Russian army had not fought since 1945 and it was difficult to visualize their methods in action. One of those directly responsible for finding an answer was Gen. Yeshayahu Gavish, head of the Training Command between 1962 and 1965. In line with the principle of rotation. Gavish was appointed C.O. Southern Command in 1965, thus going from training and tactical research to a combat assignment on the main Egyptian front; in 1967 it fell to the forces under his command to implement on the battlefield the theoretical solutions he had done so much to devise.

Gavish and his colleagues stopped at nothing in their efforts to understand Russian tactics: they analysed the voluminous Western and Russian literature on the subject, interviewed Israelis who had served in the Russian army, and even read Russian war novels hoping to glean some useful information. In an interview given three years after the war, Gavish summarised Russian tactics as follows:*

In defence, the principle is to enclose the defended area by continuous [fortified lines] deployed in depth all along the front; a brigade, for example, will deploy two battalions in front, keeping the third in the rear. This deployment requires a great deal of fire-power and a lot of armour . . . To deploy such lines, very considerable forces are needed. This is what the Russians do. They deployed hundreds [sic] of divisions in Stalingrad and Leningrad.

According to Gavish Russian methods were not suited to the Middle East where the troops would be much thinner on the ground:

* This account is based on the text of a press interview granted by Gavish on the eve of his retirement from the Army in 1970.[4]

We always doubted the ability of the Egyptians to deploy continuous [fortified] lines across Sinai since it would have required much larger forces than they had.

On the offensive, Gavish said that Russian tactics were

to surprise the enemy by concentrating large forces [which] break through wave after wave by using vast volumes of fire focused on a narrow sector [of the front]. According to this doctrine, it is essential to keep open the breakthrough point even at the expense of great loss of life, then to advance through it in order to encircle the enemy forces and destroy them.

Sound tactics must be rooted in the specifics of the situation, the ratio of forces, the strengths and weaknesses of each side and the terrain. In copying Russian tactics the Egyptians had made an obvious blunder:

We soon spotted the first weakness: the need for very large forces to defend the system of long fortified lines . . . For any chosen point of attack there would only be relatively small forces since the [Egyptian] troops would be spread very thinly . . . If a battalion is holding a line ten kilometres long, there will only be about thirty soldiers holding any one point of attack.

In other words, if the Israelis attacked on a narrow frontage they would easily gain an overwhelming local superiority. Most interesting is the account given by Gavish of how the Israelis evolved their counter-tactics:

First of all [in discussions] within the Training Command and then in wider groups where dozens of people participated, each of whom suggested this or that solution . . . We examined [rival] theories and conducted a series of exercises . . . We constructed a Russian-style deployment on a large scale and then attacked it. I remember that it was difficult to dig such extensive fortifications and sometimes we merely marked the defence lines on the ground with heavy oil . . . Officers learned [in these manoeuvres] how to control the forces in combat . . . The soldiers learned how to fight in [Russian-style] trench lines and how to move from the first trench-line to the next.

Even more than on other fronts, the Israeli offensive in Sinai relied on the shock effect of the tank battalions. The Israelis have never published the number of tanks deployed by the Armour Corps in 1967 (or for that matter on any other date), but according to estimates reproduced in the world press, the Israelis had far fewer tanks than their antagonists: 250 Centurions, 200 Patton M.48s, 200 modified Shermans with new guns and engines and 150 obsolescent AMX-13 light tanks;[5] these 800 tanks were reportedly organized into eight armoured brigades (all but one reserve formations), each presumably with two fifty-tank battalions and a third battalion of infantry. Other equally reliable estimates indicate that there were more than 800 tanks and eleven armoured brigades.[6] In fact, not all the tanks were grouped into armoured brigades; there were at least two 'mechanized' brigades with a single tank battalion (to two of infantry), and a few dozen tanks were also detached to support some infantry brigades.

Repeating a process that had taken place long before in more affluent armies, the tank battalions had become the dominant element of the ground forces but the infantry, paratroops and mechanized infantry (supervised by the Armour Corps) were still more numerous. The troop carrier of the mechanized infantry was still the ancient M.3 half-track; fitted with one heavy and one light machine-gun, each carried ten or twelve men. One mechanized battalion, about a thousand strong, was included in each armoured brigade (alongside two tank battalions) in the usual triangular pattern; other mechanized battalions served in pairs with a single tank battalion to form mechanized brigades. Since the M.3 was the only armoured carrier the Israelis had, it was also used by reconnaissance detachments as a weapon carrier (for mortars and anti-tank missiles) and as a mobile command post. Open-topped and protected only by thin (10mm) vertical armour, the M.3. was no vehicle to use in the thick of battle, but the Israelis had nothing better and had grown used to its shortcomings.

In 1956 much of the infantry had gone to war with single-shot rifles of 1898 design vintage,* but by 1967 most first-line troops were at least equipped with a modern self-loading rifle (the Belgian FN firing 7·62mm rounds). Israeli-made submachine-guns

---

* The Mauser 98/37, known in Israel as the 'Chehi' since they were originally bought from Czechoslovakia in 1948; in 1967 Chehis still equipped second-line troops (including some that were given first-line tasks). By 1967 they had all been rebored for the smaller 7·62mm N.A.T.O. cartridge on which the Israelis had standardized.

(the 9mm Uzi) were also widely issued, as in all poorer armies. Mortars, machine-guns and light anti-tank weapons were available in fair numbers, but expensive weapons, such as anti-tank missiles (manned by the artillery), were in short supply.

No longer a small unit of hand-picked volunteers, the paratroops were now fielded by the brigade. Wartime reports refer to at least three paratroop brigades. Trained infantry conscripts served in the Golani Brigade of the standing forces; a second-rate unit during the fifties, the Golani had improved beyond recognition during the sixties. Night assaults against fortified positions had been monopolized by the paratroops but, in 1960, for the first time, the Commander of Golani managed to persuade the General Staff to assign a night attack on a Syrian stronghold (Tawafik) to his unit – not without employing some sleight of hand in the process.* The troops sent into action by Golani did well, and by the mid-sixties the brigade was regarded as almost interchangeable with the paratroops. As for the reserve infantry brigades, whose troops included men between twenty and forty, recent immigrants and veteran settlers, the well trained and those who had only a basic course behind them, their standards of skill and morale varied enormously. The Jerusalem Brigade, a multi-battalion force larger than any other, was confined to static defence duties; as against this, at least one brigade was thought good enough for the most exacting of assault tasks.†

Again, there are no official figures for the number of infantry brigades deployed in 1967 and estimates vary.‡

* When the raid was being planned, the Golani C.O., Col. (later Gen.) Elad Peled, was summoned to the General Staff together with the O.C. Paratroops, Col. (later Maj.-Gen.) Rafael Eytan. Both were asked how long it would take to ready their forces for action; Peled waited until Eytan had answered and then underbid him by twenty-four hours.[7]

† See p. 247 below.

‡ The London-based Institute for Strategic Studies (I.S.S.) estimated a grand total of thirty-one brigades, of which eight armoured, one paratroop and twenty-two infantry; Nadav Safran in his book *From War to War* estimated a total of twenty-four to twenty-six brigades of which eleven armoured, four paratroop and nine to eleven infantry, as well as fourteen brigade-equivalents of local defence troops.[8] Safran's figures are generally thought to be much more accurate than those of the I.S.S.

Table 1
Unofficial Estimates of Israeli Troop Deployments in 1967

Total strength of Israeli Defence Forces	I.S.S. Press Release 6 June 1967	N. Safran *From War to War*
Troops strength (fully mobilized)	275,000	275–300,000
of which:		
1 Ground force total	no estimate	250–265,000
2 Conscripts and career professionals of the standing forces	no estimate	71,000
Total number of brigades	31	24–26
Local defence units	no estimate	Equivalent of 14 brigades (i.e. 70,000 men)
Ground forces by brigade types:		
Armoured (3,500 men each)	8	11
Paratroops (4,500 men each)	1	4
Infantry (4,500 men each)	22	9–11

In 1967 the artillery was the only branch of the Army in which several senior officers, including the commanding officer, were foreign-born. Starting with a handful of old field guns and a cadre of ex-Red Army gunners in 1948, the progress of the artillery had been smooth. Unlike the Armour Corps, whose original Russian-trained personnel was replaced as soon as the war was over, the immigrant gunners remained in command right up to 1967 and beyond; highly respected for their professional competence, they formed a group apart, with little lateral movement into other branches. The artillery was always recognized as dependable and technically proficient; its problem was that in a movement-oriented Army the value of heavy indirect fire from static positions had been underestimated. It was not until the Sinai battles of 1967 that the gunners were finally given an opportunity to show what they could do.

In the meantime, the artillery did not receive a high priority, and its equipment was mostly antiquated: cheap, Israeli-made heavy mortars (120mm and 160mm), towed or mounted on ubi-quitous M.3 half-tracks and a mass of old towed weapons of British origin (twenty-five pounders and some anti-tank eighteen pound-ers). The only modern self-propelled weapons were 155mm howitzers mounted on an Israeli-converted Sherman tank chassis and French-made 105mm howitzers (AMX-105). Both were grossly outranged by the Russian field guns of the Egyptians, but both were mobile and during the 1967 War they usually managed to come within shooting range of their targets without hindrance. The lack of long-range guns ('rifles') did not make itself felt until well after the 1967 War, when the War of Attrition (1969–71) taught the Israelis the virtues of heavy artillery in a static contest for fire superiority.

The nightmare of every defence planner is that war will come at a time of transition when plans and tasks have moved ahead of the equipment in hand. The War of 1967 caught the I.A.F. on the eve of a major re-equipment programme. With its main battle plan based on an all-out strike against enemy airpower on the ground, it needed more aircraft with substantial payloads than Israel could possibly afford, but forty-eight Skyhawk A-4H attack bombers and fifty Mirage 5 strike-fighters were on order and this could have solved half the problem. Between them, these ninety-eight aircraft could deliver up to 400 tons of bombs, rockets and cannon shells per sortie, as much as all the first-line aircraft the I.A.F. already had. Both the Skyhawks and the new Mirages should have been operational by the end of 1967; in the event, the Skyhawks did not reach Israel until several months after the war, and the Mirage 5s were never delivered owing to a French embargo. This accident of timing drastically reduced the planned strike capability of the I.A.F.; its achievements on 5 June 1967 should be seen in this perspective. According to the Institute for Strategic Studies, on that date the I.A.F. had a total of 197 combat aircraft: seventy-two Mirage IIICs, twenty Super-Mystères, forty subsonic Mystère IVs, forty obsolescent Ouragans and twenty-five Vautour IIs light bombers.*[9]

Except for the one squadron of Vautours, none of the I.A.F.

---

* The Israelis also used the Fouga-Magister jet trainer for close-support fitted out with rocket racks for tank-busting; it lacked the range, speed and payload required for strike missions against airfields.

fighters was really suitable for the low-level strike mission*
and their combined weaponload per sortie was quite small. In
spite of this severe handicap, the commanders of the I.A.F. were
confident that the pre-emptive strike could be carried out as
planned. As far as air combat was concerned, the Mirage squadrons were at a peak of preparedness and ready to take on anything that came their way. In a contest for superiority over the
battlefields, the fast 'turn around' (as little as seven to ten minutes)[10] for refuelling, re-arming, briefing and checking, would
magnify the effective strength of the I.A.F. as compared to the
slower Arab air forces; this, and the difference in pilot quality, was
expected to offset the Arabs' four-to-one superiority in the number
of combat aircraft.

The Israelis enjoyed a very special advantage in their thorough
knowledge of the MiG-21, the first-line fighter of the Egyptian,
Iraqi and Syrian air forces. In August 1966, the operational arm of
Israeli civilian intelligence carried off a major coup: an Iraqi
fighter-pilot was persuaded to fly his MiG-21 to an Israeli airfield.
(His family had been smuggled out to Israel some days earlier.)
After the 1967 War, the MiG-21 was exhibited under I.A.F.
markings with a 007 number code, as an oblique acknowledgement
of how it had been obtained. The basic performance details of this
widely used aircraft were already known from normal observation
but the Israelis had the priceless advantage of actually flying the
aircraft in mock battles against Mirages so as to discover its weak
points.

As we have seen, Israeli strategy and tactics were not meant to
be of general applicability; they were conceived in direct response
to the geographic setting and the specific nature of Arab military
forces. A 'relational' approach, such as this, is of course more
vulnerable to errors in intelligence assessments than more conservative strategies which insure against failure. A bold move
aimed with surgical precision at the enemy's weak points can
bring victory at little cost, but it can also fail disastrously if the
points of attack turn out to be much stronger than expected.
Cautious non-relational strategies and tactics, planned with wide
margins of safety all round, will not yield spectacular results since

* Flying low to avoid detection, fuel consumption is at a maximum and
the net weapon payload is sharply reduced.

forces cannot be concentrated to the same degree, but if they fail, they will at least fail 'gracefully': the safety margins which reduce the net gains also reduce the risks. The fact that the Israelis were consistently relational is an indication of their unusual reliance on intelligence. Only the gambler with inside information can rationally bet his whole stake on a single race.

Partly as a result of its presumed role in the 1967 War, Israeli Intelligence enjoys a world-wide reputation. There is no doubt that during the sixties Israeli military Intelligence developed sound analytical methods and applied sophisticated computer-assisted data-handling techniques. Headed by Aharon Ya'ariv (who by 1972 had served for a record-breaking eight years at his post), military Intelligence, like its civilian counterpart, relied on all the usual collection techniques: analysis of publications and broadcasts, photographic recce, communications and electronic intelligence, radio-traffic analysis, and even classic espionage.

Neither its modest budget nor its run-of-the-mill techniques can explain the undoubted effectiveness of Israeli military intelligence. The real explanation is probably its discipline and concentration of purpose. Intelligence organizations more than other bureaucracies tend to suffer from a proclivity to self-serving growth, and a corresponding diffusion of purpose. Their special status, and the screen of official secrecy, often breed these common bureaucratic diseases in an unusually acute form. Israeli intelligence seems to have retained its main target, the Arab world, in sharp focus and did not squander its manpower and budget on futile attempts to attain a world-wide coverage (unlike Egyptian intelligence, which was apparently working as far afield as Latin America and Western Europe). Israeli military intelligence was also spared the heavy burdens of the totally different internal security function,* which apparently preoccupied its Egyptian counterpart to the detriment of its external duties. (None of these virtues helped in 1973 when Israeli Intelligence was faced with the intractable problem of providing warning in a zero-warning situation. See pp. 339–41 below.)

* Except for the Army's Field Security, all security functions are performed in Israel by the civilian police (Special Branch) and the (civilian) Security Service.

1967: The Decision

The diplomatic crisis of May 1967 which ranged a widening circle
of Arab states, supported by the Soviet bloc, against an increasingly isolated Israel, also triggered a major domestic political crisis
within the Jewish State. In successive moves, the Egyptians massed
their troops in Sinai, expelled the U.N. Emergency Force, insti-
tuted a blockade of the Straits of Tiran and threatened a war of
annihilation while the Israeli government did nothing beyond
ordering a partial mobilization and appealing for international
action. As the confrontation escalated towards war, international
pressures and inter-party controversies were subsumed in a crisis
of confidence centred on the person of Levi Eshkol, Prime Minister
and Minister of Defence. An able consensus politician of the older
generation (he was then seventy-two), Eshkol was not an inspiring
figure and lacked the outward qualities of a war leader. As the
crisis heated up his personal qualifications as Minister of Defence
were challenged by the leaders of opposition parties, an increasingly wide segment of the press, and finally even by Eshkol's
colleagues in his own Mapai party.

At this time of supreme crisis the senior members of the officer
corps emerged as a key political pressure group. After some initial
hesitations, the generals agreed that war was inevitable and that
Israel had to strike before the Egyptians did so. This was one of
those rare occasions in which the military were agreed among themselves on what was essentially a political issue; normally their
politics are far from uniform, and lack the cohesion needed to make
an effective pressure group. In the weeks of extreme tension that
preceded the war, the generals applied their concerted influence on
the Cabinet in order to secure an early decision in favour of war. In
spite of their prestige – and the disarray of the civil power – their
intervention failed to decide the issue: Israel only went to war when
the politicians were persuaded by reasons that had little to do with
the essentially tactical considerations which preoccupied the
General Staff. The generals' demand for a pre-emptive attack
derived from their prudent assessment of the Arab threat – and
especially the vulnerability of the Air Force concentrated as it was
on a small number of virtually unprotected airbases.*

* Hardening an airbase costs about 200,000 dollars per aircraft and very
few I.A.F. aircraft were sheltered in bomb-proof underground hangars.

The Egyptian air force had a total of 385 combat aircraft; flying time from its forward airfields in Sinai to the main Israeli bases was between seven and fifteen minutes, i.e. not enough time for interception. The smaller air forces of Jordan, Iraq and Syria were less of a threat, but they did muster another 200 combat aircraft technically capable of attacking targets in Israel. On the ground, the magnitude of the threat depended on the degree of Arab participation; all Arab states declared war but not all sent troops. In the direct proximity of Israel's borders there were a total of 240,000 Arab troops, armed with at least 1,700 battle tanks and 1,300 guns, mortars and howitzers.[11] Beyond these forces, which were deployed in areas directly adjacent to Israel, there were the armies of other Arab states and the Egyptian contingent in the Yemen; given time, these forces could have doubled the effective strength of the Arabs.

The immediate threat on land was the Egyptian army in Sinai already deployed at its battle stations: approximately 100,000 combat troops supported by 900 battle tanks, 200 assault guns and 900 field guns, heavy mortars and howitzers.[12] The Egyptians apparently did not contemplate an all-out attack (their prime objective was political and could have been achieved without war), but they did plan a localized offensive across the Negev to cut off the southern Negev and seize Eilat.[13] The Syrians for their part were making ready to seize Galilee, but would only move after the Israelis had already been defeated by the Egyptians in the south. In the centre a joint Jordanian–Iraqi offensive could not be totally discounted, though it was most unlikely that their armies would go over to the offensive before the Egyptians did so successfully.

Table 2
Arab Military Capabilities on 5 June 1967[14] (collated estimates)
Air Power (Operational Combat Aircraft Only)

	Egypt	Syria	Iraq	Jordan
Mach 2 first-line fighters (MiG–21s)	125	36	48	None
Other supersonic Aircraft (MiG 19s/Su–7s)	80	—	12	None
Subsonic fighter-bombers (various)	110	40	80	21
Light bombers (Il–28s)	40	—	10	None
Medium bombers (Tu–16s)	30	None	6	None

Ground Forces (Operational and Deployed Only)

	Egypt	Syria	Iraq	Jordan
Combat and first-line support troops	100,000	65,000	20,000	55,000
Battle (and medium) tanks with guns of 75 mm and above	900	300	200	300
Other armoured vehicles mounting guns (except A.A. guns)	200	50	N.A.	30+
Artillery weapons (excluding infantry mortars and light anti-aircraft guns)	900	300	N.A.	100

On the basis of these ominous figures, the General Staff argued that further delay would expose Israel to an Egyptian pre-emptive strike, which would deprive her forces of all the advantages of tactical surprise, increase the casualty toll and cause serious damage to the I.A.F. As against these military considerations, there were sound political reasons for waiting until all diplomatic action had been exhausted. Few Israelis believed that the U.N., or the Great Powers acting outside it, would resolve the crisis peacefully, but many thought it worth going through all the diplomatic rigmaroles in order to secure American acceptance for an eventual Israeli offensive.[15] The General Staff and the entire officer corps were naturally far more impressed with the urgency of the military situation than with such diplomatic calcuations, but they failed to convince the Cabinet through two weeks of rising tension.

As always in Israeli politics, the deciding factor was the stand taken by the parties in the coalition Government, and especially Mapai. It was not until Mapai's partners threatened to leave the coalition that Eshkol finally agreed to relinquish the Defence portfolio. In the meantime, rival groups pressed the candidacy of two distinguished ex-soldiers, Yigal Allon and Moshe Dayan.

By the end of May 1967 the inevitability of war was no longer debatable. The ultimate reason for going to war was that, even if the United States could lift the blockade of the Straits of Tiran and secure an Egyptian withdrawal from Sinai, the crisis would remain unsolved since the credibility of the Israeli Army as a deterrent would have been fatally impaired. In other words a diplomatic solution would merely encourage the Arabs to renew their challenge to Israel's survival at the first suitable opportunity.

The May crisis was not only a political affair of portfolios and party rivalries. When the Egyptians moved their troops into Sinai the Israelis were already demoralized by a deep economic recession, the worst since 1948. Unemployment figures stood at an all-time high and confidence in Israel's future was undermined by an unprecedented emigration of thousands of young and better-educated Israelis. When the Egyptians expelled the U.N. force, Israelis waited for their own government to act; the closure of the Tiran straits had repeatedly been stated to be a *casus belli* but Nasser's challenge had gone unanswered. Eshkol's statements were not only conciliatory but also conveyed an impression of fumbling indecisiveness. Word got out that the Cabinet was split and unable to act. While the Arabs were proclaiming the imminence of a war of extermination, the Foreign Minister, Abba Eban, was travelling back and forth in a humiliating quest for help from Washington, London or Paris. Once the Army mobilized the reservists, only children, old men and women were left at home, and the streets of the cities were deserted. Graves for thousands of dead were dug in the cemeteries while schoolchildren were clearing out air raid shelters and digging slit trenches in parks and alongside roadways.

As the Arab build-up continued, intense fear spread in the country. Arab radios and T.V. stations, which had a wide audience in Israel, portrayed the Arabs as confident in victory while Western media relayed the common estimate that war would result in tens of thousands of dead for Israel. Meanwhile the Israeli failure to react forcefully to Nasser's spectacular coup was widely seen as evidence that not only the Cabinet but also the Army feared the consequences of war. There was talk of Russian secret weapons in Egypt, and the certain knowledge that the Egyptian air force had already used bombs filled with nerve gas in the Yemen. In the third week of May, panic-stricken housewives raided food shops, buying up their entire stock. Government announcements that there were ample reserves were disbelieved. By then even the well-informed began to doubt whether Zahal could stand up to the Arab armies. Dispersed and camouflaged, its forces and weapons blanketed by strict censorship, the Israeli Army projected no vivid images of power, as the Egyptians did with their endlessly repeated television films of thousands of vehicles advancing in Sinai. Israel had no television station but many Israelis had sets, and many watched – and believed – Arab stations. Finally, on 30 May 1967 Eshkol gave up the Defence portfolio, though he remained Prime Minister. Allon had already withdrawn his candidacy, and Dayan became Minister of Defence. His first public act established his political position for years to come. Addressing a conference for the world press which hundreds of thousands of Israelis followed on the radio, Dayan's obvious confidence, his relaxed tone and straightforward statements, made a sharp contrast to Eshkol's hesitant and circuitous phrases. With great skill, Dayan managed to convey the impression that war was not imminent, successfully deceiving the Arabs on this score, while at the same time reassuring Israeli opinion that the crisis would be solved to Israel's advantage whether in peace or by war. Asked what would happen if the Egyptians used bombardment rockets and nerve-gas bombs, he answered: 'Let them try.' Asked whether war was imminent, he said that there was still room for a diplomatic solution. It was a magnificent performance.

On Saturday 3 June newspapers around the world published news-agency photographs of Israeli soldiers on leave relaxing on the beaches with their families. Experts asserted that Israel would get along without the port of Eilat, and that war had been averted. By then the decision had already been made.

1967: War

On the morning of 5 June 1967 Israel answered the Egyptian challenge with an all-out offensive in Sinai and a devastating preemptive strike against the Egyptian air force. At 7.45 a.m. (Israeli time) the first wave of Israeli fighters struck at nine Egyptian airfields. Ten minutes after the double pair of aircraft in the first wave completed their bombing runs against each airfield, a second wave came over the target and after another ten-minute interval, a third. By 10.50 a.m. the General Staff was informed by Air Force Headquarters that the backbone of the Egyptian air force, the MiG-21 squadrons, no longer existed as operational forces. Four Egyptian airfields in Sinai (El Arish, As Sirr, Bir Gafgafa and Bir Thamad) were included in the first wave of the attack because of their proximity, although only second-line MiG-17 fighter-bombers were deployed there, but the main targets were three air bases near the Canal (Abu Suwayr, Fayid and Kabrit) and two in the Nile valley (Inshas and Cairo West) which contained most of the MiG-21 squadrons.

In each case the attack followed the same sequence. First, the runways were put out of action with delayed-action bombs. The Israelis modified standard 'iron' bombs with a retro-firing rocket device to stop them in mid-air and added a second set of rockets to accelerate their vertical dive to impact. (This to prevent the payload wastage caused by the slithering of ordinary bombs on concrete, a common occurrence with dive-bombing.) Next the same fighters went on to attack aircraft on or near the runways. Following a strict priority list, supersonic fighters were attacked first, other combat aircraft second and transports last. Bombs were reserved for runways and hangars; aircraft out in the open were mostly attacked with cannon and rockets.*

Following the initial strike, the air combat potential of the Egyptian air force had virtually been eliminated, but eight Egyptian airbases remained intact and, with them, the Egyptian bomber force. Between 8.15 a.m. and 12.30 p.m. the bomber force was totally destroyed in the second phase of the air strike.

8.15 a.m.	Bani Suwayf	Tu–16s
10.00 a.m.	Mansura	(mixed)
10.00 a.m.	Helwan	(mixed)
10.00 a.m.	Al Mazza	(mixed)
10.15 a.m.	Minya	(mixed)
12.00 a.m.	Bilbays	(mixed)
12.15 p.m.	Ghardaka	MiG–19s and MiG–21s
12.30 p.m.	Luxor	Tu–16s

While these airfields were still under attack, Iraq, Jordan and Syria responded to Egyptian claims that much of the I.A.F. had already been destroyed by sending a few bombers and fighter-bombers to attack targets in Israel. The bombing seemed to have no pattern or purpose; bombs landed on a seaside resort and a

---

* In spite of reports to the contrary, no air-to-ground missiles were used. The photos released by the I.A.F. did show rows of MiG–21s each apparently hit in the exact centre of the fuselage, but this was due to the accuracy with which the cannon shells were aimed at the fuselage fuel tanks.

village, but only one Israeli airfield was attacked – and a single transport aircraft destroyed. Between 12.45 p.m. and 3.45 p.m., two Jordanian, five Syrian and one Iraqi airbase were attacked by the Israelis. Except for the Iraqi air force (most of whose aircraft were *hors de combat* at remote airfields), this one-wave strike was sufficient to eliminate Arab airpower on the 'Eastern Front'.

12.45 p.m.	Amman (Jordan)	(mixed)
1.00 p.m.	Mafraq (Jordan)	Hunter squadron
1.00 p.m.	Damascus (Syria)	(mixed)
1.15 p.m.	Sayqal (Syria)	MiG–21s
1.15 p.m.	Dumayr (Syria)	MiG–21s
1.15 p.m.	Marj Riyal (Syria)	MiG–17s and MiG–21s
3.00 p.m.	H–3 (Iraq)	MiG–21s
3.45 p.m.	T–4 (Syria)	MiG–21s

In the afternoon of the same day, the Egyptians transferred their last operational aircraft to Cairo International, a large civilian airport used by many foreign airlines, and to a remote dispersal airfield at Ras Banas on the Red Sea coast. Between 5.15 and 6 p.m. these last two Egyptian airfields were attacked and put out of action.

In their air strike of 5 June, the Israelis did not follow the standard tactic of attacking early-warning radar first – in order to 'blind' the air defences. Most of the twenty-three radar stations in the Egyptian network were not attacked until the *afternoon* of 5 June, when the decisive phase of the air strike was already over. According to unconfirmed press reports, the Israelis did not have to destroy Egyptian warning radars sooner since they had already been neutralized by means of Electronic-Countermeasures (E.C.M.).[16]

What is certain is that Israeli pilots evaded Egyptian radar by flying below the 'radar horizon' which limits the low-level detection capability of most radar sets. This tactic is more or less radar-proof but it also reduces the range/payload. There has been no confirmation from any official source of the use of jamming or deceptive E.C.M. techniques against the radar network. Another explanation for the delay in attacking the radars is that they were not sited or used effectively; in that case the best tactic is indeed to ignore warning radars, since a preliminary strike *does* give a clear warning of an impending attack.

Another standard tactic ignored by the Israelis is to time air strikes just after dawn, when enemy anti-aircraft gunners are still adjusting to daylight. The Israelis struck at 8.45 a.m. (Cairo time), when A.A. gunners had long since adjusted to daylight. Brig.-Gen. Modechai Hod, Commander of the I.A.F. (1966–73), later explained the timing of the air strike as follows:

> The Egyptian state of alert was past its peak. It was safe to assume that the Egyptians . . . had several flights of MiG–21s waiting at the end of the runway on five-minute alert at dawn every morning. . . . When no attack had materialized within two or three hours after dawn, the Egyptians would more than likely have lessened their alert and switched off some of their radar scanners.[17] Egyptians get to their offices at 9 a.m. Striking fifteen minutes before that time would catch . . . air force commanders on their way to their offices, and pilots on their way to training courses.[18]

Short of aircraft, the I.A.F. multiplied the number of sorties carried out by each plane: according to well-informed accounts, Israeli fighters could be refuelled, re-armed and their pilots briefed for a new set of targets in seven to ten minutes. Assuming a two-way flight time of some fifty minutes, this meant that Israeli fighters attacking the complex of Egyptian airfields near the Suez Canal could be over their target for a second attack within an hour of their first strike. By spacing the waves of incoming aircraft, Egyptian airbases could thus be kept under continuous attack by the same group of aircraft which turned around to attack again and again. That this was achieved points to a ground turn-around rate much higher than most air forces ordinarily expect to achieve. Once over the target Israeli pilots made three or four low passes before releasing their weapons, ignored anti-aircraft fire and flew as slowly as possible to achieve maximum accuracy. (Some aircraft were seen flying with the landing-gear lowered in order to reduce the approach speed after diving to attack.)[19] Another economy measure applied by Israeli pilots also helped to make small payloads go a long way; they used the smallest practicable weapon against each target – cannon shells instead of rockets to attack aircraft on the ground, and rockets instead of bombs to attack 'soft' hangars.

Good intelligence could ensure that the initial wave of the air strike would be planned efficiently but, after that, it was up to the operational control officers to redirect attacking aircraft against the highest priority targets as yet undestroyed. With the target picture changing all the time as returning pilots reported kills (and attack films were developed), this meant making complex decisions in a minute or two as each follow-up strike was sent against a fresh set of targets. Apart from the physical problems of debriefing pilots, developing and scanning films, collating the information and briefing outgoing pilots in the course of a few minutes, there were delicate choices to be made: if one MiG-21 (a priority one target) remained undestroyed at a given air base, committing a sortie to it could mean that *two* MiG-19s (second-priority targets) at another air base would remain undestroyed in that wave of the attack. Since undestroyed aircraft could fly away to safety, or attack the next wave of incoming I.A.F. fighters, the exact priority assigned at any one time to each target was of critical importance.

The combined effect of these factors determined the outcome of the 5 June air strike. In the first day of the war, the Egyptians lost 122 supersonic fighters, seventy-five subsonic fighters, twenty-seven light bombers, thirty Tu-16 medium bombers (the entire force) and thirty-two transports and helicopters.[20] However certain the outcome may have appeared in retrospect, the virtually total commitment of I.A.F. aircraft to the 5 June strike involved grave risks. According to one report, only twelve Super-Mystère fighters were retained for air defence when the first wave of the attack was launched.[21] If the Egyptians had received any kind of advance warning, e.g. from Russian radar picket ships, they could have dispersed their second-line aircraft and met the heavily loaded I.A.F. fighters with MiG-21 interceptors. In that case, the Israelis could have lost their slower aircraft (Ouragans, Mystères, Vautours) in air combat; the Egyptians could then have sent their bombers and fighter-bombers to attack Israeli airfields. Most of the 452 Arab aircraft destroyed during the war (see Table 3) were hit on the ground, but there were also many air battles; the score was reportedly sixty to three in favour of Israel.[22] Israeli losses during the first two days of the war were twenty-six aircraft of all types; of these, nineteen were lost on the first day.[23] Total Israeli losses during the war amounted to forty-six aircraft, all but three lost to ground fire.

Table 3

Aircraft Combat Losses by Type and Country (5 June – 10 June 1967)[24]

	Egypt	Syria	Iraq	Jordan	Lebanon	Total
Fighters						
MiG–21	100	33	15	—	—	148
MiG–19	29	—	—	—	—	29
MiG–15/17	89	23	—	—	—	112
Sukhoi–7	14	—	—	—	—	14
Hawker Hunter	—	—	5	21	1	27
Bombers						
Tu–16	30	—	1	—	—	31
Il–28	29	2	—	—	—	31
Transports						
Il–14/Dakota	24	—	2	6	—	32
An–12	8	—	—	—	—	8
Unidentified	4	—	—	—	—	4
Helicopters						
Light (Mil–4)	1	3	—	2	—	6
Heavy (Mil–6)	10	—	—	—	—	10
Grand Total						452

Superiority in the air undoubtedly eased the Israeli victory on the ground; without it, the outcome would almost certainly have been the same, but Israeli casualties could have been much higher. Air superiority means that *all* serviceable aircraft can be put to use, including those which cannot survive in air combat; obsolete fighter-bombers, transports and armed trainers could be sent on their missions without fearing enemy interceptors, and without requiring first-line fighters for top cover. Israeli forces on the ground could advance in compact convoys without having to fear air attack, while I.A.F. fighter-bombers attacked the Arab troops on the battlefield and cut their line of retreat in depth. I.A.F. aircraft flew several thousand sorties during the few days that each front was active in turn. By bombing and strafing in close support, airpower helped the Israeli advance and sometimes bailed out troops on the ground, as in the battle of the Dotan Valley on the Jordanian front.[25]

On the other hand, the most important ground battle of the war, the breakthrough on the Rafah/El Arish axis which cracked the Egyptian front wide open, was fought and won by the Israelis during the first hours of the war when they had little air support.

1967: The Egyptian Front

The 5 June air strike was based on a fixed operational plan worked out long before, but the strategy of the ground forces and even the very nature of their objectives remained undefined until the very eve of the war. The original plan envisaged by the Israeli Cabinet called for a limited offensive to conquer Gaza and northern Sinai. The intention was to use these territories as bargaining counters to induce the Egyptians to re-open the Straits of Tiran and withdraw their forces from Sinai. This 'minimalist' plan did not satisfy Moshe Dayan, appointed Minister of Defence on 1 June 1967.

Like some others in the Cabinet, Dayan thought it imperative to destroy the Egyptian army in Sinai rather than bargain for its withdrawal since, in his view, only this would restore the credibility of the Israeli Army after the political indecision of the May crisis. Besides, Dayan feared that if the Israelis took northern Sinai, the Egyptians were liable to say (in his words): 'Keep Gaza with its 400,000 Arabs, choke on them. We will keep the Straits closed.' Brig.-Gen. Yeshayahu Gavish, O.C. Southern Command and *ex officio* commander of all ground forces on the Egyptian front, has described how the final plan was chosen:

It was on the day of Dayan's appointment or the day after. I was notified by the Chief of Staff to come and present the operation plan of the Southern Command. I was then told by Yitzhah Rabin [Chief of Staff] that after he had approved the plan, Moshe Dayan would come and I would have to present the plan to him as well. I told him that on the previous evening I had made an assessment of the situation and that I had a plan which differed from the limited one i.e. the plan for the conquests of Gaza and northern Sinai.

Rabin told Gavish that he should stick to the limited plan.

I told him [Rabin] that I would bring along the wider plan too, and he agreed to this. At 7 p.m. I presented the two plans and then the Minister of Defence [Dayan] entered. He asked Rabin: 'Chief of Staff, have you a plan, present it.' The Chief of Staff instructed me to

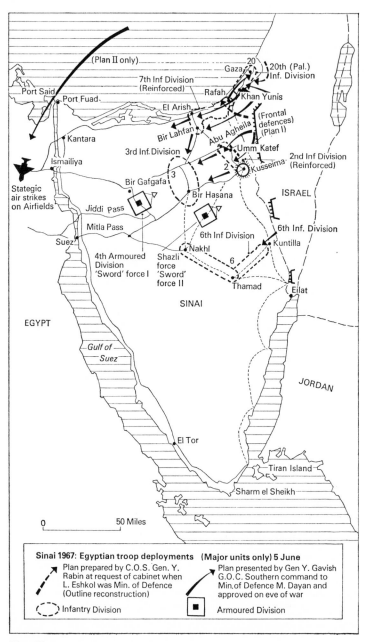

(Plan II only)

Port Said

Port Fuad

7th Inf Division
(Reinforced)

Rafah

Khan Yunis

Gaza

20

20th (Pal.)
Inf. Division

El Arish

(Frontal
defences)
(Plan I)

Kantara

Bir Lahfan

Abu Agheila

Umm Katef

2nd Inf Division
(Reinforced)

Ismailiya

3rd Inf. Division

3

2

Kusseima

ISRAEL

Stategic
air strikes
on Airfields

Bir Gafgafa

Bir Hasana

Jiddi Pass

Mitla Pass

6th Inf Division

6th Inf. Division

Suez

Nakhl

Kuntilla

4th Armoured
Division
'Sword' force I

Shazli
force
'Sword'
force II

6

EGYPT

Thamad

Eilat

SINAI

Gulf of
Suez

JORDAN

El Tor

Tiran Island

Sharm el Sheikh

0   50 Miles

Sinai 1967: Egyptian troop deployments   (Major units only) 5 June

Plan prepared by C.O.S. Gen. Y.
Rabin at request of cabinet when
L. Eshkol was Min. of Defence
(Outline reconstruction)

Plan presented by Gen Y. Gavish
G.O.C. Southern command to
Min.of Defence M. Dayan and
approved on eve of war

Infantry Division

Armoured Division

Map 12

present the plan. I asked him: 'Which of the two?' Rabin answered: 'The second' [i.e. the full-scale plan]. I presented the wider plan.[26]

The plan that Gavish presented and Dayan approved envisaged a full-scale offensive on the two major routes across Sinai, with secondary offensives against the Gaza Strip and points further south. Three divisional task forces were to cross the armistice line simultaneously (at 8.15 a.m. on 5 June), but only the northern division, commanded by Brig.-Gen. Israel Tal, O.C. Armour Corps, was to press on to attack the main enemy force just across the border, the Egyptian 7th Division entrenched in depth along the Rafah/El Arish axis. Its task was to break through the Rafah fortifications and reach El Arish so as to unhinge the northern end of the Egyptian front. The central and smallest division, with only two reserve armoured brigades under the command of Brig.-Gen. Avraham Yoffe, himself a reservist, was to penetrate the difficult desert terrain of north-east Sinai in order to cut the roads leading to El Arish. Its first objective was to ambush Egyptian forces moving up to counter-attack Tal's forces. Except for a few outposts, the route taken by Yoffe's forces was undefended, since the Egyptians thought that the terrain was impassable for heavy vehicles. The third division, commanded by Brig.-Gen. Ariel Sharon, the grand master of the paratroopers, now on the General Staff, was to envelop the Egyptian fortified perimeter astride the central Sinai route at the Abu Agheila/Umm Katef crossroads.

Advancing during the first day, Sharon's troops were only to launch their assault after nightfall in order to unbalance the Egyptian command, until then preoccupied with the northern sector of the front. The Abu Agheila/Umm Katef positions had held up the Israeli advance for three days during the 1956 Sinai Campaign; in the campaign post-mortems the Israelis attributed the failure to the fact that their forces were committed in battle in dribs and drabs. In 1967, Sharon's plan envisaged a concerted night attack by infantry, armour and heli-borne paratroopers supported by the largest concentration of artillery ever assembled in battle by the Israeli Army.[27] All three divisions were to advance across Sinai to engage and defeat the rest of the Egyptian army after stage one, but no firm plan had been formulated for the second phase of the offensive.[28]

The Egyptians followed a Russian-style 'sword and shield'

strategy in which the 'shield' forces, entrenched in fortified perimeters, were to stop the Israeli advance while the 'sword' forces moved up to counter-attack. Three divisions of infantry* supported by almost 100 tanks apiece and several regiments of field artillery held separate shield positions in depth along the main Sinai routes.[29] Two additional infantry divisions† guarded their flanks. In accordance with Russian doctrine, each shield was stretched out to the point where its flanks were covered by neighbouring forces or by 'impassable' terrain. The sword forces consisted of the 4th Armoured Division and a mechanized task force of divisional size, the 'Shazli Force', named after its commander, who was to become Chief of Staff of the Egyptian army in 1973. There were gaps between the shields, as in the north-east where Yoffe's forces were to drive through, but in each case the Egyptians were satisfied that major formations could not cross the difficult desert terrain left undefended. (Along the Rafah/El Arish axis, the Israelis tried and failed to cross the sand dunes on the southern flank.)

According to Russian tactical doctrine – and Egyptian expectations – the three shields were to stop the Israelis, or at least slow their advance, while the two sword forces, the 4th Armoured Division and the Shazli Force,‡ moved up to launch their counter-attack once the Israeli offensive had spent itself against the minefields and fortifications of the shields.

Viewed in abstract terms, the Egyptian plan was sound. Advancing Israeli forces would be decimated by the long-range fire of the artillery regiments covering the approaches to each shield; 'soft' infantry units (and the road-bound supply columns) would thus be

* The 7th Division deployed in multiple fortified lines along the Rafah/ El Arish axis, the 2nd Division in a fortified 'hedgehog' around the Abu Agheila/Umm Katef crossroads, and the 6th Division deployed in depth along the southernmost Kuntilla/Nakhl axis.

† The 20th Palestinian in the Gaza Strip on the northern flank of the 7th Division, and the 3rd Division deployed between Jebel Libni and Bir Hasane in the rear of the 2nd.

‡ The 4th Armoured Division was an elite unit manned by the flower of the Egyptian officer corps. As well as the full establishment of a Russian tank division, with more than 300 battle tanks, it had some additional infantry and artillery detachments. The three-brigade Shazli Force included an elite commando brigade, a tank brigade and an artillery brigade.

The Russian-Style 'Sword & Defence' Shield

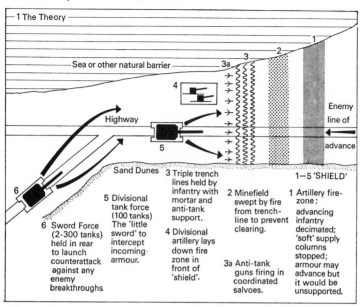

1 The Theory

Sea or other natural barrier

Highway

Enemy line of advance

Sand Dunes

1—5 'SHIELD'

6 Sword Force (2-300 tanks) held in rear to launch counterattack against any enemy breakthroughs.

5 Divisional tank force (100 tanks) The 'little sword' to intercept incoming armour.

3 Triple trench lines held by infantry with mortar and anti-tank support.

4 Divisional artillery lays down fire zone in front of 'shield'.

2 Minefield swept by fire from trench-line to prevent clearing.

3a Anti-tank guns firing in coordinated salvoes.

1 Artillery fire-zone: advancing infantry decimated; 'soft' supply columns stopped; armour may advance but it would be unsupported.

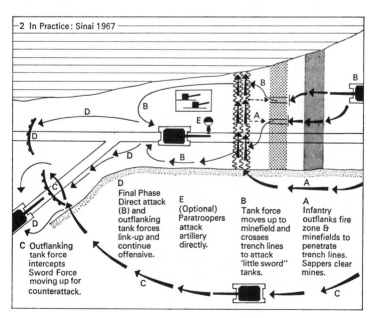

2 In Practice: Sinai 1967

D Final Phase Direct attack (B) and outflanking tank forces link-up and continue offensive.

E (Optional) Paratroopers attack artillery directly.

B Tank force moves up to minefield and crosses trench lines to attack 'little sword'' tanks.

A Infantry outflanks fire zone & minefields to penetrate trench lines. Sappers clear mines.

C Outflanking tank force intercepts Sword Force moving up for counterattack.

Fig. 4

mauled even before coming into sight of their objective. If Israeli armour continued to advance on its own it would meet the extensive minefields covering the front of the shield, and if Israeli sappers tried to clear a path through the minefields, they would come under automatic and mortar fire from Egyptian troops entrenched at the far end of the minefields.

Covered in turn by two more trench lines behind them, the Egyptian troops guarding the minefields could call down artillery fire from the main perimeter. With Israeli infantry held at bay by the fire from the trenches, the sappers would not be able to clear the minefield and the tanks could not get through; if the tanks entered the minefield all the same, they would be met by the coordinated fire from dozens of anti-tank guns.

If the Israelis overcame all these barriers and achieved a breakthrough somewhere along the trench line, they would be met by the tank and assault gun battalions attached to each Egyptian division which provided each shield with a small sword of its own. Finally, even if large formations of Israeli tanks could blast their way through minefields and artillery barrages, the 'soft' infantry and supply columns could not. As a result, these tanks would be stranded on the far side of the shields, where they would rapidly run out of fuel and ammunition. At this point, the fresh armoured units of the main Egyptian sword forces would move up for the kill.

In the first phase of the offensive, the Israeli plan dove-tailed perversely with the Egyptian, and within twenty-four hours the entire 'sword and shield' defence had collapsed. The strongest of the three Israeli formations, Tal's division with two crack tank battalions in the lead, penetrated into the northern axis through Khan Yunis in the Gaza Strip and reached the edge of the Rafah shield in less than two hours. Instead of being held up, floundering in the minefields under the direct fire of anti-tank guns, in less than ten hours its first tank battalion broke right through the Egyptian shield, reaching El Arish by the late afternoon. The Egyptians recovered and closed the road behind the advanced battalion, but by midnight the multiple barriers of the northern shield had collapsed so that supply convoys could drive through to join the tanks.[30]

The Egyptian sword duly moved up to launch its counter-attack but the advance columns of the Egyptian 4th Armoured Division were ambushed by a tank brigade of Yoffe's division which had crossed the 'impassable' gap between the two shields to cut the road up to El Arish.[31] On the central axis, the Egyptian shield at the Abu Agheila/Umm Katef crossroads was crushed by Sharon's forces in a night-long battle and the sword (the Shazli Force) did not even try to counter-attack.[32] By then Egyptian communications had been cut; it was dawn on the second day of the war and the Egyptian army was beginning to disintegrate.

Table 4
Israeli Order of Battle and Major Operations: June 1967 Egyptian Front

(Source: Authors' collation)	
G.H.Q.	Chief of Staff: Maj.-Gen.* Yitzhak Rabin Deputy Chief of Staff: Brig.-Gen. Haim Bar Lev
Southern Command	General Officer Commanding: Brig.-Gen. Yeshayahu Gavish
Northern ugdah (division)	**Operations**
G.O.C. Brig.-Gen. Israel Tal 7th Armoured Brigade. Col. S. Gonen (with 1 Patton batt., 1 Centurion batt., 1 mech. inf. batt.) 'M' Armoured Brigade. Col. M. Aviram (with 1 Sherman batt., 1 AMX–13 batt., 1 mech. inf. batt.) 'R' Force: 2 paratroop battalions. Col. R. Eytan (equipped with half-tracks supported by 1 Patton batt.)	*Day one* (*5 June*) Advance through Khan Yunis to Rafah. Breakthrough at Rafah junction. Advance to El Arish. *Day two* (*6 June*) Battle at Bir Lafhan, advance towards Jebel Libni. Col. Eytan's brigade into Gaza Strip. Reconnaissance detachment moves towards Kantara. *Day three* (*7 June*) Advance towards Bir Gafgafa. Running battles and two-brigade encirclement. Col. Eytan's brigade returns to join advance towards Kantara.

* After the war the rank structure changed with the introduction of the *Tat Aluf* rank between colonel and general ranks. With this, *Tat Aluf* became equivalent to brigadier-general and *Aluf* (held by divisional commanders) became equivalent to major-general. *Rav Aluf* held by the Chief of Staff alone became equivalent to lieutenant-general. Hence Bar Lev, Gavish, Tal, Yoffe and Sharon were all major-generals in post-1967 terms, which Rabin was the only lieutenant-general.

Northern ugdah (division)	**Operations**
1 reconnaissance detachment Divisional artillery (S.P.) Supply and Service units	*Day four* (*8 June*) Advance towards Canal after early morning Egyptian counter-attack. Armour battles on the way. At the Canal by 0030 hours.
Divisional H.Q. and Staff. C.O. Col. Herzel Shafir. Air Support: armed Fouga jet trainers	
Central ugdah (division)	
G.O.C. Brig.-Gen. Avraham Yoffe	*Day one* Col. Shadmi's brigade moves towards Bir Lafhan area. *Night* ambush of Egyptian armoured forces on El Arish road.
'I' Armoured Brigade. Col. I. Shadmi (2 Centurion batt.) 'X' Armoured Brigade. Col. X (removed from command) Centurions Divisional H.Q. and Staff	*Day two* Advance to Jebel Libni, battles on the way.
	Day three Advance to Mitla and Jiddi Passes. Blocking position at Mitla. Destruction of retreating Egyptian forces.
	Day four Advance to the Canal through Mitla and Jiddi Passes. Move down the Red Sea coast.
Southern ugdah (division)	
G.O.C. Brig.-Gen. Ariel Sharon	*Day one* advance around Umm Katef perimeter. Battles against peripheral strongholds. *Night* battle of Umm Katef.
1 infantry brigade. Col. Y 1 armoured brigade. Lt.-Col. M (1 Sherman batt., 1 Centurion batt., 1. mech. inf. batt.)	*Day two* move southwest towards Nakhl.
2 paratroop battalions	*Day three* move towards Nakhl. Col. Y's brigade sent to mop up in El Arish and Gaza Strip.
6 battalions of artillery (155mm SP and 105 SP howitzers, 25 pounders)	*Day four* Ambush of Egyptian 6th Division at Nakhl.
Combat engineers detachment	
Divisional H.Q. and Staff	

Non-divisional operations	
1. Independent armoured brigade	*Day four* advance from Kuntilla towards Nakhl to drive Egyptian forces into Sharon's ambush.
1. Paratroop task force and naval contingent (patrol boats and landing craft)	*Day three* unopposed landing at Sharm el Sheikh; heli-borne task forces occupy points on Red Sea coast
1. Dismounted brigade. Col. Y (with no half-tracks and one AMX–13 batt.). 1 detached paratroop battalion with half-tracks	*Day one* penetration into Gaza Strip. *Day two* seizure of main towns with support of Col. Eytan's paratroop brigade (of Tal's division). *Day three and subsequent* mopping up operations continue for several days. Col. Eytan's brigade returns west. Col. Y's brigade (Sharon's) comes in from El Arish after day three.

Tal's division launched its thrust towards El Arish at 8.15 a.m. on 5 June, with a two-brigade assault against the Egyptian defences at the Rafah junction, the critical hinge position between Sinai and the Gaza Strip. While a battalion of Patton tanks and two battalions of paratroopers riding on half-tracks attacked the Rafah junction from the south, Tal's spearhead force, the crack 7th Armoured Brigade of the standing army under Col. Gonen,* fought its way to the eastern edge of the Rafah shield by way of the Gaza Strip.

The massed Pattons and Centurions of the 7th Brigade overran the thin border defences manned by the 20th Palestinian Division, outfought an Egyptian tank battalion at Khan Yunis and moved south to the Rafah junction without pausing to regroup. This was an all-tank breakthrough which followed Tal's recipe; the brigade's mechanized infantry battalion was left behind in reserve at this stage. The Egyptian shield at the Rafah junction consisted of several defence lines laid out in depth for almost eight miles on

* Later Major-General. The surnames of serving officers below the rank of *Aluf* are normally classified; we shall use first name initials where surnames have not been published. Brigade numbers are also classified; we shall use arbitrary letters in most cases, the 7th being one of the exceptions.

either side of the road; minefields and trench lines were covered by strong artillery forces and manned by two brigades of infantry protected by scores of anti-tank guns concealed in the sand dunes.

When the tanks of the 7th Brigade reached the shield, Egyptian anti-tank gunners started firing, the concentrated salvoes of each battery aimed at a single tank. Also according to plan, Egyptian field artillery pounded the approaches, though armed Fouga trainers attached to Tal's *ugdah* attacked Egyptian guns with their rockets. After suffering a few losses from the guns, the Israeli tank battalions paused and regrouped for a coordinated attack. Here Tal's approach to armoured warfare really paid off: owing to their good tank gunnery, the Israelis could pick off Egyptian anti-tank guns at ranges of 1,000 metres or more, thus inducing the Egyptians to open fire too soon, giving away their positions while the range was still too long to allow their anti-tank shells to penetrate heavily armoured Centurion and Patton tanks.

By noon a local breakthrough was achieved at the junction and the 7th's lead battalion advanced rapidly, penetrating successive Egyptian defence lines to reach El Arish by the late afternoon. The tanks of the lead battalion cut across the Egyptian defence lines but could not clear them of infantry so as to open the road for the rest of the division. Advancing without infantry support, the tanks simply drove at high speed through the elaborate Jiradi defences; these lined both sides of the El Arish road for several miles with high sand dunes on one side and the sea on the other. When the lead battalion drove its tanks at full speed straight down the road, the Egyptians were surprised by its sudden onslaught and scarcely opened fire as the tanks sped past, but they soon recovered from their confusion and returned to their posts. The Jiradi could not be outflanked, and when the second battalion of the 7th Brigade attempted to follow the first, it had to fight its way through, losing more than ten tanks and its commander in the process. Once more the Egyptians recovered and it was not until the mechanized infantry of the 7th Brigade was moved forward to mop up the Jiradi defences that the supply convoys could finally drive through to reach El Arish. After the 1967 War the fighting at Jiradi was cited as evidence that Tal had erred in preaching his 'all-tank' doctrines.

'R' Brigade, under the command of Col. (later Maj.-Gen.)

1. *(Above)* Russian Jews become eastern warriors: members of Hashomer in 1907.
2. A platoon of the Palmach on the march (the picture is posed: Palmach men rarely had such neat uniforms). Pre-1948.

3. *(Opposite above)* The Battle of the Roads: a home-made armoured car with a road-block ram on the Jerusalem road, May 21, 1948.

4. *(Opposite below)* Immigrant soldiers at rifle practice. Immigrants were rarely sent into battle straight off the boats; when this happened, casualties were heavy and results meagre.

5. *(Above left)* Yigal Allon in 1948. Second and last commander of the Palmach, Allon was the outstanding field commander of the Independence war.

6. Yitzhak Sadeh, founder of the Palmach and the teacher of Israel's first modern soldiers.

7. *(Above left)* Chief of Staff 1949–52, Yigal Yadin had already served as *de facto* Chief of Staff for much of the 1947–9 war.

8. *(Above right)* Chief of Staff 1952–53, Mordechai Makleff served as Chief of Staff for only one year.

9. *(Below left)* Chief of Staff 1953–58, Moshe Dayan was the controversial and successful reformer of the Army of the 1950s.

10. Chief of Staff 1958–60, Haim Laskov was the leading theoretician and planner of the post-Independence Army.

11. *(Above left)* Zvi Zsur, Chief of Staff 1960–63.
12. *(Above right)* Chief of Staff 1963–67, Yitzhak Rabin was the architect of the modern mechanized Army of the 1960s.
13. *(Below left)* Chief of Staff 1968–71, Haim Bar Lev led the Army during the War of Attrition (and supervised its post-1967 reorganization).
14. Chief of Staff 1972–74, David Elazar's reputation suffered from the early reverses of the 1973 war.

15. *(Opposite above)* Commander of the I.A.F. 1953–58, Dan Tolkowsky originated the concept of an all-fighter air force with an original doctrine of its
own.

16. *(Opposite below)* Israel Tal was the great innovator of the Armour Corps.
His methods were very successful in 1967 but they were largely invalidated
in the 1973 war.

17. *(Above left)* The paratroopers, old style: Captain Harari ready to jump.

18. During his long tenure as Chief of the Israeli Air Force 1958–66, Ezer Weizman shaped the Air Force that decided the outcome of the 1967 war.

19. *(Left)* The creator of the Army's paratrooper force, Ariel Sharon was a brilliant and controversial tactician and combat leader in the heroic style.
20. *(Above right)* Chief of the Intelligence Branch 1964–72, Aharon Ya'ariv masterminded the Intelligence success of the 1967 war and retired in time to avoid the failure of 1973.
21. In charge of the Egyptian front in 1967, Yeshayahu Gavish was a cool and resourceful field commander whose talents were sorely missed in 1973.

22. *(Above left)* In charge of the central ugdah on the Sinai front in 1967, Avraham Yoffe was a practitioner of the Indirect Approach both in 1956 and 1967.

23. *(Above right)* A fighting commando soldier in the heroic mould, Rafael Eytan led the paratroop force in the 1967 Rafah battle and revealed far broader command talents as the Golan theatre commander in 1973.

24. Jerusalem 1967: street fighting with tanks. Shermans giving fire-support to the paratroopers on the approaches to the Old City.

25. Reservists checking a border track for mines. The man with the probe has an UZI 9mm sub-machine gun. The support group rides an ancient M.3 half-track.

26. A battalion of Israeli-converted diesel Centurions on exercises, Sinai 1970.

27. *(Above)* Delicate and too light for the job, the Mirage IIIC was turned into a precision strike-fighter by the Israeli Air Force.
28. The artillery became a lead branch during the War of Attrition. A 155mm howitzer mounted on a Sherman chassis.

29. (*Above*) The Navy comes into its own: an Israeli-made Gabriel seaborne anti-ship missile, semi-active homing.

30. The quest for self-sufficiency: a Soltam 155mm self-propelled howitzer made in Israel with a Sherman chassis and an imported gun assembly.

31. *(Above)* An Iraqui anti-aircraft battalion destroyed by IAF air strikes on the approaches to Kuneitra Syrian Front, October 1973.

32. Captured Russian-built Katyusha bombardment rockets in 1973. Neither these nor the conventional guns of the Israelis sufficed to outweigh the superior fire-power of Egyptian artillery.

33. *(Above)* Crossing the Canal, 1973.
34. The grandmaster of the paratroopers and the focus of controversy, Ariel Sharon across the Canal with his men, Egypt 1973.

35. In the hour of crisis Minister of Defence Moshe Dayan faces the ill-fated
G.O.C. Southern Command, Shmuel Gonen: Sinai battle headquarters,
October 1973.

Eytan, was a task force of paratroopers mounted on half-tracks supported by a tank battalion. Tanks and paratroopers lost touch with each other during the advance and fought a confused and bitter battle of piecemeal assaults against the southern half of the Rafah shield. At one stage Col. Eytan and his command group were almost overwhelmed by a local counter-attack; the size of the Egyptian forces in the area had been under-estimated and, since most of the tank contingent went off on its own, the paratroopers were exposed to the counter-attacks of Egyptian armour.[33] It was not until after 7 p.m. that the southern half of the junction defences were cleared; by then the advance battalion of Col. Gonen's brigade had already reached El Arish at the far end of the axis.

Tal's third brigade was a reserve armoured unit equipped with second-line modified Shermans and AMX-13 light tanks under the command of Col. Aviram. According to the divisional plan this 'M' Brigade was to make its way across the sand dunes south of the Rafah-El Arish road; its task was to support the other two brigades by making flank attacks against the southern edge of the Egyptian shield at the appropriate moment. This time Russian tactical doctrine and the reality on the ground were well matched: 'M' Brigade found the terrain virtually impassable; its progress was slow and the supply columns were quite unable to negotiate the sand dunes. When Tal ordered 'M' Brigade to launch a flank attack against the main axis, its tanks and troop carriers failed to get through: the 7th Brigade reached El Arish while 'M' Brigade was still struggling through the sand dunes without having fired a shot.

The capture of El Arish was to have been a combined air–sea–ground operation, with a brigade paradrop and an amphibious landing to bypass the Jiradi defences in advance of the arrival of Tal's tanks. Spearheaded by the 7th Brigade (which fought virtually alone from Rafah onwards), the progress of Tal's division was so rapid that the paradrop and landing were cancelled by mid-morning. Tal had won a clear victory but his was not a neat battle. In the words of a colonel on Tal's staff:[34]

It is hard to find even one commander in Tal's *ugdah* who operated according to plan. Almost all the plans were foiled during the fighting, but all objectives were attained in full – and faster than expected.

Sinai 1967 : The Northern (Rafah-El Arish) Axis.

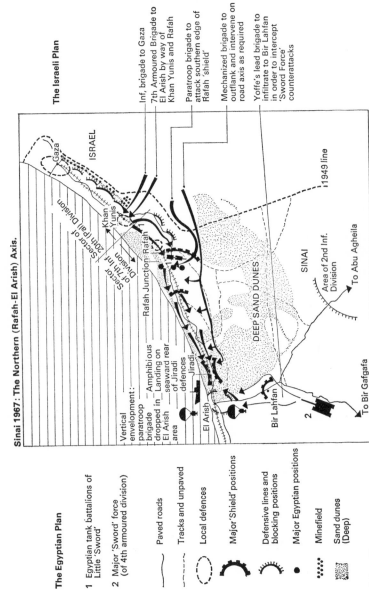

The Egyptian Plan

1 Egyptian tank battalions of Little 'Sword'

2 Major 'Sword' force (of 4th armoured division)

——— Paved roads

- - - Tracks and unpaved

⌒ Local defences

◖ Major 'Shield' positions

⌒⌒⌒ Defensive lines and blocking positions

● Major Egyptian positions

⋮ Minefield

▦ Sand dunes (Deep)

The Israeli Plan

Inf. brigade to Gaza

7th Armoured Brigade to El Arish by way of Khan Yunis and Rafah

Paratroop brigade to attack southern edge of Rafah 'shield'

Mechanized brigade to outflank and intervene on road axis as required

Yoffe's lead brigade to infiltrate to Bir Lahfan in order to intercept 'Sword Force' counterattacks

Map 13

Of the three brigades of Tal's division, the reserve armoured brigade commanded by Col. Aviram saw no fighting at all and spent the first critical day *hors de combat* in the sand dunes; the second, Col. Eytan's paratroop force, lost part of its Patton battalion escort on the way – and its men fought dozens of uncoordinated engagements among the sprawling trench lines and gun positions in the southern half of the Rafah shields. Even Col. Gonen's crack tank force failed to remain concentrated in a solid 'mailed fist' formation; for several hours its lead battalion was cut off beyond Jiradi and in danger of running out of fuel and ammunition. What saved the day was the leadership of unit commanders who never paused to reorganize, or to search for their mother formations. In accordance with Tal's standing orders, they continued to fight and advance towards the divisional objective: El Arish. When Col. Eytan's battalion of Patton tanks lost touch with his mechanized paratroops, neither stopped to find the other; both went on to fight separately. One company of the Patton battalion advanced right across the southern half of the Rafah shield, reached the main road, linked up with a battalion of the 7th Brigade, and spearheaded its second thrust through Jiradi, and all this because of a communications breakdown.

The heroes of the day were the troopers of the 7th Brigade, and especially the tank commanders. With their heads and shoulders exposed above the turret armour (standing orders required it for better vision), they guided their tanks through a curtain of enemy fire, sniping at anti-tank guns, crushing trench lines and fighting tank duels without a break from morning till late at night. Many were killed, including one of the two battalion commanders, decapitated by a shell as his tank led the second assault through the Jiradi defences.

Tal's division reached its stage one objective, El Arish, not in twenty-four hours as planned, but in just over half this time. On the way it defeated ten infantry battalions, five tank battalions and four artillery regiments of the Egyptian army.* Many of these

* Egyptian deployments on the northern axis (Khan Yunis/Rafah/El Arish), 5 June 1967.
Khan Yunis: one (Palestinian) infantry brigade. Rafah town: one (reduced) National Guard brigade. Rafah Junction to Jiradi: 7th Div. H.Q. 16th Mech. Brigade: three motorized battalions, one tank battalion (18 T-34s),

units were badly under-strength (and their tanks were second-line T-34s or Stalin IIIs), but they had the enormous advantage of defending well-protected trench lines with minefields, tank obstacles and wire all around. Tal's division had fought and won – and remained virtually intact; next day at dawn the 7th Brigade resumed its advance.

While Tal's forces had to defeat a whole series of Egyptian defence lines to advance across the forty miles from the Israeli border to El Arish, Sharon's division on the central axis faced a single and very large fortified perimeter around the Abu Agheila and Umm Katef crossroads. This was the central shield of the Egyptian defence; it controlled the roads leading across Sinai to Ismailiya (by way of Bir Gafgafa) and to points south along the Canal through Bir Hasaha and the two passes across the mountains: Jiddi and Mitla. The Abu Agheila/Umm Katef defences were centred on a large blocking position of three continuous trench lines at Umm Katef, facing the Israeli border; their flanks rested on deep sand dunes on both sides of the system and the concrete-lined trenches were protected by extensive minefields, barbed wire fences and tank obstacles.

Behind the triple trench line, manned by a reinforced infantry brigade, there was the artillery with some 70 field guns, pre-ranged on the approaches to the shield; the artillery was protected by its own trench perimeter facing the sand dunes all around. (This was a single thin line of trenches, since the terrain was, as usual, 'impassable'.) Five outer strongholds, also protected by minefields, blocked the tracks leading to the perimeter from north, south and east. The troops manning the shield were equipped with anti-tank weapons, but their main defence against an Israeli tank breakthrough was a force of sixty-six medium tanks (T-34s) and twenty-two heavy tank-destroyers (Su-100s). This mobile force, the small sword attached to the 2nd Division holding the Abu Agheila/Umm Katef defences, was to be used

---

one artillery regiment. 11th Inf. Brigade: two inf. battalions, one tank battalion (21 Stalin IIIs), one artillery regiment. 49th Art. Brigade: two artillery regiments (36 guns). Div. Tank Batt. 213: 17 T-34s. Jiradi to El Arish: 112th Inf. Brigade: two inf. battalions, two tank battalions (26 mod. Shermans). 57th Art. Brigade: 24 guns. Coastal Art. Battalion: 8 guns. A.A. artillery units. El Arish town: one (reduced) National Guard brigade.

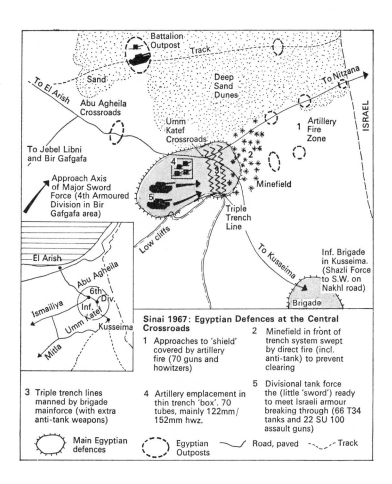

Sinai 1967: Egyptian Defences at the Central Crossroads

1 Approaches to 'shield' covered by artillery fire (70 guns and howitzers)

2 Minefield in front of trench system swept by direct fire (incl. anti-tank) to prevent clearing

3 Triple trench lines manned by brigade mainforce (with extra anti-tank weapons)

4 Artillery emplacement in thin trench 'box'. 70 tubes, mainly 122mm/152mm hwz.

5 Divisional tank force the (little 'sword') ready to meet Israeli armour breaking through (66 T34 tanks and 22 SU 100 assault guns)

Main Egyptian defences ⬭   Egyptian Outposts ⬭   Road, paved ⌣   Track --.-

Map 14

according to the tactics which the Egyptians had learnt from the Russians and which the Russians had copied from the Germans: the tanks were to remain mobile inside the main perimeters and between the five strongholds, ready to engage any Israeli forces which broke through while they were still weakened by recent combat, short of supplies and trapped between the trench lines and their minefields.

Sharon's division, like that of Tal and Yoffe, crossed the Egyptian border early on the morning of Monday, 5 June but it did not engage the enemy main force until late at night, when its forces converged on the Umm Katef perimeter at nightfall. (Though in the course of the day a battalion of Centurions had taken one of the outer strongholds and set up blocking positions astride the roads leading to Umm Katef.) In the evening, a reduced battalion of paratroopers were positioned by helicopter a few miles north of the Egyptian artillery perimeter. At 11.30 p.m., after a slow and exhausting march through the sand dunes, the paratroopers reached the thin perimeter around the Egyptian guns. They met with little opposition, crossed the trenches and assaulted the gun-crews at close range with submachine-guns and hand grenades. With this, the shield lost its fire support.

During the day, six battalions of Israeli artillery had moved up towards Umm Katef, ranged their guns, and then remained silent. The Israelis had to come well within the range of Egyptian artillery since their 155mm and 105mm howitzers and twenty-five pounders were grossly outranged by the 122mm field guns of the Egyptians. At 10.45 p.m., when the paratroopers at the opposite end of the perimeter were about to attack, Israeli artillery opened fire with a concentrated barrage on the guns and trench lines. Sharon, a former commando soldier who had fought many times without even mortars in support, was amazed by the power of his own artillery: 'For half an hour the fire was tremendous . . . I have never seen such fire in all my life.'[35]

A battalion of Shermans from the *ugdah*'s armoured brigade moved up during the afternoon along the highway to Umm Katef until it faced the minefields in front of the triple line of the Egyptian trench system. According to the Egyptian plan, the Israeli tanks were expected to enter the minefields to be destroyed piecemeal by artillery and short-range anti-tank weapons, but the

Israelis simply took up firing positions opposite the Egyptian trenches, stayed well clear of the minefields, and waited.

Sharon's infantry brigade drove to battle on mobilized civilian buses and then advanced on foot across deep sand dunes on the northern flank of the trench lines. There, the Israelis waited silently until 10.30 p.m. when they broke through the thin flank of the trench system, split into separate groups and entered the three lines of trenches. One infantry group was assigned to each of the trench lines and the vanguards carried coloured torches to mark their progress as they ran down the three miles of trenches, fighting hand-to-hand all the way. The light of these torches showed the tanks waiting in front of the minefield exactly how far the infantry had reached, and they opened fire aiming their shells just ahead of the running infantrymen.

As soon as the northern segment of the trench system was taken, the minefield in front of it was tackled by sappers who could now work without being exposed to the fire of the Egyptians. When a path was cleared, the Shermans drove across the minefields, over the trenches and fanned out inside the perimeter to engage the Egyptian tank force. Egyptian tanks were attacked from the front and then from the rear when the Centurion battalion (which had escorted the blocking forces to their positions) swung back to fight Egyptian armour from the west, while the Sherman battalions attacked from the east.

Any failure of coordination could have led the two groups of Israeli tanks to fight each other as they converged on the Egyptian tank park from opposite directions in the dark. This entire battle, with its simultaneous attacks of infantry, tanks, artillery and paratroopers, required rigid adherence to very detailed plans from soldiers whose forte had always been improvisation. Extreme precision was in fact achieved: the outflanking Centurion unit drove past the paratroopers without incident, while the artillery shelled Egyptian positions all over the battlefield without hitting any of the several Israeli forces within it.*

---

* The complexity of the plan apparently worried Sharon's superior, Brig.-Gen. Gavish, G.O.C. Southern Command. Just before the attack was launched (at 10 p.m. on 5 June) it was suggested to Sharon that he should wait until daylight, when air support would be available and tactical co-ordination would be far easier. Preliminary air strikes would certainly have

By morning on 6 June, the Egyptian shield on the central axis was defeated, though sporadic fighting was still continuing across the vast battlefield. Just before dawn, Yoffe's *ugdah* sent one of its two armoured brigades through the Nitzana/Abu Agheila road which the shield was to have blocked. Yoffe's other brigade, a reserve armoured unit commanded by Col. Shadmi, a business executive in civilian life, had already fought its first battle. On 5 June, while Tal's division was advancing along the northern Rafah/El Arish axis and Sharon was preparing for his night battle on the central axis, the Centurions of Col. Shadmi's brigade struggled across the sand ridges between the two. This gap between the northern and central shields of the Egyptian array was virtually undefended; once again the terrain was deemed impassable by the Egyptians, at any rate for major formations. In taking this route, the Israelis accepted the hazards of the terrain and a day-long struggle through soft sand, in order to avoid a frontal attack and, by the same token, gain the advantages of tactical surprise.*

At nightfall, Col. Shadmi's Centurions finally reached the road connecting El Arish with the interior of Sinai and Bir Gafgafa (where the Egyptian sword forces were deployed) and took up ambush positions just south of Bir Lafhan. By then Tal's forces had already broken through the eastern end of the shield, but only the lead battalion of the 7th Brigade had reached El Arish; Jiradi was still closed and its position was precarious. The arrival of the fresh tank forces of the Egyptian 4th Armoured Division could have tipped the scales since Israeli supply columns could not get through Jiradi to refuel and restock the tanks at El Arish. Two Egyptian brigades, one armoured and one mechanized, duly moved up to launch the planned counter-attack of the 'sword

* In 1956 the then Col. Yoffe led his 9th Brigade over the most nearly impassable of all terrains to reach Sharm el Sheikh from the north; in 1967 it was Yoffe again, this time as an *ugdah* commander, who followed the 'indirect approach'.

simplified his task, but Sharon, the man who had pioneered the paratroop night raids, decided not to wait; Gavish followed Israeli practice in leaving the decision in the hands of the man on the spot.[36]

and shield' defence, but before they could reach their prey at El Arish, they were stopped by Col. Shadmi's Centurions. At 9 p.m. the lead tanks of the Egyptian sword were ambushed by the Israelis and the two sides fought a night-long tank battle. Next morning the surviving Egyptians turned back. Its two complementary elements having been kept apart, the Egyptian defence system collapsed.

After twenty-four hours of non-stop fighting the Israelis had achieved their primary objective: the destruction of the northern and central shields. On the morning of 6 June Tal's leading 7th Brigade linked up with Yoffe's 'I' Brigade, after Gonen's tanks had defeated the Egyptian defences at Bir Lafhan, the last barrier between the two Israeli pincers. With this, the pincers closed around a vast pocket which contained the fragments of two Egyptian divisions (the 7th Infantry on the Rafah/El Arish axis and the 20th Palestinian in the Gaza Strip). Sharon's forces had by then defeated a third Egyptian division (the 2nd at Abu Agheila/Umm Katef), but the major part of the Egyptian army was still at large: the 4th Armoured Division, the 3rd and 6th Infantry Divisions and the Shazli Force. The second phase of the Israeli offensive was about to begin.

The strategic goal of the Israelis remained the destruction of the Egyptian army as a fighting force. As Gavish and his three *ugdah* commanders, Tal, Sharon and Yoffe, met to consider the problem on 6 June, it was clear that they could not hope to destroy the enemy by a conventional broad-front advance along the major highways, since the Egyptians would simply escape westwards and across the Canal. Nor could they trap the enemy by outflanking manoeuvres across country, since off-road movements are very slow in the difficult desert terrain of Sinai. Gavish's solution was original: fast tank detachments were to advance as rapidly as possible along the roads, fight their way *through* the retreating Egyptians, overtake their convoys and set up road blocks astride the routes leading out of Sinai.[37]

For the Egyptians, there were only three highways leading to the Canal and safety since the El Arish/Kantara road was already closed: the Bir Gafgafa/Ismailiya road, the Jiddi Pass to its south, and the third and southernmost road to Suez by way of the Mitla

Pass. Gavish's plan called for the closure of all three exits as soon as possible. Tank forces from Tal's 'M' and 7th Brigades were assigned to the Bir Gafgafa/Ismailiya axis while Yoffe's 'I' Brigade was sent to the Jiddi and Mitla Passes, 100 route miles to the south-west. The Air Force was now available for support: its task was to prevent the escape of Egyptian formations by attacking their road-bound convoys. In 1956 the I.A.F. had attacked east to west, in effect pushing the Egyptians out of Sinai; this time it was ordered to attack traffic in the western half of Sinai in order to slow down the Egyptian retreat, thus forming the anvil for the hammer of the ground forces.

Gavish's plan was a strategic solution but it also had a great tactical advantage. As in the case of Col. Shadmi's ambush south of Bir Lafhan, it combined the strategic offensive with all the advantages of defensive tactics. The Israelis, if they succeeded in making their way through the Egyptians, could take up blocking positions at the exits which the retreating Egyptians would then have to overwhelm in order to make good their escape. In other words, the advancing Israelis would have the lesser task of static defence while the retreating Egyptians would be forced to attack. Liddell Hart described this phase of the offensive as the subtlest and most effective application of the 'indirect approach' in the record of modern warfare.[38] Military historians, mindful of the offensive–defence stage of many battles of encirclement, may dis-agree. What is certain is that the second phase of the Israeli offensive led to the utter defeat of an army almost four times as large as Rommel's was on the eve of El Alamein, and in forty-eight hours instead of six months.

The plan may have been brilliant but its implementation was far from easy. Both sides were trying to use the same roads across Sinai, narrow strips of asphalt from which it was impossible to deviate for long stretches. Both sides tried to avoid combat, the Egyptians because their goal was to reach the Canal; the Israelis because they were equally eager to reach their blocking positions. Nevertheless, running battles (in the literal sense) took place all along the way. Israeli tank detachments racing westwards often had to fight their way through retreating Egyptian convoys; some-times the two sides drove side by side separated by nothing more than the dust of the desert. On occasion, Israeli and Egyptian

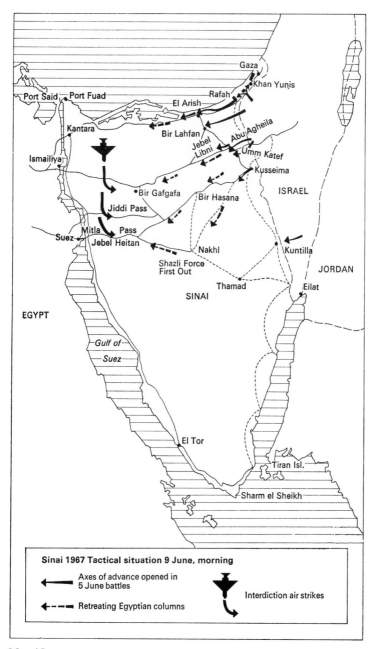

Gaza
Khan Yunis
Port Said — Port Fuad
Rafah
El Arish
Kantara
Bir Lahfan
Abu Agheila
Jebel
Libni
Umm Katef
Ismailiya
Kusseima
ISRAEL
Bir Gafgafa
Bir Hasana
Jiddi Pass
Suez
Mitla
Pass
Jebel Heitan
Nakhl
Kuntilla
Shazli Force
First Out
JORDAN
Thamad
Eilat
EGYPT
SINAI
Gulf of
Suez
El Tor
Tiran Isl.
Sharm el Sheikh

Sinai 1967 Tactical situation 9 June, morning

◄━━ Axes of advance opened in
      5 June battles

◄━ ━ ━ Retreating Egyptian columns

Interdiction air strikes

Map 15

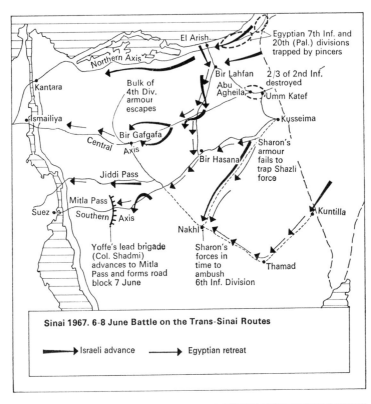

Egyptian 7th Inf. and
20th (Pal.) divisions
trapped by pincers

El Arish

Northern Axis

Bir Lahfan

2/3 of 2nd Inf.
destroyed

Kantara

Bulk of
4th Div.
armour
escapes

Abu
Agheila

Umm Katef

Ismailiya

Kusseima

Central

Bir Gafgafa

Sharon's
armour
fails to
trap Shazli
force

Axis

Bir Hasana

Jiddi Pass

Mitla Pass

Suez

Southern

Axis

Kuntilla

Nakhl

Yoffe's lead brigade
(Col. Shadmi)
advances to Mitla
Pass and forms road
block 7 June

Sharon's
forces in
time to
ambush
6th Inf. Division

Thamad

Sinai 1967. 6-8 June Battle on the Trans-Sinai Routes

➤ Israeli advance ——➤ Egyptian retreat

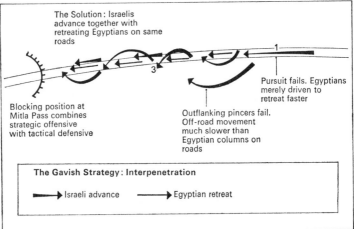

The Solution: Israelis
advance together with
retreating Egyptians on same
roads

1

3

Pursuit fails. Egyptians
merely driven to
retreat faster

Blocking position at
Mitla Pass combines
strategic offensive
with tactical defensive

Outflanking pincers fail.
Off-road movement
much slower than
Egyptian columns on
roads

The Gavish Strategy: Interpenetration

➤ Israeli advance ——➤ Egyptian retreat

Map 16

vehicles were actually intermingled on the same stretch of road: at one time an Israeli armoured unit found itself moving in the midst of a larger Egyptian force. The tanks advanced peacefully together for several moments until the Israeli commander gave a curt order to his men: 'Wheel off sharply to the right of the road, and shoot up every tank that remains on the road.'[39]

The Israelis had to fight a series of minor engagements to clear the strongholds holding out on the Egyptians' second line of defence, but their main problem was to keep the leading tank detachments supplied with fuel and ammunition. Battle tanks such as the Patton and Centurion consume about half a ton of fuel in one day of fighting, and each tank battalion needs more than a dozen heavy tanker-trucks to keep it moving for a day of battle. Unlike the well-protected tanks, the unarmoured fuel trucks of the supply units could not fight their way through the retreating Egyptians. There was no way of clearing the large bodies of Egyptian troops from the roads without a substantial delay – and to do so would have defeated the whole purpose of the plan.

Col. Shadmi's brigade, ordered to block the Mitla and Jiddi Passes on the third day of the war, had to advance more than a hundred miles through what was still enemy territory and its supply units could not keep up; the battalion sent to the Mitla continued to advance, but as it did so tank after tank ran out of fuel. It finally reached the Pass with only nine tanks, of which four had been towed for the last stretch. This handful of tanks, supported by a few infantry and mortar carriers which got through some time later, held out in front of the Mitla Pass for eighteen hours (till 10 a.m. 8 June) against the desperate attacks of Egyptian troops trying to enter. As each Egyptian column reached the entrance to the pass, it was ambushed in turn and fought a futile battle unaided. (The pass was already blocked by burnt-out vehicles.) The Egyptians caught in front of the Mitla never regrouped to launch a combined assault, and it was this total organizational collapse that enabled the small Israeli detachment to destroy the far larger Egyptian forces (including several dozen tanks) which reached the pass in wave after wave.

Tal's forces tackled the central route across Sinai leading to Ismailiya by way of Bir Gafgafa. The Pattons and Centurions of Col. Gonen's 7th Brigade, manned by conscripts and career officers, once again took the brunt of the fighting. Advancing from Jebel Libni on 7 June, the third day of the war, together with the AMX-13s and Shermans of 'M' Brigade, Gonen's forces fought a series of minor battles against the strongholds and rearguards of the Egyptian 3rd Infantry Division. The prize was the Egyptian 4th Armoured Division with its modern T-54 and T-55 battle tanks, but instead of counter-attacking, it retreated ahead of the Israelis. The relentless advance of Tal's forces culminated in the afternoon with a vast divisional pincer movement around the camps, depots and airstrips south of Bir Gafgafa where the 4th Division had been deployed. In a classic battle of encirclement, the Israeli tank battalions moved off the road, advanced with inner and outer pincers and linked up again on the highway west of Bir Gafgafa, but they only caught rearguards and stragglers. Parts of the 4th Division was trapped and destroyed, but much of the division had already fled; for all their speed the Israelis had failed to overtake the Egyptians.

At midnight on 7 June, Tal's *ugdah* was poised on the central highway to the Canal just forty miles away. After three days and two nights of virtually non-stop fighting, four of the five tank battalions under Tal's command* were resting, refitting all over the vast battlefield, and the fifth, a reserve battalion equipped with AMX-13 light tanks, was posted astride the Ismailiya highway to guard against Egyptian counter-attacks.

At 3 a.m. on 8 June the Egyptians launched their only 'strategic' counter-attack of the whole war. Sixty modern T-55 battle tanks attacked the light-tank battalion whose 75mm guns could only penetrate their armour at the shortest ranges. The Israelis lost several vehicles but held out, until the indefatigable 7th Brigade moved up to the rescue. The Egyptians were trying to dislodge the Israeli blocking force in order to rescue their troops stranded on the far side, but this one determined attempt to counteract the Israeli offence–defence strategy failed.

Sharon's *ugdah* had less armour than those of Tal and Yoffe

---

* Two Patton and one Centurion battalions of the 7th Brigade including the Patton battalion that had fought at Rafah initially with Col. Eytan's brigade; and the Sherman (modified 105mm gun) and light AMX-13 battalions of 'M' Brigade. Tal's forces also included the two mechanized battalions organic to the brigades.

and was correspondingly less mobile; it was not until 8 June, the fourth day of the war, that Sharon's men reached Nakhl. The Shazli Force, which had been deployed south of Umm Katef, had long since retreated but Sharon's tanks and mechanized infantry trapped the columns of the 6th Division (originally deployed along the Kuntilla/Nakhl road) which were trying to retreat towards Mitla.* A fresh Israeli brigade entered the fight at this stage, advancing westwards from the border and driving the Egyptians into Sharon's ambush at Nakhl. As in the case of the Mitla battle, the Egyptians failed to regroup for an attack off the march; the Egyptian 6th Division, with 100 tanks and two brigades of infantry, was almost totally destroyed at Nakhl.

On the northernmost axis of Sinai, from El Arish to Kantara, the road cuts across the coastal sand dunes without a single junction or turn-off to connect it with the interior of the Peninsula. Here, the fighting was entirely separate from the great tank battles of the interior. After the conquest of El Arish, while Tal's two armoured brigades moved south-west, the 'Granit Force', a special task-force of elite reconnaissance troops, was sent due west towards Kantara and the Canal. Joined on the third day of the war (7 June) by Eytan's two paratroop battalions,† the reconnaissance force, supported by a Patton company, advanced along the 100 miles to the Canal totally isolated from the rest of Tal's division.[40]

As the Israelis drove westwards from El Arish, they met only minor ambushes but, less than ten miles from the Canal, the Egyptians put up a really determined resistance with a mixed task force of battle tanks and commando troops. The Egyptians held out for several hours supported by the remnants of their air force. Their resistance came to an end when Israeli jeeps fitted with recoilless rifles outflanked the Egyptian tanks on one side, while Israeli tanks delivered an assault on the other, in an original tactical combination of 'hard' and 'soft' forces.

* Where the road had been blocked the day before. It is noteworthy that the Nakhl ambush surprised the Egyptians in spite of the fact that by then the Israelis had already reached the Suez Canal at the far side of Sinai. The Egyptian military communications system had broken down, and these forces were probably relying on the misleading news bulletins of Radio Cairo.

† Which had fought in the southern half of the Rafah junction on day one and in the Gaza Strip on day two.

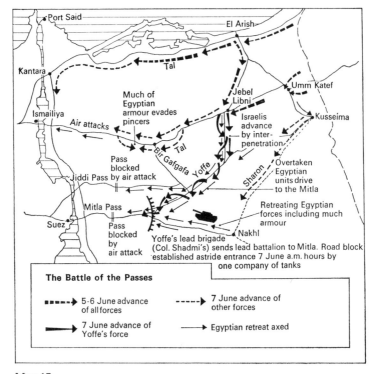

Map 17

Egyptian resistance having collapsed with the retreat of the last survivors across the Canal, the Israelis reached their finishing line on the morning of Thursday, 8 June, the fourth day of the war. Israel's strategic goal was not to reach the Canal at all but to destroy the Egyptian army in Sinai. Had they reached the Canal too soon the Israelis could have triggered a diplomatic intervention by the Great Powers and this in turn could have led to the imposition of a premature U.N. cease-fire. As it was, when the first Israelis reached the Canal at Kantara, battles were still raging in the rest of Sinai and major Egyptian formations were still at large. The forces on the ground had outrun their goals. Dayan had set a finishing line at the passes, and did not want the Canal to fall into Israeli hands. But when the 'noble stallions'

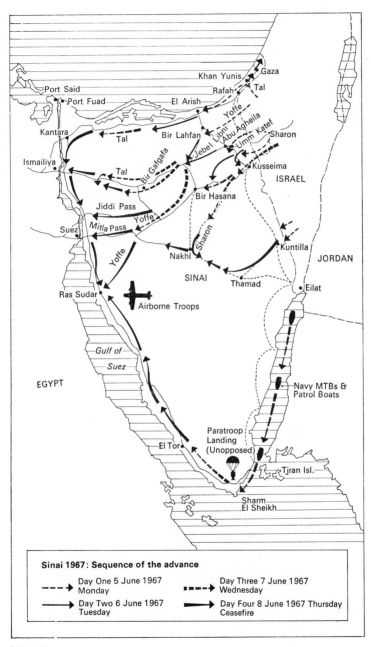

Port Said
Port Fuad
Kantara
Ismailiya
Jiddi Pass
Suez
Mitla Pass
Ras Sudar
EGYPT
Gulf of Suez
El Tor

Tal
Tal
Tal
Bir Gafgafa
Yoffe
Yoffe
Yoffe

Khan Yunis
Rafah
El Arish
Bir Lahfan
Jebel Libni
Abu Agheila
Umm Katef
Kusseima
Bir Hasana
Nakhl
Sharon
Thamad
SINAI

Gaza
Tal
Yoffe
Sharon
ISRAEL
Kuntilla
JORDAN
Eilat

Airborne Troops
Navy MTBs & Patrol Boats
Paratroop Landing (Unopposed)
Tiran Isl.
Sharm El Sheikh

Sinai 1967: Sequence of the advance

--→ Day One 5 June 1967
      Monday

--■-■-→ Day Three 7 June 1967
         Wednesday

──→ Day Two 6 June 1967
      Tuesday

━━► Day Four 8 June 1967 Thursday
      Ceasefire

Map 18

advanced beyond the line, Dayan failed to insist on his prudent and far-sighted limit.

The capture of Sharm el Sheikh, the Red Sea outpost which had been the ostensible cause of the war, was uneventful. A pair of Israeli motor torpedo-boats found the whole area deserted on the third day of the war and a planned air–sea operation with air-dropped assault units, navy-landed light tanks and air strikes in close support was cancelled. The paratroop flight arrived on the scene as planned, but the transports simply landed on the airfield which the Egyptians had left intact. (An Egyptian brigade had been holding the area.) Heli-borne paratroops then took control of the western coast of Sinai moving up from Sharm el Sheikh until they met Yoffe's forces which had driven through the Mitla Pass and then down the coastal road. With this, the ring of Israeli forces around the Sinai Peninsula was closed.

In the rear the Gaza Strip had been taken by a brigade of dismounted mechanized infantry* (with a battalion of AMX-13 light tanks) and a detached paratroop battalion. Virtually indefensible, and cut off by the breakthrough at Rafah as from noon on the very first day of the war, the Gaza Strip was not a strategic objective for the Israelis. The troops deployed to defend the area, Palestinian volunteers of the 20th P.L.A. Division, were scattered over a long defensive perimeter, and had no real offensive potential. Nevertheless, the Israelis had to secure the Strip and disarm the Palestinians. Assisted by Col. Eytan's paratroop brigade with its Patton battalion (during the second day only) the Gaza task force quickly seized the roads and dominating positions in the Strip, overwhelming the roadblocks and strongholds in the area. Sniping continued for days from the excellent cover of the narrow alleys in the towns and the stone walls around groves and orchards. Packed with 400,000 desperate Palestinians liberally supplied with small arms, the Gaza Strip was less a military than a police problem, and one which remained unsolved until long after the June War.

---

* This brigade (two half-track battalions and a light tank battalion) was deprived of its half-tracks by Tal who gave them to Eytan's paratroops. The latter were not specialists in armoured infantry operations but they were thought to be 'better fighters'. After the war, this switch was the prime exhibit in the criticism directed against Tal, accused of having neglected the mechanized infantry. See p. 295 below.

By the night of 8 June the Israelis had achieved their final objective: caught between the blocking positions at the western end of
Sinai and the mobile forces advancing from the east, the Egyptian
army had disintegrated. The Egyptian High Command ordered a
general withdrawal, making no further attempt to control its troops
in Sinai. Ambushed at the Mitla and Jiddi Passes, encircled at Bir
Gafgafa, trapped on the road to Nakhl, divisions, brigades,
battalions and finally even companies and platoons disintegrated.
Abandoning their tanks and troop carriers, their field guns
and rocket launchers, officers and men at first tried to escape in
trucks and jeeps; exposed to ceaseless air attacks, they left their
road-bound vehicles and continued on foot in small leaderless
groups.

The Israelis held the length of the Canal but made no systematic
attempt to capture prisoners. On this front, the war was over
even before the U.N. cease-fire was proclaimed on Friday, 9
June.

1967: The Jordanian Front

When the Israelis went to war against Egypt they expected a Syrian
attack but remained confident that Jordan would not intervene.[41]
The Israelis believed this although King Hussein of Jordan had
signed a military pact with Egypt on 30 May 1967, and though, on 3
June, it was announced that an Egyptian general, Abdel Munaim
Riad, had been placed in command of the Jordanian front, where
the Iraqis were also deploying a division. The official Israeli estimate was that Hussein would ride out the crisis without risking an
attack on Israel.

Accordingly, the deployment of Israeli forces on the Jordanian
border was precautionary and purely defensive. The large but
second-string reserve brigade attached to the Jerusalem Command,
manned by Jerusalemites defending their own city, had little
striking power; many of its troops were poorly trained or over
age and it had almost no armour, and few heavy weapons. Along
the entire armistice line in Samaria there were only two other
Israeli brigades of reserve infantry with small tank and anti-tank
detachments; the latter were deployed astride the possible invasion
routes into the coastal plain. In the north-east corner of Samaria

there was a third formation of infantry whose main task was to deceive the Jordanians by posing an apparent threat to the Jordan Valley; it too had little striking power. Southwards, Judea was the responsibility of Southern Command. Fully engaged as it was against the Egyptians, the Command kept only a small infantry force in reserve. The only armoured force available to the Central Command was the Harel reserve mechanized brigade (with one Sherman battalion) commanded by Uri Ben Ari of 1956 fame.[42] The sum total of these forces was adequate for a territorial defence but not for a large-scale offensive. When Jordan did enter the war, the brunt of the fighting fell on forces hurriedly switched from other fronts: an *ugdah** commanded by Brig.-Gen. Elad Peled from the Northern Command, and a reserve paratroop brigade originally assigned to the planned El Arish air drop on the Egyptian front.[43]

The Jordanian campaign was improvised in the midst of the fighting in pursuit of changing (and expanding) objectives. Actually there were two distinct campaigns, one in Samaria which climaxed with the capture of the town of Nablus, and one in Jerusalem. In Judea, the southern half of the West Bank, the Jordanian position was untenable once East Jerusalem had fallen, and the Bethlehem–Hebron area was in fact occupied without a shot being fired.

Three separate Area Commands fought an unplanned campaign with improvised task forces, and the coordination of the different formations was far from perfect. In the Jerusalem sector, Ben Ari's mechanized brigade broke through the outer perimeter of Jordanian defences west and north of the city, while the paratroops fought a separate battle against an inner arc of Jordanian fortifications on the northern edge of Jerusalem. In the meantime, the Jerusalem Brigade conducted its own equally distinct operations on the southern edge of the city. A sense of extreme urgency (first to rescue the Mount Scopus garrison, then to seize the Old City) and the lack of firm central coordination led to unnecessary casualties.

On the morning of 5 June 1967, Jordanian artillery opened fire on Jewish Jerusalem, an Israeli airfield in the north and on the suburbs of Tel Aviv (with 155mm 'Long Tom' long-range guns).

* It consisted of one armoured, one mechanized and one infantry brigade.

Table 5

Israel Order of Battle and Major Operations: June 1967 Jordanian Front
(Source: Authors' collation)

G.H.Q.	Chief of Staff: Yitzhak Rabin Deputy Chief of Staff: Haim Bar Lev
Northern Command	**Operations**
G.O.C. Brig.-Gen. David Elazar *ugdah*, G.O.C. Brig.-Gen. Elad Peled 1 armoured brigade, Col. U (Pattons) 1 mechanized brigade. Lt.-Col. M. (Shermans and infantry on half-track carriers) 1 infantry brigade	*Day one* (*5 June*) *Evening.* Lt.-Col. M's brigade and additional infantry move towards Jenin. Infantry feint down Jordan valley. *Day two* (*6 June*) Col. U's brigade crosses border and fights its way towards Tubas. Lt.-Col. M's brigade fights defensive battle at Kabbatya junction. *Day three* (*7 June*) Col. U enters Nablus in the morning after night battle. Lt.-Col. M's forces reach Nablus later in the day. Col. U sends detachments to the Jordan river.
Central Command G.O.C. Brig.-Gen. Uzi Narkiss	
Jerusalem Brigade Col. E. Amitai (infantry, multi- battalion)	Fights in Jerusalem; occupation of Judea.
1 mechanized brigade Col. U. Ben Ari (Shermans)	Breaks through to heights dominating Jerusalem area and West Bank roads. Conquers Ramallah, occupies Jericho and lower Jordan Valley.
1 paratroop brigade Col. M. Gur	Attacks fortifications of East Jerusalem, street fighting, takes Mount Scopus and Old City.
1 reinforced infantry brigade	Advances along Latrun road towards Ramallah.
1 infantry brigade	Advances in Qalqilya and Tulkarem areas towards Nablus.

The Israelis still thought that this was a gesture of Arab solidarity and not the start of a full-scale attack.[44] Prime Minister Eshkol sent a message to King Hussein through the U.N. staff in Jerusalem making it clear that, so long as Jordan did not intervene, she would not be attacked. Towards noon the Jordanians seized the U.N. headquarters building in the no-man's-land between Jewish and Arab Jerusalem.[45] By then the Israelis had realized that they would have to fight a full-scale war against the Jordanians even if only to silence their artillery. The Jordanians had a total of eight brigades deployed for action; the Iraqi forces were still on the way to the front.*

When the enclave on Mount Scopus came under heavy shelling, the Israelis decided to launch a limited attack to open a corridor to it across north Jerusalem. This could be used to evacuate the garrison, but control of the area could be most useful for offensive purposes as well since Mount Scopus and the adjacent Mount of Olives dominate the whole of Arab Jerusalem as well as the roads linking it with Samaria and the Jordan Valley. At noon, in one of the improvisations that shaped the course of the campaign, G.H.Q. ordered a battalion of paratroopers to Jerusalem; when the Jordanians attacked the U.N. headquarters building (at 2 p.m. on 5 June) a second battalion of the same paratroop brigade was called in, and by 4 p.m., the whole brigade, commanded by Col. Gur, was on its way to Jerusalem.

Uri Ben Ari's brigade was ordered to move up from its base on the coastal plain at 1 p.m. Five-and-a-half hours later, Ben Ari's armour reached the Jerusalem area, turned off the highway a few miles before the city and crossed into Jordanian territory. Superbly led, this mechanized brigade overran the small Jordanian fortified position on the way and continued to advance all night, reaching the crest of the mountain ridge west of Jerusalem by dawn

* One Jordanian infantry brigade was in Judea and another was in position in the fortifications around East Jerusalem. Four infantry brigades were deployed along the borders of Samaria, and a striking force of two well-equipped armoured brigades (with M.47 and M.48 Patton tanks and modern M.113 carriers) was stationed in the Jordan Valley, one in the Damya bridge area in the north and the other near Jericho. Two battalions of Egyptian commandos had been airlifted to Jordan and by 5 June they were in place at Latrun; Iraqi armoured units were building-up near the Jordan River bridges.[46]

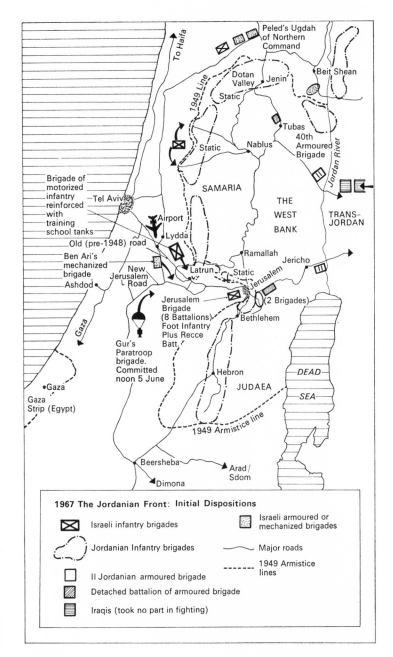

1967 The Jordanian Front: Initial Dispositions

⊠ Israeli infantry brigades	▨ Israeli armoured or mechanized brigades
Jordanian Infantry brigades	Major roads
☐ II Jordanian armoured brigade	- - - - 1949 Armistice lines
▨ Detached battalion of armoured brigade	
▤ Iraqis (took no part in fighting)	

Map 19

on Tuesday, 6 June. The terrain was hilly and the road very narrow; this slowed Ben Ari's progress to a crawl after the rapid movement into battle straight off the march. While the mechanized brigade was advancing, another Israeli force, a motorized infantry brigade supported by a tank detachment, advanced on a wider arc west of Jerusalem along the road from Latrun to Ramallah. This was a second line reserve brigade, intended for static defence only, but its commander wangled permission to advance and did so boldly, reaching the Ramallah area even before Ben Ari's forces had broken through from the other side.

The first Israeli forces to cross into Jordanian territory were those of Peled's division of the Northern Command; Brig.-Gen. David Elazar,* the G.O.C., was not prepared for a campaign against Jordan:

When the war broke out on the fifth of June, the Command was all set for defence on both fronts (the Syrian and the Jordanian). To our surprise, when the war broke out there was little fire from the Syrian sector . . . and, again to our surprise, fire was directed at us from the Jordanian front as from the early hours of 5 June.

About noon I was ordered to open an attack on the Jordanian sector in order to stop their fire . . . The attacking forces were not in the jumping-off areas, but in the relatively distant assembly areas, when the order came through at noon. We went into a typical attack, regrouping while in movement, and the first forces crossed the border shortly after 5 p.m.[47]

Although the Israelis had experienced strategic surprise on this front, it was soon the turn of the Jordanians to be surprised tactically. The sudden Israeli onslaught caught the Jordanians entirely unprepared. Lt.-Col. M, who commanded one of the three brigades of Peled's division, described the initial phase of the advance as follows:

We crossed the border at 1700 hours and penetrated deep into enemy territory. At the front line there were batteries of anti-tank guns . . . The tanks swept through and passed the line of anti-tank guns. Only then did the gunners wake up and open fire with light arms.[48]

As Peled pointed out after the war, the rapid response of his forces was not merely a question of physical speed:

* Chief of Staff as of January 1972.

The speed with which we entered the battle is not only expressed in the travelling speed of vehicles, but also in the speed of coordinating plans, the ability to improvise at all levels . . . down to the platoons facing targets and assignments for which they were not always prepared.[49]*

Judea and Samaria, the two halves of the so-called West Bank, are mountainous, with few low-lying valleys. The few roads carved out of steep and rocky hills are very narrow and it is rarely possible to travel cross-country. Peled's forces converged on Nablus, the key to the control of Samaria, from two directions, but the main attack, which turned out to be decisive, came from the rear. An armoured brigade commanded by Col. U advanced through Tubas along the eastward road to Nablus, thus reaching the town from the Jordan Valley–Nablus road. To get there, the Israelis had to a fight a tough tank battle on the way to Tubas, after which their subsequent advance was almost unopposed, since the Jordanians did not expect an Israeli attack from the east; indeed, they were waiting for reinforcements which were supposed to come from that direction.

'U' Brigade (with Patton tanks) took a serious risk in advancing through the narrow Tubas–Nablus road with no infantry cover for its flanks, but the gamble paid off: at 9.30 a.m. on 7 June a tank company, the brigade's reconnaissance detachment and Col. U with his staff simply drove into Nablus without a shot being fired. The Israelis were astonished at what awaited them once they entered the town. 'I saw that the inhabitants were greeting us with great joy . . . Thousands stood at the entrance of Nablus waving white handkerchiefs and applauding.'[50] The applause did not last very long. The people of Nablus had mistaken the dust-covered Israelis for the Iraqi reinforcements which were supposed to be coming up from the Jordan valley.

Suddenly something happened and the whole picture was changed. One of the officers wanted to take away a rifle from an Arab who stood next to us. The Arab refused to surrender his rifle and the

---

* Something of an intellectual, Elad Peled was in charge of the National Defence College until the June War. After the war the College was disbanded for manpower-economy reasons. Peled retired from the Army in 1968 and is now Director-General of the Ministry of Education.

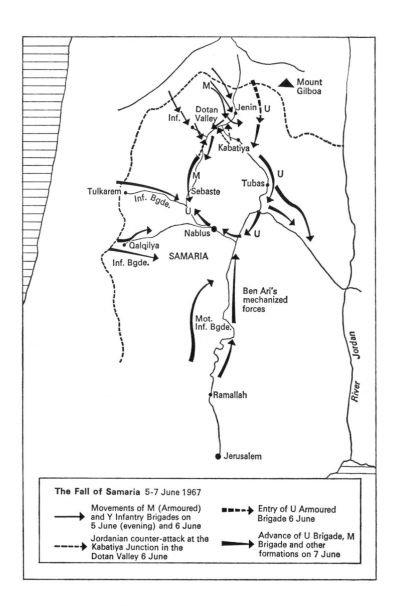

The Fall of Samaria 5-7 June 1967

→ Movements of M (Armoured) and Y Infantry Brigades on 5 June (evening) and 6 June

▪▪▪▶ Entry of U Armoured Brigade 6 June

--→ Jordanian counter-attack at the Kabatiya Junction in the Dotan Valley 6 June

➤ Advance of U Brigade, M Brigade and other formations on 7 June

Map 20

officer shot a volley into the air. Within seconds the streets were empty. The population disappeared, and sniping started immediately.[51]

Peled's infantry and his mechanized brigade commanded by Lieut.-Col. M (which had crossed the border so easily on the first evening of the war), had to fight all night to penetrate the anti-tank defences around Jenin. On the next day Col. M's forces were almost overwhelmed[52] by a Jordanian counter-attack. In Jenin, the Jordanian defence was both determined and skilful. As usual, the static elements, anti-tank guns and entrenched infantry were more effective than the mobile element, a number of Jordanian tank companies equipped with Pattons, which should have been able to defeat the greatly inferior Shermans of Col. M's tank battalion. On the morning of 6 June Jordanian troops were still holding out in Jenin when Col. M's brigade was warned by the divisional command that a fresh formation of Jordanian Pattons was approaching from the east. This was the most effective counter-attack launched by any Arab army during the war. More than fifty Pattons of the Jordanian 40th Armoured Brigade under the command of the outstanding soldier on the Arab side, Shaker Ben Zaid, advanced to the Kabbatya junction just south of Jenin and attacked the rearguard of 'M' Brigade. In a deliberate shoot–move–attack, Jordanian Pattons shot up the scattered Israeli mechanized forces which had been left behind at the junction when 'M' Brigade looped round to attack Jenin. At this point the bulk of 'M' Brigade was still embattled in Jenin town.

When the Israelis started to pull out their tanks to counter-attack at the junction, the Jordanian troops in Jenin began to fight with renewed intensity, holding up the extrication of Lieut.-Col. M's tanks. The divisional artillery stemmed the Jordanian assault at the junction with its accurate long-range fire, but could not rescue the forces trapped in the area. When Lieut.-Col. M's tanks finally reached the scene, the Jordanians attacked them in turn and the Israelis came near to defeat. By then they had fought non-stop for almost twenty-four hours, they were short of ammunition and utterly exhausted. It was the I.A.F. that saved the day for the Israelis; its air strikes stopped the Jordanians and forced them to withdraw. At dawn on 7 June Lieut.-Col. M's battered forces resumed their advance towards Nablus.

Col. U's brigade, the second prong of Peled's right–left attack, also had to overcome a strong Jordanian tank force before making its unopposed entry into Nablus. (Unlike 'M' Brigade, this force was armoured with two tank battalions.) It avoided a frontal advance by driving cross-country from Mount Gilboa to the Jenin–Tubas road during the early morning of 6 June, and continued to advance along the road until blocked by a force of Jordanian Pattons. Col. U's tanks fought and manoeuvred all day but at dusk the road to Tubas was still closed by the determined resistance of Ben Zaid's armour. As night was falling, the Israelis called down an air attack and ranged their guns, but Col. U decided not to launch an immediate attack; he also decided not to wait until dawn although with daylight his men would have the powerful support of the Air Force. In fact, Col. U chose the least convenient of the alternatives open to him, a night attack:

> We could well visualize their feelings. We ourselves were very tired from the physical and mental strain which we had experienced, and there was no shadow of a doubt in my mind that this was also true of the enemy, particularly after the strikes of the Air Force. In the dark we hoped to attack with some surprise effect. I estimated that they would lie down a bit to rest and perhaps we could catch them while they were not in their tanks.[53]

When the attack was launched, the Jordanian tank crews were duly caught sleeping on the ground alongside their Pattons, and were quickly overwhelmed. A few hours later Col. U's men reached Nablus.

By his timing, Col. U could exploit the 'indirect approach', achieving surprise in time if not in space, but when political considerations allow no choice in timing, and when topography restricts the scope of manoeuvre, 'the line of least expectation' cannot be exploited. The reserve paratroop brigade sent to Jerusalem on 5 June launched a frontal assault against Jordanian fortifications on the northern edge of the city without the benefit of surprise. Believing that a U.N. cease-fire could stop the fighting at any time, and anxious about the fate of the Israeli garrison on Mount Scopus, the paratroopers of Col. Gur's brigade were sent into action on the first night of the war with little artillery support, without a proper briefing and with no street maps. In line with Israeli command doctrine, the deputy Chief of Staff, General Haim Bar

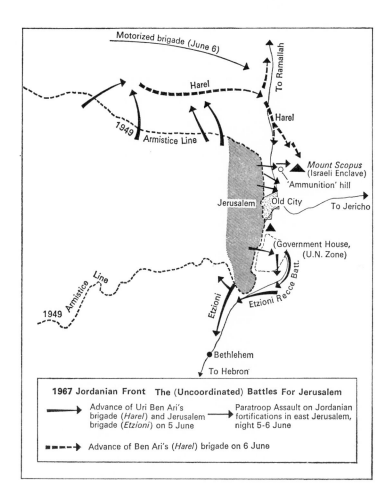

1967 Jordanian Front   The (Uncoordinated) Battles For Jerusalem

➤ Advance of Uri Ben Ari's brigade (*Harel*) and Jerusalem brigade (*Etzioni*) on 5 June

➤ Paratroop Assault on Jordanian fortifications in east Jerusalem, night 5-6 June

▪▪▪➤ Advance of Ben Ari's (*Harel*) brigade on 6 June

Map 21

Lev (Chief of Staff, 1968–71), allowed Col. Gur to choose the time of the attack. Apart from a general sense of urgency, his decision was probably influenced by the paratroopers' preference (and specialized training) for night assaults against fortified positions.[54]

When the attack was launched, the Israelis came under mortar and machine-gun fire as soon as they entered the tangle of wired minefields in the no-man's-land between Jewish and Arab Jerusalem. Many were hit even before they reached the Jordanian positions and, when they did so, the paratrooper assault broke down into a series of uncoordinated hand-to-hand fights which lasted until the morning.

One by one, Jordanian trench and bunker positions were taken by small groups of soldiers, who fought with little or no central direction from Brigade H.Q. On the next day, 6 June, Gur's men took the dominating heights of Mount Scopus and the Mount of Olives together with some of Uri Ben Ari's tanks. The Jerusalem Brigade began to advance on the southern side of the city, making slow progress. By 6 p.m. on 6 June, the Old City was virtually surrounded, but the Israeli government did not overcome its political hesitations until 5 a.m. on 7 June when Haim Bar Lev, the deputy Chief of Staff, finally allowed the paratroopers and the Jerusalem Brigade to take the Old City. He added,

> We are already being pressed for a cease-fire. We are at the Canal. The Egyptians have been carved up – don't let the Old City remain an enclave. [i.e. a Jordanian enclave][55]

Shortly before 10 a.m. on 7 June, the Jews conquered 'the holiest of their holy places', the western (or 'Wailing') Wall of the Second Temple, which had last been in Jewish hands nineteen hundred years before.

From a strictly military point of view, the conquest of the town of Ramallah between Nablus and Jerusalem was of greater importance than the fighting in Jerusalem. After a slow advance over the hilly terrain to the west, Ben Ari's men reached Ramallah towards dusk on the evening of 6 June. Splitting off combat units in all directions as if he had an army rather than a mechanized brigade in his charge, Ben Ari sent some of his forces south towards Jerusalem, east to Jericho and north to Nablus after having used shock tactics to take Ramallah:

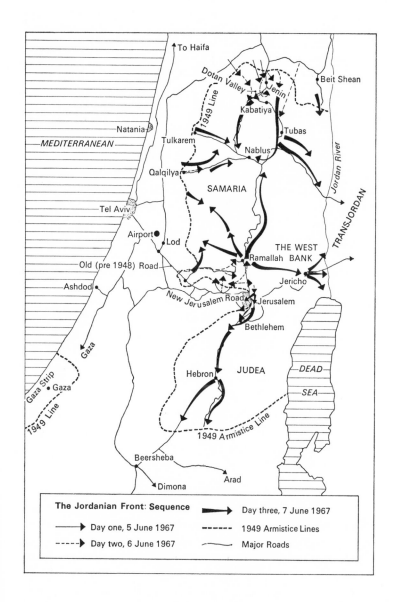

To Haifa

Dotan Valley

1949 Line

Jenin

Beit Shean

Kabatiya

Natania

Tulkarem

Tubas

MEDITERRANEAN

Nablus

Qalqilya

Jordan River

SAMARIA

TRANSJORDAN

Tel Aviv

Airport

Lod

THE WEST
BANK

Old (pre 1948) Road

Ramallah

Ashdod

Jericho

New Jerusalem Road

Jerusalem

Gaza

Bethlehem

Gaza Strip

Hebron

JUDEA

DEAD

Gaza

SEA

1949 Line

1949 Armistice Line

Beersheba

Arad

Dimona

The Jordanian Front: Sequence

Day three, 7 June 1967

Day one, 5 June 1967

1949 Armistice Lines

Day two, 6 June 1967

Major Roads

Map 22

We decided to go into Ramallah with a battalion of tanks, shooting at all sides as far as possible. We crossed and recrossed the city several times and it slowly fell silent. We cleared out of it at night and took up positions to the north and the south. By morning (7 June) there was no resistance and the town was mopped up.[56]

With Nablus already in Israeli hands, Samaria was now secured; southern Judea, which had been held by a single and thinly spread Jordanian brigade, fell to a detachment of the Jerusalem Brigade with scarcely a shot being fired. Advance units of Ben Ari's ubiquitous brigade moved down into the Jordan Valley to Jericho and the brigade thus completed the conquest of Judea and Samaria well before the Kingdom of Jordan accepted the U.N. cease-fire, at 10 p.m. on 7 June, after three days of fighting.

1967: The Syrian Front

Confined to a narrow sector only forty miles long, the fighting between Israel and Syria lasted for less than thirty hours; the decisive first stage of the Israeli offensive was concentrated on a still narrower frontage and saw only two brigades fully committed for a single day. Nevertheless, the Syrian campaign of 1967 is one of the most interesting episodes in modern military history. For one thing, it provided a far more valid test of Russian tactics in action than the Egyptian campaign. In Sinai, the Russian 'sword and shield' defences were improperly applied: Egyptian forces were too thin on the ground, the 'shields' overstretched and their flanks uncovered. But in Syria the front to be defended was shorter* and the flanks fully secured.

Most importantly, the Syrian border ran along the edge of the Golan Heights, some 2,000 feet above Israeli territory; the steep and denuded slopes of the plateau provided a superb natural defence for the Syrian shield, especially since for almost one-third of its length the border was fronted by Lake Tiberias. With four reinforced infantry brigades in the first line (Banias to Fiq) the shield was thick enough to match the prescriptions of Russian tactics. Again, unlike Sinai, the terrain was particularly suitable

---

* In relation to the size of the forces involved. The Syrians had seven brigades to cover 60 kilometres of front; the Egyptians had about twenty brigade-equivalents to cover the entire Sinai in depth.

Table 6
Israeli Order of Battle and Major Operations: June 1967 Syrian Front
(Source: Authors' collation)

G.H.Q.	Chief of Staff: Maj.-Gen. Yitzhak Rabin Deputy Chief of Staff: Brig.-Gen. Haim Bar Lev
Northern Command	General Officer Commanding: Brig.-Gen. David Elazar
1 armoured brigade: Col. A Avraham Mendler* (Two Sherman tank battalions, 1 mechanized inf. batt.) Engineering troops in support	*Day one* (*9 June*) Force 'A' (Lt.-Col. B) direct advance to Qala by way of Sir Adib. Force 'B' (Col. A) turns off at Sir Adib, fights at Zaoura and turns south to Qala. *Day two* (*10 June*) advance to Kuneitra.
1 infantry brigade (Golani): Col. Y (Three battalions, reconnaissance detachment, tank unit)	*Day one* assaults on first line of Syrian strongholds at Tel Fakhr Bourj Babil, Tel Azaziyat and at the approaches to Rawyie. *Day two* mopping up and occupation of Kuneitra.
Paratroops and infantry detachments	*Day one* Capture of front-line strongholds opposite Notera Banot and the Ya'acov bridge. *Day two* mopping up.
1 armoured brigade: Col. U (Pattons)	*Day one* Advance to Rawyie. *Day two* Battle east of Rawyie, advance to Kuneitra.
1 mechanized brigade: Lieut.-Col. M (Shermans)	*Day one* Penetration in the wake of the *Golani* to Banias and Masa'ada; capture of points to the north.
Ugdah forces: Brig.-Gen. Elad Peled. Infantry units, heli-borne paratroopers, mechanized forces, tank detachments in support	*Day two* Unopposed advance in southern sector of Golan plateau on Fiq–El Al Rafid–axis.
Northern Command artillery forces	*Day minus four* (*5 June*) to *day one* (*9 June*) counter-battery fire. *Day one* Indirect fire in close support.

* Mendler was killed in October 1973 while serving as Commander of the Armoured Forces in Sinai with the rank of Major-General for defence works and over the years the Syrians had built a formidable chain of fortifications on the plateau and its slopes. According to a professional account:

> Bunkers and pillboxes were rooted deep in the rocky soil, and a network of interlocking positions continued well to the rear of the first line ... Every strongpoint was lined with masonry, with heavy slabs of concrete overhead. Above ground, exposed to the direction of a possible Israeli attack, were only narrow firing ports. Ammunition and equipment were also stored in subterranean bunkers. The positions were linked by deep and well-supported communication trenches. Around everything were fields of barbed wire sown with mines.[57]

A total of 265 field pieces covered the approaches to the fortified line and Syrian gunners enjoyed a commanding position over territory below. (The range of their guns actually exceeded the width of Israeli territory in the northern sector of the border.) To attack the Syrian shield, the Israelis would have to climb the slopes under continuous artillery and machine-gun fire; they would have to overcome the heavily fortified defence line and – if they got that far – they would then face the counter-attacks of the tank battalions* attached to the front-line brigades. Behind all this there was still the main 'sword' force of three Syrian brigades (infantry/armoured/mechanized) ready to move up to counter-attack.

The I.A.F. flew more sorties on the Syrian front than any other; dive bombing could not destroy the well-built fortifications but all daylight troop movements were interdicted by Israeli fighter-bombers. This being so, the sword forces could not remain mobile and the defence lost its flexibility, becoming all shield, with no offensive back-up. The Syrians thus had no way of closing the breaches made by the Israelis while the latter could send in reinforcements to follow up successful breakthroughs.

During the first four days of the war, the Israelis were heavily engaged on other fronts and an offensive against Syria was ruled out on military grounds alone. Brig.-Gen. David Elazar, G.O.C. Northern Command, had sent the *ugdah* of Elad Peled against Jordan keeping only two brigades deployed on this front as against the seven or more of the Syrians. As from the morning of 5 June

---

* A battalion of T–34 tanks or Su–100 tank destroyers was attached to each of three front-line brigades.

the Syrians started to shell the towns, villages and highways in the border areas. The Israelis replied as best they could with counter-battery fire but their artillery was too weak to silence Syrian guns. On the second day of the war the Syrians cautiously attacked four border villages; the assault forces were small and they were thrown back by the settlers and army detachments that came to their aid.

When Peled's division with its three brigades once again became available for action, following the Jordanian collapse, the Israelis continued to hesitate, mainly for political reasons. With Egypt and Jordan defeated, time was running out for an attack on Syria. The Soviet Union had already suffered a major blow in the catastrophic defeat of its Egyptian ally; it now threatened intervention to protect the Syrian regime, the most promising of its Arab clients. By 8 June Northern Command was ready to launch a dislodging offensive but some members of the Cabinet, especially Minister of Defence Moshe Dayan, feared that Israel would be forced to suspend the offensive half-way, after losing many casualties but before breaching the formidable Syrian defences. All through 8 June the Israelis hesitated while Syrian shelling continued unabated, the Russians threatened and the U.S. government made no attempt to reassure the Israelis; its acquiescence in Israeli military action was at an end. Domestic political pressures eventually prevailed over Russian threats. In the words of the most authoritative inside account:

Ahdut Haavodah, the left-wing party heavily dependent on the kibbutz movement [many of whose settlements had long suffered from Syrian shelling], strongly urged the government to take an immediate decision ... leading the 'doves' was the Minister of Defence, Moshe Dayan. He strongly opposed any action against Syria ... Such a step, he asserted, would be one of extreme irresponsibility. The Syrian front would be the hardest to break, the one that would cost Israel the highest rate of casualties. Syria, moreover, was backed to the hilt by the Soviet Union, and an attack on her could lead to consequences over which Israel would not have any control.[58]

Late on 8 June Syria accepted the U.N. cease-fire, hoping to forestall the Israeli offensive; but early next day, Dayan finally gave the word to Brig.-Gen. Elazar, and within a few hours the offensive was in full swing.

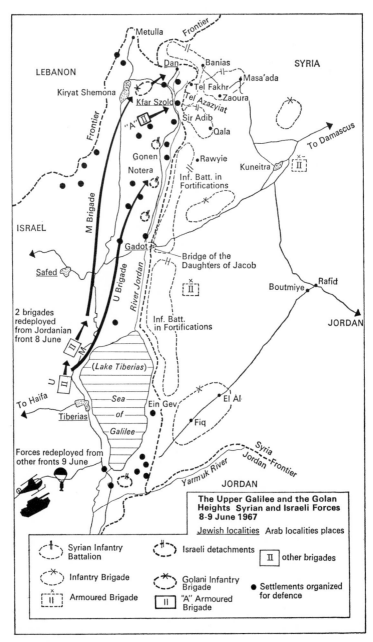

The Upper Galilee and the Golan Heights Syrian and Israeli Forces 8-9 June 1967

Jewish localities Arab localities places

Symbol	Meaning
Syrian Infantry Battalion	
Infantry Brigade	
Armoured Brigade	
Israeli detachments	
Golani Infantry Brigade	
"A" Armoured Brigade	
II other brigades	
● Settlements organized for defence	

Map 23

The fighting on this front saw the unprecedented use of tanks to spearhead attacks while climbing one-in-eight slopes. But most Israelis are not interested in the finer points of tactics and for them the most striking lesson of the Syrian campaign was the performance of the Golani Brigade, conscript infantry of the standing forces. The Golani troops came from the poorest segment of Israeli society and a majority were high school drop-outs, the children of Jews from North Africa and the Middle East. Many Israelis had long feared that the young men of the 'Second Israel' would not stand up to the test of battle.

When the offensive began on the morning of 9 June, two battalions of the Golani (under Col. Y) were sent to attack the strongholds in the Banias area. After crossing the border with tanks and troop carriers in the lead, the riflemen had to continue alone on foot, since their tanks and half-tracks were stopped by mines and artillery fire. From their fortifications, the Syrians kept the Israelis under heavy fire as they walked over the minefields, formed human bridges over barbed wire fences, rushed machine-gun nests and fought their way into trenchlines. Running and shooting from the hip, Golani troops penetrated the strongholds and fought hand-to-hand until Syrian resistance ceased. One battalion commander, his deputy and several company officers were killed.

The initial assault of the Israeli offensive was made by a reserve armoured brigade (with rebuilt Shermans) commanded by Col. A, which set off from the Kfar Szold area at 11.30 a.m. on 9 June. In this sector, the climb to the plateau was particularly difficult: in their constant search for the line of 'least expectation', the Israelis had chosen the steepest and rockiest part of the border, calculating that it would be less heavily defended than the rest. The terrain was in fact so difficult that at first Col. A's tanks had to advance in the wake of engineers' bulldozers which opened a path for them after the sappers had cleared the mines just across the border The entire brigade, spearheaded by a battalion of thirty-five Sherman tanks, had to advance slowly in single file under heavy artillery fire.[59]

The lead battalion lost its way a few minutes after crossing the border and advanced frontally against the major anti-tank positions in the Qala area instead of bypassing them as had been planned. The commander of the battalion, Lieut.-Col. B, who was riding in the fifth tank of the column, was wounded in the neck and

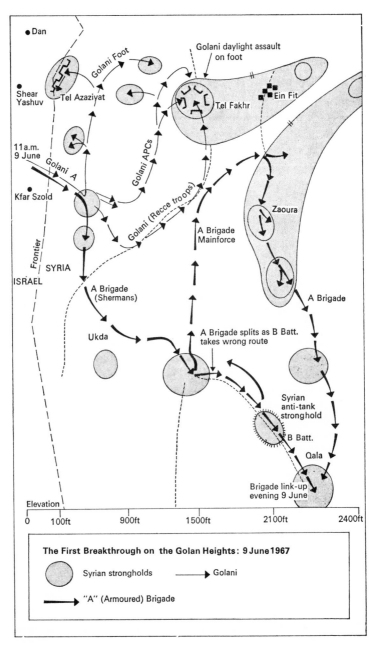

The First Breakthrough on the Golan Heights: 9 June 1967

Dan

Golani Foot

Golani daylight assault on foot

Ein Fit

Shear Yashuv

Tel Azaziyat

Tel Fakhr

11 a.m. 9 June

Golani A

Golani APCs

Kfar Szold

Golani (Recce troops)

A Brigade Mainforce

Zaoura

Frontier

SYRIA

ISRAEL

A Brigade (Shermans)

A Brigade

Ukda

A Brigade splits as B Batt. takes wrong route

Syrian anti-tank stronghold

B Batt.

Qala

Brigade link-up evening 9 June

Elevation

| 0 | 100ft | 900ft | 1500ft | 2100ft | 2400ft |

Syrian strongholds — Golani

"A" (Armoured) Brigade

Map 24

Maj. R, in charge of the reconnaissance unit, took over command. After a few minutes, Maj. R was mortally wounded, and command of the battalion passed to a lieutenant in charge of the lead company. This twenty-five-year-old reserve officer led the Shermans through successive Syrian fortifications. His force was decimated by the very heavy anti-tank fire, but it continued to advance without pause. Tank after tank was hit, the lieutenant was wounded and his force progressively reduced until only two Shermans still led by the lieutenant finally went over the edge of the plateau at Qala village, 2000 feet above Kfar Szold.

The rest of the brigade, under Col. A, had meanwhile turned off to attack Zaoura area on its planned roundabout route to Qala; the lieutenant, the two tanks, and his men were alone. At dusk, Syrian tanks appeared at the opposite end of the village, but the situation was saved by the belated arrival of I.A.F. planes. The lieutenant had begged for air support much earlier, but poor communications and a temporary bottleneck in aircraft availability delayed the intervention of the I.A.F. Shortly afterwards, Col. A's main force entered Qala village from the north after having fought a difficult battle on the way.

The strategy of Gen. Elazar was to open as many breaches in the Syrian line as possible in order to disguise the main thrusts and prevent a concentration of enemy forces against them. This was essential since after a daylight battle up the slopes his forces would be tired and much weakened by nightfall; the Syrian sword brigades could then counter-attack the exposed bridgeheads on the plateau, and at night the Air Force would be of little use. For this reason, while the lead brigade was fighting its way to Zaoura and Qala, three battalions of the Golani and separate infantry and paratroop detachments attacked the Syrian line at four major points north and south of Col. A's jump-off position in the Kfar Szold area. Syrian resistance was fierce; but by nightfall the shield had been breached at Zaoura, Qala and in the Banias area where the Golani troops had fought.

Early next morning (10 June), the Israelis were poised for a front-wide advance from Banias in the north to the Yarmuk river in the south, where the borders of Israel, Syria and Jordan met. The Israeli plan called for a concerted drive on Kuneitra to cut off the Syrian forces deployed along the border, with a second line of

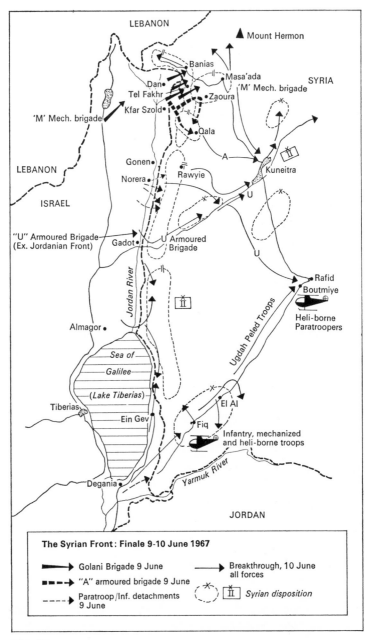

LEBANON

▲ Mount Hermon

Banias

Masa'ada
SYRIA
'M' Mech. brigade

Dan
Tel Fakhr
Zaoura

Kfar Szold
'M' Mech. brigade

Qala

LEBANON
Gonen
A

Rawyie
Kuneitra
Norera
U

ISRAEL

"U" Armoured Brigade
(Ex. Jordanian Front)
Gadot
U Armoured
Brigade
U

Jordan River
Rafid
Boutmiye

Heli-borne
Paratroopers

Almagor

Ugdah Peled Troops

Sea of

Galilee

(Lake Tiberias)
El Al

Tiberias

Fiq

Ein Gev
Infantry, mechanized
and heli-borne troops

Degania
Yarmuk River

JORDAN

The Syrian Front: Finale 9-10 June 1967

➤ Golani Brigade 9 June

➤ Breakthrough, 10 June
all forces

▪▪➤ "A" armoured brigade 9 June

➤ Paratroop/Inf. detachments
9 June
Ⅱ *Syrian disposition*

Map 25

advance south of Lake Tiberias to the Rafid junction. Once both had been taken, the pincers were to close along the road linking the two. By then, the forces on this front were augmented by two brigades ('U' and 'M') which had already fought on the Jordanian front under Elad Peled's *ugdah*. Demonstrating the flexibility of this type of formation, Peled's *ugdah* had detached the two brigades and had become a roof command for a paratroop battalion (which had fought on the Egyptian front), infantry forces and a tank detachment. Peled's forces, held up by heavy artillery fire on 9 June, was to advance on the Tel Katzir–Rafid road, while two armoured brigades ('A' and 'U'), a mechanized brigade ('M') and the Golani advanced farther north along the roads leading to Kuneitra.

Just as the second phase of the Israeli offensive was about to begin, Syrian resistance collapsed. Until then, Syrian troops had fought with great determination but now they abandoned their positions on the whole front and started a panic flight towards Damascus. At 8.45 a.m. on 10 June Radio Damascus had announced that Kuneitra had fallen, several hours before the Israelis got there. A variety of explanations have been suggested for this premature and most uncharacteristic Syrian statement. The most plausible is that the Syrian government wanted to induce the Great Powers at the U.N. to impose an immediate cease-fire, hoping to stop the Israeli offensive in its tracks. In any event, the broadcast implied that the Israelis had already cut the line of retreat for the Syrian troops still at the front, and it was apparently this announcement that precipitated the collapse.

Kuneitra was captured by the Israelis at 2 p.m. on 10 June without a shot being fired* and by 6 p.m., when the U.N. cease-fire came into effect, the Israelis had reached the invisible but very real limits on their advance which were set by political considerations.

A crescendo of Russian threats (implicitly backed up by American warnings) ruled out a further advance towards Damascus, less than forty miles away.

---

* The Syrian government newspaper, *Al Thawra*, wrote next day that the defence of Kuneitra had been 'heroic, the most honourable fighting known to modern history, even greater than the Russian defence of Stalingrad'.[60]

1967: An Overview

Even before the last shots of the 1967 War were fired on the bleak plateau of the Golan on Saturday, 10 June, it was evident that the Israeli Army had won a great victory. Sinai, Judea and Samaria, and the Golan Heights had been captured in six days; much of the Egyptian army and air force had been destroyed, the Jordanian and Syrian armies thoroughly defeated. And all this had been achieved at a relatively low cost in human casualties, fewer than 700 dead and less than three thousand wounded.

June 1967 Casualties (ground forces only)[1]

	Egyptian Front		Jordanian Front		Syrian Front	
	Killed	Wounded	Killed	Wounded	Killed	Wounded
Israeli Losses	275	800	299	1,457	115	306
Arab Losses	10–12,000	20,000?	1,000	2,000	2,500	5,000

Israeli casualty figures are exact except for a small number of wounded who subsequently died. Figures for Arab casualties are crude estimates.

The magnitude of the victory, its breathtaking speed and low cost, surprised most outside observers and many Israelis too. The Soviet government, deeply implicated in the crisis that triggered the war, had apparently estimated that the Israelis would not even dare to challenge the Egyptian army in battle; reportedly their assessment was that if war did break out, it would result in a stalemate.[2]

The Russian mistake in the analysis of Israeli *intentions* was probably due to a faulty reading of Israel's internal situation; they seem to have exaggerated the impact of the 1965–6 economic crisis (and the resultant political malaise) on the morale and national cohesion of Israeli society. Their intelligence analysts must have counted the number of tanks, guns and aircraft deployed on both sides and reached the obvious conclusion that the Arabs were superior.[3] Having trained the Egyptian, Syrian and Iraqi armies to use their equipment according to their doctrines, it was naturally very difficult for the Russians to accept the superiority of Israeli training and tactics.

In the West too, estimates of the relative military capabilities were badly off the mark, with one major exception. The American National Intelligence Estimate, revised shortly before the war, expected the Israeli Army to defeat any combination of Arab armies, even if the Arabs attacked first.[4] World public opinion expected a bloody and inconclusive war or even an Israeli defeat; among the well disposed there was fear for the fate of Israel. Most military commentators who declared themselves in the media said that a war would probably end in a stalemate. Even when the June War had actually started some of these attitudes persisted. On the first day, while the Arabs claimed to have shot down dozens of Israeli aircraft, Israeli communiqués spoke only of bitter fighting with invading Egyptian forces. In the early morning of 6 June the Israelis broke their self-imposed silence and gave a detailed rundown of the results of the air strike but most Western commentators dismissed this communiqué, taking the view that the truth must lie somewhere between Arab and Israeli claims.*

Some observers apparently misjudged the relative military capabilities of the two sides, even *after* the war.[6] Typically they argued that the outcome of the war might have been different if the Arabs had attacked first; in their view, Israel's victory was due to the success of the surprise attack against Egyptian airfields. In other words, it was a single well-timed blow that determined the outcome of the war. But the success of the Israeli Army on all fronts and in widely different combat environments indicated that its superiority had far more fundamental causes than the early acquisition of air superiority.

Perhaps the most obvious was the higher average level of technical skill of Israeli manpower. While learning by rote and acting

* Various analyses of the press and T.V. coverage of the war have been made. In these it is hard to find even one commentator who believed the official Israeli announcement on the results of the air strike.[5]

by standard drills can satisfy many skill requirements, the successful operation of advanced weaponry in combat also requires some
real technical ingenuity. Tactical problems become more subtle as
weaponry increases in complexity, while the time available for
each action-decision is progressively reduced. In this respect
Israel, as the more developed society, had a built-in advantage over
her Arab antagonists for, if ultra-modern weapons can be acquired
overnight, the skills required for their successful use can only be
learned more slowly.

Educational shortcomings certainly played a role in the Arab
defeat but a much smaller one than is commonly thought. If Arab
fighter-pilots have obvious difficulty in mastering their complex
machines, Arab riflemen, tank drivers, gunners and radio operators are not notably less efficient than their Israeli counterparts,
given adequate training. In 1967, as in later years, differences in
technical skill between Arab and Jews have been much less significant than differences in *social* conduct.[7]

From the pair of infantrymen who advance in tandem, where
one runs forward while the other exposes himself to give covering
fire, to the attack manoeuvre of a tank baattalion, modern mobile
war requires not only team-work but also active solidarity between
the troops. The first man takes the greater risk of running forward
because he trusts the other will share in the risk, and also reduce
it by attempting to pin down the enemy with his fire. Every modern
army must depend on voluntary cooperation and *mutual risk-
taking* since mobile war cannot be waged by ordering about
visible blocs of men in the manner of eighteenth-century foot
regiments. And mutual risk-taking can only derive from the deeply
felt solidarity of men who trust each other with each other's lives.
A common hatred for the enemy is not enough. Yehoshafat
Harkaby, once head of Israeli Military Intelligence and now a
widely respected academic, has explained Arab military weakness
in these terms:

> The crucially important factor in the Arab defeat [of 1967] must be
> sought in the weakness of the social links which join Arab to Arab.
> Because of this defect in the social fabric, each Arab soldier, in the
> critical moments of combat, finds himself fighting not as a member of
> a team, but as an abandoned individual. Consequently, each indi-
> vidual tends primarily to look after himself, and the unit disintegrates.[8]

The social defect that induces the anomie observed in Arab soldiers under stress has been described as 'amoral familism' and it is by no means unique to Arab society. Its root cause is perhaps the nature of economic relationships in static societies where, except for windfalls, the overall output does not increase from year to year, since there is no technical progress. Men will co-operate in organized groups if they expect cooperation to yield more than the sum of their individual efforts. But if men feel that more for one can only come from a reduction in the share of another, each will refuse to cooperate since he may well become that other.*

The 'amoral familist' sees social relations (other than those within the family) as a zero-sum game: any gains must be somebody else's losses; he will therefore refuse to make sacrifices for others on behalf of common group goals. Nor will he believe that others will be willing to make sacrifices on behalf of the group. Expectation becomes reality since it is self-fulfilling: as brave as any in individual terms, Egyptian soldiers fail to act bravely in groups since each man does not trust the other to share in, and thus reduce, the collective risks faced by the group. Not trusting his fellows to give him covering fire as he advances against the enemy, the single soldier fails to move; seeing his reluctance to accept risks on behalf of the group, the others are confirmed in their mistrust of collective action.

A brave individual can break the circle within any one small group – and armies are vast collections of many small groups – and thus transform negative individualism into solidarity. The principal duty of junior officers is to do just that: by risking his own life the officer should induce his men to do the same – on behalf of the group. But in Arab society the peasant sees the landlord and office-holder as his natural enemies. Conscripted into the army, the peasant–soldier sees his officers in the guise of the landlords and tax-collectors familiar to village life. Just as they expect the tax-collector to be corrupt and make him so by constantly offering him bribes, the peasant–soldiers expect their officers to be indifferent to

---

* This is why in static societies peasants commonly refuse to join farm cooperatives. Believing that their share of the total output can be no greater than what they could have produced by themselves, they refuse to take the risks of cooperation such as favouritism in the distribution of benefits.

their fate, and make them so by failing to respond to their leadership.

These entrenched attitudes do not affect the performance of peasant–soldiers in *static* warfare where each man can be assigned a fixed firing position and an individual task. The Egyptian soldier has frequently fought steadfastly and well in such conditions. But in *mobile* warfare, where mutual confidence is indispensable if one man and one unit are to advance while another man and another unit risk *their* lives in order to reduce the risk for both, the deep mistrust of the amoral familist paralyses the army. Men advance against fire only because of the inner compulsion of their mutual solidarity, unless forced to do so by the whips of their officers as in pre-Napoleonic armies. Where this solidarity does not exist, effective mobile warfare is impossible. Men will run forward against the enemy's fire because their buddies are doing so, and each man feels that he 'cannot let his buddy down'. The amoral familist has no buddies: under stress, he will behave as a solitary individual and no group cohesion underpins the discipline to which he is subjected.

In practice this means that Arab peasant armies can only be viable military forces in static warfare, where each man can fight on his own and the whole is no more than the sum of the parts. (The most impressive feature of Egyptian planning in 1973 was the combination of the strategic offensive – the virtually unopposed crossing of the Canal – with the tactical defensive, so that the troops were only required to fight in a static manner to defeat Israeli counter-attacks, which they did – until the second week of the war.)

Another of the intangible requirements of clean mobile war is truthful reporting on the radio links which are the nerves of modern armies.[10] The disposition to falsehood is a standard subject of national invective and therefore a difficult topic to discuss. Having registered his reservations Harkaby went on to analyse the effects of false reporting on the Arab military:

If the channel of communication in the armed forces becomes a channel for communicating exaggerated reports and lies . . . none of the levels [of command] . . . can act from knowledge of the situation. Decisions therefore are faulty. Subordinate levels are caught in a vicious circle: on the one hand, they know that the command prefers to receive favorable reports – even if this is false boasting – and responsively, they supply them. On the other hand, they cannot trust the orders of their command since they know that they are based on incorrect data.[11]

In 1967 this particular weakness had the gravest consequences for the Arabs. The Israelis wanted to delay the imposition of a U.N. cease-fire until the outcome of the war had been decided; they therefore tried to conceal the results of the initial air strike for as long as possible, without worrying about the effects on national morale. At a time when almost every Israeli was either fighting or glued to his transistor, the 'Voice of Israel' news bulletins deliberately conveyed the impression that the Israelis were doing nothing more than 'containing' powerful Egyptian attacks; there was no mention of the decisive air strike until eighteen hours after the event. Egyptian broadcasts spoke of entirely imaginary victories until the very end. This certainly contributed to the fatal confusion of the Egyptian forces in Sinai; their military communication networks had broken down and they had to rely on the misleading news bulletins broadcast over Radio Cairo.[12] After the 1967 War it became known that even Nasser himself was not told of the destruction of the Egyptian air force until several hours after the event.[13] Moreover, even when the full extent of the Israeli victory had become known to Nasser, the Egyptian leader persisted in his refusal to accept the U.N. cease-fire (which could have saved much of the Egyptian army) for reasons of national 'honour' and personal prestige.[14] (In 1973 Egyptian reporting had improved very sharply but this did not prevent the command débâcle that made the Israeli counter-offensive possible. By then, false reports were once again manifest in Egyptian command channels.)

At a more technical level, the Israelis had another inherent advantage: internal lines of communication. The Israeli Army could switch forces from one front to the other with relative ease while the prime force on the Arab side, Egypt, had no overland contact with the other Arab belligerents. The *ugdah* commanded by General Elad Peled, originally assigned to the Syrian front, was switched against Jordan within hours of that country's entry into the war; forces of this *ugdah* later took part in the seizure of the Golan Heights less than forty-eight hours after the Jordanian cease-fire.[15] The paratroop brigade that fought in Jerusalem, originally deployed in the south, was sent to the sector (in mobilized civilian buses) during the first day of the war and went into battle on the same night.[16]

The Israelis could use this geographic advantage to maximum effect because of the great physical mobility of their forces and their exceptional command flexibility. Brigades with thousands of men and hundreds of vehicles, poised to carry out a planned task, could be diverted at a moment's notice without catastrophic disruption. The ability to switch attacks from one point to another, to change plans in the midst of combat and interpret unusual intelligence correctly are all aspects of command flexibility – Israel's long suit. The readiness of officers and men to take responsibility so as to improvise order out of the chaos of war was the key to this flexibility.[17] Purposeful action was achieved by focusing the confused energies of loosely organized forces and not by the meticulous execution of brilliant plans.

In the Arab armies, junior officers are used to operating on the basis of written orders rather than on their own responsibility; in combat they seemed to lack the personal initiative and mental flexibility required by a fast-moving mechanized war. When plans were disrupted, most Egyptian units broke down into a leaderless mass of individuals; their officers could pass on orders but failed to provide leadership in the absence of specific guidelines. In this respect, Dayan's 'collapse theory', the basis of his strategy in 1956, was to a considerable extent validated in 1967 – after having been disproved in 1956.[18]

The difference between the two wars fought in Sinai, little more than a decade apart, reflected the changed circumstances of both sides. In 1956, the Egyptians were able in many cases to fight static and defensive battles from within their well-prepared strongholds, in accordance with detailed plans prepared in advance. The Israelis for their part failed to concentrate their forces effectively so that they lacked the weight of armour and the fire-power to dislodge the Egyptians from their fortifications. In 1967, on the other hand, the Egyptians moved into Sinai only three weeks before the war broke out, too short a period of time for the slow and meticulous preparation that the Egyptian army needs to fight effectively. Further, the Egyptians kept changing the deployment of their forces to counter Israeli re-deployments, and their cumbersome logistic organization failed to keep up with these moves. (This may have been a deliberate use of the Israelis' comparative advantage in flexibility.) As Egyptian units were moved from place to place, their supply trains were left behind or sent to the wrong place. Plans were disrupted and the resultant confusion was not offset by initiatives from the men on the spot. A specific example of how damaging this rigidity could be is quoted in a well-informed account of the prelude to the 1967 War:

A typical case was that of one of the battalions of a reserve brigade which had moved to El Arish at the end of May. Shortly after arrival, they were given marching orders to Bir Hasane, although the brigade headquarters remained in El Arish. They bivouacked in the vicinity of Bir Hasane in an open area. They had neither water nor food – apart from their battle rations, which they were forbidden to touch. Communications did not function, and they had no ammunition. But they were told that the brigade headquarters would soon arrive and then all deficiencies would be rectified. For forty-eight hours the men waited impatiently for H.Q. and supplies to arrive, under the burning sun, *with no orders and nothing to do.* By that time many of the troops were in a state of near-collapse and there was still no word or sign from brigade headquarters. The battalion commander gave the order to open battle rations and dig in. The following day, 5 June, the battalion was attacked from the air. *The dug-outs were not ready* and many, including the battalion commander, were killed. *They had not even known that fighting had broken out.*[19] (our italics)

In 1967, as in 1956, the tactics of the Israeli Army were marked by a striving for mobility and a constant search for the element of surprise. If the style was the same, actual methods were quite different and there was no uniformity in the tactics of 1967. On the Egyptian front it was as if each of the three divisional formations was bent on demonstrating the virtues of its own quite distinctive tactical approach. General Tal's division smashed the strong Egyptian deployment along the Rafah/El Arish axis with its spearheads of relentlessly advancing armour; it relied almost exclusively on the massed battle tanks of Gonen's 7th Brigade which outfought the successive strongholds blocking its path. Tal's division had the supporting fire of a detachment of self-propelled howitzers as well as armed Fouga trainers in close support, but most of its fire-power came from the guns of its own tanks; the artillery and the mechanized infantry played a secondary role in its battles.[20] The operations of Yoffe's division were most reminiscent of 1956. Like Uri Ben Ari in 1956, his lead brigade, commanded by Col. Shadmi, infiltrated across a desert gap between the Egyptian shields without meeting any substantial resistance. And Col. Shadmi's forces, like those of Uri Ben Ari in 1956, outran their supply lines; the small advance detachment that managed to reach the Mitla Pass on its own wreaked havoc even while its supply position was desperate.[21]

Sharon's division used a most unlikely combination of all possible types of forces and tactics. The composition of this *ugdah* was quite different from that of the other two: it included an infantry brigade, two paratroop battalions, the largest artillery force ever assembled by the Israeli Army, and a single armoured brigade. Sharon's forces neither infiltrated between the Egyptian shields nor attacked them with massed armour on the move. Instead, they fought a meticulously planned set-piece battle whose delicate combination of fire and movement would have delighted any staff officer addicted to sand tables and war games. Sharon combined heli-borne paratroops, foot infantry, tank battalions and concentrated artillery fire in a concentric attack totally unlike anything the Israeli Army had ever done before. The conduct of the battle was rigidly centralized, unplanned movements were ruled out, and there was very little scope for command initiative except at the very top.

Sharon's use of massed artillery was a major innovation for the Israeli Army. Israeli fire tactics at Umm Katef (and elsewhere) were to concentrate heavy volumes of fire on specific targets for a short period just before or during the attack itself. Lengthy artillery barrages in the Russian manner were ruled out. Short, sharp artillery attacks do not need vast quantities of ammunition, but they do depend on the ability to reach and hit specific targets. In a war of movement this requires mobile, self-propelled artillery so as to keep within range of moving targets and evade counter-battery fire. In contrast to this, the Egyptians followed Russian artillery doctrine, which emphasizes the value of lengthy and heavy barrages launched from static positions. Such tactics require a great deal of ammunition and a vast tube capacity, but the guns and howitzers need not be self-propelled: their fire is to move across the battlefield but the weapons themselves remain static. Accordingly, the Egyptians deployed several hundred towed field guns and howitzers in Sinai; they had no self-propelled field artillery at all.*

Another feature of the 1967 War was the limited role of the Israeli infantry; foot soldiers were rarely used for classic infantry assaults and infantry formations only conducted independent operations where the terrain excluded the use of armour. Except for the Golan infantry on the Syrian front and the paratroop brigade that fought in Jerusalem, no infantry brigade was given an independent operational role; the mechanized infantry battalions organic to the armoured brigades were mostly confined to mopping-up operations. At first sight the disappearance of the infantry as an independent force may simply be attributed to mechanization which has altered the ratio between infantry and armour. In fact, the diminished role of the infantry in 1967 concealed a basic innovation over the grand tactics developed during the Second World War.

By 1945, the German practice of concentrating tanks and other armoured vehicles into self-contained Panzer formations capable of sustained penetrations in depth had been imitated and developed by the Russian and Western armies into a two-phase tactical system which became the conventional military wisdom of the post-war period. Tanks were to be used to support the infantry and vice-versa, but tank and infantry *formations* were seen as essentially distinct and meant for different tasks. As in the great battles of the Eastern Front, armoured divisions were to penetrate the enemy front and push out fast columns that would become the outer pincers of the encirclement, while 'infantry armies' mounted direct assaults on the slice of front under attack. While the infantry armies stayed behind to surround the enemy troops caught in the pocket, the armoured divisions were to be extricated from the battle as soon as possible and sent forward to form a new set of pincers. On the defensive too, infantry and armoured forces were to operate as separate arms, with the infantry manning shields or

---

* Whether they fully accepted the Russian doctrine or not, they had little choice in the matter, since their Russian arms suppliers have no self-propelled artillery, except for anti-tank (A.S.U. series) and anti-aircraft (Z.S.U. series) weapons.

'hedgehogs' (independent, all-round perimeters), while armoured forces were to be deployed in the rear ready to counter-attack.

Although the Israelis did not follow any single tactical system during the 1967 War, the prevailing tactics were those of Tal's *ugdah*, and these represented a new stage in the integration of armour and infantry. For one thing, with the building-block *ugdah* system, there were no separate 'armoured' and 'infantry' divisions, let alone 'corps' or 'armies'.

Tank battalions, mechanized infantry, artillery and motorized infantry together with support and service units were integrated into single *ugdah* formations; each *ugdah* controlled *all* the forces along any one axis of advance. In Tal's division, the tank battalions acted as the 'mailed fist' whose task was to open a breach in the enemy defences; mechanized infantry forces followed in their wake to widen the breakthrough points by clearing enemy gun lines and trenches. Their additional task was to keep the breach open in the event of enemy counter-attacks. Along this axis of advance came the first-echelon supply columns bringing up fuel and ammunition to keep the tanks and troop-carriers rolling. With the second wave there came also the recovery teams whose task was to extricate and repair fighting vehicles, and the medical evacuation groups. The ordinary (i.e. nonmechanized) infantry, riding trucks or mobilized civilian buses, made up the third wave; its task was to take over the mopping up so as to release the mechanized infantry while securing the route of advance for the second-echelon supply columns. Roadbound and virtually unarmed, these supply columns could not advance until the infantry had thoroughly cleared roads and assembly points against last-ditch enemy resistance and since the first-echelon supply units had to shuttle back and forth to replenish their vehicles, the logistic system could break down if the second-echelon supply columns were left too far behind. Support forces such as the engineers and the artillery, rear H.Q. elements and service units, moved along the axis, sometimes just behind the mechanized infantry and sometimes well to the rear with the second-echelon supply columns.

This 'conveyor-belt' system allowed the spearhead tank battalions to advance continuously since they were sustained by the supply, evacuation and recovery units that followed in their

Fig. 5

Armour and Infantry in World War Two: The meaning of Armour – Infantry Cooperation

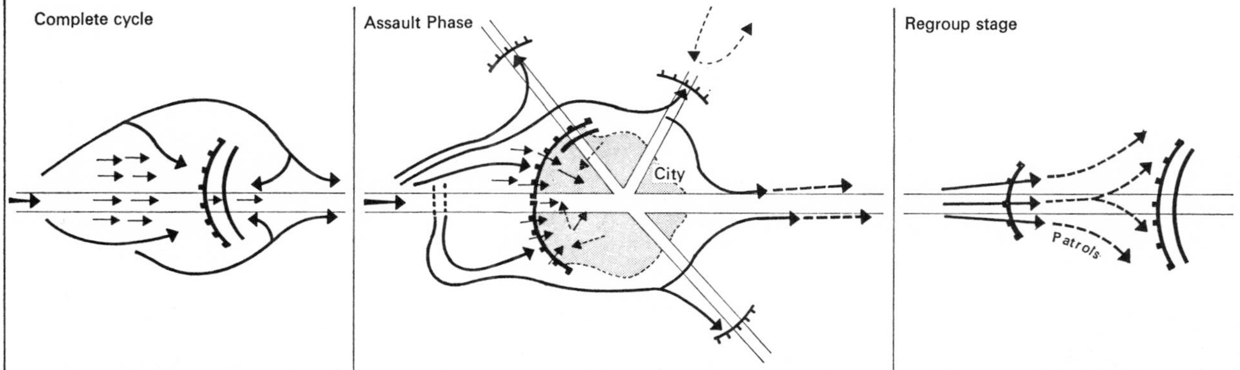

Complete cycle

Armoured Divisions send out pincers ⋂ to cut off enemy and reach rear of his defences ⋂. But major assaults carried out in cooperation with infantry ↑↑. Defences cannot simply be bypassed since roads must be cleared for the road-bound supply columns ↑. Hence the speed of the advance is set by the speed of the infantry, and *not* of the tank forces.

Assault Phase

Armour cooperates (in the direct assault) with the Infantry. It also acts independently (a) to guard against flank attacks and (b) to reconnoitre the road ahead.
So long as the axis is not secured, the supply columns cannot follow and the advance cannot be sustained much beyond the supply limiting line ┇┇┇

Regroup stage

While the axis is still unsecured, armour can advance with light forces and even take minor defences off the march. It cannot attack major defended positions At this stage, the offensive force (Armour, infantry and support) must therefore regroup, reorganize and wait until a supply line is established.

Fig. 6

Armour and infantry in Sinai 1967, Northern Axis.
The 'conveyor-belt' integration of armour, infantry and logistic support
(Artillery/Engineers etc. not shown)

Complete Cycle

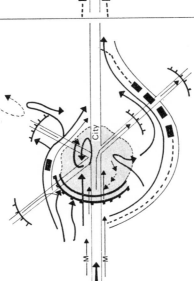

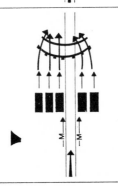

Tank Battalions ⟶ attack on their own remaining concentrated to do so. They are immediately followed by mechanized infantry battalions ▬ and by first-echelon supply mini-columns equipped with cross-country vehicles. The 'conveyor belt,' of first-echelon supply, repair and recovery and medevac is sustained in turn by main (road bound) supply columns ⟵ for which the infantry (motorized) —M→ secures the so far uncleared roads. Hence the speed of the advance is set by the tank battalions, and *not* by the infantry.

No attempt is made to clear the City of all organised opposition. Tank Battalions ⟶ go in and out with Mech Inf ⟶ and bypass City together with first-echelon supply and support ▬ . Mopping up is left to the motorized infantry with tank/artillery detachments in support. If City holds out, cross-country supply vehicles maintain a link ▬▬▬ to sustain the advance.

Advance continues at tank tactical speed until conveyor-belt can be stretched no more. But flexibility of system allows advance (with decreasing spearhead) to continue while enemy opposition in City is being reduced. Once road is secured, supplies are rushed to replenish the first echelon of the conveyor belt.

wake. It is this 'linear integration' that explains the apparent disappearance of the infantry as a front-line combat force. The infantry did fight, but only in the wake of the tank battalions. Its role was undramatic but still essential: without the infantry-operated 'conveyor-belt' the advance of the tank battalions could not be sustained for long. Although the conveyor-belt concept is not new, it is clear that Tal's Armour Corps had achieved a major tactical innovation (pre-1973 view). Tanks were originally developed during the First World War as support weapons for the infantry; during the Second, armoured *formations* acquired the status of independent forces alongside the infantry; in Tal's *ugdah* the process was taken a step further and the infantry was actually subordinated to the tank forces. As a result, the pace of the advance was limited only by the mobility of the tank forces and not by the lesser mobility of the infantry. The difference is not in the mechanical speed of movement (infantry vehicles are faster) but in the actual speed of advance against enemy fire. The apparently cumbersome heavily armoured battle tank[22] is more likely to advance rapidly than the mechanically faster light vehicles which cannot move at all in the presence of gunfire.

In spite of the undoubted success of his *Ugdah*, and of the armoured forces on all fronts, Tal's concept came under attack following the 1967 War. Some commentators claimed that Tal had concentrated all his attention (and the corps' resources) on the tank battalions, neglecting the mechanized infantry; this, they argued, could have dire consequences in the future. The critics pointed out that on the eve of the 1967 War Tal had handed over the half-tracks of one of his mechanized brigades to Col. Eytan's brigade; the latter had no armour training but its men were considered to be 'better fighters'. According to his critics, this proved that Tal had bled the mechanized infantry of its better manpower to the point where even he himself preferred to have paratroopers fighting alongside his tanks, instead of the mechanized infantry supposedly trained for this very task.

Tal's critics went on to argue that his all-tank tactics could have failed against a more determined enemy.[23] Instead of fleeing after the first Israeli tanks had broken through, more resilient troops (e.g. Russians) would have closed the breaches made by the tanks, thus blocking the flow of 'soft' troops and supplies that came in the wake of the tanks. At this point the tank battalions would no longer be able to advance since they would have to return to re-open the breakthrough point once again. In other words, without strong mechanized infantry forces to clear and hold the break-through points against enemy counter-attacks, the 'conveyor-belt' could be cut in two, and neither half would be of much use without the other. According to the critics, the mechanized infantry needed better equipment and more select manpower than it had received under Tal's priorities, if it was to stand up to the test of a future war that could involve the presence of Russian troops. (Although the tactical scenario was quite different, the critics' case was sub-stantially proved by the 1973 War: 'all-tank' approach to warfare proved to be quite inadequate.)

As a serving officer, Tal* could not reply to his critics but his view was apparently that they had missed the point. In building the forces of the Armour Corps up to 1967, more for the mechan-ized infantry inevitably meant less for the tank forces and, since the enemy was Arab and not Russian, the tank battalions could safely be given an overriding priority. Against the specific enemy at hand, only mopping up would be needed after the tanks had broken through – and there was therefore no need to weaken the tank spearheads in order to build stronger follow-up forces (but see the Jiradi episode p. 240 above).

The only offensive action mounted by the Israeli Navy during the 1967 War was the raid of its frogmen-commandos against Egyptian naval bases at Alexandria and Port Said. The frogmen penetrated the harbours and reportedly damaged a number of vessels. Since the Egyptian navy played no role in the war the defensive strength of the Israeli Navy was not tested.

In 1967 the Navy was caught in the midst of a major re-equip-ment programme: its two N-class destroyers were obsolescent while its radically new vessels, a flotilla of twelve Saar fast patrol-boats armed with Gabriel anti-shipping missiles, had not yet been delivered.† The Commander of the Navy in 1967, Rear-Admiral

---

* Promoted to Chief of the General Staff branch in 1972.

† The German-designed Saar boats have a displacement of 240 tons (full-load), a 45 knot maximum speed and a range of 800 n. miles at 30 knots. The Israeli-developed Gabriel anti-shipping missiles have a maximum range (with boosters) of twenty-two miles (normal range or around twelve

Shlomo Errel, has described the predicament of his corps in these terms:

> When the first missile boats appeared in Egypt during the early sixties the Israeli Navy was faced with a dilemma. Its equipment was insufficient and obsolete while the countries that were prepared to sell warships to Israel, or to build them for her, had nothing to offer which could deal with the Egyptian threat. The strengthening of the Egyptian navy was not confined to missile boats and any Israeli reply also had to take into consideration the modern destroyers and submarines supplied by the Soviet Union.[24]

Errel went on to say that the naval weapons available in the West were quite unsuitable given the small scale of the Israeli Navy. If Western destroyers could defeat the destroyers and submarines of the Egyptian fleet, there was no counter-weapon (other than airpower) for the Russian-built missile boats. The Israelis therefore decided to strike out on their own to develop an anti-shipping missile system. The results of this development programme only became apparent after the 1967 War when the Saar/Gabriel system was deployed. This combines a fast but really seaworthy vessel (the Russian boats are only meant for inshore waters) with the powerful Gabriel surface-to-surface missile.

With its new weapons the Navy could finally develop a specifically Israeli answer to its problems, as the ground and air forces had done long before. Abandoning its previous posture, of a Great Power navy in miniature, the Israeli Navy became a far more effective force once its Saar boats became operational in 1969 (as was clearly shown in 1973).

Unlike the Navy, the Air Force had received the highest priority for men and budgets while in the Army's strategic planning its role was central. Nevertheless, until 1967, only within the I.A.F. itself was there a realistic appreciation of just how effective a weapon had been forged. In 1956, Ben Gurion had insisted that only foreign fighter squadrons could protect Israeli cities against Egyptian air attacks. Dan Tolkowsky, the Air Force Commander, had wanted to strike at Egyptian airfields at the very outset of the

---

miles) and a 230 lb. warhead, capable of sinking destroyer-sized vessels with one hit. Each Saar boat can carry up to eight Gabriel launchers.

campaign without waiting for Israel's 'junior partners', but his advice had been rejected.[25]

On the eve of the 1967 War many otherwise well-informed Israelis in the government, and even in the Army, had misgivings about the claims made by the Air Force. When the Commander of the I.A.F., Brig.-Gen. Mordechai Hod, told the Cabinet that the entire Egyptian air force would be destroyed before it could bomb Tel Aviv, this statement was regarded as little more than a boast. Even within the Army and at fairly senior levels Hod's claim was disbelieved; there was much anxiety about the Egyptian bomber threat especially in conjunction with the use of gas-filled bombs. Actually the I.A.F. estimate was conservative. At a lecture given at the Staff and Command course when he was still the I.A.F.'s Commander, Brig.-Gen. Ezer Weizmann was asked how long it would take to destroy the Egyptian air force on the ground. He referred the question to a major on his staff who said that it would take three or four hours. Weizmann thought that this was too optimistic and gave his own estimate of twelve hours.

After 1967 the tendency to underestimate the I.A.F. was replaced by its opposite: many came to see in the I.A.F. an all-purpose weapon which could achieve any and all goals. In the next four years the Israelis were to receive a full education in the limitations of air power.

Zahal in the Seventies

At an official press conference held in Tel Aviv three days after the end of the 1967 War, Gen. Ariel Sharon concluded his statement with these words:

We managed to finish it all, and after our success this time, I am very much afraid that by the [time of the] next war we are all going to be too old, and the next generation will have to take care of it, because we have now completed everything in such a way that the enemy is not going to be able to fight for many, many years to come.[1]

When Sharon spoke, the Egyptian military establishment had just been shattered by the war, the Jordanian army had been reduced to a few battered infantry battalions, and the Syrians had lost the Golan Heights, their main military asset. As against this, Israeli ground forces were almost intact, and the Air Force had lost only forty-six aircraft (all but three to ground fire) and fewer pilots. Most important, Israel had acquired a far more defensible territory. Radar facilities in the Sinai Peninsula could now provide adequate early warning of incoming aircraft, while forward airfields could cut flying time to Egypt down to a few minutes.[2] As for defence on the ground, Sinai provided a broad protective shield of desert itself, guarded by the best possible anti-tank ditch, the Suez Canal.

The new cease-fire lines with Jordan were equally advantageous. Instead of a tortuous and hilly borderline, which in places reduced Israeli territory to a narrow ten-mile corridor between the mountains and the sea, the new border north of the Dead Sea was now the straight line of the Jordan River valley. From Lake Tiberias to Jericho, the cease-fire line provided little natural cover for infiltration, always the main threat on this sector. As for conventional military threats, the occupation of Judea and Samaria tripled the width of Israeli territory and provided a mountain barrier against invasion from the east. Since a full-scale Jordanian attack had always been unlikely, the principal advantage of the new cease-fire line was that it was far shorter with 185 instead of 350 miles to guard.

Given the state of the Arab armies in the aftermath of the June War, the Israelis may be excused for having believed with Sharon that there would be no more war for a long time to come. But in 1967, as twice before, Israel's military victory had far-reaching political repercussions, which entailed in turn new military dangers. Just as the defeat of the Palestinians in 1948 had triggered the May invasions of regular Arab forces, Israel's victory in 1967 was followed by a sharp escalation in the degree of Russian intervention. The credibility of the Russians as reliable patrons had been compromised by the utter defeat of their Arab clients in June 1967; after the briefest hesitation, the Russians reacted. By sea and by air large quantities of weapons were delivered to Egypt and Syria; within a month seventy per cent of the equipment losses were made good.[3] With the hardware, there came Russian 'technical advisers' and plain military officers; from 3,000 before the war their number increased to 10,000 or more by the end of the year. Until the 1967 War Russian advisers had served only as technical specialists or at higher staff levels, but after it, they were present in each Egyptian battalion and air force squadron.

When the 9 June cease-fire came into effect, the Egyptian air force had practically ceased to exist. Within three months, it was provided with more than two hundred new Russian aircraft, and hundreds of its men were sent to the Soviet Union for pilot training. In replacing the lost equipment, there was also a more or less automatic upgrading in quality: Second World War vintage T-34 tanks were replaced with newer T-54/T-55s (which before had appeared only in first-line tank units); more capable Sukhoi-7 ground-attack aircraft replaced the older MiG-17s destroyed by the Israelis, and first-generation MiG-15s were phased out in favour of additional MiG-21s.

Nevertheless, two years later, when air battles started once again over Egypt, the I.A.F. quickly achieved total superiority in the air. A first Egyptian attempt to deploy a barrier of Sam-2 (Guide-line) anti-aircraft missiles along the Canal was foiled and Israeli

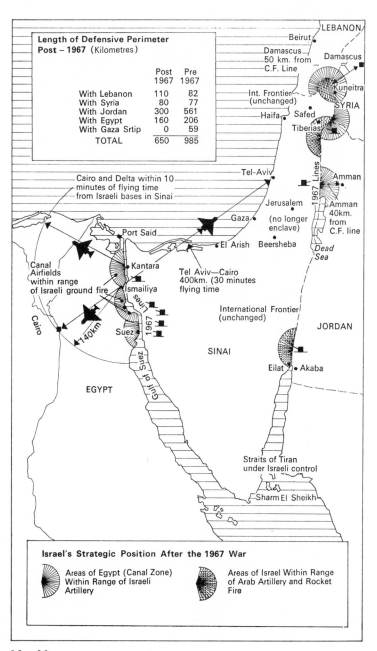

Length of Defensive Perimeter Post – 1967 (Kilometres)

	Post 1967	Pre 1967
With Lebanon	110	82
With Syria	80	77
With Jordan	300	561
With Egypt	160	206
With Gaza Srtip	0	59
TOTAL	650	985

LEBANON

Beirut

Damascus 50 km. from C.F. Line

Damascus

Kuneitra

SYRIA

Int. Frontier (unchanged)

Safed

Haifa

Tiberias

Cairo and Delta within 10 minutes of flying time from Israeli bases in Sinai

Tel-Aviv

1967 Lines

Amman

Jerusalem (no longer enclave)

Amman 40km. from C.F. Line

Gaza

Beersheba

Dead Sea

Port Said

El Arish

Canal Airfields within range of Israeli ground fire

Kantara

Tel Aviv—Cairo 400km. (30 minutes flying time)

Ismailiya

International Frontier (unchanged)

JORDAN

Cairo

1967 Lines

140km

Suez

SINAI

Eilat

Akaba

EGYPT

Gulf of Suez

Straits of Tiran under Israeli control

Sharm El Sheikh

Israel's Strategic Position After the 1967 War

Areas of Egypt (Canal Zone) Within Range of Israeli Artillery

Areas of Israel Within Range of Arab Artillery and Rocket Fire

Map 26

fighter-bombers struck at targets on the west bank of the Canal and deep into Egypt without meeting any effective opposition. Whenever Egyptian fighters attempted to intercept them, the Israelis had no trouble in shooting them down. In three years of sporadic air combat up to August 1970 it lost only two (Mirage) fighters, as against more than sixty MiG-21s, the best Russian interceptor in the theatre.*[4]

Once again, the Russians reacted by escalating their intervention. By April 1970 a new air-defence system based on SAM-3 (Goa) missiles, operated by Russian crews, was deployed in Egypt along with several Russian air force fighter squadrons equipped with the advanced MiG-21J. The missile batteries and the fighter patrols, originally deployed in the Egyptian interior, were gradually pushed forward to the Canal and in July 1970, shortly before the cease-fire, the Russian air force fought its first air battle since the end of the Second World War. The I.A.F. shot down four Russian-piloted MiG-21Js, with no loss of its own, but this victory could not assuage Israeli anxieties. The possibility of a drastic Russian retaliation for this humiliating defeat could not be excluded. In 1970, as twice before, it seemed as if Israel's military victory had only extended the scope of the conflict: from Palestine to the Arab world, from the Arabs to the Russians and their client states.

Except for the first few months following the June 1967 cease-fire, Israel and Egypt were involved in fighting of one sort or another until the next cease-fire, imposed by Russo-American agreement in August 1970. On the Jordanian, Syrian and Lebanese fronts, the fighting continued, but it was sporadic and characterized by low-key guerrilla operations. This 'War of Attrition' went through several distinct phases, but had a single unifying theme: for the first time the Israeli Army was fighting a defensive war whose results could not be decisive even in purely military terms.[5]

What made the post-1967 fighting so inconclusive were the

* Between July 1967 and May 1973 the kill ratios were as follows:

	Air-to-air	Ground-to-air	Total
I.A.F. losses	2	25	27
Arab losses	125	37†	162

† (Of which 13 to I.A.F. Hawk missiles.)

severe political restraints on the Army's freedom of action. The Israelis had accepted limited war as a fact of life ever since 1948 but, now that their relative military power was so much greater, its frustrations were correspondingly more intense. During the June War, the Israelis could not fully exploit their victory over the Syrians because Russian threats kept them from taking Damascus, although, according to the G.O.C. Northern Command, Brig.-Gen. David Elazar, the Syrian capital could have been captured in thirty-six hours.[6] The invisible limits imposed by political realities meant that Israel could not transform her military victories on the battlefield into a finite, political victory. And later, during the War of Attrition, political constraints forced Israel into a defensive posture. The rules of the game were that the Israelis could not cross the cease-fire lines in order to reach the interior of Egypt, Jordan or Syria and so impose a settlement, or even to counter-attack effectively. Air attacks and raids were permissible but neither super-power would tolerate a full-scale offensive on the ground. In the very first instance of large-scale fighting on the ground, the Karameh operation of March 1968, the Israelis suffered twenty-eight killed and sixty-nine wounded because of their failure to take this constraint into account when the operation was being planned.[7]

Counter-Guerrilla: Jordanian and Lebanese Fronts

On 21 March 1968 an Israeli task force of armour and heli-borne paratroops seized the Jordanian town of Karameh in a two-pronged spoiling operation against a concentration of Palestinian (mainly Fatah) irregulars. The latter failed to put up an effective resistance but the Israelis came under fire from Jordanian tanks and guns stationed in the hills above the town. The commander of the Israeli task force was forbidden to advance into the hills, while his tanks could not silence Jordanian fire from their unfavourable position on the valley floor. Retreating under fire, many Israelis were hit and two tanks were left across the river. One hundred and fifty irregulars and twenty-five Jordanian soldiers were killed, as against twenty-eight Israelis, but Arab public opinion was told that a full-scale Israeli invasion had been foiled; Karameh was accordingly seen as a great victory. Moreover, although it was the

Jordanian army, and not the guerrillas, that had inflicted most Israeli casualties, the battle was captured by the Fatah propaganda-machine.[8]

The Fatah claimed that it had succeeded in defeating the Israelis when all Arab armies had failed; on the basis of this fabrication it launched a successful fund-raising and propaganda campaign which portrayed the Fatah as the 'wave of the future' and the final arbiter of the Arab–Israeli conflict. The myth of military prowess was not exposed until the collapse of the irregulars three years later; in the meantime it formed the basis of their prestige in Arab (and non-Arab) eyes.

The post-1967 cease-fire line between Israel and Jordan was identical with the pre-1948 international border between Palestine and the Kingdom of Transjordan. From the densely populated Beisan Valley south of Lake Tiberias it bisected the lower Jordan Valley and the Dead Sea, continuing virtually as a straight line to the shores of the Red Sea. Between 1968 and 1970 the northern segment of the line, which followed the meandering course of the Jordan, became the scene of a ceaseless struggle between the Israelis and the Palestinian guerrillas. Both sides of the Jordan Valley are arid, with almost no vegetation right up to the western watershed on the hills of Judea and Samaria; settlement is limited to irrigated oases, of which the largest is Jericho. On both sides the population is Arab: on the west the Arabs of Judea and Samaria under Israeli military rule following the 1967 War, and on the east the Arabs of Transjordan, many of whom are of Palestinian origin. In the first phase, which began shortly after the 1967 War, the Fatah sent men and weapons across the Jordan to establish sabotage networks among the Arabs of Judea and Samaria. As the Fatah and its competitors* gathered momentum, increasing numbers of infiltrators were sent across, with excellent automatic weapons, very little training, and guides familiar with the many caves and gullies of the Jordan Valley.

Owing to the successes of guerrilla–terrorist movements,† from Algeria to Vietnam, there is a widespread tendency to exaggerate the effectiveness of this type of politico-military warfare. Many

---

* Its main rival was the 'Popular Front for the Liberation of Palestine'; by 1970 there were more than twelve rival organizations.

† Rural guerrilla plus urban terrorism.

observers predicted that in the Fatah the Israeli Army was facing an enemy against which all its tactical brilliance would be of no avail. In particular, it was said that the Palestinian guerrilla movements would inevitably succeed in gaining the support of the population in the occupied territories. The networks of covert civilian members ('the subversive base') would then supply food, shelter and information to the guerrilla arm of Fatah, so that it could strike at Israel from within. Israeli repression and acts of reprisal would follow, inevitably playing into the hands of the guerrillas by heightening the discontent of the occupied populations. In the words of a seemingly authoritative survey, Israel was in for 'a renewal of . . . inter-communal friction – the sniper at the upper window, the grenade lobbed into the coffee house'.[9] There was going to be a new war between Israel and the guerrillas for which 'Israeli military talents would provide no solution'. But the Israelis did find a solution; its essence was their refusal to play their allotted part as repressive occupiers.

Within the occupied territories, the military Government, personally controlled by Moshe Dayan through a few hand-picked aides, followed a policy of extreme liberality. Jordanian-appointed mayors and their local government, police forces, laws and regulations were all left unchanged.* No attempt was made to control freedom of speech and it was made clear to all that the military Government did not expect 'collaboration'. The basic guideline of Dayan's policy was to minimize interference in the lives of the population; another was to encourage the recovery and then the growth of the local economy, especially its agricultural base. This involved not only technical and financial aid, but also the highly original 'open bridges' policy which allowed the movement of people and goods between the occupied areas and Transjordan – though Israel and the Kingdom of Jordan were in a state of war.[10] Two-way travel was permitted for Arabs even though Israelis were excluded from Jordan, and this traffic was almost unaffected by the sporadic outbreaks of fighting along the cease-fire line.

On occasion, trucks loaded with produce crossed the river while, a few miles away, Israeli and Jordanian forces were exchanging

---

* The one instance of interference was the deletion of anti-Jewish and anti-Israeli statements from schoolbooks. At first overambitious, the cuts were later scaled down to eliminate only the most offensive statements.

fire. It is typical of the highly personalized style of the military government that this unconventional policy was devised by relatively junior officers in Samaria and endorsed as official government policy only at a later stage. While the economic policies improvised by the military government were successful (they resulted in unprecedented prosperity for Arab agriculture whose output doubled by 1969), the poorer segments of the population benefited most from their free access to jobs in the high-income Israeli economy. In spite of terrorist threats, by 1969 thirty thousand Arab workers commuted daily from Gaza, Judea and Samaria to Israeli factories and farms.

The liberality of the military government and its economic measures were meant as incentives for the local population to avoid all contact with local terrorists and imported guerrillas. Arab patterns of life could continue very much as before; except for small, almost symbolic patrols, Israeli troops were kept out of sight, partly to assuage Arab sensitivities. All this was one side of the policy coin; swift and severe sanctions were the other. Active terrorists or guerrillas were imprisoned, and suspects were deported across the river without trial; the most effective sanction was perhaps the demolition of houses owned by terrorists and those that gave them aid and comfort.

This was a fitting punishment since it affected primarily the wealthier segments of the Arab population – which were also those that had gained least from the incentives. Landowners, lawyers and former officials of the Jordanian government had suffered a loss in both social status and economic power since Arab workers and peasants could now turn to the high-wage Israeli labour market and were no longer at their mercy. Although Jordanian law, still in force, did provide for capital punishment, the military courts followed Israeli legal practice in this respect and never applied the death penalty.[11]

Instead of community-wide reprisals – whose only effect is to drive passive elements into the arms of rebellion – the Israelis in most cases patiently tried to find those responsible for terrorist acts. Arabs living under the occupation quickly realized that the efficiency of Israeli security intelligence would avert undeserved punishments and – in most cases – identify terrorists and their active supporters. As a result, the General Security Service, the civilian branch responsible for security intelligence, was perhaps the main protagonist of the struggle against the Fatah and its rivals. Security agents penetrated the terrorist networks in Judea and Samaria so thoroughly that by the spring of 1968 the Fatah was left with only passive sympathizers; all its operational networks had been demolished. With this, *local* terrorism became episodic, and its ultimate results insignificant except in the Gaza Strip; there the military government and the General Security Service were much less successful. Until 1971, terrorist networks operated almost undisturbed and grenade attacks were a daily occurrence. But if the Israelis failed to control terrorism, the terrorists failed to use the Strip as a base for attacks on Jewish-inhabited territories.* They also failed to exert *political* control over the Gaza population. In 1969 ten thousand, and by 1970 twenty thousand Arabs living in the Strip daily went to work in Israeli factories and farms, in spite of all the appeals from the Palestinian organizations which stressed that Arab workers were releasing Israeli manpower for military service.

When the General Security Service penetrated and destroyed its hastily organized cells in Judea and Samaria, the Fatah made the first of its retreats. Instead of emulating the Vietcong in building local, self-sustaining, terrorist and guerrilla cells through a slow but solid process of subversion, the Fatah sacrificed its future for the sake of quick results. Lacking a genuine subversive base, it sent armed guerrillas from across the Jordan. Not being local men, these imported guerrillas inspired little confidence in Arab towns and villages; as strangers they were particularly vulnerable to detection and some made themselves unwanted by their tactless behaviour. More important, this tactic was a poor substitute for the creation of real fish-in-water guerrilla forces, since it was vulnerable to standard military counter-measures. To reach the towns and villages of Judea and Samaria, Fatah operatives† had to infiltrate across the cease-fire line.

The topography of the torrid valley of the Jordan, the deepest depression in the world (1,200 ft. below sea level), shaped the

---

* Except for the placing of mines in the fields of kibbutzim directly adjacent to the strip.

† Fatah men were paid on scales much higher than those prevailing in the Jordanian or Israeli armies.

tactics of both sides. To cross the Jordan undetected, the guerrillas moved at night in groups of a dozen or so; if they managed to elude Israeli ambushes and patrols along the Jordan, which is easily forded at many places, they had only a few hours of darkness to cross the open ground west of the river and to reach the shelter of wadis or caves. Once there, the guerrillas had to hide until nightfall, when they could resume their march to the towns and villages of the West Bank still several hours away. Each day at dawn the Israelis patrolled along the river looking for the tracks of guerrilla bands that had crossed during the night; knowing how far they could have walked during the night, the Army sent small foot, jeep and helicopter patrols to search wadis and caves within a semicircle drawn from the crossing point. These 'chase missions' ended in gunfights between the small groups ranged on either side. Initially the Israelis suffered frequent casualties in these fire-fights including some senior officers who insisted on leading the pursuit units personally.

Mobile patrols and pursuit tactics were supplemented by an increasingly sophisticated anti-infiltration barrier running from Lake Tiberias to the Dead Sea with mined strips, fences, surveillance devices and a variety of classified equipment. At first uncontrolled, infiltration was eventually contained and finally virtually eliminated. By 1970 the Jordanian cease-fire line was effectively sealed; Israeli casualties decreased from an average of thirty per month in 1969 to five in the second half of 1970 as fire-fights became rarer, and it became evident that the Palestinian organizations had failed to sustain guerrilla action in the West Bank through infiltration.

Often willing to hide and feed guerrillas, the population of the occupied areas refused to take an active part in sabotage activities.[12] A lack of discipline, and the failure to conduct *political* subversion in depth, eventually deprived the Fatah and its rivals of even this limited cooperation. In their frequent and increasingly relaxed contacts with Arab town and village leaders, Dayan and the district military governors made it clear that they did not demand or expect active collaboration with Israeli security forces, but they also pointed out that cooperation with the guerrillas would be severely punished. This left a safe middle ground on which the occupied population was content to stand. The guerrillas for their part were too weak to use terror in order to discipline the reluctant. The Fatah, the Popular Front for the Liberation of Palestine and their dozen smaller rivals imitated the mannerisms of the Vietcong and the Algerian F.L.N. but lacked perseverance in political indoctrination and the stomach for terrorist compulsion.

Lacking the indispensable subversive bases within the occupied population, in the spring of 1970 the guerrillas made their second strategic retreat. In northern Galilee and the Beisan Valley, the unchanged demarcation line left Jewish-inhabited areas directly adjacent to the border, and within easy range of barrage rockets and mortars. The guerrillas now began shelling Israeli towns and villages from the sanctuary of Lebanese and Jordanian territory; the Katyusha rocket* emerged at this time as the typical weapon of the Palestinian irregulars, marking their decline from guerrillas to little more than the unwanted auxiliaries of the regular forces of Jordan and Lebanon.

Katyusha rockets are inaccurate, but the objective of the guerrillas was to terrorize civilian settlements, and they were not concerned with accuracy.

The guerrillas were quite openly operating on Jordanian territory, but the Israelis could not cross the border because of political constraints arising from American support for the Jordanian regime. The latter claimed full sovereign rights but refused to accept responsibility for guerrilla attacks emanating from its territory. As a result, the guerrillas could go on firing rockets and mortars at Israeli villages with impunity; that this tactic was totally ineffectual in terms of their long-term aims did not reduce the human anguish and material losses suffered by the Israelis living near the border. With political constraints foreclosing a direct answer to guerrilla shelling, the Israeli Army resorted to an indirect strategy based on the principle of graduated response. When border villages were shelled, Israeli artillery shelled Jordanian army positions; when the town of Beit Shean was hit by rockets, the Israelis used long-range guns to shell the Jordanian town of

* Originally developed by the Russians during the Second World War, Katyushas are unguided fin-stabilized rockets fitted with large explosive warheads, and fired from portable tripods or from multi-tube launchers mounted on trucks or tractors.

Irbid; when Jordanian or Iraqi artillery opened fire in support of the guerrillas, the Israelis responded with air strikes against the offending batteries.

This graduated 'price-list' was tacitly recognized by the Jordanians who began to exercise some degree of control over the guerrillas. The security situation of the Israeli port town of Elat on the Red Sea provided the best example of this type of tacit understanding. Elat is an important tourist and transport centre for Israel, but the adjacent town of Aqaba is Jordan's only port and therefore relatively far more important. The Jordanians were understandably anxious to ensure its safety and took strict security measures to prevent guerrilla attacks against Elat. One incident occurred all the same: on 8 April 1969 Elat was shelled with Katyusha rockets. The Israeli response was an immediate air strike against the port of Aqaba. No more attacks on Elat took place.

In Lebanon, as in Jordan, the government did not sponsor or encourage guerrilla activity, but it was unwilling or unable to control the territory over which it claimed sovereignty. At first the Palestinian organizations used Lebanese soil only for their fund-raising and propaganda offices; later they began to make Beirut the organizational base for terrorist attacks against Israeli civilian aircraft at European airports. When terrorists coming from Lebanon, some of whom carried Lebanese passports, attacked El Al aircraft at European airports, the Israelis responded in December 1968 with a commando raid against Beirut International Airport.*

The commandos† were instructed to destroy all Arab-owned aircraft in the airport without damaging any (non-Arab) airliners; they had also been given strict orders to avoid any casualties, even if the Lebanese were to resist and open fire.

When the Israeli commandos, some forty in all, descended from their helicopters right on the main airport runway at 9.30 p.m. on

---

* The event which triggered the Beirut raid was an attack on an El Al airliner at Athens Airport on 25 December 1968; a few months earlier, on 23 July, an El Al airliner had been hijacked to Algiers. In both instances Lebanon was implicated.

† Here described as commandos, their formal designation is 'reconnaissance' troops.

the night of 28 December, panic broke out in the crowded passenger lounges. Arabic-speaking Israeli soldiers controlled the crowds, giving instructions via hand-held loudspeakers. At the same time, another group of commandos escorted passengers who had already boarded Arab-owned aircraft back to the passenger lounge. Thirteen Arab aircraft, including nine jetliners, were blown up after being thoroughly searched to ensure that no passengers were left on board. Although there were vast secondary explosions from their fuel tanks when the T.N.T. charges were set off, no other aircraft parked on the tarmac was damaged, and there were no casualties. Even when some Lebanese policemen opened fire, the Israelis managed to intimidate them by firing in the air and refrained from shooting back. The airport is only two and a half miles from Beirut and motorized units of the Lebanese army were sent to the scene of the raid almost at once. The Lebanese column was intercepted by another squad of commandos which had set up a road block on the way to the airport. Again, there was no shooting and no casualties. The Israelis released some smoke canisters and this was enough to stop the Lebanese from advancing any further. At 10.30 p.m., one hour after they had landed, the commandos returned to Israel.

Although the Beirut raid was later criticized in the Israeli press because of its political repercussions,* there was little doubt that on a purely technical plane the operation was virtually perfect. It is notoriously difficult to control commando-style operations, and in an airport crowded with panic-stricken passengers and replete with highly inflammable aircraft and fuel dumps, operational control required an extraordinary degree of precision.†

But the Beirut raid did not induce the Lebanese government to control the guerrillas operating on its territory. When the Palestinian organizations were sealed off by the Jordan Valley barrier, they

---

* De Gaulle's government used the occasion to impose a total arms embargo; the U.S. complained, and Israel was criticized even by the Pope (who had remained silent when blood was spilled but chose to protest against the destruction of property).

† According to the foreign press, the forty-odd commandos were led by Brig.-Gen. Rafael Eytan – a legendary figure in Israel, one of Sharon's original paratroopers, and Chief Officer of Paratroops and Infantry. (In 1973 Eytan distinguished himself as a divisional commander on the Golan Heights.)

began to stage attacks from Lebanon. Again, they were unable to penetrate Israeli territory in depth and failed to establish subversive networks among the 250,000 Israeli Arabs of central Galilee. Again they opted for a second-best tactic: the shelling of Israeli settlements from adjacent Lebanese territory, as well as shallow but occasionally successful infiltration. Once more, the Israelis could not respond with decisive military counter-measures since Lebanon's Western friends put pressure on the Israeli government to avoid attacks on her territory. The only way of protecting the border villages would have been to establish a layer of Israeli-controlled territory wider than the range of guerrilla weapons* but political constraints made this impossible at this stage.

Although the sporadic and inaccurate bombardment of Israeli towns and villages did not cause heavy casualties or much damage, the Israeli leadership felt that some kind of reaction was imperative, if only for the morale of the local population, which includes a high percentage of recent immigrants from North Africa and the Middle East. Instead of air strikes or commando raids, the Israelis decided to try out a new, low-cost tactic which would not result in politically explosive battles or heavy casualties. On 12 May 1970 an Israeli mechanized column raided the Fatah camping grounds on the slopes of Mount Hermon just across the Lebanese border in order to disrupt guerrilla operations by capturing weapon stocks. Advancing with noisy tanks and carriers in broad daylight no surprise was possible; the guerrillas merely left their bases only to return once the Israelis had withdrawn. After the ambush of a schoolbus and the killing of twelve Israelis including eight young children on 22 May 1970, the Israelis decided to ignore foreign pressures and began to patrol on *both* sides of the border.[13] Pairs of Israeli tanks crossed the border in daylight along with a few soldiers on foot and took up commanding positions to observe and intercept guerrilla movements near the border. At night, the same objective was achieved by ambushes on the Lebanese side of the border. In this way Israelis could maintain effective military control of a strip of Lebanese territory without a formal occupation,

---

* Katyusha rockets vary in size and range from the 20 km. BMD-25, which weighs 450 kg. to the 8.2 km. RM-130 which weighs 26 kg. The most popular types with the Fatah seems to have been the BM-21 (range is 15 km., weight 46 kg.).

and without interfering with the Lebanese population in the area. After some formal protests, the Lebanese government tacitly accepted these patrols and the Lebanese army made no attempt to intervene.

The Syrian cease-fire line was the quietest of all, although Syria remained the most verbally militant of Israel's neighbours. The Syrians gave political and propaganda support to the Palestinian organizations and sponsored one of their own, the Saeka, but though the Syrian army gave logistic help for guerrilla operations mounted from Jordanian and Lebanese soil, it kept a tight control over the guerrillas on its own territory. Behind a barrage of strident propaganda, the Syrians were most careful to avoid trouble with Israel, in spite of the very large concentration of forces they deployed along the cease-fire line.*

Since the Syrian government actually controlled its territory and all the armed forces on it, the Israelis could develop a tacit *modus vivendi* with it more easily than with Jordan or Lebanon. This was based on the mutual understanding that any violation of the cease-fire would trigger a proportional Israeli response; the Syrians were very careful to avoid such violations unless they had some weighty political reasons for doing so, and whenever they staged an incident to serve Syrian purposes in inter-Arab politics, they accepted the inevitability of Israeli retaliation. A spectacular though entirely harmless exchange was the 'war of the booms' in January 1970. On 23 January 1970 a Syrian MiG-21 fighter flew over the Israeli city of Haifa at supersonic speed and low altitude, thus producing a loud 'sonic boom'. On the evening of the same day, Israeli Phantoms flew over several cities from Damascus in the south to Aleppo in the far north, their height being such as to produce particularly powerful sonic booms.

Not all the incidents between Israel and Syria were as harmless as this. When the Syrians orchestrated a border incident to coincide with an Arab summit meeting in June 1970, the Israelis reacted on 26 June with a spoiling attack against the very large concentrations of Syrian tanks and artillery along the cease-fire line. Thirty Syrian tanks were destroyed (and an assault gun captured)

* In May 1970 it was reported that the Syrians had no fewer than 900 battle tanks deployed, about the same number as the Egyptians had in Sinai in 1967.

as against no Israeli tank losses. Another Israeli tactic was to send heli-borne raiders into Syrian territory to sabotage remote installations and shell army camps with light mortars. Since the targets were a long way from the front, such raids were thought to have a powerful psychological impact on the Syrians.

The Jordanian, Lebanese and Syrian cease-fire lines were described by Arab media as the 'Eastern Front', but from the Israeli point of view all three presented only a problem of 'current' security in the border areas themselves. It was only on the Egyptian front that Israel faced a serious strategic threat.[14]

The Egyptian Front: War of Attrition

Until the autumn of 1968 Nasser's Egypt made no real attempt to dislodge the Israelis from Sinai by military means. Confident that what they had lost in war would be made good by international diplomatic action, the Egyptians were content to harass the Israelis, hitting at targets of opportunity while waiting for a 'political' solution. Equally deluded, the Israelis at first occupied Sinai without preparing for its defence, believing that Nasser's discredited regime would soon be replaced by a new leadership ready to negotiate a peaceful settlement.

When more than a year had passed and neither of these expectations had been realized, the Egyptians began a systematic offensive on the Canal front. They could not force a crossing of the Canal; even if their forces could get across in the face of Israeli air superiority, not even the most optimistic Egyptians could contemplate a straight fight between Israeli and Egyptian armour with any degree of equanimity. Plentifully supplied with guns and howitzers by their Russian patrons, the Egyptians tried instead to force an Israeli withdrawal by using artillery fire to inflict unacceptable casualties to the forces along the Canal.

The Israelis responded to this static offensive by fire with a two-pronged strategy: to *absorb* the weight of enemy fire-power they constructed increasingly elaborate fortifications; to *deflect* the Egyptian offensive they launched de-stabilizing attacks on all sectors other than the Canal, relying on all tactics bar the conventional. Heli-borne commandos raided targets of value deep within Egypt, frogmen–commandos attacked naval vessels and isolated positions by the sea, and even armour took part by staging

an amphibious raid on the Egyptian coast south of the Canal.
From August 1969, the Israelis relied increasingly on air power to
contain Egyptian fire on the ground; the Russians in turn introduced air defence forces, and this second phase of the fighting
culminated in duels between Israeli fighters and Russian missiles.
By August 1970 both sides recognized the stalemate by accepting
a new cease-fire sponsored by the United States; Israel's strategic
and territorial position was now such that a stalemate, which
would have been catastrophic in 1967, was equivalent to a qualified
victory.

When the cease-fire had come into effect on 10 June, 1967, the
Israeli Army found itself in control of the Sinai Peninsula but had
no clear political guidance on the duration and purpose of the
occupation. Port Fuad and its causeway at the northern end of the
Suez Canal were east of the waterway, whose mid-line was generally understood to mark the cease-fire line, but for purely technical
reasons the Israelis made no move to occupy either. The causeway,
a narrow roadbed with the Canal on one side and impassable mud
flats on the other, thus became a no-man's-land between Egyptian-
held Port Fuad and the Sinai mainland.

A dispute over this strip of land triggered the very first engage-
ment of what eventually became the War of Attrition. On 1 July
1967, two Egyptian platoons took up positions astride the causeway; on the evening of the same day, the Israelis moved up tanks
to dislodge them and then established a stronghold a few miles
south of Port Fuad. This was to remain the northern limit of
Israeli-held territory along the Canal.[15] The skirmish turned out to
be only the first of a series, all caused by conflicting Israeli and
Egyptian demarcations of the cease-fire line. The Israelis held that
the line should run straight down the middle of the Canal and that
both sides, or neither, should be free to use the waterway. The
Egyptians fired at Israeli boats on the Canal while attempting to
sail their own. The real issue was not navigation but the rights of
the two sides in deciding on the re-opening of the Canal; accordingly it was worth fighting for. After several shooting incidents, a
typically negative *status quo* emerged: neither side was to use the
Canal.

Until October 1967, holding the line along the Canal was little
more than a boring routine for the Israelis; the troops built

shallow earthworks with no hard fortifications. There was only one major incident during this period, the sinking of the Israeli destroyer and flagship *Elat*. On 21 October 1967 the *Elat* was on a routine patrol along the Sinai coasts when it was hit and sunk by a Styx missile fired by Egyptian boats from within Port Said harbour. The small Israeli Navy had only two destroyers to patrol 560 miles of coast-line (as against 150 before the war) and on her patrol of the north Sinai coast, the *Elat* was operating totally without support. The sinking, with the loss of forty-seven dead and missing, was a major act of war and the Israelis responded accordingly. The Egyptians may have thought that a reprisal against Port Said would be inhibited by the presence there of several Russian warships, but the Israelis once again avoided a stereotyped response and instead struck at a far more valuable target. On 24 October 1967, three days after the sinking of the *Elat*, Israeli guns shelled the Egyptian oil refineries at Suez and set the storage tanks on fire.*

The first bout of shelling did not exhaust the hostage value of the refineries and the Israelis shelled them again whenever the Egyptians broke the rules of the game. It was only in 1969, when the Egyptians inaugurated the War of Attrition, that the refineries finally lost their hostage value since the Egyptians no longer attempted to repair them. By then it also became clear that the Egyptian government was willing to sacrifice the cities along the Canal – a far more valuable hostage than the refineries. (600,000 inhabitants were evacuated according to official Egyptian figures.)

The *Elat*-refineries exchange established a new *status quo* along the Canal which lasted for eleven months. On 8 September 1968 the war entered a new phase when the Egyptians unleashed a prepared artillery barrage along sixty miles of the Canal, from Port Tewfik in the south to Kantara in the north. Thousands of shells were fired, ten Israelis were killed and eighteen wounded. Several weeks later, on 26 October 1968, the Egyptians repeated

* It seems likely that the Egyptians thought that the refineries were protected by the tacit *modus vivendi* which covered the oil-producing areas in the Red Sea: the Israelis worked the offshore oilfields at Belayim, while the Egyptians and their American partners continued to operate the El Morgan fields a few miles away. Both oilfields continued to function normally throughout the War of Attrition.[16]

their move, killing thirteen Israelis by a massive artillery barrage; two more were killed in an Egyptian ambush on the same night. The immediate Israeli reaction was another bout of shelling against Suez, Ismailiya and the refineries, but it was evident that the Egyptians had already discounted their loss; this move did not amount to an adequate retaliatory response.

The first phase of desultory and purposeless cease-fire violations had come to an end. The Egyptians now had a strategy and a goal: to prevent the consolidation of the cease-fire line into a permanent border by frequent attacks, in order to stimulate outside diplomatic intervention. Until then, the Israelis had thought in terms of occupying the line, but now they were faced with the problem of actively defending it against a purposeful offensive.

The deployments of the two sides along the Canal were entirely different in size and design. The Egyptians massed tens of thousands of men and several hundred heavy mortars, howitzers and guns in a series of fortified lines laid out in depth behind the Canal. The Israelis only kept a few thousand men on the other side of the water and instead of continuous trench lines, they built a chain of small strongholds from Ras el Eish in the north to Port Tewfik in the south (the so-called Bar-Lev line). Each stronghold was quite small and self-contained having a detachment of two or three tanks in lieu of artillery emplacements; in fact the aim was merely to provide shellproof shelter for lookouts and patrols. The strongholds could offer little protection to the interior of Sinai and were not meant to serve as defensive shields. The prime weapons of the defence were offensive, highly mobile armoured columns of battalion size whose task was to destroy the bridgeheads established by an Egyptian invasion force. Normally kept well in the rear – beyond the range of Egyptian artillery – the armoured columns were trained to advance rapidly in the event of a Canal-crossing offensive in order to seal off and destroy the bridgeheads and thus cut off any Egyptian spearheads that penetrated into the Sinai. (In 1973 there were only 600 men in the strongholds and only two tank battalions in the second line.)

Since the Egyptians had many more artillery weapons, and since they generally outranged the Israelis (who had no proper guns, only shorter-ranged howitzers), the latter could not hope to defeat or even contain the Egyptian artillery offensive by conventional means, i.e., counter-battery fire. But nor could they absorb the casualties that the shelling was inflicting. By dint of constant construction efforts, often under fire, the strongholds were kept shellproof in the face of heavier and heavier attacks, but the outbuildings, the patrols and above all the supply detachments that kept contact with the strongholds remained vulnerable. Something had to be done, and in the first of many tactical expedients, the Israelis launched a commando raid against a target of value deep in Egyptian territory. On 31 October 1968, five days after the second artillery barrage, a detachment of heli-borne paratroopers sabotaged two important bridges spanning the Nile and a new power transformer at Naj Hammadi, deep into Egypt and hundreds of miles from the Canal front.[17] The message of the raid was clear: if Israeli troops in the front line were vulnerable, so was the whole vast interior of Egypt. The raid was meant as a deterrent and also to induce a shift in Egyptian military resources, from offence to defence, and from the Canal to the interior. After Naj Hammadi there were no more Egyptian artillery attacks of any size until the beginning of March 1969. If the Naj Hammadi operation was indeed the cause of this interval, the raid may well have been the most cost-effective operation in the history of the Israeli Army: during those four months, 'hard' reinforced-concrete strongholds were built on the front line. Without this added protection, the Israelis could not have held the Canal over the next two years without heavy casualties.

The Army had no prior experience in positional warfare and had never built elaborate fortifications. The building of a static defence line went against all the professional instincts of the Israeli military. Steel and concrete fortifications are very expensive and resources spent on them would mean less for the mobile forces. A number of senior officers led by Maj.-Gen. Israel Tal, still O.C. Armour Corps, therefore advocated a strategy of elastic defence which would leave almost no Israeli forces within Egyptian artillery range, thus dispensing with the need for strongholds.[18] Their solution was to keep strong mobile forces in the rear, ready to advance against any Egyptian attempt to cross the Canal. But at the political level it was feared that the Egyptians could establish some sort of bridgehead on the Israeli side, and then invoke political intervention at the U.N. in order to freeze a new *status quo*.

From the purely military point of view, it was feared that the Egyptians could hold back the mobile forces by a screen of heavy fire from their massed artillery on the far side of the Canal, while the invasion forces dug in.

For these reasons, Minister of Defence, Moshe Dayan, and the new Chief of Staff, Haim Bar Lev (1968–71), decided to build shell-proof strongholds. Apparently the Egyptians did not realize the significance of the massive work of construction that went on round the clock which their front-line troops must have seen and heard; when the Egyptians resumed large-scale shelling in March 1969, it was too late: the strongholds were ready and their concrete could not be penetrated. A very heavy Egyptian barrage on 8 March 1969 resulted in the death of a single Israeli soldier, as against the thirteen lost in the 26 October attack.

In March 1969 there came a major turning point in the War of Attrition. Egyptian artillery attacks* and commando raids increased in frequency and magnitude; primarily directed against the 'soft' supply traffic linking the strongholds with the rear and mobile patrol units, Egyptian attacks exacted an almost daily toll of casualties. By relying on artillery barrages and commando raids rather than attempting a moving offensive, the Egyptians chose the kind of warfare that suited them most. Their numerical superiority in artillery, and their far higher tolerance for casualties, gave them a clear advantage especially since the qualitative gap between the two sides was far narrower in static conditions, where Israeli tactical ingenuity and command flexibility were of little consequence. The Israelis refused to accept the rules of the game chosen by the Egyptians and responded by taking to the air. If it had to be a contest for fire superiority, the Israelis meant to use their Air Force in the role of 'flying artillery'. On 28 July 1969, the Israelis launched a daring commando raid against the southern hinge of Egyptian anti-aircraft defences at Green Island just south of the Suez Canal. Israeli frogmen scaled the perimeter wall, overwhelmed the defenders and destroyed anti-aircraft guns and radar installations. These obstacles having been removed, the Israeli air offensive began.

* The Egyptian Chief of Staff, General Abdel Munaim Riad, was killed together with a number of his entourage (some allegedly Russian) in an exchange of fire on 10 March 1969.

Attacking anti-aircraft guns and missiles first, road convoys and artillery batteries later, the I.A.F. lost only one aircraft in a long series of low-level strikes between July and December 1969. The Sam-2 (Guide-line) missiles and the large numbers of radar-directed anti-aircraft guns west of the Canal were poorly coordinated at first and could not even protect themselves, let alone prevent Israeli tactical bombing which inflicted heavy losses on the Egyptians and sharply reduced the volume of their artillery fire.

In September 1969, after the first month of the air offensive, the Israelis launched another of their typical de-stabilizing raids to force the Egyptians to switch more of their military effort away from the Canal. Israeli frogmen sank two Egyptian torpedo boats in their home port (Ras Sadat) on the night of 9 September; the boats had been used to patrol the northern shores of the Gulf of Suez and, with their destruction, the coast was quite literally open. Early next day, an assault team of tanks and troop-carriers was taken to the Egyptian side of the Gulf by landing craft. After making an unopposed landing, the Israelis travelled down the coastal road at speed, shooting up Egyptian trucks and jeeps and destroying installations in their path. According to reports in the foreign press, the column consisted of half a dozen Russian vehicles captured in 1967, identical to those used by the Egyptians. In nine hours spent on Egyptian soil, in broad daylight, the raiders travelled more than thirty miles down the coastal highway south of Suez without ever being stopped; two wounded were evacuated by helicopter and the whole force re-embarked at Ras Zafrana, returning safely to the Israeli side of the Gulf.[20] The total disarray of the Egyptian units holding the area (none warned the other as each was attacked in turn) and their heavy losses had profound repercussions. The Egyptians attempted to retaliate by launching a large-scale air attack against Israeli positions in Sinai on 11 September 1969, but seven Egyptian MiG-21s, one Mig-17 and three Su-7 jets were shot down for no I.A.F. losses. A few days later, the Egyptian Chief of Staff was replaced after only six months in office.

By September 1969, as in 1967, Israel had achieved total superiority in the air and this time without the benefit of a pre-emptive strike.[19] As part of a Russo-Egyptian attempt to exact a higher cost for Israeli air strikes, a relatively advanced type of low-level Russian radar (P-12) had been introduced earlier in the year. Anxious to examine this new equipment in order to devise counter-measures, the Israelis sent a force of reconnaissance troops to seize a P-12 station near Ras Gharib on the night of 26 December 1969. Heavy-lift helicopters were flown in, and a team of engineers worked most of the night to dismantle the heavy radar equipment into helicopter loads. The Israelis worked without interference; several of the Egyptians guarding the radar had been taken prisoner while those who managed to escape failed to alert Egyptian units stationed near by. The frequency range, agility and electronic countermeasure devices of radar systems are among the few really valuable military secrets that cannot be uncovered by visual reconnaissance and this raid was an intelligence coup of the first order.

In March 1968, Nasser had proclaimed the beginning of the 'stage of liberation';[21] one year later on 31 March 1969 he formally repudiated the U.N. cease-fire and announced the beginning of the 'preventive defence stage'; finally, on 23 June 1969, he declared a War of Attrition.[22] Nevertheless, the Egyptians failed to dislodge the Israelis from the Canal by inflicting unacceptable casualties on their front-line troops.* In the meantime, as against this, Egyptian losses in equipment and men had been very considerable. One estimate is 30,000 casualties from June 1967 to January 1970. Israeli air power had sufficed to offset the Egyptians' numerical superiority on the ground, especially in artillery forces; the Canal strongholds could therefore hold out since Egyptian fire-power was contained by Israeli tactical bombing. Its cost in terms of I.A.F. aircraft shot down was surprisingly small, considering the density of Egyptian anti-aircraft guns. From June 1967 until January 1970, the I.A.F. lost only fifteen aircraft on *all* fronts; of these, two were lost in air combat, the rest having been shot down by anti-aircraft fire from the ground.

At first the Egyptian air force tried to intercept Israeli fighter-bombers, but by the end of 1969 they gave up the attempt, after

---

* The Israelis lost a total of 244 killed and 699 wounded on the Egyptian front between June 1967 and January 1970.[23] Considering the very large volumes of fire which were exchanged, these figures testify to the effectiveness of the fortified strongholds.

suffering heavy losses.* The effectiveness of the Israeli air offensive is graphically demonstrated by the decline in the monthly casualty figures for the Egyptian front. From 106 dead and wounded in July 1969, before the start of the air offensive, the monthly totals of Israeli casualties were as follows: August – sixty-five; September – forty-seven; October – fifty-six; November – thirty-nine; December – thirty.[25] The Israelis were clearly gaining the upper hand and it became evident that the Egyptians could neither launch an offensive across the Canal nor force the Israelis to withdraw by exploiting their low tolerance for casualties.

Having used air power successfully to contain Egyptian artillery attacks, the Israelis now decided to employ it for a far more ambitious, political purpose. With the introduction of the two-seat heavy-weight Phantom F-4, the I.A.F. now had its first supersonic aircraft capable of delivering substantial weapon loads (up to seven tons) at long ranges; a true multi-mission aircraft, the Phantom also had the speed (Mach 2.4) and high acceleration required for air-combat. As a result, Phantoms could be used for precision bombing in depth without needing an umbrella of interceptors. On 7 January 1970, the I.A.F. launched the first of a series of bombing raids against military bases in the Nile Valley, close to Cairo and well beyond the Canal area. Although the targets were still purely military, it was realized that such attacks differed in kind from the tactical strikes along the Canal.

The bombing of depots and supply bases near Egyptian cities could disrupt Egyptian logistic support for the forces deployed along the Canal; it could also force the Egyptians to disperse their anti-aircraft forces, until then concentrated near the Canal. But it also had a political purpose: to weaken Nasser's standing as a war leader for the Egyptians and the Arabs at large by further reducing his credibility. In the face of all historical evidence on the counter-productive morale effects of bombing some Israelis may even have hoped to bring about Nasser's downfall.[26]

For a time it seemed that all these different purposes were being achieved. Egyptian attacks along the Canal fell off quite sharply;†

* Between July 1967 and January 1970 the Egyptians lost 60 aircraft (mostly first-line MiG–21s); the Syrians lost 14.[24]

† During the second week of the offensive the Egyptians opened fire 48 times as against 85 times in the previous week, and this trend continued.

the bombing of depots and bases destroyed large quantities of high-cost supplies and Egyptian troops along the Canal were visibly affected by supply shortages. But the political effects of the bombing campaign were far less favourable to the Israelis. Critics, both in Israel and abroad, claimed that deep penetration bombing would only strengthen Nasser's position by stimulating a sense of national solidarity around his person. Others, including some members of the Cabinet, objected on moral grounds, especially after the Abu Zabaal incident (12 February 1970) when an Israeli Phantom bombed a factory by mistake, killing eighty-six civilians. And then there were those who feared that the Russians would step in to avert Nasser's downfall. Some critics were content to rest their case on all three points. The claim that Nasser's position was being *strengthened* by the bombing campaign was soon disproved. On 22 January 1970, Nasser made a supposedly secret visit to Moscow, to plead for help; the Russians apparently responded with their first direct, but still limited, intervention in the conflict.

The Israeli Prime Minister, Golda Meir, later admitted that the possibility of direct Russian intervention in response to the bombing campaign had not even been taken into consideration when the I.A.F. plan was discussed.[27] Some members of the Cabinet, including the Minister of Defence, Moshe Dayan, later argued that the deepening Russian involvement was the logical consequence of the failure of the Egyptian War of Attrition, and could not be attributed to the bombing campaign.[28] Few found this explanation convincing.

In March 1970 it was reported that Sam-3 (Goa) anti-aircraft missile batteries manned by Russian crews had appeared in Egypt. Not long after, the Israelis reported the presence of Russian-manned MiG-21J interceptors. (Lacking data-link units, pilots and controllers had been overheard talking in Russian.) By the end of June no fewer than 120 MiG-21Js were integrated with fifty-five Goa missile batteries to form the Russian-operated* core of a new air defence system, which at this stage covered the Egyptian heartland in the Nile Valley. For tactical air defence, the Goa is a far more effective weapon than the Guideline previously deployed in

---

* Egyptian air defence forces were reportedly placed under the command of Col.-Gen. V. V. Okunev, detached from his post as Commander of the Moscow P.V.O. (air defence) district.

Egypt and the improved 'J' version of the MiG-21, manned by Russian pilots, was certainly more formidable than Egyptian air force MiG-21s. Above all, the tactical coordination of radars, missiles, A.A. guns and fighters added up to a major threat. If the weight of Russian equipment and the political threat symbolized by the presence of Russian crews could negate the I.A.F.'s ability to operate over Egyptian soil, there would no longer be a counterweight to the massed artillery on the far side of the Canal. Beyond the immediate military threat there loomed the prospect of further intervention. The Russians had crossed a crucial threshold in sending their own missile troops and pilots to Egypt, and the Israelis could not be certain that additional forces would not follow.

The basic axiom of Israeli strategy, originally laid down by Ben Gurion, was that the Army should be ready to fight against any combination of Arab states at all times, but that Israel should not, under *any* circumstances, risk a direct military conflict with a Great Power.[29] When the Russians chose to introduce their forces into Egypt, and when it became clear that the United States would not react, the Israelis faced a decision of supreme importance. Some argued that the only way of discouraging further Russian intervention was to make the depth of Israeli resolve quite unambiguous by attacking and destroying the Russian forces in Egypt. Others held that the Russians could not tolerate such a blow against their prestige; instead of cutting their losses, they would send more men and arms against Israel.[30] Veterans of three wars and countless crises, the Israelis now opted for caution; they decided to stop deep-penetration bombing, thus giving up their control over Egyptian air-space beyond the Canal area. At the same time, the Israelis made it clear that they would resist any Russian attempt to extend the air defence system towards the Canal.[31] Until 30 June 1970, two months after the last deep-penetration raid, the Russians seemed to have accepted the tacit agreement offered by Israel, but on that day two Israeli Phantom F-4 fighters were shot down by new batteries only twenty-five miles from the Canal.

Overlapping Goa and Guideline batteries had been moved into the Canal area literally overnight, to provide a thick air defence shield forty miles long. It was obvious that this shield could in turn cover the next forward step which would extend the killing radius of the missile belt right up to the banks of the Canal. The 'electronic summer' forecast by the Minister of Defence, Moshe Dayan, had come about. In the Russian system, 'improved Guideline'* batteries suited for high-altitude interception were protected against low-level strikes by Goa missiles, faster and more agile; both relying on ground-based search and tracking radars, the eyes of the system. Anti-radar deception, jamming and warning electronic countermeasure devices were the key to defeating the Russian system; the I.A.F. acquired such equipment but it still lost a total of five Phantoms between 30 June and 7 August, when a new cease-fire was imposed at the initiative of the U.S. government.

Exceptionally dense, with more than 1,000 A.A. guns as well as some six hundred missile launchers, the anti-aircraft belt from the Canal to Cairo was a formidable obstacle since each Israeli aircraft was exposed to the attack of more than a dozen missiles when striking at each battery. For more than a month a ceaseless struggle between aircraft and missiles continued; the Egyptians lost thousands of dead while attempting to move the missiles forward day after day. The Israelis were slowly being pushed back but continued their separate bombing offensive against the Egyptian artillery batteries near the Canal. While Phantoms were struggling to hold back the moving missile belt, the Skyhawk A-4s and other fighter-bombers dropped unprecedented tonnages of ordnance on the ground forces menacing the Israeli strongholds along the Canal.

Russian missile troops were active and fighting, but in their Egyptian uniforms their undeclared role could be denied. Not so for the MiG-21Js of the Russian air force. Beginning with the immediate Cairo area, their patrols were gradually extended until, in July 1970, Russian fighters attempted to intercept Israeli aircraft near the Canal. At first I.A.F. pilots were ordered to avoid combat but on 30 July 1970, Israeli and Russian fighters clashed head on. Four Russian MiG-21Js were shot down and a fifth damaged, as against no Israeli losses. Next day, the Commander-in-Chief of the Soviet air forces, Marshal P. S. Kutakhov, reportedly flew into

---

* The Guideline is a command-guided missile; the improved version is more agile.

Cairo to investigate the humiliating defeat of his men. Meanwhile, the much-maligned pilots of the Egyptian air force were said to be celebrating. However gratifying its results, the 30 July air battle had seen Israel in direct conflict with a global and nuclear power; this was not an experience the Israelis wanted to repeat.[32]

After 1,141 days of inconclusive warfare the fighting between Israel and Egypt was brought to an end when a new cease-fire came into effect on 7 August 1970. Sponsored by the U.S. government and endorsed by the Soviet Union, the cease-fire included a total military stand-still over a fifty-kilometre belt on either side of the Canal. Within ten hours the standstill was openly and massively violated by the Russians and Egyptians whose troops moved missile batteries right up to the Canal. This, and the lack of a forceful Israeli or American reaction, seemed to confirm the widespread view that the cease-fire indicated an Israeli defeat. Accordingly, it was generally expected that Israel would soon withdraw from the Canal without obtaining the negotiated settlement that remained her key political goal. Between June 1967 and August 1970 Israel had lost on all fronts 594 soldiers killed and 1,959 wounded, in addition to 127 civilians killed and 700 wounded; these losses seemed very heavy to the Israelis, especially since nothing was seemingly achieved in three years of fighting.

In retrospect the August 1970 cease-fire appeared in a different light. It soon emerged that the Russians and Egyptians had accepted the cease-fire not in exchange for tacit political concessions but because of dire military necessity: while public attention was focused on the I.A.F.'s losing battle against the missile belt, Israeli tactical bombing was inflicting devastating casualties on the Egyptians, reportedly 300 per day during the very last phase. It later transpired that in August 1970 front-line Egyptian forces were on the verge of total collapse.

By successfully resisting the Russian military threat, the Israelis had achieved the goal that eluded them in 1956, a political consolidation of their military gains. Arab diplomatic action at the U.N., in Europe, and in concert with the Soviet Union continued nevertheless, but it had become obviously futile; the Israelis could not be dislodged. The Arabs' attempt to secure an Israeli withdrawal with no compensating political concessions on their part had failed. In 1973 after a further war this still remained so, for, if the Egyptians were still demanding an Israeli withdrawal, they were now prepared for the first time to offer meaningful political concessions – just how meaningful it is too early to tell as of this writing.

The Army in the Seventies

To sustain the pressure on all fronts, but primarily to contain the Russo-Egyptian offensive, the Israelis had to deploy an unprecedented defensive effort after 1967. The length of male conscript service (thirty months as of 1967) was increased to three years,* the annual period of reserve duty was raised to two months or more for some combat troops, and many over-age reservists were re-assigned to the active forces.

For a full-employment economy whose growth was chiefly limited by the shortage of manpower this was a very heavy burden. As for direct budgetary costs, these amounted to no less than 5,000 million Israeli pounds for the fiscal year 1970–71, more than a quarter of the total G.N.P., and *450* per cent of the last pre-war figure of fiscal 1966–7. Foreign currency expenditures increased even more, from 160 million U.S. dollars in 1966–7 to over 800 million in 1970–71.[33]

But Israel fought the War of Attrition without the restrictions typical of war economies. Resources were channelled to defence by competitive pricing, while the country enjoyed a virtually unrestrained consumption boom (the number of private cars doubled between 1967 and 1971), a major investment spurt in industry and an increase in building that brought the number of housing starts to 50,000 dwelling units in 1971. There was no rationing, no austerity and no serious attempt to control the use of resources through central planning. According to the tenets of 'Zionist' economics, deficit budgets, foreign loans, inflation and devaluation are all preferable to central controls that would have limited the rapid increase in the standard of living and the growth of the economy. Over and above the other calls on her resources, Israel absorbed more than 100,000 new immigrants in the four

* Female conscription remained 20 months but a higher proportion of girls was actually conscripted.

years after the June War. In 1971, a new migration from the Soviet Union began; for the first time since the October Revolution, Jews were allowed to leave the Soviet Union and by 1972 they were arriving at the rate of almost 1,000 per week. In that year also the protests of poor sections of the population led to an expansion of the welfare programmes, including the distribution of some virtually free housing.

Financially unsound but dynamic as ever, the economy continued to grow. In their more sober pronouncements, Arab spokesmen had pointed out that, even if the Fatah and the Egyptians could never hope to defeat Israel on the battlefield, they would certainly cripple her economy and discourage immigration. Even these seemingly feasible goals were not attained. Economic growth and immigration were both at a much higher level in 1969–72 than in the five years prior to 1967.

The Ministry of Defence, under Moshe Dayan since 1967, had to share out the human and material resources at its disposal between a broad range of security programmes. From the building of reinforced concrete shelters in all border settlements, to the provision of security guards wherever terrorists could strike, substantial resources were absorbed by the struggle against the Palestinian guerrilla organizations. That the shelling, mining, bombing and grenade attacks of thousands of their men caused less than one hundred civilian deaths over a three-year period, belies the magnitude of the security burden they imposed. At the opposite end of the spectrum, there were the long-range weapon development programmes, which competed with current defence needs, just as defence as a whole competed with civilian needs.

By blocking the delivery of fifty Mirage-5 fighter-bombers even before the 1967 War, France had served notice on her best customer that she would no longer be a reliable source of arms. In January 1969 France completed her political realignment by imposing a total embargo on all weapon sales to Israel while negotiating to sell weapons to Iraq. By their endless hesitations in supplying weapons to Israel, while the Russians were airlifting them to Egypt, the Americans reminded Israel of the dangers of depending on others for essential military equipment. Unable as yet to put battle tanks and jet fighters into production, the Ministry of

Defence and its industrial affiliates resolved to obtain at home whatever Israeli factories could produce, while initiating a series of major development programmes for the future production of battle tanks, jet fighters and military electronics.

According to press reports, by 1972 the aircraft, missile and electronic concern I.A.I. (Israel Aviation Industries) had re-engined Mirage and other French-built aircraft, developed and produced the first sea-borne anti-shipping missile operational in the West, the Gabriel, and was in the process of developing a new jet fighter based on the Mirage pattern. (A Swiss court stated in 1969 that an Israeli military attaché had purchased illegally a large quantity of Mirage blueprints.) Unconfirmed reports claimed that I.A.I. was engaged in the production of short-range ballistic missiles, apparently code-named Jericho, with a presumptive range of 300 miles.

Ta'as, the weapon-production affiliate of the Ministry of Defence, set out after 1967 to make Israel self-sufficient in light arms and all types of ammunition. In addition, with the Army's Ordnance Corps, Ta'as and its sub-contractors re-engined Centurion and Patton M.48 tanks (with U.S.-made diesel engines) to increase their range, while Patton M.48s were upgunned and standardized with the powerful 105mm gun already mounted on the Centurion (produced under U.K. licence). Two new weapons, a 160mm heavy mortar mounted on rebuilt Sherman chassis, and a 90mm anti-tank gun mounted on half-track carriers, were produced for the artillery. Russian T-54 and T-55 battle tanks, supplied via the Egyptian army, were also re-engined and up gunned with 105mm guns to provide the Armour Corps with another hundred tanks – and, for once, at little cost to the Israeli tax-payer. Other Russian weapons, such as BTR-151 and BTR-40 wheeled troop carriers, 122mm and 130mm guns and truck-borne rocket launchers, were put to use without much more than refurbishing. The inevitable press reports also disclosed that Israel was in the process of developing a new battle tank of original design; here at least the size of Israeli tank forces would make domestic production no more uneconomical than in Britain or France.

The Ministry of Defence, much enlarged since 1967, was also responsible for nuclear weapon research and development. Competent observers agreed that by 1969 Israel had acquired the 'option': whether nuclear weapons were assembled or not would therefore depend on a political decision rather than on technological limitations. Israel's official position was still the Delphic pronouncement that 'Israel would not be the first to introduce nuclear weapons into the region', but it became apparent that given the non-nuclear balance of forces Israel had no real incentive to deploy nuclear weapons. (In spite of claims to the contrary this remained so after 1973.)

For all their efforts, the Israelis did not achieve self-sufficiency. At the cost of almost a billion U.S. dollars, and after endless struggles with the intricate bureaucracy in Washington (and its dilatory counterparts in other countries), Israel acquired after 1967 a formidable armoury of new weapons from abroad. The Air Force took the lion's share, receiving twin-jet Phantom F-4E (and RF-4E) multi-purpose fighters, Skyhawk A-4E (and H) light attack aircraft, Super-Frelon and CH-53 (Sea Stallion) heavy assault helicopters, and AB-205 utility helicopters as well as Hercules H-130E transports. Electronic warfare and radar devices, maintenance rigs and repair equipment, intercept and anti-radar missiles were also purchased, at great cost but with fewer political problems than with the much-advertised Phantom fighters. According to the Institute for Strategic Studies, the I.A.F. had built up a force of 432 combat aircraft by the summer of 1972, as against 275 in 1967.*

In terms of bombing capabilities (net tonnage over 'average' target ranges), the I.A.F.'s growth was dramatic: each Phantom can deliver up to seven metric tons of bombs and even the lightweight Skyhawk can deliver more than three, as against less than two for the Mirage IIIs of 5 June 1967. The Navy acquired during

* (Though I.S.S. figures must be used with caution.) I.S.S. figures as of 1972 (The military balance 1972–3): [Authors' notes]

Fighters	96 Phantom F–4E and 6 RF–4E; 50 Mirage IIIC; 9 Super-Mystères [Figures low]
Fighter-bombers	27 Mystère IVA; 30 Ouragan [Both deleted]
Light bombers	125 Skyhawk A–4 (E and H); 10 Vautour
Transport, fixed-wing	20 Noratlas; 10 Stratocruiser; 10 C–47; 2 C–130
Transport, rotary-wing	12 Super-Frelon; 10 CH–53; 30 AB–205; 20 Alouette
Anti-aircraft missiles	8 Hawk batteries with 48 launchers

this period its first custom-built warships, a flotilla of twelve Saar fast patrol boats equipped with radar, sonar and guidance electronics for their Gabriel missiles; three coastal submarines (500-ton class) were ordered from British shipyards, but no attempt was made to replace the destroyer *Elat* lost in combat. (A submarine, the *Dakar*, was lost in 1968 in transit, with all hands.) More potent than ever before, the Navy still remained a coastal defence force with limited capabilities.* (This statement was partially disproved by the surprising showing of the navy in 1973.)

The self-sufficiency programme benefited the ground forces sooner than either the Air Force or the Navy, but they too received much new equipment imported from abroad and primarily from the U.S. The Armour Corps† received Patton M.60A1s; these were its first new battle tanks ever, delivered fully equipped and fresh from the factory, instead of being second or third hand discards of other armies. Already fitted with the 105mm guns and diesel engine with which the secondhand Patton M.48s were fitted only after 1967 (except for a single company), this latest version of the Patton series was much superior to the M.48 in armour and optics.† The War of Attrition much increased the tactical role of the Artillery Corps even though Israel refused to limit the fighting to a straight contest for fire superiority on the ground. Primarily supplied with Israeli-made weapons since 1967, including the new 160mm SP mortar, the artillery also received new equipment from abroad: U.S.-built 155mm SP howitzers (M.109) and long-range 175mm SP guns (M.107). For the first time the artillery

* According to the I.S.S. it comprised two old model submarines, a single Z-class destroyer (the *Yafo*), sixteen small patrol boats, the twelve Saar boats, and ten landing craft.

† Israeli tank strengths, I.S.S. figures, summer 1972: [Authors' notes]
950 Centurions; 450 Patton M.48s; 100 T–54/T–55s (captured, Russian).
   All the above stripped and rebuilt with new diesel engines, new wiring and optics as well as high-velocity 105mm British-pattern guns. [Collation of I.S.S. data.]

New Patton M.60A1s [100% by 1973]
200 rebuilt Sherman M.4s (medium-velocity French-pattern 105mm guns).
1,000 rebuilt M.3 half-track carriers.
New M.113 U.S.-built carriers; ZIL–151 wheeled carriers (captured, Russian).
Israeli-made 90mm anti-tank guns on rebuilt M.3 carriers; various A.C.s.

received brand-new weapons (other than mortars) and for the first time it acquired long-range guns. Apart from these purchases, the artillery was the principal beneficiary of the weapon harvest of June 1967: excellent Russian field pieces (122mm howitzers and guns: 130mm guns) and useful truck-borne launchers for Katyusha-type bombardment rockets. Also captured in large numbers were small calibre anti-aircraft cannon and 57mm anti-tank guns. Many of these weapons were found intact and pressed into service. Later a number were selected as standard issue, refurbished by the Ordnance Corps, supported with training and supplies, and absorbed into the regular and reserve forces.

The infantry and paratroop forces were supplied with Israeli-made weapons but here too 'free imports' of captured equipment were added, including large numbers of AK-47s, the standard Russian assault rifle (Kalashnikov). In some brigades infantrymen had gone to war in 1967 with bolt-action rifles no better than those of the armies of 1914; by 1972 all combat troops had self-loading or automatic rifles as well as more and better anti-tank weapons.

The 1,141 days of the War of Attrition raised a large number of new organizational and tactical problems for the Army; some required drastic measures, and all had to be solved under the ceaseless pressure of war. For the pilots, the last year of combat meant round-the-clock operations 'with no sabbath, no family, no rest'. Facing the challenge of a steady technical escalation by the Russians, the I.A.F. kept pace by absorbing much new equipment while it was already under severe strain in its attempt to remain in control of the air. Hundreds of pilots and thousands of ground crews were trained in 1968–70 to handle totally new aircraft. Electronic warfare, a minor concern until 1967, became a field of primary importance. Intricate electronic warfare techniques had to be learnt from scratch, new equipment put into service and specialists trained under the constant pressure of the new missiles and new radars introduced by the Russians at short intervals until virtually all their air defence expertise, developed for strategic purposes over two decades, was thrown into the battle. Often near the breaking point, the small body of airmen had to find a way of growing in size and sophistication while retaining its qualitative edge. It was only after the August 1970 cease-fire that the I.A.F. recovered its balance, re-establishing the small-group cohesion and high technical standards that had been its hallmark before 1967.

The War of Attrition required an even more radical adjustment from the ground forces to a totally new strategy of territorial defence. Built to defeat enemy forces in swift battles of movement, the Army had to hold the 1967 lines without ever being allowed to counter-attack in depth on a large scale. In the General Staff Maj.-Gen. Ariel Sharon, G.O.C. Southern Command (1969–73), insisted on the need to preserve an offensive orientation by launching canal-crossing attacks but he was usually overruled. (Some raids did take place.) In 1968–70 the Army had to devise new tactical methods, retrain officers and men, absorb much new equipment – and do all this while fighting a conventional war on one front and counter-guerrilla war on three. The Engineer Corps, which had hardly built a stronghold until 1967, was made responsible for the construction of the so-called Bar Lev line along the Canal, the anti-infiltration barrier on the Jordan and many new roads, camps, depots and airfields. The Armour Corps and the Artillery Corps had to maintain large combat-ready forces in Sinai while at the same time training many new men to handle equipment much more sophisticated than ever before. The conflicting demands of training and 'readiness' were so acute that at times reserve tank battalions were allowed to manoeuvre their tanks for only one day out of thirty. For the Quartermaster branch of the General Staff and the units under its supervision, the post-1967 lines presented a totally new problem. Designed to fit the small size of pre-1967 Israel, when all points were within a few hours' travel of its central bases, the Army's supply organization had to provision forces across the width of Sinai and not for a few days, but seemingly permanently. Supply depots had to be extended and stock levels increased many times over, while lines of communication doubled and tripled in length. (In 1973 it turned out that stocks were still too low for safety.)

All branches of the Army were chronically short of manpower*

* According to the I.S.S. (1972), the ground forces comprised 11,500 career men, 50,000 conscripts (including women) and up to 213,500 reservists; assuming that one twelfth of the latter were in uniform at any one time, the total number in the ground forces at any one time was about 80,000. The Air Force, according to the same source, consisted of 10,000

and remained so even after the length of conscription was increased, many more girls were inducted, the career establishment expanded and the length of annual reserve duty doubled or tripled. Always poor in material resources, the Army had never regarded manpower as the limiting factor. On the contrary, as the most abundant resource, it was freely substituted for scarce supplies and limited funds and there was no great pressure to use manpower efficiently. The War of Attrition changed this situation radically; manpower became the most valuable of all resources and the true limiting factor in the growth of the combat forces. Army planners recognized the change: girls were substituted for potential combat soldiers serving as drivers and auxiliary police; over-age reservists were recalled for active duty instead of being left to the Local or Civil Defence. But the efficient management of manpower would also have required radical changes in established Army methods and, most difficult of all, in habits. Even after three years of war many officers continued to run their units as if manpower was still plentiful, and many reservists could complain that they had to leave their familes and jobs for nearly sixty days or more each year only to be left idle during several days of each recall owing to Army mismanagement.

The conflicting demands of force-building on the one hand and daily operations on the other were all the more acute because of the new defensive tactics that were coming to the fore. The price of change is disruption, and the changes required by any reforms had to be superimposed on those required by the new territorial and strategic conditions as well as by the influx of new equipment. In some cases, force-building and operations could be combined: air strikes along the Canal were far better bombing training for the Air Force than anything that could be obtained on the ranges; the artillery also trained its crews in action. Compromise solutions could also be found: garrisons for Judea and Samaria were provided by the simple expedient of moving training courses from central Israel to the well-appointed camps left behind by the Arab

career men, 1,000 conscripts and 9,000 reservists; the Navy of 3,500 career men, 1,000 conscripts and 500 reservists. (These figures should be treated with caution.)

Legion. In most cases, however, the dilemma could not be evaded. Tank forces could not be trained in large formations if tanks (with many maintenance hours left over) were also to be ready to repel an invasion. Infantry troops distributed in small detachments on the Canal and in the Jordan Valley could not at the same time be trained in large formations for mobile war. Nor could pilots learn the intricacies of E.C.M. in the classroom when every available man was urgently needed for combat.

For all this, the margin left over for force-building was sufficiently large to make the Army of 1972 a far more capable force than the one of 1967 both absolutely and – what is more important – relative to its enemies. (This is not clearly disproved by the 1973 War: after the initial shock it was the self-imposed casualty constraint that limited the scope of Israeli military action. Even so, the Syrians were badly defeated and the Egyptians lost more ground than they gained.) Its training was far more intensive and much improved by the lessons of 1967; most of its troops, civilian reservists, accumulated more days of active service in the three years following the War of Attrition than in all the years till 1967. The Arab armies, manned by long-service regulars or conscripts, could gain no proportionate benefit. The quality of Israeli equipment in 1967 was such that there was plenty of room for instant improvement by the simple substitution of standard modern weapons for those built twenty or thirty years before. This in itself increased capabilities very considerably, whereas the Arab armies were already so well equipped in 1967 that in many areas improvements could only be marginal.

Just as important perhaps was the added competence of the post-1967 officer corps which had acquired the experience of the mobile war of June 1967 and the War of Attrition. The increased prestige of the Army attracted an even better class of candidate for the career cadre than before; this was of crucial importance, since many more junior officers were retained in the career after their period of conscription (but not after the 1970 cease-fire). Many middle-rank officers who would ordinarily have been released were also retained in the professional service. This led to a promotion bottleneck above the *Aluf Mishne* (colonel) level. The problem was soon solved by the creation of a new rank *Tat Aluf*, (equivalent to brigadier-general)* which released the colonel rank for newly promoted officers.

Not all the Army's command problems could be solved so easily. Day-to-day operational problems and some of the post-1967 reforms required major changes in the structure of commands and formations. One of these was the creation of a new command echelon in charge of the 'Armoured Forces in Sinai'. Responsible for the control of the day-to-day operations along the Canal, this command was headed by an officer of general rank.

Within a few years of the 1967 War most of the senior commanders who had led the Army to victory were replaced to make way for new men. Yitzhak Rabin, the Chief of Staff, was replaced six months after the war by Lieut-Gen. Haim Bar Lev who was in charge throughout the War of Attrition. After four years, Bar Lev was in turn replaced by the man who had headed the Northern Command in 1967, Lieut-Gen. David Elazar, whose number two was Maj.-Gen. Israel Tal, former Commander of the Armour Corps. The heads of three out of four General Staff branches, all three Area Commanders, and most corps and branch heads, were also replaced, sometimes twice over, in the five years following the 1967 War.† By 1972 there were only two officers of general rank still in the posts they had held in 1967: Aharon Ya'ariv, Head of the Intelligence branch, and Mordechai Hod, Commander of the Air Force, and both were about to retire.

By then the Army of Israel was very different from the one which had fought and won in 1967. It had a new body of commanders, a changed structure and soldiers whose outlook, experience and training were quite different from those of 1967. Seldom has a victorious army undergone such a radical transformation so soon after its men and methods had proved so successful in battle.

* With this change, the two higher ranks, *Aluf* and *Rav-Aluf* (the latter held only by the Chief of Staff) were upgraded to the equivalent of Major-General and Lieut-General respectively.

† Maj.-Gen. Ariel Sharon replaced Gavish as G.O.C. Southern Command and was replaced in turn by Maj.-Gen. Shmuel Gonen (Gorochish) in 1973. (Gonen had commanded the 7th Brigade in Tal's division in 1967.) Maj.-Gen. Mordechai Gur replaced Elazar at Northern Command and was replaced in turn at the end of 1972 by Maj.-Gen. Yitzhak Hoffi. At central Command, Rehavan Ze'evi replaced Narkiss in 1969 and was replaced in turn by Maj.-Gen. Yona Efrat who had commanded the Golani brigade in 1967. (See Appendix 2.)

The October War*

At 2.15 p.m. on Saturday 6 October 1973, the sinister wail of powerful air raid sirens broke the silence of Yom Kippur, the Day of Atonement, the sabbath of sabbaths, holiest day in the Jewish calendar. Activated at Air Force headquarters, the country-wide alarm had been triggered by the sudden appearance of dozens of aircraft on the early-warning radar screens. No air raids took place in the cities; the crowds which left the synagogues to descend into the shelters, provided by law in every building, need not have done so.* The aircraft, Egyptian and Syrian MiG-21 fighters and SU-7 fighter-bombers, were on their way to bomb and strafe front-line strongholds, advanced armour bases and artillery batteries on the Golan Heights and along the Suez Canal. But when the sirens were heard, Israelis everywhere switched on their radios and, with this, the country's nervous system came to life. Interspersed with short and unrevealing news bulletins, there came the code words of the mobilization call signals, and men began to leave homes and shelters to join their reserve units at the assembly points.

Normally there are no broadcasts on Yom Kippur, a day of prayer and fasting. Radio and television stations are shut down, as is every public facility and every place of business. Everyone is at home or in nearby synagogues; even the irreligious refrain from driving, and Israel's usually crowded roads are quite empty. In retrospect, this was to be of considerable military significance: the Arabs had chosen the only day in the year in which any ready forces could drive to the front unimpeded by traffic, and the only

* On the first day of the war, a Tu-16 ('Badger') bomber launched a Kelt stand-off missile towards Tel Aviv, but both were shot down in flight. Later there was an equally abortive bombing attack against the Haifa refineries.

day in the year in which reservists could unfailingly be found at home or close by.

By the time the sirens were heard, the war had begun. In the Golan Heights, Syrian mechanized columns spearheaded by 800 battle tanks were advancing under the cover of a heavy artillery barrage towards the 1967 cease-fire lines held by the scattered outposts and detached tank groups of two Israeli brigades. At the Suez Canal, the first wave of Egyptian troops was crossing the water in amphibious BTR-50 armoured carriers, tracked assault boats, rubber dinghies and self-propelled pontoons. Facing them across the water were the widely separated strongholds of the 'Bar Lev' line. Built to provide shellproof housings for front-line pickets and patrols on the very edge of the Canal, the strongholds were never meant to repel an all-out offensive by themselves, but only to cope with the heavy artillery barrages and infrequent commando raids of the 1969–70 War of Attrition.

Each consisted of a cluster of concrete bunkers and observation posts, both covered by a high mound of sand held in place by wired slats. Only one stronghold had the fire slits and gun pits typical of conventional fortifications. The rest relied on assigned tank pickets for their fire-power and were in essence no more than shelters for small (fifty/hundred man) infantry detachments. Since the 1970 cease-fire, and in the last year in particular, the line had been thinned out. Many strongholds were unmanned on 6 October, and there were only 450 men holding the line along the entire Suez Canal. Behind them, there were the tank elements of an armoured brigade; another two brigades were also in Sinai, but quite far behind the front.

In the immediate aftermath of the Arab offensive, informed Israelis were shocked to discover how small were the forces deployed on the two fronts that came under attack. After all, it had been widely known that the Egyptians had a combat-ready force of no less than five first-line infantry divisions, two tank divisions and several independent brigades on the west bank of the Suez Canal. At a rough count, this amounted to a twelve to one superiority over the Israeli forces in Sinai, and a thirty-six to one superiority over the front-line forces. As for the Syrians, it was widely known that they had three infantry divisions (fully mechanized) and two tank divisions in the forward line, with at least 800 battle tanks in jump-off positions just across the Golan cease-fire lines.

In retrospect, it seemed inexplicable to many Israelis that the government and General Staff had decided to thin out the front-line forces, accepting such a gross imbalance of strength. But bringing the front-line forces to full strength would hardly have helped; on the contrary, it would merely have increased the ultimate casualty toll – unless the reserves were mobilized, thus changing the entire balance of forces. Without a mobilization, the General Staff could only share out the monthly allotment of reservists and the seven or so trained brigades of the standing army between three fronts; putting conscripts on the line would mean giving up the time needed for training.

In October 1973 as always before, Israel's defence strategy was based on the two-stage combination of small standing forces on the front with the rapid mobilization of the reserves to man combat formations and fill out the skeleton support forces. Some selected reserve troops could be mobilized in roughly twenty-four hours, but it was accepted that it would take three days or so to bring the bulk of the reserve forces to combat-ready status and to transport them to the front with their heavy equipment. In the south, the Sinai was a shield but also a logistic barrier: tanks and self-propelled guns would have to wait their turn as the heavy truck transporters travelled to the front and back again at 15 m.p.h., a twenty-four-hour turn-around even under optimal conditions. Alternatively, in an emergency, tanks and SP guns could travel to the front on their own tracks, but this would wear out their treads, exhaust their crews and ruin the road surfaces for those who followed. Many units did just that in the first days of the October war.

In October 1973 as before, the indispensable early warning needed for a mobilization of the reserves was to be provided by Intelligence, both 'strategic' warning of the enemy *intention* to attack, and 'tactical' warning, i.e., the detection of actual physical preparations for an attack. The warning function was clearly recognised to be the overriding mission of Israeli Intelligence, military as well as civilian. Both Maj.-Gen. Ya'ariv (who finally retired as head of the Intelligence branch of the General Staff in 1972) and his successor, Maj.-Gen. Elihau Zeira, frequently described the provision of attack warning as their 'number one problem'. There is a theory on the subject, which is popular in professional circles. According to this, the problem of warning is that the 'signals' (i.e., the true data) must be detected in the mass of the 'noise' (i.e., the welter of false and irrelevant information) that flows into the Intelligence-gathering system. Intelligence bureaucrats are forever calling for better ways of filtering out the 'signals' from the 'noise' by refining analytical procedures. All this is very plausible, but it is also quite misleading: a closer look reveals that as far as the 'strategic' warning of intentions is concerned, there is actually *no* difference between 'signals' and 'noise' – except in retrospect. There is no true and false data; in a deeper sense, all strategic warning data is 'noise'.

If, for example, the Israelis had actually overheard President Sadat of Egypt ordering his generals to launch an offensive on 6 October by means of a well-placed spy or hearing device, this information would have been the true 'signal' according to the theory. The problem would then have been only to identify it as such in the mass of contradictory 'noise' emanating from other sources. But if the Israelis *had* received the signal, and if they had successfully filtered out the 'noise', they would no doubt have mobilized the reserves and alerted the front-line forces. A large-scale mobilization cannot be kept secret, and it would have induced Sadat to postpone the D-day of his offensive until such time as the Israelis relaxed their alert and demobilized the reserves. Thus, the 'true' signal would have been falsified, and the 'noise' – according to which the Egyptians would *not* attack on 6 October – would have been proved to be true. Thus, 'strategic' warning is not so much a problem capable of solution as a snare; in fact, the conventional theory is only of significance to the historian, who may indeed be interested in searching for the first indications of an event that has *already taken place*. For the Intelligence professional, the theory is of no use, any more than 'strategic' warning itself. Prudent defence planners will work on the assumption that enemy moves simply cannot be predicted, thus ignoring intentions and focusing on actual capabilities.

In principle, the problem of 'tactical' warning is much simpler, a matter of making sure that air reconnaissance, communications intelligence and visual surveillance are properly employed to keep track of enemy preparations so as to give timely warning of an impending attack. Normally, this should provide a guarantee against surprise: even allowing for the extra time needed for the prior recall of the reserves, the Israelis could deploy faster than the Egyptians. But by October 1973, even a perfect Intelligence system could no longer have given any real 'tactical' warning to the Israelis: by then, the Egyptian and Syrian armies had long been ready for the offensive. Ever since the spring of 1973, assault forces had been deployed at their jump-off positions, missile and gun batteries had been placed on continuous alert, and supply echelons had been moved to the forward line. In fact, the two armies had been poised for an attack for several months. In other words, 'tactical' warning had come – and gone – long before the offensive of 6 October. There were still some last-minute logistic preparations, but spotting these could, at most, have given a few hours of warning to the Israelis, certainly not enough for mobilization.

The Israelis were thus in the exceedingly dangerous position of having to rely on a reserve structure that required a two- or three-day warning period in a situation where there could be no real warning at all. There was only one complete solution to this predicament: to mobilize the reserves, wait awhile, and then launch a full-scale preventive attack to destroy the vast array of front-line forces deployed by Egypt and Syria. The Israelis could not call out the reserves and then do nothing. A full-scale mobilization would empty factories and farms, bring production and development to a stand-still, and, if prolonged, would eventually reduce the country's standard of living to the poverty level. On the other hand, a limited mobilization of selected reserve units on a rotating basis, which *could* have provided an effective defence of the fronts, was certainly feasible even if costly. But this 'partial' solution was not adopted. As we shall see, this was due to a fundamental error of judgment, at the core of Israel's deterrent strategy.

While mobilization-without-war was ruled out on economic grounds, there were sound political reasons for rejecting the alternative of preventive war. Reasonably enough, Golda Meir's government had decided that Israel could no longer afford the political risks of striking first. Faced with the rising power of the

Soviet Union, faced with a Europe slipping into a flaccid neutralism, and with the new political threat of Arab oil-diplomacy, Israel had to rely more than ever on the United States. And there, a dangerous, isolationist mood was already apparent. Irrespective of the circumstances, a preventive attack was bound to antagonize public opinion, and make it yet more difficult to obtain American military support. Thus, the mobilization-and-war option was also ruled out. The Israelis were now caught in an insoluble dilemma. Without fully realizing its implications, they were now in a defensive posture that was essentially passive: the Army could only wait for an attack, absorb the first blows as best it could, and then strike back once the mobilized reserves reached the front. In adopting this posture, the Israelis may have overestimated its political merits, but preventive war or even a *pre-emptive* attack (i.e., one launched when the enemy attack is already in motion) would certainly have further deepened Israel's diplomatic isolation.

In January, in May, and in September 1973, there were strong indications of an impending Arab offensive; there was both 'strategic' and 'tactical' warning. On two of these occasions, the Israelis refrained from mobilizing the reserves but, in May, a partial recall was ordered. No war took place, and the Army was criticized for the unnecessary expense. In the first days of October, there was another wave of warning indicators, but inevitably, the evidence was not conclusive. On Thursday, 4 October, word reached Israel that the families of Russian military advisors were being evacuated from Egypt and Syria; although previous Intelligence assessments had stressed the assumption that the Arabs would not attack because the Soviet Union opposed a war (in order to preserve the *détente,* of course) this new signal did not bring about a basic re-assessment of the situation; there was no mobilization, but the standing army was placed on alert. On the next day, Friday, 5 October, Yom Kippur eve, there were further ominous warnings; once again, no mobilization was decreed, but the mobilization offices were alerted and conscripts who had expected to go home were surprised to see their holiday leave cancelled. Finally, on Saturday, 6 October, in the first hours of the morning, 'tactical' intelligence came into its own; the Egyptian and Syrian armies were plainly preparing for an offensive. These and other indications were read to mean that a two-front attack was to be expected at 6 p.m. that evening.

The Chief of Staff, Lt.-Gen. David Elazar, who had succeeded Haim Bar Lev at the end of 1972, asked for a full-scale pre-emptive strike by the Air Force. First the Defence Minister, Moshe Dayan, and then the Prime Minister, Mrs Golda Meir, turned down his request. An emergency meeting of the inner cabinet ('Golda's kitchen cabinet') was called for 8 a.m. But although 'irrefutable' information* had reached Israel by 4 a.m. at the latest, the decision to mobilize was neither immediate nor complete. It seems that it was not until after 9 a.m. at the earliest that a large-scale (but not full) mobilization was decreed. At the same time, the Prime Minister passed word to the Egyptians and Syrians through U.S. diplomatic channels that Israel would not strike first. This could have helped to avert a war started by miscalculation but, in this instance, war was fully calculated, if only by one side. The only effect of the Israeli message may have been to induce the Egyptians and Syrians to anticipate their attack, thus invalidating the information that suggested a 6 p.m. zero hour. The Israeli Cabinet met and deliberated on that fateful morning but by the time the decision was made to mobilize the first-line formations, the Arab offensive was less than five hours away. For the troops on the front, the decision could no longer make much of a difference, since no reinforcements could reach them in time.

At the tactical level, the new situation created by the Arabs' permanent readiness to strike should have resulted in a basic change in Israel's defence plan for the Sinai, but no change was made. In a zero-warning environment, the former plan that called for a *pre-attack* redeployment to bring the supporting armour to the front, should have been changed to a permanent forward deployment, but it was not. The two brigades held in the interior of Sinai were only ordered to advance to the front when the Egyptians had already attacked and, by then, it. was too late.

---

* The Israelis received no warning from American Intelligence sources as some press accounts were later to claim. When the final warnings reached Israel, an attempt to compare notes with U.S. Intelligence was made through the Israeli Foreign Minister, Abba Eban, who was then in New York. But Eban was unable to contact the U.S. Secretary of State in useful time.

Moreover, instead of instructing the small infantry detachments in the Canal strongholds to evacuate their positions in the event of a large-scale offensive – which could have saved hundreds of men from death or captivity – standing orders for a resolute defence remained in force. During the War of Attrition the strongholds had been isolated from time to time by heavy artillery barrages, and they had also been attacked by commandos, but none was ever abandoned. But in the new zero-warning environment, in which a large-scale offensive was possible, a stolid defence of the Bar Lev line was no longer feasible or desirable.

When the Egyptians began to cross the Canal, at 1.45 p.m. on 6 October, the strongholds came under heavy artillery and air attack. The shellproof bunkers proved their worth and the attacks were largely ineffective. But this did nothing to prevent the invasion: Egyptian troops crossed in large numbers in the wide undefended tracts between the few strongholds that were manned – less than twenty in a hundred-mile frontage. A fire barrier, based on the use of petroleum to set the Canal waters on fire, remained unused, apparently for fear that the Egyptians would then resort to gas (the Egyptians had used lethal gas in the Yemen). Lacking in artillery, the strongholds left behind as islands in the rear of the Egyptian invasion could not interfere with the enemy build-up. Quickly coming under close-range attack by large numbers of Egyptian infantry, some strongholds were overrun. In some cases, the troops were reportedly caught entirely unprepared, resting or doing their laundry. It seems that the state of alert that prevailed in Tel Aviv by 9.30 a.m. that morning was not communicated – or enforced – on the front; possibly the stronghold detachments were acting on the basis of an earlier Intelligence warning according to which an Egyptian attack was expected at 6 p.m. If so, instructions to rest and relax during the day would have been appropriate.

Also caught by surprise were the few artillery batteries and tank battalions held behind the front whose mission was to give teeth to the defence by giving covering fire or taking up prepared positions along the Canal. The initial Egyptian air attack, shallow and short as it had to be in order to avoid air-combat with Israeli fighters, sufficed to destroy most of the few long-range guns held in the rear to give remote covering fire to the strongholds.

Egyptian air attacks also inflicted considerable damage to the tank forces deployed on the Baluza-Ras switch road which runs parallel to the front. Still more serious in its consequences was a basic error in the Area Command's defence plan. When the Egyptians began to cross the Canal, the tank forces were duly sent forward; they split into small detachments and began to travel towards their prepared fire positions overlooking the Canal. Hull-down in their firing pits, the tanks could have shot up the pontoon bridges being built on the Canal, sunk the assault boats and given covering fire to the strongholds. But the Israeli tanks never reached their carefully sited firing positions. They were ambushed on the way by the accurate long-range fire of wire-guided anti-tank missiles. Southern Command should have ordered the tanks forward *before* the Egyptian attack, in a permanent readiness response to a zero-warning situation, or not at all.

On the ground as in the air, the Egyptians neatly foiled the initial response of Israel's quick-reaction forces and found a way of overcoming the continued weakness of the Egyptian army in mobile warfare. Although the Egyptians had almost two thousand tanks ready to cross the water, and although the first pontoon bridges were built within an hour and a half of the first attack, the Egyptians made no attempt to move their tanks across the Canal to fight Israeli armour with their own. Even with a ten to one numerical superiority, they were apparently determined to avoid tank-to-tank combat. Instead, having crossed the narrow (3–400 feet in most places) waters of the Canal, the advance elements of the Egyptian army moved only a mile or two into the interior. Large numbers of Egyptian infantry men equipped with portable Sagger anti-tank missiles and hand-held RPG recoilless launchers then took up ambush positions as a human anti-tank barrier astride the approach routes to the Canal. When the Israeli tanks came down the approach roads in the reflex-like reaction that the plan called for, and which the Armour Corps' operational doctrine inspired, they were hit by a hail of anti-tank weapons fired by troops that they could not even see. Very few tanks survived to retreat to the switch road running behind the front. Normally fired at ranges of around two kilometres, the Sagger missiles were very accurate, and their hollow-charge warheads could penetrate even the thickest frontal armour of Israeli Pattons and Centurions. The operator need only keep the target in his sights and align the missile's position flare with the target; the Sagger, though a sophisticated weapon, is thus very simple to operate. In this manner, the Egyptian invasion plan combined the strategic offensive of the Canal crossing with strictly defensive tactics immediately afterwards; it negated Israel's undiminished superiority in fast-moving and sharp-shooting armour by opposing to it Egypt's superiority in foot infantry that could be deployed – and if needs be sacrificed – in large numbers, and which was equipped with modern anti-tank weapons on a lavish scale.

The wire-guided anti-tank missile is not a recent innovation. Early French-made models (SS-11, Entac) have been in service since the mid-fifties. Nor is this weapon, any more than the short-range 'bazooka' rocket launcher or the recoilless RPG, a total answer to the modern battle tank, any more than the machine-gun was a total answer to the infantry. It certainly does not make the tank obsolete. What it does mean, however, is that the *unsupported* tank is no longer a viable weapon and that the 'all-tank' method of armour warfare, where the solid phalanx of a tank battalion relies mainly on its own mobility and gunfire to breach enemy defences, is indeed obsolete. As discussed above at some consider-able length, by 1973 Israel's armour doctrine was based precisely on the 'all-tank' approach to mobile warfare. The validity of this doctrine, associated with Maj.-Gen. Israel Tal, and endorsed with some enthusiasm in the above text (written prior to the October war) was undermined by a subtle but basic error which has already been pointed out by Tal's critics in the post-1967 debate on armour tactics. It was not due to simple ignorance. Tal and his successor, Maj.-Gen Avraham Adan, head of the Armour Corps since 1972, were both fully aware of the large numbers of anti-tank missiles in Arab hands, and of their lethality; more than six years before the October war, two Israeli Pattons were dest-royed in a fire-fight by Snapper ('Schmell') missiles in a July 1967 incident along the Canal. The mistake was not technical, but the result of a basic error of judgement; as we shall see, the same error was the root cause of the failure of Israel's defensive strategy as a whole.

Aside from the two tank battalions held on the Baluza-Ras Sudar switch road, which were virtually out of action by the first evening of war, the only quick-reaction weapon available to the Israelis was the Air Force, the sole branch of the Army which is combat-ready at near full-strength at all times. (Though it too relies on reservists to pilot second-line attack aircraft and for technical support.) In October 1973, as before, Egyptian or Syrian fighters could not survive air combat with Israeli Phantoms and Mirages.* During the 1967 War, the air combat score had been sixty to three, a twenty to one ratio as between all Arab air forces and the Israelis; from the 1967 War to 1 May 1973, the score was 125 to two, and between 2 May 1973 and the *end* of the October war, the ratio was again of the order of twenty to one or better; of the 104 Israeli aircraft lost in combat, less than ten per cent were shot down by Arab fighters. As against this, the vast majority of Arab aircraft shot down (420 or so), were lost in air combat, including 13 Syrian Mig-21s which fell victim to an Israeli air ambush in a pre-war incident. Actually, the Egyptian air force, with its 600 fighters and fighter-bombers as well as forty-six bombers (and 194 helicopters) was never fully committed to battle in the 1973 War; the Egyptians made no real attempt to dispute Israel's control of the air, just as Israel did not attempt to strike at the dispersed and well-protected bases of the Egyptian air force. Most air clashes took place when Israeli fighters succeeded in intercepting Egyptian fighter-bombers, making shallow penetrations of the airspace and, in these unequal contests, the Egyptians did not fare any better than they had in 1967 or during the War of Attrition.

But the well-balanced Egyptian invasion plan also included a remedy for Israel's superiority in air combat. It was not just that the Egyptians were equipped with large numbers of Russian-built anti-aircraft missiles, including the new low-level Grail (SA-7) and the multi-level Gainful (SA-6), but rather that both the strategy and tactics of the entire offensive were successfully designed to absorb and negate the impact of the Israeli Air Force, which with its estimated 162 Skyhawk A-4s, 127 Phantom F-4s, sixty–seventy

* According to press reports, a first squadron of Israeli-built Mach 2 fighters – the Barak – was also operational in the October war.

Mirages and fifty Super-Mystères (and fifty–two helicopters), should have been several times as powerful as in 1967.

The first element in the Egyptian anti-air strategy was the unrewarding nature of the targets presented to Israeli air power. The Egyptian invasion plan did not rely on armoured thrusts or agile manoeuvres on the ground; from one end of the Canal to the other, Egyptian troops simply crossed the water in large numbers and then built pontoon bridges to link the bridgeheads with the rear. Air attacks on pontoon bridges are not worth the price in aircraft shot down; the bridges were bombed again and again, only to be rebuilt within the hour by the replacement of destroyed pontoon sections with new ones. As for the invasion force itself, this was a mass of dispersed infantry, steady troops that held their ground. Only very heavy and sustained air attacks could have made an impression on this amorphous array of men who filled in losses and closed gaps as soon as they occurred.

It was the second, strategic element in the Egyptian plan which insured that Israeli air attacks could be neither heavy nor sustained: the simultaneous Syrian invasion of the Golan Heights was calculated to deflect much of Israel's air power from the southern front. The Syrian tank columns were, from the start, a much more urgent threat than the Egyptian invasion of Sinai; with Syrian tanks only a short drive from the towns and villages of eastern Galilee, the Air Force was called in to stop them at all costs, in order to avert a massacre of the civilian population. It is not clear at the time of writing whether the sacrificial role of the Syrian army was recognized as such in the joint plan of the Arab offensives. What is certain is that, in the first seventy-two hours of war, the Syrian tank forces on the Golan acted as a gigantic decoy for the Egyptian invasion, absorbing most Israeli air attacks during this period.

Having thus diluted the threat of Israeli air power, and reduced its impact by their broad-front tactics, the Egyptians were also well prepared to exact a heavy price in aircraft shot down. Both Egyptians and Syrians deployed large numbers of Gainful (SA-6) twenty-mile range anti-aircraft missiles; guided by radar command from the ground, the SA-6 also has an infra-red (IR) homing device for final intercept that is not easily decoyed by flares, as some older IR missiles were. Since very little was known about the search and tracking radar of the SA-6, and since it could make rapid changes in frequency, the SA-6 radar could not be blinded or deceived by the jamming and deception electronic-counter-measure equipment (ECM) in service with the Israeli Air Force. The Israelis did not even have the simplest of defensive ECM for the SA-6, a detection 'black box' to alert the pilot that his aircraft is caught in the tracking web of the radar. Moreover, since the SA-6 accelerates to a speed of Mach 2.8 (while fighter-bombers invariably fly subsonic when making ground strikes) evasion manoeuvres would in any case have been very difficult. One technique the Israelis developed was to fly a cross in the sky, with one aircraft intersecting the exhaust trail of the other, so as to make a 'hot spot' in the sky to attract the heat-sensing IR homing device of the SA-6. Needless to say, this requires split-second precision flying and an immediate response, since there are only a few *seconds* between the observed launch of the missile and its arrival to target.

In the Russian-designed air defence systems of the Egyptians and Syrians, the SA-6 was interlaced with the older twenty-mile range Guideline (SA-2) and the faster seventeen-mile range Goa (SA-3). Although less effective than the SA-6, which has truly advanced features, these less sophisticated weapons also exacted their price by forcing the Israelis to carry ECM equipment instead of useful weapon loads, and by forcing aircraft to fly at low altitude where they were vulnerable to the SA-6 and the array of other low-level air defences. These included the short-range Grail (SA-7) missile. Encountered in Vietnam as a hand-held weapon guided by an easily fooled IR system, the SA-7 emerged in a different guise in the Middle East, with new and efficient IR filters that could no longer be spoofed by firing flares to simulate the hot exhaust of the target aircraft. Moreover, the SA-7 could follow first-line forces right into the combat zone, since it was mounted (in eight-barrel launchers) on a armoured chassis. Fired in salvos of four or eight, the SA-7s were lethal to aircraft that came within their range. Israeli pilots could avoid one missile, and then a second or third, only to be hit by one more. While the SA-2, SA-3, SA-6 and SA-7 missiles complemented each other, and scored 'invisible kills' by forcing aircraft to fly into each other's lethal zones, the missiles taken together had the effect of forcing Israeli aircraft to fly as low as possible, and so right into the lethal range of the many anti-aircraft guns attached to each ground formation. The most effective was the self-propelled quadruple 23mm AA cannon (ZPU-23-4); with its ('Gun Dish') radar, the ZPU-23-4 is the most effective weapon of its class, world-wide. But even the old 37mm AA cannon and the 14.5 heavy machine-guns, found in every ground unit, could be very dangerous when fired *en masse* at aircraft coming in low to avoid the missiles. In all, these weapons accounted for more than half of the Israeli aircraft lost in combat.

Faced with the powerful bomber force of the American Strategic Air Command, the Soviet Union has historically invested much more effort in anti-aircraft defences than has the United States, which has only had the rather small 'Long Range Bomber Force' of the Soviet Union to deal with. As a result, the Soviet Union has a very large inventory of anti-aircraft weapons. Even so, the Egyptians and Syrians were supplied (and re-supplied) so lavishly for the October war that the Russians were forced to strip their own front-line AA units in order to keep the Arabs supplied with SA-6 and SA-7 missiles. In the end, it was the sheer *number* of the missiles fired that made the difference. There is reason to believe that, in the October war, the Arab armies fired more surface-to-air missiles than there are in the *entire* inventory of European N.A.T.O. forces.

Except for the latest additions, the Israelis had already faced the Egyptian missile belt during the War of Attrition, when a total of twenty-five Israeli aircraft were shot down, mostly in the last few months of fighting until the August 1970 cease-fire. Only the SA-6 with its agile radar and the SA-7 with its sophisticated IR filters (in an otherwise simple weapon) came as a genuine surprise. The Israelis certainly knew that the Egyptian missile belt could provide effective air cover for Egyptian forces on the ground up to ten miles into the Sinai, and that the volume of AA fire would be very heavy. But in the face of the threat the Israeli Air Force held fast to its belief in a combination of simple ECM equipment and sophisticated evasion tactics. An experiment with pilotless bombardment drones, which had looked very promising as low-cost strike weapons against missile batteries, was apparently abandoned, possibly because the United States refused to sell essential components or because of budgetary reasons. The United States certainly refused to sell its better ECM equipment – on security grounds – as well as certain newer weapons such as the 'extended-range Walleye' and the Lance ground-to-ground missile, both of which could have been very useful to attack missile sites at long range.

American restrictions on weapon sales, a sharp contrast to Russian generosity, and the always tight budget limitations, both prevented the acquisition of much protective equipment. But there also seems to have been a strong bias in the Air Force against the technological 'high road' solution, and a measure of over-confidence in the ability of Israeli pilots to improvise defensive tactics in the face of new weapons. What is certain is that priority was given to the purchase of new aircraft so that the Air Force entered the October war with almost 200 Mach 2 fighters and 200 fighter-bombers but with no commensurate ECM capabilities. Even the simplest expendable ECM such as 'chaff' (thin metal-coated strips released in the air to confuse enemy radars) was in short supply, and became a priority item in the wartime airlift of military equipment from the United States. One lesson of the October war was that an ounce of ECM is worth a pound of additional aircraft, in the presence of dense and sophisticated air defences. And by 1973 the air defences over the Canal were the thickest and most effective ever deployed, notably superior to those of Hanoi at the time of the last American bombing offensive.

The Egyptian combination of fixed air defences and the Syrian decoy as well as the resilience of the targets was distinctly success-ful: until the Israelis crossed the Canal and attacked the AA weapons on the ground, in the second week of war, the Air Force was unable to bring its striking power to bear. As in the case of the human anti-tank barrier on the ground, the Egyptian anti-aircraft complex could be no more than a static and range-limited response to a mobile and dynamic threat. It was no sub-stitute for effective air power, and could give no support to the troops on the ground. Above all, by being fixed on the wrong side of the Canal, its outer range of ten miles or so set a finite limit on the depth of the Egyptian penetration into Sinai – until there was time and secure ground enough to move the entire system one step forward.* In any case a forward move would *dilute* the system, since there would be the same number of weapons to cover a larger airspace. In the end, the Egyptian failure to develop a fighter force able to hold its own in air combat imposed an unavoidable penalty. Aptly described as a 'Maginot Line in the Sky', the Egyptian air defence system was effective but inflexible, notably in being highly vulnerable to attack on the ground: the same weapons that kept the Israeli Air Force at bay for ten days were quickly knocked out by a few paratroopers and tanks once the Israelis crossed the Canal.

The utter defeat of Israel's quick-reaction tank force along the Canal during the first hours of war and the virtual neutralization of the Air Force made the situation on the Canal front quite critical. There was very little to stop the Egyptians had they tried to move forward to the Baluza-Ras Sudar switch road and beyond it to seize the Sinai passes at Jiddi and Mitla. Until the armour in Sinai came up to the front, both passes were held by scratch forces, conscript infantry brought in from training courses and a few surviving tanks. But the Egyptians did not move. As before, the Egyptian army proved to be steadfast on the defensive but slow and hesitant on the offensive. Neither in Cairo at G.H.Q., nor at the divisional headquarters on the Canal, nor among the forces in Sinai, was there any realization of the momentary weakness of the Israelis. This is not surprising. The collapse of the front-line defences was so sudden and unexpected that neither side fully understood what the new situation implied for several days. In the meantime, the fleeting opportunity open to the Egyptians was lost for good.

The two senior officers in charge of the Canal front were both representative of the new breed of tank commander which had come to the fore since the 1967 War. The forces normally held in Sinai (three brigades) came under the control of Maj.-Gen. Avraham Mendler, Commander of the Armoured Forces in Sinai, in effect a divisional command for whatever forces happened to be on the front. The officer in charge of Southern Command,

---

* In theory, the most powerful element of the system, the SA-6, was as mobile as its tracked carrying vehicles but, in practice, the need to calibrate radars and build protective emplacements sharply reduced the mobility of these weapons.

ex-officio commander of the front in the event of war (when most of the army would be under his control), was Maj.-Gen. Shmuel Gonen (Gorodish). Both had been outstanding brigade commanders in 1967, Mendler on the Golan in charge of A brigade, and Gonen in Sinai in charge of S brigade in Tal's division. Both had been promoted twice since then to full general rank. Mendler was about to finish his tour of duty when the war broke out, and Gonen was new at his post, having taken over at Southern Command in July. By the end of the first week of war, Mendler was dead and Gonen was no longer in charge.

Mendler and Gonen were the men on the spot when the Egyptian offensive began, and when the failure of the initial counter-attacks revealed the inadequacy of the all-armour approach to the defence of Sinai. Although everything that went wrong was inevitably personalized, it does seem that neither officer understood the implications of the Egyptian offence/ defence strategy, and its successful answers to Israeli superiority in tank warfare and air combat. When the two brigades in the rear and the advance elements of the hurriedly mobilized divisions reached the front on Sunday, 7 October, a fresh armoured brigade was sent forward to execute a classic cut and thrust tank assault towards Kantara, as if nothing had changed. With little artillery support, this tank force was ordered to penetrate and cut off the northern sector of the Egyptian front; the tanks never made it. Many were hit and stopped by anti-tank missiles fired at long range and where some tanks did manage to penetrate, coming into close contact with the Egyptians, instead of the brittle and static enemy they had expected they were met by a shifting mass of infantrymen armed with hand-held RPGs, who decimated the unsupported and thinned-out tank detachments of the Israelis.

It was not until the afternoon of Monday, 8 October, seventy hours or so after the beginning of the war, that Mendler, Gonen and their staff understood the new threat posed by the Egyptians. In the morning, the newly mobilized forces on the northern sector, a division commanded by Maj.-Gen. Avraham Adan, Tal's successor as commander of the armour corps, had repeated on a much larger scale the errors of the first two days of war. Attempting to advance to the water line at Kantara in order to cut through, in a ninety degree turn to the south to reach the Firdan bridge opposite Ismailiya in a classic envelopment manoeuvre, Adan's division failed just as miserably as the garrison battalion on 6 October, and the quick-reaction brigades on 7 October: one of Adan's two tank brigades lost more than three-quarters of its tanks and the second was also badly hit. By then almost 400 tanks had been lost on this front.

A second divisional offensive had also been planned for that day. It was to be mounted by an over-strength armour-paratroop division deployed in the central sector under the command of Maj.-Gen. Ariel Sharon, grand master of the paratroopers in the fifties, divisional commander in 1967 and now a civilian reservist who had left the Army to enter politics in July 1973. Even more ambitious than Adan's abortive offensive in the northern sector, Sharon's mission was to move his forces south towards Port Tewfik, breach through the Egyptian lines on the Sinai side and cross the Canal at Suez to penetrate the rear of the Egyptian front in a south-north advance on the west bank of the Canal. Sharon's forces were travelling on the Baluza-Ras Sudar switch road towards the jump-off point opposite Port Tewfik when the offensive was called off. Word of Adan's failure, and with this an understanding of the new tactical situation, had at last reached Southern Command. This was the moment of truth for the Israeli Army in Sinai.

From the battalions decimated in the initial counter-attacks, to the divisions newly arrived in Sinai, and then to the command post of Maj.-Gen. Gonen, the truth had finally filtered back, and with it came the realization that the quick solution of all-armour attacks would no longer work. It took some time yet for the realization to reach G.H.Q. in Tel Aviv. On that same Monday evening, the Chief of Staff, Lt-Gen. David Elazar, spoke to journalists and TV cameras in a full-dress news conference. He seemed confident of a quick victory in the 1967 style, and spoke of 'breaking the bones' of the Arab armies, unusual bombast for the man and a sharp departure from the restrained language favoured by Army spokesmen. Had Elazar's press conference taken place a few hours later, he would no doubt have spoken very differently, since by then the truth had reached G.H.Q. (Though at that moment in time it was imperative to discourage the Jordanians from intervening in the war and Elazar's press conference may also have reflected this need.) A classic credibility gap was thus created. The men at the front knew that the war was going badly and, for a while, the optimistic official communiques and news broadcasts on the radio were distrusted. The bitter joke of those days was that the Egyptians had learnt from the Israelis how to fight, and that the Israelis had learnt from the Egyptians how to lie. Characteristically, for many soldiers this proved to be the most demoralizing experience of the war, more so than the initial defeats themselves.

The shock of defeat, the desperate plight of the troops still holding out in the Canal strongholds cut off behind Egyptian lines, and the failure of imagination and leadership at Southern Command, precipitated a leadership crisis. Ariel Sharon, who concealed one of the finest tactical minds in the Army behind the carefully cultivated image of a simple fighting soldier, was not in sympathy with Gonen, who had just taken over his last post as G.O.C. Southern Command, and who was his junior. (In 1967 Gonen had been a brigade commander, a post that Sharon had already held in 1956.) Although Adan did not have Sharon's explosive personality and was not so outspoken, he too was uncomfortable serving under Gonen, who had once served under him. Above all, Gonen and his staff had failed. The inner war cabinet, in which Yigal Allon played an important part as both Deputy Prime Minister and as a considerable military expert in his own right, responded to the disarray of Southern Command by appointing the former Chief of Staff, Haim Bar Lev, as the *de facto* commander. (His formal title was only that of 'representative of the General Staff'.) A skilful tactician, and a conciliating man, Bar Lev also had the stature the job needed. As Minister of Trade and Industry, a post he had taken up in 1972 when he left the Army to enter politics, Bar Lev had been something of a failure, but back in uniform he resumed a military career of unbroken success. Another figure from the past was also at Southern Command, serving as area chief of staff: Uri Ben Ari, now a Brig.-Gen. in the reserves. Israel's tank warfare pioneer who had done so well as a brigade commander in both 1956 and 1967 – but had never reached general rank – was thus present when Israeli armour entered a new and painful phase of development under fire.

By then the basic strategy of the war had been determined.

It was decided that the main effort of both air and ground forces would be concentrated on the Golan front in order to push the Syrians back to the 1967 cease-fire lines, and destroy their forces in the field. By the same token, the forces in the Sinai would have to remain on the defensive as far as possible. This meant that the beleaguered strongholds of the Bar Lev line could not yet be reconquered nor their men extricated. The order to evacuate or surrender at discretion was finally given, but by then the men could no longer find a safe passage through tens of thousands of Egyptians concentrated in the narrow invasion salient west of the Canal. Some did escape nevertheless; one stronghold, on a pier at Port Tewfik at the southern end of the Canal, held out against repeated attacks and only surrendered after eight days, when the Egyptians agreed to bring representatives of the International Red Cross to the scene. Only one stronghold held out until relief came, the 'artillery' stronghold on the eastern causeway to Port Fuad, with which the Israelis affected a link-up after three days. The others were all overrun or surrendered and the men within were either captured or massacred. Once the major Egyptian crossings had taken place, the strongholds were of no further use to the Israelis and the troops left behind were a pure loss. In this respect, it is fortunate that the Israelis did *not* have the time to bring their infantry detachments to full strength. When it was decided to leave the strongholds to their fate, the open radio-telephone network was still carrying the desperate pleas of their men all over the front. It was a terrible decision to have to take.

The great question raised anew by the bitter experiences of the first days of the war was one which has already been discussed at some length in the text above written before the October war. Was there a 'new Egyptian' or at least a radically improved Egyptian soldier? In the immediate aftermath, Western media and much of Israeli opinion would have answered with a categorical yes. Those who had portrayed the Egyptians, and indeed all Arabs, as cowards and incompetents, now went to the opposite extreme. Racist invective was replaced by an almost uncritical admiration: the Egyptian soldier of 1973 suddenly emerged as not only very brave (there was talk of 'Chinese human wave assaults') but also very much at ease with the complex technology of his Russian missile weapons. The authors of this book were, at least in this respect, in the happy position of seeing their pre-war views confirmed. As it was pointed out in the original text above, the Egyptian soldier is as brave and steadfast as any as an individual but there are basic weaknesses in Egyptian, and Arab, *group* behaviour. The distinction is basic and it has a direct operational implication: on the defensive, where each man can carry out his task on his own in a fixed role or position, and there is therefore no need of officer leadership or small-group solidarity, Egyptians have historically fought rather well. In 1948, the Israelis regularly failed to capture even small Egyptian strongholds where these were held by soldiers in prepared positions who could fight on their own by standard drills. In 1956, repeated Israeli attacks on the Umm Katef/Abu Agheila defences in central Sinai were costly failures. Even in 1967 when there was a catastrophic collapse induced by the shock of surprise, Egyptian troops some-times fought tenaciously as at the Jiradi defences in front of El Arish; and the soldiers of Jordan's better army fought better still.

But wars cannot be won by remaining on the defensive. Al-though the virtually unopposed one-bound leap over the Canal (followed by strictly defensive tactics) of the Egyptian invasion almost managed the feat, in order to win one must advance, manoeuvre and attack. And for these, officer leadership, coordina-tion and small-group solidarity are indispensable. In the many commando raids and local attacks, and in the one large-scale Egyptian offensive of the 1973 War, the fatal lack of these qualities was apparent as it was in 1948, 1956 and 1967, even though in the October war the Egyptians did have the powerful morale boost of a clear-cut success in the first days of fighting. Except for a few more or less fortuitous successes (including the successful ambush of an Israeli tank battalion caught in an ambush as it was unload-ing the tanks from their transporters), Egyptian commando raids were a dismal failure; most of the dozens of commando teams sent into the Sinai were killed or captured, or else failed to find their targets.*

More important, and much more significant, the defeat of the

* An entire battalion heli-borne to attack Sharm el Sheikh on the first night of the war was shot down in the air.

full-dress Egyptian offensive of 14 October was due to the same inability of officers to control fluid troop movements, and the same failure of group solidarity and command discipline that was observed in previous wars. Finally, the success of the Israeli Canal-crossing offensive which was to end in the encirclement of the so-called Third Army at Suez,* and in a near disaster for the entire Egyptian army (that was only averted by the cease-fire), was due to the total inability of the Egyptian commanders at every level, from the brigades to the G.H.Q. in Cairo, to cope with a fluid and rapidly evolving tactical situation. In this respect 1973 was no different from 1967.

For all their limitations in mobile warfare, the Egyptians certainly never deserved the ill-informed and malevolent ridicule to which they were subjected. There were, and are, severe educational shortcomings that all Arab armies must overcome, but these are not an insuperable obstacle. Through intensive training, simple privates had learnt by 1973 to use their wire-guided anti-tank missiles very effectively, and rather less simple technical troops had learnt to calibrate AA radars and operate the missile launchers. This should not have come as a surprise; during the War of Attrition the ever-increasing technical skill of the Egyptian army was perfectly obvious. Israeli defence planners did not generally share the uninformed view of Arab inferiority propagated by the media (Western more than local) which part of the Israeli public had also come to share. But they, and specifically the Minister of Defence, Moshe Dayan, did come to believe in something very similar to the 'Collapse Theory' that was already put forward – and sharply criticized – in 1956. Never spelled out in so many words, this belief was implicit in the dominating assumption that guided Israeli defence policy between the 1970 cease-fire and 1973: the Egyptians would not start a war because any Canal-crossing offensive would be quickly defeated by the quick-reaction forces in the *early stages of build-up*.

Since Dayan and his associates believed that the regular forces in Sinai together with the Air Force would suffice to bring about

* The Egyptian army was organized in three corps, with three or four divisions each: Second Corps held the northern sector down to the Great Bitter Lakes, Third Corps the south and First Corps was in the rear.

the collapse of an Egyptian offensive, Israel's entire strategy was not based on the active *defence* of the fronts but rather on deterrence – hence the small size of the garrison units in Sinai and on the Golan. Any strategy of necessity combines both defence and deterrence (since to defend one needs forces which also deter *ipso facto*, while to deter one needs forces which must have some inherent defence capability) but in the post-1970 period the degree of defensive preparedness along the fronts was allowed to decline, and increased reliance was placed on deterrence. Increasing belief in the deterrent power of the ready forces on the ground and in the air was apparent in the 1973 decision to reduce the length of conscript service from thirty-six months to thirty-three, and in the reduction of the annual reserve recall from the 1968–71 norm of sixty days or more, to the pre-1967 level of a month or so. It was largely because of this that the forces deployed on the front on 6 October 1973 were so small.

With such great and critical reliance on deterrence, and with such a thin defence, it was imperative to make quite sure that the conditions required for the successful deterrence of an attack were fulfilled: that the Air Force and the armour ready on the ground could indeed inflict devastating blows in the early stage of an Arab offensive; that the Egyptians did *not* come to believe that even a fresh defeat was preferable to continued inaction. Actually these were only the *minimum* conditions of deterrence, all of which had to be satisfied to make deterrence possible.* None were. The failure of Israel's deterrent policy was due to a catastrophic miscalculation and not to a subtle error of judgement. Belief in deterrence need not prevent a temporary increase in the strength of the defence at times of particular tension. But a deterrent frame of mind, based in this case on the underlying belief in the fragility of Arab armies, does tend to work against a sense of urgency in strengthening the degree of 'insurance' provided by an active defence when the risk of war seems greater than usual. Confident in the deterrent power of the Army, Dayan and his associates tended to discount the ominous warnings that contradicted their expectations. Thus Dayan reportedly resisted requests to reinforce the fronts, to mobilize early and, in the end, to mobilize fully.

* These were necessary but not sufficient conditions. The latter include rationality in adversary decisions, in the formal sense.

Above all, Dayan's position led the Israeli government to reject the only way out of the 'no-preventive-war' and 'no-mobilization-without war' dilemma, which was of course to mobilize some part of the Army on a permanent basis.

It must be recognized, however, that Dayan and his associates did not shape Israel's defence policy in a vacuum. Their decisions were not the product of blind belief in deterrence, or even in the 'Collapse Theory'. Dayan, his fellow Ministers and his civilian and military subordinates were all captive to the atmosphere of overconfidence that pervaded Israeli society, and they were also under pressure from a public opinion that was loud in its demands for an ever-rising standard of living and for more social welfare. Subject to these insistent demands, and deceived by the apparent tranquillity of Israel's borders in the wake of the 1970 cease-fire the Israeli government gave way and agreed to reduce the human and financial burdens of defence preparedness. From the high point of 1970, when defence expenditures amounted to twenty-six per cent of the country's total G.N.P., or $483 per capita (much the highest figure in the world) there was a significant decline; the 1973 figure would have been of the order of twenty per cent of G.N.P. (As a percentage of total government spending, defence expenditures declined from 43.7 per cent in 1970 to just under thirty-two per cent in fiscal year 1973–3.) And within the defence budget there was a shift in emphasis from current forces to weapons for the future.

A population with the fully developed consumption appetites of Europe had sustained a major consumer boom ever since 1967, in spite of the highest income and sales taxes in the world. Moreover, social welfare expenditures had sharply increased. The poor had become more articulate, and the immigrants were once again coming in large numbers. In terms of the size of Britain's population, the new Russian immigration was equivalent to 75,000 a month; in terms of the U.S. population, the equivalent figure was of the order of a quarter of a million each month. The arrival of Russian Jews fulfilled a deeply felt hope, but it also accentuated the demands of Israel's poor. In spite of the generous aid that Israel continued to receive from Jewish communities the world over, the provision of homes, jobs, education and welfare to the new immigrants and the poor was a crushing burden on the

Israeli economy, and one which had the effect of eroding the priority of defence.

Deterrence is cheaper than defence, above all in the critical area of manpower. Israel's 'high-pressure economy' was chronically short of qualified manpower, and the drastic fifty per cent cut in the length of the annual reserve call thus affected a critical bottleneck, with direct and beneficial effects on the level of production and exports. Part of the resources saved by shifting to a strategy of more deterrence and less defence were absorbed by the civilian economy but part were redirected *within* the defence establishment. Dayan and his associates also had to choose between the needs of current defence and those of *long-run* security; keeping fewer troops on the line released men and funds for civil society but also for weapon development and production. Self-sufficiency in equipment was clearly the key to long-run security, and Israeli defence planners were constantly forced to choose between the needs of the future and those of the Army in the field. There are no official figures but the investment in the self-sufficiency programme was very considerable; according to press reports in 1973 Israel was on the verge of producing both jet fighters (the so-called Barak) and battle tanks of local design while new weapons already in production included SP howitzers (the Soltam L-33, a 155mm conversion), the Galil automatic rifle, the Shafrir air-to-air missile and the Reshef class of long-endurance missile boats. In fact, by the October war, Israel was producing a wider range of artillery and infantry weapons, of missiles and electronic equipment, of aircraft and battle tank and gun conversions, than any country in the world except for Sweden and the great powers. The investment, in specialized machinery and imported know-how, in research and development, and in construction, was very extensive; by 1973 the complex of Israeli research establishments and defence industries was engaged in a broad-front effort that covered the full spectrum from nuclear physics to mechanical engineering.

This phenomenal scientific and industrial endeavour was wholly disproportionate to the size and resources of Israel, whose population is no larger than that of a medium-sized Western city and poorer than most. Inevitably, the needs of the future were paid for out of the necessities of the present. Not only was the

Army's manpower thinned out, but also ammunition and spare part stocks were reduced on the assumption that a war would only require a few days of actual fighting, and not very intense fighting at that. The capital costs thus saved were considerable; also reduced was the replacement stocks of those items which have a limited shelf life. But the risk was also considerable, and it materialized with a vengeance in the October war; by the time the American airlift began, the Israelis were running out of many kinds of ammunition and air ordnance.

Even in retrospect, it is not certain whether the better policy would have been to cripple the defence self-sufficiency programme by keeping 'adequate' stocks of ammunition: for the tank force alone, a thirty-day re-load stock of 105 mm shells would have required the purchase or manufacture of two and a half million rounds of ammunition at a cost of about 250 million dollars, not counting cyclical replacement for wastage. As against this, it does seem that the stock levels of the Army were far too low for even a minimal degree of 'insurance' against error. Here, as in the very small size of the forces assigned to the front, there was an elementary lack of prudence, whose ultimate cause was the fundamental error of judgement of those who believed in the 1973 version of the 'Collapse Theory'.

In 1973, as in 1956, there was a direct link between the 'Collapse Theory' and the role of the tank forces. But this link had undergone a curious reversal. In 1956, Dayan had wanted to keep Ben Ari's 7th Armoured Brigade out of the campaign because he believed that the Egyptian army in Sinai would collapse anyway, once the major fortifications were by-passed and their roads to the rear were cut off. Tanks, he felt, would only slow the advance of the fast, half-track and truck-borne infantry columns on which the offensive was to be based. But, in 1973, the tank battalions of the garrison brigades on the front, together with the Air Force, were expected to be the *principal instruments* of the expected collapse of an Egyptian or Syrian invasion attempt. Believing the enemy's forces to be essentially fragile, trusting in the ability of the Air Force to overcome the missile barrier, and in the ability of the tank forces to defeat Egyptian forces on the ground, Dayan and his associates felt secure with the very thin defence that would itself collapse in October 1973.

The failure of the initial counter-attacks on the Canal and even more of Adan's counter-offensive of Monday, 8 October, naturally called into question the validity of the armour doctrine and operational method; formulated and advocated by Maj.-Gen. Israel Tal, the 'all-tank' doctrine had shaped not only the Armour Corps but, after 1967, also the entire army. Discussed above, in some detail (pp. 186–92), Tal's doctrine stressed the independent and self-sufficient role of tank forces. Relying mainly on their own accurate gunfire, on constant forward movement, and on concentration into all-tank 'mailed fists', the tank battalions were trained to fight as the cutting edge of the ground forces, who were now reorganized around them into 'conveyor belt' formations, whose task was to support the advance of the tanks, which pulled forward the entire array. In the post-1967 re-organization of the Army, the loose Ugdah framework was abandoned in favour of conventional divisions and, owing to the armour orientation that came to the fore after 1967, these new divisions were, in essence, tank divisions (the basic divisional structure was made up of two tank brigades and one mechanized infantry brigade, as well as some organic artillery). These divisions could accommodate additional paratrooper or infantry units, but their main combat forces were the two tank battalions of each brigade. Moreover, the tank battalions were stripped of some of their organic mechanized infantry and mortars. In fact, they were almost pure all-tank formations. Everything thus depended on the tank spearheads, since most of the combat forces were now armoured, and since the mechanized infantry was manned, trained and equipped to fight mainly in a subordinate role; its major task was in fact to mop up in the wake of the tanks.

The Israelis were perfectly well aware of the existence and effectiveness of the Russian anti-tank missiles deployed in large numbers by the Arab armies. They also knew that Egyptian and Syrian troops were armed with short-range RPG weapons, down to the squad level. But it was believed that, if the tank spearheads advanced rapidly in a solid wedge, so as to minimize the 'surface' exposed to fire, pausing only to shoot accurately at the source of enemy fire, the tanks would still penetrate the curtain of anti-tank fire and break up enemy formations at short range. As we have seen, what actually happened was that first the front-line battalions, then the advance brigades, and finally, Adan's divisional forces sent their tanks forward, only to have them decimated by long-range missile fire; when the tanks did manage to reach the Egyptian lines they were surrounded by a mass of infantry firing RPG shells off the shoulder. Lacking any infantry, the Israeli tanks were helpless.

The human anti-tank barrier deployed by the Egyptian army to shield their long and very narrow invasion salient utterly defeated the all-tank tactics of the Israelis. But this did not mean that the tank had finally become obsolete. For there is, and has long been, a remedy: the use of tanks in *mixed* forces fighting with mixed tactics, as opposed to the all-tank forces and all-tank tactics of Israel's armour doctrine. The most obvious answer to the anti-tank missile threat is to provide a rolling barrage of artillery fire to sweep the axis of advance, firing air-burst fragmentation shells over the top of the advancing tanks; self-propelled mortars and artillery moving with the main force in the rear can clear the ground of the unprotected anti-tank missile crews. On the flanks, the tank battalions themselves can do much to blind these visually-guided missiles by putting down smoke screens using their pro-jector tubes (usually affixed to the sides of tank turrets) and self-propelled mortars organic to the tank battalion. Naturally, such tactics require a good deal of artillery in the division as well as mortar companies in each tank brigade and battalion. They also require a generous supply of ammunition, since the ground ahead must be swept to the depth of anti-tank missile range which, in the clear air of the Middle East, means two miles or more. But the ordinary mortar is still a very effective counter to the sophisti-cated anti-tank missile, and if the Israelis had deployed them and used them well (mortars were once an Israeli speciality), they could have done much to defeat Egyptian anti-tank tactics.

To protect the tanks from attack at close range by hand-held rockets or recoilless weapons, and to provide a screen around tank forces resting, refuelling or regrouping, infantry is needed too, not behind, but right with the tanks. Clearly, it would not do for the Israelis to fight the mass of Egyptian infantry on their own. Whether Tal's armour doctrine was right or wrong, the Israelis could never copy the Egyptians and throw thousands of men into battle to clear the ground for each armour assault. Nor was the orthodox version of armour-infantry cooperation of any use. Having foot infantry march alongside the tanks would not only slow down the speed of advance to the slow pace of men walking cross-country, but clearly it would also be insufficient; an infantry close escort can only provide protection for a few hundred yards ahead and around the tanks, much less than the range of anti-tank missiles. Outside the shallow infantry screen, enemy missile crews could still fire their weapons without hindrance. And if the infantry screen is made deeper, this orthodox version of armour-infantry cooperation would break down into the mass infantry solution with its mass casualties. Clearly, what the Israeli army needed was a strong mechanized infantry, high-grade troops with good quality armoured and fully tracked carriers that follow battle tanks across country and into all but the heaviest fire. Sheltering behind the mass and firepower of the tanks in the event of tank-to-tank clashes, the infantry in its carriers could move out and ahead of the tanks when the major threat was presented by enemy infantry armed with anti-tank weapons. In such a mixed combat-team, tanks and carriers could powerfully assist one another and advance together; on the defensive, and when pausing to regroup or rest, the infantry could leave its carriers to provide a guard force for the tank leaguer. In each of their tank brigades, the Israelis did have a mechanized infantry battalion but, as Tal's critics pointed out after the 1967 war (pp. 295–6), within the armour corps the mechanized infantry was accorded a low priority in both manpower and equipment. In 1973 there was not enough of it, and not enough of what there was matched the quality of the tank forces. In 1967 the tank battalions had not yet become predominant, if only because there were not enough tanks. But in 1973 the Israeli Army deployed at least 1,750 battle tanks (less than either the Egyptian or Syrian but more than the British *and* French tank forces combined). Except for a few infantry and paratrooper brigades, the standard Israeli combat formation was the tank brigade, with two battalions of tanks, and one of mechanized infantry. There was thus a built-in numerical imbalance.

Moreover, a major implication of Tal's doctrine (strongly endorsed in the original text) was that the mechanized infantry could be provided with inferior manpower and inferior equipment,

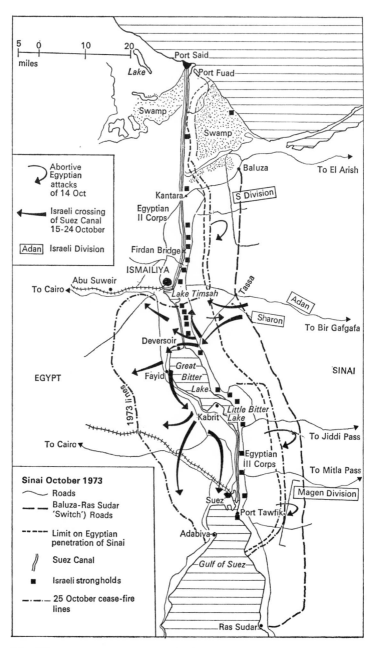

Map 27

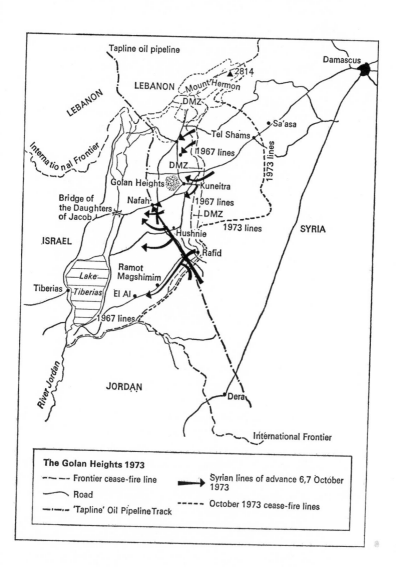

Tapline oil pipeline

Damascus

LEBANON

LEBANON

Mount Hermon

▲ 2814

DMZ

Sa'asa

Tel Shams

1967 lines

DMZ

Golan Heights

Nafah

Kuneitra

1967 lines

DMZ

1973 lines

1973 lines

SYRIA

Bridge of
the Daughters
of Jacob

Hushnie

ISRAEL

Rafid

Lake
Tiberias

Ramot
Magshimim

Tiberias

El Al

1967 lines

River Jordan

JORDAN

Dera

International Frontier

International Frontier

The Golan Heights 1973

- - - - Frontier cease-fire line

▬▶ Syrian lines of advance 6,7 October 1973

Road

'Tapline' Oil Pipeline Track

- - - - - October 1973 cease-fire lines

Map 28

since its only task was to mop up and guard for the tanks. While most tank battalions were equipped with carefully rebuilt M.48 Pattons and Centurions standardized on high-velocity 105 mm guns and new diesel engines, most of the mechanized battalions were still equipped with the ancient and poorly armoured M.3 half-track carrier.* A sizeable number of new M.113 carriers were bought after 1967, mainly because a fully enclosed vehicle was needed to cope with the threat of gas warfare. But although far superior to the half-track, the M.113 is not a combat carrier since its armour is thin and it has no built-in weapon turret; to fight, its crew must stand in open hatches, totally unprotected above the waist. Had the mechanized infantry been rated as important as the tank forces, ways could have been found of supplying it with better fighting vehicles as well as more and better manpower. For one thing, even fully-fledged combat carriers are much easier to develop and produce than battle tanks.

Because of the primacy of the tank forces, and the belief that they could cope with all threats more or less on their own, the entire defence of the Canal rested on their effectiveness. Part of the small artillery contingent on the front was destroyed in the initial air attack of 6 October (including a battery of long-range 175 mm guns); when the reserves were mobilized, priority was given on the scarce heavy transports to the tank forces. Thus, when the tank-based defence collapsed, the front was initially reinforced with more tank forces which were no better suited to the task of fighting Egyptian tank-killer teams than those which had been defeated on 6 and 7 October. The organic mortars, the self-propelled artillery and the mechanized infantry needed to make up mixed combat teams capable of defeating the new threat, did not arrive until later and not in adequate numbers. In fact, the all-tank armour doctrine had distorted not only the Canal defence plans, but also the entire structure of the Israeli army.

---

* The Israeli tank force still included some much-modified Sherman A-4s now awaiting conversion to mortar or gun carriers; there were also captured T-54 and T-55 Russian tanks converted and re-armed with 105mm guns. After 1970 a number of M.60 Pattons were purchased from the United States, but the bulk of the force consisted of locally modernized M.48 Pattons and Centurions. (All the Pattons were brought up to M.60 A.1 standards, and all the Centurions were brought to Mark 10 standards.)

Another of the profound but indirect changes brought about by the ascendency of the tank element was manifest in the army's tactics and operational method. In the aftermath of the October war, paratroop officers complained that their colleagues in the Armour Corps 'do not *plan* their battles'. Thinking in terms of the 'concentric' battles typical of their set-piece operations of the past, where the attacking forces converge on a single objective in a carefully planned assault on a static enemy, paratroop officers felt that the tank commanders simply advanced and attacked without thought or method. In fact, when armoured forces are fighting well, they are fighting on the move; their optimal tactic is indeed the improvised concentration against – and through – a weak point in the enemy line revealed by the success of local penetrations which cannot be predicted in advance. In the manner of water descending down a slope which flows into the faster rivulets, tank forces on the move find their own direction in the course of the battle itself, breaking through the line and out to the rear in a manner that cannot be planned in advance.

But the complaints of the paratroop officers had a grain of truth: when their fluid assault tactics were defeated by the Egyptian offence/defence strategy with its human anti-tank barrier, the highly specialized officers typical of the Armour Corps were slow to re-think their tactics and slow to realize the need for artillery support and for the mixed combat-team approach; nor did they take easily to the careful planning that a combined infantry, artillery and armour operation requires. Instead, for the first three days of the war in Sinai, unsupported tank battalions were thrown into battle even though the real targets of any armour assault could not be reached anyway. The supporting artillery, and the missile and gun AA forces that protected the shallow Egyptian front in Sinai were on the far side of the Canal as were the lines of supply, the headquarter units, and the armour deployed by the enemy. Hence, the tank assaults were not only costly, but futile; to cut through Egyptian lines was not enough, since to break out in the soft rear – and to engage Egyptian armour – the Israeli tanks would have had to cross the Canal and this they could not do for the lack of bridging equipment and a secure crossing point.

Although there were plenty of imaginative tank officers, both among career men and reservists, intellectual breadth of understanding was not the quality stressed in selecting the officers of the Armour Corps. Following Tal's lead, officers were promoted for their technical expertise, for their attention to detail and for their ability to enforce 'technical' discipline. These men had concentrated on the formidable problems of training thousands of conscripts and reservists of no special aptitude to keep complex and delicate tank machinery in running order. These were men who had made tank gunnery a fine art, and whose own specialized skills had to compensate for the lack of the long-service troops that man the tank forces of most armies. In the October war, Israeli tank troops, who had been civilians until a day or two before, outmanoeuvred and outfought their Arab counterparts who had undergone years of continuous training. (In 1967, owing to the pre-war crisis period of full mobilization, reservists had received two weeks of refresher training before being sent into combat.) But some of the middle echelon of Lt-Colonels and Colonels in the Armour Corps, the brigade and battalion commanders of the October war, showed a lack of tactical inventiveness and mental adaptability. In a sense, this was one of the hidden costs of mechanization, manifest in the distinctly superior performance of the remaining paratroop officers and their units.

By 1973 most infantry brigades had been converted to armour; as distinct from at least seventeen brigade-equivalents of armour, there were reportedly only three paratroop and a few first-line infantry brigades, including the Golani, the training brigade of the conscript infantry. Much of the rest of the infantry, 'motorized' with conscripted civilian buses or trucks, was made up of second-line troops. (Forces of this kind, including the large but low-grade Jerusalem Brigade, supplied the stronghold detachments along the Canal, as well as the covering force for the Jordanian front.)

Another of the indirect consequences of mechanization was that the Israelis virtually abandoned their traditional speciality of night-fighting. Day after day the official communiqués of the October war concluded their account of the previous day's fighting with a brief phrase that displeased veterans of the Palmach and the paratroopers: 'Our forces had a quiet night'. Group morale, junior officer leadership and small-unit initiative are much more important in night-fighting than in daylight when larger forces can be brought to bear and when troop movements can be controlled much more easily. Close combat is more likely, field-craft is more important and, especially in the desert, navigation and map reading are crucial. In all of these specialities, the Israelis were particularly strong and the Arabs rather weak. Ever since the days of the Palmach the Israelis had exploited their ascendancy in night-fighting: in 1948 to compensate for their lack of heavy weaponry and especially artillery, and in the paratroop raids of the fifties in order to minimize casualties.

In 1967, at the battle of Umm Katef, Ariel Sharon had demon-strated that a precise orchestration of fire and movement, as between infantry, tanks, artillery and heli-borne paratroopers, was possible on a divisional scale and at night, with a hundred times as many troops as in the night raids of the fifties. Indeed, the night battle at Umm Katef was one of the outstanding successes of the 1967 War. Thus, Sharon's division, with its mixture of forces, provided an alternative model to Tal's all-tank approach, and one which was not explored deeply enough by the Israelis, as the 1973 War was to show. As against this, there was the record of the night paratroop assault on East Jerusalem which had broken down into a confused and costly battle, and one which later seemed almost unnecessary since Uri Ben Ari's tanks were advancing towards the all-important dominating heights around the Old City while the paratroopers were fighting and dying in the valley below.

In the October war, the Israelis hardly fought at night, except for some small paratroop operations, some (very successful) commando raids, and Sharon's night crossing of the Canal in the second week of the war. To some extent, the heavy cost of the paratroop attack on East Jerusalem may have discredited para-troop night assault tactics and night fighting in general. But more important, no doubt, was the natural daylight cycle typical of mechanized operations supported by a powerful air force. Attack aircraft are many times more effective in daylight than at night, even if equipped with advanced sensors (which most Israeli aircraft did not have), and tank forces fight best in good visibility when targets can be seen at long range and when rapid cross-country movements are possible. And so Israeli tank forces fought in daylight and used the night for refuelling, re-arming, maintenance and rest. One of the lessons of the October war is thus that an army based on armoured forces is largely limited to daylight operations. There is no question of the Israelis reverting to 1948-style light infantry and night-attack tactics (even the mixed combat-teams would be heavy in armour), but perhaps an entirely new concept may emerge from the October war: the '24-hour' division which would field 'tank-heavy' mixed combat teams in daylight, and infantry-based teams at night, so as to keep the enemy under continuous pressure. Even if not much damage is done, night infantry raids and probing attacks can keep the enemy from sleeping and this can quickly degrade the effectiveness of armoured troops who must be well rested to remain fully alert.*

The record of the fighting on the Golan Heights can serve as an excellent corrective to hasty verdicts inspired by the initial Israeli defeats in Sinai. The Syrians, too, launched their attack between 1.45 and 2 p.m. on 6 October; like the Egyptian, the Syrian offensive began with a massive artillery barrage. But instead of infantry, the Syrians relied primarily on armour, and instead of the one-bound leap of the Egyptians followed by an immediate switch to the defensive, the Syrians launched an estimated 800 tanks in a battle of continuous penetration. As well as being a decoy for the Egyptian attack – whether the Syrians knew it or not – the Syrian invasion was a determined attempt to seize the plateau of the Golan and, no doubt, to move beyond it to Galilee below if possible.

Once the fighting moved back beyond the 1967 cease-fire lines and into Syria proper at the end of the first week of war, the outlines of the Syrian invasion plan could still be read on the

* One version of this new-style formation would be a 'square' division of two tank brigades and two infantry brigades, the latter equipped with combat carriers but also trained to fight on foot. With light and heavy mortars in each battalion and brigade, with its own organic artillery, the square division could defeat armour with armour, and defeat anti-tank troops with smoke barrages and air burst shelling; it could also fight set-piece concentric night battles with its infantry supported by armour.

ground in a long trail of wrecked tanks. The main concentration of Syrian armour was deployed against the southern half of the plateau, with one thrust on the Rafid–El Al axis to southern Galilee and another, deeper thrust from south to north along the right-of-way of the Tapline pipeline to Nafah (on the main road from the bridge of the Daughters of Jacob to Kuneitra) and beyond. While this mainforce attack was to slice the Golan from side to side, Kuneitra also came under very heavy direct attack, and a further thrust was aimed at the central bridge – Nafah–Kuneitra axis from the north-east just below the foothills of Mount Hermon. In a separate operation, the Syrians seized the Israeli outpost on the crest of Mount Hermon with a heli-borne battalion of paratroopers. The Israeli garrison brigade holding the southern half of the Golan Heights never had a chance. Its tank detachments and small outposts were quickly overrun by the massed attack of Syrian tanks. In twos and threes, the tanks attached to this brigade opened fire against entire battalions of Syrian tanks converging on their positions. Although no statistical analysis of the more than 1,000 battle tanks left on the Golan by Syria and her allies is as yet available, it seems that the Israeli tanks did very well indeed. But they could not stop the concentrated Syrian thrust down towards El Al and along the pipeline route that cut across the rear of the brigade sector. Already scattered in the many outposts of a thin deployment, the garrison brigade was cut into shreds by the onrush of Syrian tanks; the brigade command post was overrun and the brigade commander was killed, as were many of his officers.

For all this, the tanks of the garrison brigade showed the worth of the area defence plan: ready at their prepared firing pits sited to give overlapping fields of fire, the tanks were used to maximum advantage to hit the Syrians at long range. On the Canal, by contrast, the tanks were not in their prepared positions when the attack began, and were ambushed on the way, when belatedly ordered to move forward to their assigned fire positions. An even greater contrast to the failure of the tank units in the south was the outstandingly successful defence of the central bridge Nafah Kuneitra axis by the 7th Brigade, the crack 'school' brigade of the Armour Corps manned by career officers and trained conscripts. Headed by Col. Y, who emerged as one of the heroes of the

October war, this brigade implemented Tal's doctrine of concentrated mass and long-range fire with great success. By concentrating the bulk of his forces instead of scattering them to meet attacks at every point on the line, Col. Y kept up a powerful mobile defence against the heavy Syrian attacks which continued for three days. Confronted by the deep Syrian penetration which reached Nafah (command post for the divisional commander, of which more below) and by Syrian attacks on the north-east sector at the opposite side of the central axis, Y's brigade counter-attacked on the flanks and even managed to achieve local superiorities by keeping the tanks concentrated. The outcome was that the hundred or so tanks of this brigade destroyed perhaps three times their number of Syrian tanks. Moreover, the 7th Brigade was not sacrificed in the process.

On the Golan, as in Sinai, the regular 'garrison' forces and their immediate reinforcements came under the control of a front-wide divisional commander. In the south this was Avraham Mendler of the Armour Corps, commander of 'Armoured Forces in Sinai'; on the Golan, it was Brig.-Gen. Rafael Eytan, in peacetime Chief Officer of Paratroopers and Infantry and himself a taciturn paratrooper of legendary bravery. Eytan's command post was at Nafah (a small army camp on a low hill under which the command bunker was built), directly in the path of the Syrian armour on the southern sector as it cut through the thin lines of the garrison brigade south-west towards El Al on one axis, and north towards Nafah itself, on the other. By all accounts Eytan, unlike his counterpart in the south, quickly understood the scope and nature of the attack, though in fairness it must be pointed out that the Syrian offensive was by far the more conventional of the two.

Although the Air Force intervened in full strength, flying its vulnerable Skyhawks right into the killing range of the Syrian missile belt to attack the advancing armour columns (it lost thirty aircraft in one day), neither air power nor the small forces on the ground could stop the invasion; the numerical imbalance was simply too great.

While Col. Y's brigade was fighting to defend the crucial Nafah–Kuneitra axis against converging attacks from three directions, Eytan in his command bunker was coordinating the battle in the Golan and directing the flow of reinforcements together with his superior in the rear, Maj.-Gen. Yitzhak Hoffi – another paratroop officer and Gonen's counterpart at Northern Command. With the forces in Kuneitra barely holding out under very heavy frontal tank assaults and artillery fire, with the northeast sector of the Golan also under attack, with the Syrian advance towards El Al and southern Galilee becoming steadily more dangerous, and with the major armour thrust advancing rapidly towards Eytan's own headquarters at Nafah, the situation on the Golan Heights was desperate. Rapid though it was, the flow of hurriedly mobilized reservists seemed agonizingly slow; Eytan in his command bunker was calculating the course of the battle in minutes. The great danger was that the Syrians would reach the edge of the plateau overlooking the Jordan valley. Once there, their fire positions would dominate the steep and totally exposed roads winding up to the Golan Heights and thus cut off the front-line forces from the reinforcements coming up from the Jordan valley.

There was no time to assemble the reservists at their depots, to allow the grouping of men into their units and to deploy the forces in an orderly manner. Instead, small groups of tanks, odds and ends of infantry and artillery, in fact any ready forces, were all sent to the front as soon as they had collected their equipment in the reserve depots and were prepared to move, and sometimes when they were not. Officers stood in the assembly camps putting together tank crews anyhow: a gunner, a loader, a driver, and a tank commander would be made into a crew, sent to the front as fast as they could travel, and frequently into action straight off the march. Instead of the designated platoons, companies, battalions and brigades, improvised forces were reaching Eytan's command in dribs and drabs.

While Eytan was directing the flow of reinforcement to the front, Syrian tanks reached Nafah. Down in his bunker, Eytan was in cool command of the battle while Israeli and Syrian tanks were fighting it out above him. After the Syrian retreat, there were wrecked Syrian tanks in a semicircle around Nafah Hill, the nearest perhaps *ten* yards from the wire fence. In the meantime, at the other end of the front, the Syrians had reached Ramot Magshimim, a religious farming village on the road to El Al, one of a number of civilian settlements established on the Golan

Heights since 1967. (Its inhabitants, like those of all other Golan settlements, were evacuated ahead of the advancing Syrians, thus avoiding a certain massacre.) With Nafah holding out, the Syrian advance towards the central axis was deflected to the west, more dangerous yet, since the Syrians could then reach the vital central road from the bridge of the Daughters of Jacob to Nafah and Kuneitra at a point still nearer to the edge of the plateau. In spite of massive confusion, the reserve forces were beginning to reach the front much faster than could have been expected. Nor did Hoffi at Northern Command, or Eytan under fire at Nafah, throw these forces into battle in reflex-like counter-attacks as in the south. Instead, the reinforcements were deployed in an improvised but sound containment action focused on the vital Nafah–Kuneitra highway.

In the end, the Syrian tanks were stopped just short of the old Customs House dating from Mandatory times. A few minutes more, and they would have cut off the road to Kuneitra and reached positions overlooking the steep ascent from the gorge of the Jordan; at this point, Syrian tanks were three miles from the bridge of the Daughters of Jacob, their main objective. Had they reached the bridge, had Y's men broken down under the strain, had Eytan lost his nerve, the Syrians could have made the recapture of the Golan Heights a much longer and much more costly operation than it was. And they could have broken out into the thickly populated upper Galilee with its thousands of civilians.

On 30 October 1973, a few days after the final cease-fire, Rafael Eytan received a richly deserved promotion to Major-General. After the war, many Israelis remarked the fact that both Eytan and Hoffi were paratroop officers while the counterparts in the south were tank commanders; but the remarkable performance of Col. Y shows that the comparison is more suggestive than valid.

Following the collapse of the frontal defences along the Canal, the Egyptians had established a foothold in Sinai, holding a long strip, five to seven miles deep, all along the Canal. Although their first pontoon bridge was built within an hour and a half of the initial crossing, most of the Egyptian armour was kept on the west bank of the Canal until several days after the crossing. It was plain that the Egyptians were not ready to follow their initial success with a drive for the Sinai passes. Their firm and prudent intent was rather to remain under the umbrella of the missile batteries whose decreasingly effective range extended for ten miles or so into the Sinai. Nor did the Israelis have much reason to attack. The decision to concentrate on the Syrian front first was made on Monday, 8 October; fighting along the Canal would thus be inconclusive at this stage. The best tactics open to the Israelis were, rather, to retreat, hoping to lure the Egyptians deeper into Sinai beyond the forward edge of their missile cover and beyond the effective range of their artillery, still massed on the far side of the water. Had the Israelis retreated and the Egyptians advanced, their solid array of forces would have been diluted, their AA cover thinned out, and their supporting artillery fire weakened. But a cumulative error of planning prevented the Israelis from following this ideal tactical course. Over the years, a cluster of bases, depots, air defence and intelligence facilities had been allowed to grow in the areas between the Sinai passes and the Canal. This uncontrolled growth sharply increased the costs of any retreat since it would have entailed the loss of valuable facilities. (There were also morale costs and the political risk that a premature cease-fire would leave the Egyptians in control of a deeper and more consolidated front.) As a result, no real tactical use was made of the geographic depth of Sinai. Instead of the fluid tactics of a flexible defence, with partial retreats followed by counter-attacks on the flanks, tactics calculated to throw the slow and methodical Egyptian command off balance, the Israelis were forced to defend the ground.

During the first week of war, while the Syrian army was throwing its reserves into the battle in a futile attempt to stop the inexorable drive that was pushing its forces out of the Golan, the Egyptians did not move to relieve the pressure on their allies. But by the end of the week Syrian appeals for help had become frantic, and the Egyptians anticipated by two days a planned offensive towards the Sinai passes. On Sunday, 14 October, the Egyptians finally launched a front-wide offensive spearheaded by more than a thousand tanks. Again, the Israelis should have allowed the Egyptians to advance as deep as they would. But again, a certain degree of anxiety, as well as the ill-located forward facilities, forced the Israelis to meet the Egyptian attack in advanced positions well to the west of the passes. As a result, the

Egyptians were hit too hard and too soon for maximum effect. Even so, more than 250 Egyptian tanks were quickly destroyed. Unable to bring their infantry forward, the Egyptians were forced to engage in tank-to-tank combat with predictable results: no more than a dozen Israeli tanks were hit. But the opportunity for a much more conclusive victory was missed; the battle lasted for only a few hours, in many places not even one. The Egyptians retreated back towards the Canal and could not be tempted to attack again, in spite of all manner of retreat manoeuvres on that day and the next, Monday, 15 October. By then, as we shall see, the fighting on the Golan Heights had reached a natural conclusion in front of the invisible political limit shielding Damascus. The Egyptian offensive had come too late for the Syrians. They had managed to hold on to only one small outpost within the 1967 cease-fire lines, an isolated position on the crest of Mount Hermon lost by the Israelis on the first day of war. But while the Syrians had failed in their attempt to reconquer the Golan Heights, the Egyptians were still in firm control of the entire east bank of the Canal.

There were, by now, four mobilized divisions in the Sinai under Bar Lev's effective command (Gonen was not officially replaced until after the cease-fire): Adan's reconstituted division, Mendler's former command, now organized as a division under his designated successor, Maj.-Gen. Kalman Magen (who took over when Mendler was killed in an artillery barrage), an over-strength four-brigade division under Ariel Sharon, and a fourth division deployed in the northern sector (here described as S division).

Sharon had been agitating for an early crossing of the Canal even before the Egyptian attack of 14 October, preferring a combined spoiling-attack-and-penetration to his superiors' scheme for a counter-attack followed by a crossing. Sharon was afraid that a manipulated cease-fire ordered by the Security Council would freeze the existing lines; his superiors, Bar Lev at Southern Command and Elazar at G.H.Q., wanted to wait until the bulk of Egyptian armour had crossed the Canal, thus denuding the west bank. In their view, this was essential to ensure that a bridgehead would not come under heavy attack in the early phases of build-up. In the late afternoon of Monday, 15 October, the Israeli Canal-crossing offensive began. Magen's division was to contain the Egyptian Third Corps on the southern sector between the Bitter Lakes and Port Tewfik (and prevent a breakout to the south towards Ras Sudar, the Belayim oil fields and the road to Sharm el Sheikh), while S division was to keep the Egyptian Second Corps under pressure in the northern sector between Ismailiya and Kantara. Sharon's division, with its two paratroop brigades and two armoured brigades, was to break through the Egyptian front to the Canal, send a holding force across on boats and tank pontoons, secure the crossing point on both sides, cover the erection of a tank bridge, and open the way for Adan's armoured division whose task was to exploit the crossing. Once on the other side, Adan's armoured division and as many follow-up forces as could be sent over were to attack AA missile sites, and gun batteries, and the massive concentration of artillery that was supporting the forces on the east bank from its firing positions on the other side of the water. It was expected that this would unhinge the entire Egyptian front since it would strip the vast array of front-line forces of their air-defence and artillery support and open the way for a two-pronged encirclement of the entire Egyptian army. It could be another Cannae, a total tactical victory.

Sharon executed the first half of his mission with a characteristically complicated series of manoeuvres; a first armoured force was sent due west from Tassa in a 'cover and deception' manoeuvre, and also to pin down the front of the Second Corps forces in the area; a second formation, an armoured brigade, swung round the south of the road from Tassa to the Canal (which reaches the Canal just north of the Great Bitter Lake) and then moved due north on another road that parallels the east bank of the Canal. Not wanting to have the wide waters of the Great Bitter Lake behind their narrow front, the Egyptians had concentrated their army in Sinai on either side of the lake, Second Corps to the north and Third Corps to the south, and the Sinai shore of the lake was thinly held. Thus the second force found little opposition on its way until it began to move north along the Canal. But then it was engaged by increasingly strong Egyptian armour and infantry forces as they gradually turned to face the unexpected attack from the south. This was exactly what Sharon had intended. Engaged in battle with the second force, the Second

Corps forces could not move to the south in order to cut the road from Tassa to the Canal. On the road, a third tank force and a brigade of paratroopers riding in half-tracks was waiting to cross. There were still some Egyptian road blocks between them and the Canal, but the second force sent a detachment of tanks backwards towards Tassa to attack the road blocks from the rear. Once the second force secured the dangerous northern flank and cleared the road to the Canal, the paratroopers were ready to cross. By then, it was night.

With the Egyptian Second Corps forces engaged in battle to their north, and with the placid waters of the Great Bitter Lake to the south, the half-tracks of the paratroopers drove to the Canal preceded by a contingent of tanks to clear the way. Once at the Canal, bulldozers breached the sand bank (reportedly at a spot where the solid mass of sand had been weakened for just this purpose long before the war) while the paratroopers crossed the Canal waters on rubber boats. It was 1 a.m. on the night of 15–16 October. Instead of the strong opposition they had expected, the paratroopers found the west bank of the Canal almost undefended. In the meantime, a fierce battle was raging on the east bank, and Egyptian artillery fire was blanketing the area, sending shells plunging all around and into the Canal. A battalion of tanks began crossing just after dawn on self-propelled pontoons. By then, the paratroopers themselves had destroyed four Egyptian tanks found in the area, and had dealt with what little opposition there was. Although the actual crossing point was virtually undefended (logically enough, since this was supposed to be the safe rear of the Egyptian front), the Egyptian defences further north along the Canal were manned. The troops within were to act as a second line of defence behind the Canal front; they were alert to the possibility of an attack from across the water, but not from their own side. Not only did the Egyptian troops fail to attack the paratroopers in the bridgehead, but they were also caught by surprise as the Israelis moved from bunker to bunker, attacking each one in turn.

At this point, with the bridgehead apparently secure and being steadily expanded as the tanks and paratroopers spread out to find and attack targets, a bridge should have been built on the Canal to allow the crossing of Adan's fresh and uncommitted division. But while the west bank of the Canal was almost tranquil, Egyptian troops of Second Corps were launching fierce southward attacks on the east bank towards the crossing point. Egyptian infantry armed with the ubiquitous wire-guided missiles and RPGs infiltrated to the Tassa-Canal road while artillery kept it under heavy fire. The bridgehead was secure enough, or at any rate, not coming under attack, but the crossing point on the *east bank* was being fiercely contested. A specially built tank-capable bridge of novel design broke down en route and failed to reach the crossing-point; other bridge equipment was not available on the spot, but the road was under such intense fire that, even if the equipment had been ready in place and on time, it is improbable that it could have survived the passage to the Canal through a hail of shells, anti-tank missiles, rockets and small arms fire.

The task of Sharon's oversize division had been to straddle *both* sides of the water in order to secure passage for Adan's armoured forces to the west bank of the Canal. But when in the course of Tuesday, 16 October, the southward pressure of Second Corps continued to threaten the road to the Canal, Bar Lev at Southern Command, and Elazar at G.H.Q., refused to send Adan's division across the Canal. After the war, Sharon accused his superiors of an excess of caution; this, he felt, had deprived Israel of a complete victory since the whole time-table of the offensive was slowed down, and the cease-fire at the U.N. thus stopped the Israelis in mid-stride. From the first, Sharon was with the small body of troops on the west bank of the Canal (with a command group carried on six M. 113 carriers); after the war he told visiting newsmen that it was the failure of his superiors to come to the scene that was the root cause of their blunder. Had they been on the spot, had they seen with their own eyes how easy it was to advance against the Egyptians in disarray, they would have sent across Adan's forces for a quick and massive exploitation of the crossing.

Although there were political* undertones in his statement, Sharon's polemic basically reflected a difference in viewpoints. He was the man on the spot, but *his* spot was the west bank of the Canal where the Egyptians were behaving true to form in failing

* Sharon had become a prominent figure in the Liberal Party and had done much to organize the Likud opposition block.

to respond to the threat of the crossing. With each Egyptian formation following its prepared plans with dogged persistence and great rigidity of purpose, there was a command vacuum around Sharon's men. Different Egyptian battalions and divisions were reporting the hit-and-run attacks of Israeli forces on the west bank; at different levels of command, Egyptians thus knew that there were Israelis on their side of the water, but they did not know how many or where, since Sharon's forces were moving in wide-ranging attacks. Above all, no one Egyptian command was given responsibility for re-establishing a continuous front along the *west* bank of the Canal. And no Egyptian command assumed the responsibility to do so on its own; each had its assigned task, and it would have required risk-taking initiative to do something that had been neither ordered nor planned, i.e., to locate, contain and eventually destroy the Israeli bridgehead. Hence, Sharon and his men were *not seriously attacked* throughout Tuesday, 16 October. Unable to cope with the unexpected, unable to comprehend a vague and fluid tactical situation, the Egyptian command was paralysed and took no concerted action while there was still time.

But the situation was entirely different on the east bank of the Canal where a fierce battle was underway. There, the Egyptian Second Corps did have a clear-cut mission, to hold the ground west of the Canal to a depth of X miles, to defend against Israeli attacks, and to maintain contact with Third Corps whose main body was in the Port Tewfik sector at the southern end of the Canal. And Second Corps carried out its assigned mission by launching heavy armour and infantry attacks in a southward direction to re-establish contact with Third Corps. Faced with a tangible enemy, instead of the phantom presence on the other side of the water, the Egyptian command made a strong response; throughout Tuesday, 16 October and into the night there were bloody battles between the troops of Second Corps and Sharon's east bank forces, primarily the containing armoured brigade and a second brigade of paratroopers. Just north of the crossing point there was a former experimental farm that the Japanese had helped to develop; this 'Chinese farm' became the scene of bitter fighting between armour and infantry on both sides as the Egyptians tried to choke off the crossing point while the Israelis were trying to widen it in order to open a secure path for the follow-up forces.

In a sense, therefore, it was Sharon who was not 'on the spot'. From the viewpoint of his superiors, the essential *sine qua non* of the Canal-crossing offensive was to establish a secure crossing point, and one wide enough so that passage would be safe for the flow of forces and supplies to the other side of the water. With intense fighting continuing just north of the road, with the entire area under heavy artillery fire, Bar Lev at Southern Command as well as Elazar at G.H.Q. could not allow Adan's forces to cross over; they could have been cut off at any time. Nor was it much good to send forces across if a steady flow of fuel and ammunition could not be kept up; the tanks and carriers of Adan's division could perhaps make a run for it under fire from artillery and from the Second Corps troops near the road, but the 'soft' fuel tankers and ammunition trucks could not. Moreover, with many bridge elements broken down on the way, others hit in combat, and others still in the process of assembly, there was no incentive to commit all available forces to clear the road to the Canal on Tuesday, 16 October. To do so would have left no major forces in reserve to oppose an *eastward* attack on either sector of the Canal and both Second Corps and Third Corps could still launch powerful attacks. The very fact that Sharon met with such weak opposition on the west bank was due to the eastward deployment of the Egyptian army, and this still presented a major threat to the holding forces of Kalman's division in the south and S division in the north. It was not until the afternoon of Wednesday, 17 October that Adan's division finally crossed the Canal over heavy pontoon bridges, some thirty-six hours behind schedule. When the Egyptians belatedly realized that the Canal crossing was not a raid, but an offensive, their artillery began intensive barrage of the entire crossing area; Katyusha rockets fired at long range, gun and mortar shells from both sides of the Canal, and even air attacks turned the area into an inferno but failed to destroy the bridges or cut off the bridgehead.

In the meantime, the Israeli foothold on the *west* bank of the Canal was being steadily extended. Sharon's forces were moving north along the west bank, clearing Egyptian infantry from stronghold to stronghold; the Egyptians still expected attacks from the front and not from the south along their own side of the water. Sharon's northward drive towards Lake Timsah and Ismailiya was also exposing the rear of the Egyptian forces on the *east* bank of the Canal and these began to retreat under the concerted attack of the Israeli forces on both sides of the water. Eventually, the Israelis took control of both banks of the Canal almost up to Lake Timsah; cut off from the forces of Second Corps, those of Third Corps also fell back so that the Israelis were also left in control of the eastern shore of the Great Bitter Lake, as well as the ten mile sector between the lakes. The Egyptians, for their part, retained hold of a strip of Sinai from Lake Timsah to the Port Fuad causeway in the north, and of a second strip in the south from the confluence of the Great and Little Bitter Lakes to a few miles below Port Tewfik.

But, of course, the tactical situation was dominated by the fighting on the west bank of the Canal. In sending out his forces in raiding parties on the first day to attack missile sites and every target of opportunity from road-side fuel dumps to entire convoys (still moving in the area in ignorance of the Israeli crossing), Sharon had shown a deep, intuitive understanding of his enemy. Virtually cut off from the rear for a day and a night, Sharon's small force on the west bank (perhaps two thousand men and thirty tanks) should have remained on the defensive. With a large mass of Egyptian forces still on their own side of the water, the Israelis should have dug in a defensive perimeter and prepared to meet Egyptian attacks as best they could. But Sharon apparently sensed immediately that it would be wrong to play the battle by the book. In fact, had he concentrated his forces in an Alamo by the Canal, chances are that the Egyptians would have *located* the threat, which would thus have been made tangible and static. Instead, it was Sharon's decision to spread out his forces and attack; not only did this enable them to cut part of the missile belt at its vulnerable roots but it also deprived the Egyptians of a target. The Egyptian command thought that only a small raiding party had crossed the Canal on Monday night because there was no visible concentration of Israeli forces at the bridgehead. The Egyptians assumed that this was so because the Israelis had retreated; in fact, the bridgehead was almost empty because they **had** advanced.

Adan's forces crossed the water later than planned, too late according to Sharon, but they still enjoyed some residual element of surprise since the Egyptian command was slow to cope with the new threat on the west bank of the Canal. Between the main force crossing and the first cease-fire of 22 October, the Israelis fought to extend the bridgehead into a widening bulge, against the growing resistance of the Egyptians who were moving more and more of their forces against them. Nor did the Israelis rush to advance; commanders at all levels were being careful, perhaps too careful, to reduce casualties to an absolute minimum. While Sharon's forces slowly fought their way northward towards Ismailiya in the rear of Second Corps, Adan's division and the forces that followed in its wake* began to advance due west on a secondary road that leads to Cairo, and due south on the western shore of the Great Bitter Lake along a road that leads to Suez in the rear of Third Corps, past the Fayid and Kabrit air bases.

Although the Israelis were not moving very fast, their three-pronged advance was threatening to encircle the entire Egyptian deployment east of the Canal. It was not until 18 October at the earliest, a full three days after the initial crossing, that the Egyptians realized the gravity of their predicament. (This is when the desperate attempts to interdict the bridges began.) In the next four days, while the Israelis continued their slow but relentless advance, the Egyptians tried to redeploy their forces to contain the bulge. It was at this critical stage of the war that all the rigidities of the Egyptian war machine exacted their full penalty. Lacking in a genuine air capability, the Egyptians had substituted fixed air defence based on missiles. Once the missiles in the growing bulge held by Israeli troops were destroyed, the Egyptians, for all their 600-odd fighters and fighter-bombers, could not prevent the Israeli Air Force from operating in full strength. Flying low across the narrow crossing point, Israeli fighter-bombers could operate almost freely over the bulge to support the forces on the ground; as the latter gradually advanced and rolled back the air defences still further, the Air Force exploited

---

* A fifth division was formed with forces redeployed from the Golan and detached from other formations. At one time, Sharon's division appears to have grouped no less than five brigades, two over the norm.

the widening gap in the missile array (though the long slant range of the missiles allowed their coverage to spill over the bulge on the ground). When Egyptian fighters did try to intervene, dozens were shot down in air combat. Israeli troops on the ground also destroyed several aircraft each day, since their pilots had not learnt the attack-evasion tactics that Egyptian air defences had so forcefully taught the Israelis.

Since the forces lacked the tactical flexibility essential for modern mobile war, the Egyptians had fought Israeli armour with static anti-tank infantry. This had worked very well in the initial crossing phase, but now the Egyptians were faced with Israeli striking forces that could break out in any direction to the south, north and west, and they could not hope to mass anti-tank infantry to cover each and every possible line of advance. The Israelis were moving northwards and threatening the main line of supply to the Second Corps, the road and railway from Cairo to Ismailiya; they were advancing to the south and threatening the Cairo–Suez Road in the rear of the Third Corps; they were moving west and threatening Cairo itself. Politically, a march on Cairo was out of the question; almost certainly it would have triggered a Russian intervention. But the Egyptians could not be sure and they had to cover that front too. What they needed was, therefore, a truly mobile army and flexible command system; in other words, an army with thousands of junior officers and N.C.O.s able to take the initiative and act on their own, men who could direct mobile forces in a fluid battle of movement to locate the Israelis, engage them in combat and stop their advance. This, for all their mass of mobile equipment, the Egyptians did not have. Well trained to carry out slow and methodical manoeuvres, their forces could not fight an improvised battle of movement. Had they tried to emulate the fluid tactics of the Israelis, the Egyptian divisions would merely have disintegrated into an uncoordinated mass of leaderless troops.

Thus, the only recourse open to the Egyptians was to ask their Russian patrons to procure a cease-fire. After having expressed their 'disinterest' in a cease-fire while their clients were doing well, the Russians now moved fast. After a hurried visit to Moscow by the U.S. Secretary of State, a cease-fire resolution was duly introduced at the U.N. Security Council to come into

effect on 22 October. As late as five hours before the announcement was issued in New York, Israeli divisional commanders on
the west bank were still told to fight slowly and methodically, so
as to minimize casualties, since there would be plenty of time to
finish the job. The United States, they were told, would not allow
the Arabs and their Russian patrons to start a war when they
chose to do so and to switch it off just as the Israeli counter-
offensive was getting off the ground. The fighting did in fact
continue; the Egyptians could not really control all their scattered
forces on the west bank, while the Israelis, stopped in mid-stride,
were all too eager to resume their advance. In the end, direct
Russian threats of military intervention finally brought the fighting
to an end on 25 October.

By then the Israelis had reached to within three quarters of a
mile of the main Cairo-Ismailiya highway, the major supply link
to Second Corps and the entire northern sector of the Canal. The
Israelis had also cut the three highways linking the southern half
of the Canal sector to Cairo, encircled the Egyptian Third Corps
(with an estimated 25,000 first-line combat troops), seized the
commanding ridge of the mountains overlooking Suez and the
Cairo–Suez road, taken the port of Adabiya on the African coast,
and widened their salients between these points into a bulge much
larger than the strips of Sinai held by the Egyptians. All this was
still short of a Cannae but, by any standards, it was a major
military victory; no one doubts that, given another few days, all
the Egyptian forces in Sinai would have been encircled. Instead,
there came a second cease-fire, the product of the Russian threat
of direct troop intervention, of American hopes for a durable
peace (which a complete victory would undermine, or so it was
said) and Israeli hesitations in either dismissing the hope of peace
or outfacing Russian threats.

As well as demonstrating that the Arabs could indeed begin and
end wars just as it suited them, an accurate reflection of Israel's
political weakness,* the 25 October cease-fire also proved Sharon
wrong. His criticism of the General Staff and Bar Lev (Dayan was
explicitly exempted) implied that Israel was fighting on a time-

* And of America's failure to adhere to any fixed principles of conduct,
and of the European determination to pursue the paths of self-interest in
the narrowest and most short-sighted terms.

table that was short, which was true, but which was also fixed, which was not true at all. Had Adan's forces and the rest crossed the Canal sooner, had they broken out north and south faster, the Egyptians would have asked for Moscow's help sooner, and the cease-fire would have come sooner too. As a result, the post-combat situation would not have been much different than it was. The real problem was not the prudence of the General Staff but, rather, the willingness of the Russians to go to any lengths to prevent an Arab defeat.

The invisible political barrier that protected Cairo and, indeed, the Egyptian army, much better than its own strength could do, was also evident on the road to Damascus. But during the first days of war this was the least of the Israelis' worries. The rapid, if sometimes chaotic, inflow of reservists was easing Eytan's balancing act at his exposed forward headquarters in Nafah when, on Monday, 8 October, the Syrians sent an additional two divisions with an estimated 500 battle tanks into battle. Col. Y's 7th Brigade was doing wonders by barely holding on to the Nafah-Kuneitra road; the Syrians were in Kuneitra itself and in the southern sector had penetrated much deeper so that they held a rough triangle deep within the cease-fire lines, with one side on the Rafid-El Al road and another along the Tapline right-of-way to Nafah. The garrison brigade was fragmented into isolated pockets of resistance with no commander, almost no ammunition, and no possibility of concentrating its troops into a counter-attack striking force. Col. Y's 7th Brigade had not suffered devastating losses like its counterparts in Sinai, but it was fully committed in strenuous, round-the-clock combat; its holding operation was still hanging by a thread.

By then, the initial quick-reaction force structure, nominally a division headed by Eytan, had given way to the full-mobilization order of battle, three divisions, one under the command of Eytan (who took over the northern sector), another under Maj.-Gen. Dan Lanner, a kibbutz-member reservist and Palmach ⁺veteran who had commanded a battalion in one of the most desperate battles of 1948 (his last career post had been commander of the 'Armoured Forces in Sinai'); and a third division which, like the others, grouped three brigades, divisional artillery, engineers and service units, under the command of another Palmach veteran,

Maj.-Gen. Moshe Peled. While Eytan's forces fought to recapture the ground lost in the north-east sector and in Kuneitra, and Lanner's division counter-attacked from the central road in the general direction of Rafid, Peled's forces moved to recapture the southern El Al-Rafid axis. There was a great sense of urgency. The many beleaguered outposts left behind in the Syrian rear were at the mercy of any determined attack. In fact, the outposts, mostly manned by twenty soldiers or so, were rarely attacked in full force, even when they kept adjacent roads under fire to interfere with Syrian movements. Instead, small groups of Syrian tanks would approach them from time to time and open fire in a desultory fashion; in response, the Israelis would fire their few bazooka rockets, knocking out a tank or two. With this, the Syrians usually gave up the assault. It was in this manner that most of the Israelis, cut off in the outposts, survived. (As elsewhere, the notable weakness in anti-tank weapons reflected the pervasive assumption that the infantry could invariably be best protected by assigned detachments of tanks, instead of more and better anti-tank weapons of their own.)

After a day of heavy artillery barrages on both sides, the forward drive of the Israeli divisions was accelerated on Thursday, 11 October. By the afternoon, Kuneitra was once again in Israeli hands and, later that night and on the next day, the Israelis began to advance beyond the 1967 cease-fire lines into Syria proper. At this stage, the rescue mission had been accomplished, and concern for the beleaguered troops gave way to the overriding goal of minimizing casualties. It was felt that any territory captured was liable to be lost in a post-war settlement, if there was one. If there was not, the additional territory would still not be worth the cost in human blood. Any weapons destroyed would quickly be resupplied by the Rusxians, and any Syrian troops killed would be of small significance to the rulers in Damascus and quickly replaced. Of course, this attitude, however admirable and humanitarian, exacted a tactical price: commanders oppressed by the thought of the casualties already sustained, and fearful of more, would tend to be cautious, and caution is not always appropriate against a slow-moving and rigid enemy.

For all their caution, the Israelis continued to advance until Sunday, 14 October, reaching the hill of Tel Shams on the

Kuneitra–Damascus road, opposite Sa'sa, a village twenty-two miles from Syria's capital city of two million people. It was on that day that the Egyptians launched their much-awaited offensive in Sinai; driven by frantic Syrian appeals to anticipate their planned attack by two days, the Egyptians finally attacked but could no longer save their allies from defeat. By then, the Syrians had lost all the ground they had captured on the Golan Heights except for the Israeli outpost on the crest of Mount Hermon. Syria's other allies could not be of much help either. Fortified by a peculiar Iranian promise of non-interference, the Iraqis sent first one division and then another to help the Syrians. A token force of Moroccan infantry was already there and, in the second week of the war, King Hussein of Jordan intervened too – but with great circumspection. While the 186 miles of the Jordan–Israel cease-fire line remained absolutely quiet (both sides even allowed the traffic across the Jordan to continue), Hussein ordered first one, and then a second, armoured brigade to Syria where they held part of the line in the southern sector.* The Jordanians, including the 40th Brigade of 1967 fame (p. 267), did not try very hard to seek combat, while the Israelis concentrated their drive into Syria on the northern sector, thus almost avoiding combat with Hussein's forces. (The result is a very peculiar cease-fire line that includes a suggestive 90 degree angle between the northern and southern sectors of the front.)

The Iraqis, by contrast, did enter the battle though, not strictly speaking, of their own volition. As their troop convoys drove towards the front across north-east Syria, on the night of October 13, they came under attack from an Israeli raiding force of elite 'reconnaissance' troops some seventy miles north-east of Damascus. Having penetrated unnoticed during the night, the Israelis blew up a bridge on the Iraqi line of advance; when the Iraqi convoy stopped the Israelis opened fire from ambush positions, setting fire to trucks and blowing up tanks. Continuing on its journey, the same convoy fell victim to further attacks identical to the first. The Iraqis' failure to change over from a

* Unkindly, it was suggested that while King Hassan of Morocco sent two battalions of troublemakers to fight and die, Hussein sent his best and most disciplined troops to make sure that they would not fight. In reality the Jordanians did fight.

travelling to a combat advance proved to be a token of the quality of these troops; the one Iraqi division that was actually sent into battle was largely destroyed in the first few days of combat.

The intervention of the Iraqis (who provided a second division for the defence of Damascus) enabled the Syrians to try their hand at a counter-offensive. This came on 16 October, but it was quickly defeated. With this, the Syrians gave up the attempt to recapture a symbolic foothold on the Golan Heights or even to drive the Israelis out of Syria proper. Nor did the Israelis try to conquer more territory; by the second week of the war, the General Staff had shifted the main effort to Sinai; troop reinforcements, newly repaired tanks recovered from the field, extra artillery shells and most of the new weapons that were arriving in the U.S. airlift (the first transports landed on 14 October), were all being sent to the south. So were some units initially deployed on the Golan, including a substantial body of armour. Aside from the redeployment to Sinai, and the obvious political risk, the Israelis also had a tactical reason for not advancing on Damascus. The Syrians had turned the entire belt of territory between the 1967 cease-fire lines and the outskirts of Damascus into a fortified zone. By a geologic fluke, the terrain is marked by a long series of low but steep ridges of hard, basalt rock which form a multiple anti-tank barrier more formidable than any of the man-made variety. Off-road movement is very slow, and the broken terrain quickly wears out the steel tracks of armoured vehicles. Moreover, in each ridge along the way, the Syrians had built concrete gun positions dug into the basalt rock; these could only be knocked out by a direct hit in the narrow firing slit since they were entirely bomb-proof. A force advancing on the Damascus road as it turns and climbs one ridge after another would thus face the gun positions of the next ridge directly ahead, which could cover every inch of the road in direct line-of-sight fire. Conspiring with nature, the Syrians thus provided themselves with an ideal defence in depth, a multiple barrier which would decimate stage by stage an armoured force attempting a straightforward advance on Damascus. Each defended line could be outfought, at a price in blood and time, but it could neither be rushed nor outmanoeuvred.

The conquest of Damascus would have turned the October war

into a catastrophic defeat for the Arabs, comparable to Timur's destruction of Baghdad. At the time, Arab experts disagreed in their estimate of the possible consequences, some claiming that it would energize the Arabs into an all-out holy war and others asserting that it would throw them into a deep and paralysing despondency. The Israeli government was not disposed to make the experiment; a march on Damascus would have been very costly in casualties, not to speak of the near-certainty of Russian intervention. But the Israelis did keep up the pressure on the Damascus road and their creeping advance during the second week of the war compelled the Syrians to concentrate their forces where they could be hit hardest. True to form, the Syrian government did not bother to publish casualty lists after the the October war, but an official Syrian statement published abroad suggested that Syrian losses amounted to 30,000 men, including several hundred civilians killed by Israeli bombing raids. This is probably too high but it is certain that Syrian casualties were in excess of 12,000 killed, entire formations were destroyed, and not merely driven to flight as in 1967.

Israeli forces also made a secondary advance due east of the 1967 lines south of the Damascus road. Here they drove a broad wedge into the Syrian front whose apex was only seven miles from the Damascus–Dera'a highway which connects the Syrian capital with the southern region of the country and which is the sole road link between Jordan and Syria. In the event of further Jordanian interventions on the Syrian front, control of the road would have been of considerable significance; as it was this further penetration of Syrian territory counted for little.

Of greater tactical significance was another acquisition of the October war, the 9,223 feet high peak of Mount Hermon, if only because its conquest was one more factor in the 'rehabilitation' of the paratroopers in the Israeli Army. After having been the elite and the model of the Army of the fifties, the paratroopers had declined in importance in step with the rising ascendancy of the Armour Corps; in 1967 they were virtually eclipsed. But in the conquest of Mount Hermon, as in the crossing of the Canal and in several smaller operations on both fronts, the paratrooper style of combat, with its stress on tactical ingenuity and careful planning, again came to the fore. On Saturday, 20 October, young conscript troops of the Golani brigade attempted to retake the Israeli outpost on the crest of Mount Hermon which was just within the 1967 cease-fire lines of which it formed the north-east corner. Lost to a force of heli-borne Syrian paratroopers on the first day of the war, the outpost was now held by a battalion of these elite troops who were ensconced between the boulders on the crest which dominates the Israeli-built road. As it climbed towards the crest, the Golani force came under accurate sniper and mortar fire; thirty Israelis, including a battalion commander, were killed and the attack was called off.

On the crest of Mount Hermon there was another Syrian battalion, holding a second outpost further to the east beyond the 1967 lines and some three hundred feet higher than the first; still further to the east and still nearer to the peak there was a third outpost manned by a smaller company-sized Syrian force. The peak itself was undefended. On the following day, Sunday, 21 October, the Golani force was to try again to take the first outpost in a night attack. But before this attack took place a battalion of paratroopers was sent to seize the peak of the Hermon at 9,223 feet, almost two thousand feet higher than the captured Israeli outpost assigned to the Golani troops. To do this, the paratroopers had to contend with the second Syrian battalion outpost as well as with the company deployed between this outpost and the peak. But while the Golani force tried the direct approach, the only one possible overland, owing to the difficult terrain, and then attacked at night in order to minimize the impact of Syrian fire, the paratroopers chose to attack in the early afternoon, in full daylight and in full view of the enemy. But in a classic demonstration of superior fieldcraft and tactical ingenuity, the paratroopers found a weak spot in the Syrian defence. Helicopters loaded with paratroopers flew to the Hermon and deplaned the paratroopers on the *reverse* side of the slope, just below the edge of the crest. The Syrians could watch the entire operation but could not stop the Israelis who were beyond the range of their small arms. Nor could the Syrians fire accurately with their mortars, the key weapon of mountain warfare, since they could not *correct* their fire; the Israelis were out of sight in 'dead ground' and as each mortar shell flew over the crest the Syrians could not tell whether it had found its target or fallen harmlessly in the valley below. The paratroopers waited till nightfall, having spread out on the reverse side of the crest, and then seized both Syrian positions as well as the peak of Mount Hermon. In the entire operation the paratroopers lost only one man, wounded. At nightfall the infantry conscripts of the Golani made their second attack on the battalion outposts within the 1967 lines. Once again they came under accurate sniper fire but this time they persisted until they reached and seized their objective once the Syrians were driven to flight. According to unofficial reports, Golani casualties were in excess of seventy dead for a total of more than one hundred on both attacks. (For the young conscripts of the Golani and even more so for their officers the losses of the October war as a whole were catastrophic; reportedly all but one of the battalion commanders in the brigade were killed and the one surviving battalion commander was wounded.)

The great and surprising success of the October war was undoubtedly the new missile Navy with its twelve French-built Saar class boats and two (the first of ten) Israeli-built Reshef boats (which at 410 tons of displacement are much larger). Both types rely primarily on the Israeli-built Gabriel missile for surface fire-power but they also mount rapid-fire guns, 76mm auto-loaders and, on some of the Saar boats, smaller 40mm cannon. With their 76mm guns fore and aft, and with their battery of Gabriel missiles, the Reshef boats can outrange and defeat much larger warships as well as being much faster. Out to horizon range, the Gabriel missile proved itself to be accurate and deadly during the naval clashes of the October war, while the limitations of the missile boats (i.e., their weak anti-submarine and anti-aircraft armament) were of no consequence since the boats never came under submarine or air attack. With their speed and agility, and their shallow draft, the missile boats would make very difficult targets for conventional torpedoes, but like all such warships they can offer only a limited resistance to air attack.

In 1967 the Navy was still what it had always been, a small-scale replica of a great power navy and thus inherently poorly suited to Israeli needs since it could provide no significant striking power. Its two old destroyers were no match for the Russian-built boats of the Egyptians (which sunk one of the two, the *Elat*, in October 1967). As recounted earlier in text (p. 92) the

Israelis finally developed a viable concept for an 'organic' navy in the later sixties, a naval force of missile boats and small submarines that could be integrated in the operations of the rest of the Army. Planned under the aegis of Rear-Admiral Errel around the twelve Saar boats built in France to Israeli specifications, trained and developed under his post-1967 successor as Navy commander, Rear-Admiral Botzer, the missile-boat navy finally went to war under the newly appointed Rear-Admiral Benyamin Telem.

From the first the Israelis went over to the offensive, seeking out and destroying Syrian and Egyptian Osa and Komar missile boats and shelling fuel dumps and installations in Syrian harbours. On the first night of the war, Israeli missile boats engaged Syrian warships and pursued them right into the outer harbour of Latakia, the main Syrian port, sinking three Osa boats for no loss of their own. On the next day, the Israelis engaged the Egyptians off Port Said, sinking another three missile boats in a clash which damaged one Israeli boat. In these and subsequent battles the Russian-built Styx missiles of the Osa and Komar boats of the Arab navies proved themselves to be distinctly inferior to the Gabriels, notably in their vulnerability to intercepting fire. Flying subsonically to their targets high above the water, Styx missiles could be shot down in the air – in one case by machine-gun fire – unlike the Gabriels which fly just above the waves in a sea-skimming course.

In a relatively long war, in which the security of commercial sea lanes was for the first time of direct military significance, the success of the Navy in the October war had a strategic import. By sinking most if not all Syrian missile boats, and by driving Egyptian warships into the shelter of their harbours, the Israeli missile flotilla secured the 216 nautical miles of the Israeli-held Mediterranean coast and a sea area out to Crete 500 miles away, thus assuring a safe transit for Israeli shipping.

In the Red Sea the Israelis had no missile boats, and kept only some U.S.-built Swift-class patrol boats as well as a few torpedo boats and landing craft based at Elat and Sharm El Sheikh. Even so, the navy went over to the offensive, sinking one small Egyptian warship (a DeCastro-class patrol boat) and attacking Egyptian harbours at Ras Gharib and Ras Zafrana.* These

* Penetrating right into the two harbours with their main engines switched

colourful exploits could not alter the naval situation in the Red Sea which was dominated by the Egyptian blockade of the Bab-el-Mandab straits between Ethiopia and South Yemen at the remote confluence of the Indian Ocean and the Red Sea. Hundreds of miles beyond the reach of Israeli airpower,* past the long and unfriendly coasts of Sudan and Saudi Arabia, a flotilla of Egyptian destroyers based in Aden barred the way to shipping sailing to and from Elath. Once again the Red Sea route to the east – and the oil tanker route from Iran – was closed to the Israelis, and this time it was no use controlling Sharm el Sheikh since the ships would be stopped long before they entered the Gulf of Aqaba. Deprived of any access to any port in the area (Ethiopia broke diplomatic relations with Israel during the October war) the Israelis could only have broken the blockade with a major air-sea operation that would have entailed disproportionate risks, political as well as tactical. (It would have required the deployment of missile boats round the long Cape route and the seizure of an island base for an air strip; even if all went well the operation would have been a logistic nightmare.)

To some Israelis the Egyptian blockade of the Bab el Mandab was symbolic of the futility of territorial acquisitions, since it invalidated the official rationale for retaining Sharm el Sheikh in a post-war settlement. To others, the fact that the blockade was called off by the Egyptians in exchange for the transit of food and water to the encircled Third Corps was evidence that the only instrument that mattered was the Army, and its ability to defeat the enemy in battle.

All Israelis were forced to ponder on their country's diplomatic isolation; in the entire vast area of the Indian Ocean Israel could not count on a single friend, and could count on very few in the entire world. From Morocco to Iraq and south to Yemen,

* Air refuelling is of course technically possible but it would have been exceedingly hazardous to send the vulnerable tanker aircraft through hostile airspace for hundreds of miles. Moreover, it is doubtful whether a one-shot attack with limited ordnance could have opened the straits: even the smallest warships would suffice to enforce the blockade against unarmed tankers and merchant ships.

off, the Israelis caught the Egyptians by surprise on the night of 14–15 October and attacked the shipping inside at close range with cannon and grenades.

hostility to Israel and the Jewish people had become the unofficial state religion of the Arab world. Beyond this, the diplomatic leverage of Arab territories, Arab numbers, Arab oil and Arab money had drawn a vast circle of enmity around Israel, so that during the October war both China and the Soviet Union, both India and Pakistan, France as well as Britain and states large and small from the Vatican to North Korea could agree in supporting the Arabs, and in presenting a blank wall of hostility to three million Israelis. In the light of this, the Israeli government's refusal to allow the Army to strike first seems almost pathetic. It averted neither a British arms embargo nor the charge of aggression; from Poland to Uganda well-informed governments agreed that Israel had treacherously started the war.

A nation other than the Israelis could have taken pride in the military successes of the October war; at the time of writing, Israeli troops are within twenty-two miles of Damascus while the Egyptian government is insisting that Israel *return* to the 'lines of 22 October' – and these lines are not somewhere between Gaza and Tel Aviv but rather between Suez and Cairo. On a different count, the Israelis returned 8,301 prisoners for 232 of their own, and were still hoping to return 368 Syrians, 13 Iraqis and 6 Moroccans for less than half that total of Israelis in Syrian hands. But for the Israelis the casualties of the war, 2,412 dead and 508 missing, at the time of writing, mattered much more than any victory large or small. In their unfashionable concern for human lives, the Israelis failed to enjoy the glory of victory as Arabs were doing from Morocco to Iraq.

For the Army as a whole the October war had all the qualities of a defeat except for its substance. The post-war period will certainly witness widespread changes of men, of doctrines, of tactics and of structures. Beginning with a formal judicial enquiry into what was still regarded as an Intelligence failure, rather than a failure of policy, broadened by a General Staff investigation of the initial defeats at the Canal, a comprehensive and agonizing reappraisal of the every aspect of the Army is now underway. If the American peace initiative launched in the wake of the October war were to fail, if Israel will be forced to fight yet again, a new and different Army will do the fighting, as different from that of 1973 as the Army of 1967 was different from that of 1948.

Notes

CHAPTER 1 Origins

1. See Government of Israel, *Iton Rishmi* (Official Gazette), 1948, Appendix A, p. 9.

2. 4,017 soldiers and more than 1,000 civilians were killed in the 1948 War (Y. Harkaby in *Ma'arachot* (the official journal of the Israel Defence Forces), No. 166, March 1965, pp. 5–11).

3. The security problems of the Jewish population in Palestine during the last years of the Ottoman rule are described in detail in Michael Assaf, *Ha-Yechassim Ben Yehudim Ve-Aravim Be-Eretz Israel 1890–1948* (*Jewish–Arab Relations in Palestine 1890–1948*), Tarbut Ve-Chinuch, Tel Aviv, 1970, pp. 9–83.

4. For the history of *Hashomer* see *Sefer Toldot Ha-Haganah* (*The History of the Haganah*), Vol. I, Ha-Sifria Ha-Zionit and *Ma'arachot*, Tel Aviv, 1956, pp. 113–312; Shlomo Shva, *Shevet Ha-Amitzim* (*The Tribe of the Brave*), Tel Aviv, 1970.

5. See *Sefer Toldot Ha-Haganah*, Vol. I, pp. 811–13.

6. For a description of the political conditions in Palestine during the twenties and early thirties see H.M.S.O., *Palestine Royal Commission Report* (Cmd. 5477), July 1937; E.S.C.O. Foundation for Palestine, *Palestine, a Study of Jewish, Arab and British Policies*, Yale University Press, New Haven, 1947; Bernard Joseph, *British Rule in Palestine*, Public Affairs Press, Washington, 1948; and Albert M. Hyamson, *Palestine Under the Mandate 1920–1948*, Methuen, London, 1950.

7. The origins of the Haganah are described in *Sefer Toldot Ha-Haganah*, Vol. I, pp. 624–70.

8. See 'Minutes of the Proceedings of the General Conference of the Jewish Workers of Palestine' (The Founding Conference of the Histadrut), December 1920, quoted in *Sefer Toldot Ha-Haganah*, Vol. II, pp. 1,263–4 (Hebrew). See also Eliahu Golomb, *Hevion Oz*, Ha-Sifria Le-Noar, Jerusalem, 1947.

9. For the political and ideological development of the Labour–Zionist movement see M. Breslavski, *Tnuat Ha-Poalim Ha-*

Eretz Israel (*The Israeli Labour Movement*), Vol. I, 1955; Vol. II, 1957; Vol. III, 1959; Vol. IV, 1963, Hakibbutz Hameuchad, Tel Aviv; Peretz Merhav, *Toldot Tnuat Ha-Poalim Be-Eretz Israel* (*History of the Labour Movement in the Land of Israel*), Sifriat Poalim, Merhavia, 1967; and Zvi Even Shoshan (Rosenstein), *Toldot Tnuat Ha-Poalim Be-Eretz Israel* (as above), Vol. I, 1955; Vol. II, 1966, Am-Oved, Tel Aviv; for a survey in English see Walter Preuss, *The Labour Movement in Israel*, R. Moss, Jerusalem, 1965.

10. For detailed descriptions of these organizations and their functions see The Jewish Agency for Palestine, *The Jewish Case Before the Anglo-American Committee of Inquiry*, Jerusalem 1947; and Moshe Attias, *Knesset Israel Be-Eretz Israel* (*The Israeli Assembly in the Land of Israel*), Ha-Va'ad Ha-Leumi, Jerusalem, 1944.

11. See *Sefer Toldot Ha-Haganah*, Vol. II, pp. 16–423; and Yossef Avidar, *Ba-Derech Le-Zahal* (*On the Road to Zahal*), Ma'arachot Publishing House, Tel Aviv, 1970, pp. 46, 60–67.

12. *Sefer Toldot Ha-Haganah*, Vol. II, pp. 423–33. The split as seen by one of the Haganah leaders is described in Avidar, op. cit. For the minority viewpoint see David Niv, *Ma'arachot Ha-Irgun Ha-Zvai Ha-Leumi* (*The Struggles of the Irgun Zvai Leumi*), Vol. I, Klausner Institute, Jerusalem, 1965.

13. *Sefer Toldot Ha-Haganah*, Vol. II, pp. 722–34; and Niv, op. cit., Vol. II.

14. The title of a book by David Ben Gurion, *Me-Ma'amad Le-Am* (*From Class to Nation*), Davar, Tel Aviv, 1933.

15. See *The Palestine Royal Commission Report*, 1937.

16. Avidar, op. cit., pp. 78–99.

17. A political central command known as *Mifkadah Artzit* was formed in the summer of 1931 but the day-to-day activities of the Haganah were guided by the 'National Coordinator' – a position held in succession by two Mapai party activists, Dov Hoz and Shaul Meirov-Avigur. See Avidar, op. cit., pp. 60–77.

18. The development of the Haganah during this period is described in detail in *Sefer Toldot Ha-Haganah*, a comprehensive survey of the subject. The editorial work was supervised by a committee which included the late President of Israel, Y. Ben Zvi, as well as three of the leaders of the Haganah, S. Avigur, I. Galili and E. Galili – as well as the editor, Dr Y. Skutzki, and the chief editor, Professor B. Dinoor. For a history of Jewish military organization from the I.Z.L. point of view see Niv, op. cit.

19. See *Sefer Toldot Ha-Haganah*, Vol. II, pp. 723–4, 833–50; Avidar, op. cit., pp. 126–7.
20. The beginnings of the *Nodedet* were described by its initiator, Yitzhak Sadeh, 'Ha-Nodedet' in Bracha Habas (ed.), *Me'Oraot Tarzav* (*The 1936 Disturbances*), Tel Aviv, 1938, pp. 518–19.
21. For a comprehensive account of the organization of the *Notrim* and of the relations between the Jewish national institutions and the British authorities in this context, see Gershon Rivlin, *La-Eash Ve-La-Magen* (*The Fire and the Shield*), Ma'arachot Publishing House, Tel Aviv, 1962.
22. See Yigal Allon, 'Moreshet Ha-Fosh' ('The Heritage of the Fosh'), in Z. Gilad (ed.), *Sefer Ha-Palmach*, Vol. I, Hakibbutz Hameuchad, 1953, pp. 49–53.
23. See *Sefer Toldot Ha-Haganah*, pp. 729–34. Later, in July 1938, a neutral chairman was appointed to the National Command. The first such was a Professor of Architecture and a former Russian army officer, Yohanan Rattner. See Avidar, op. cit., pp. 150–51.
24. For contrasting assessments of Wingate's role in Palestine and with central Haganah men, see Moshe Sharett, 'Ha-Mefaked Ha-Bilti Memuneh' ('The Unauthorized Commander'), in *Ma'arachot*, No. 83, 1954; Eliahu Golomb, 'Hayedid' ('The friend'), *Ma'arachot*, No. 83, 1954; and Ya'akov Dori, 'Hirhurim al Mif'alot Wingate Ba'Aretz' ('Thoughts on Wingate's Achievements in Israel'). *Ma'arachot*, No. 87–8, January 1955 (first published in *Ma'arachot* 25–6). For a comprehensive account of Wingate's activities in Palestine see Christopher Sykes, *Orde Wingate*, Collins, London, 1959.
25. See Yehuda Bauer, *Diplomatia U-Makhteret Ba-Mediniut Ha-Zionist 1939–1945* (*Diplomacy and the Underground Struggle in Zionism 1939–1945*), Sifriat Poalim, Merhavia, 1963, pp. 52–61, 84–94. Dr Bauer's study includes an account of the development of the *Haganah* since 1939, a period which is not covered in the volumes of *Sefer Toldot Ha-Haganah* published so far.
26. Wingate had first suggested a plan for the defence of a Jewish state in Palestine in 1937. See *Ma'arachot*, No. 83, 1954.
27. For Sadeh's military thought see Yitzhak Sadeh, *Ma Khidesh Ha-Palmach* (*What Did the Palmach Innovate?*), Sifriat Poalim, Merhavia, 1950.
28. See H.M.S.O., Cmd. 6019 (The 1939 White Paper). For the implications of the White Paper for the *Yishuv* and the response of the Jewish leadership see Bauer, op. cit., pp. 21–94.
29. For the history of 'Aliah B' see Jon and David Kimche, *The*

Secret Roads, Secker & Warburg, London, 1954; and Braha Habbas, *The Gate Breakers*, Herzl Press and Yoseloff, New York, 1963.

30. See Avidar, op. cit., pp. 128–50; and *Sefer Toldot Ha-Haganah*, pp. 851–80.

31. See Bauer, op. cit., pp. 51, 84–5, 123–6.

32. The Him was in fact the original militia of the Haganah composed of registered members with little training. Of 30,745 Him men in 1944, only 4,372 were designated as 'trained'; Bauer, op. cit., p. 60.

33. See Avidar, op. cit., p. 150–55; and Bauer, op. cit., pp. 48, 84–5, 116–18.

34. Forty-three of the Haganah's most experienced men (who were instructors at one of the first platoon commanders' courses) were arrested in September 1939. The group, which included Moshe Dayan and Moshe Carmel, was released after 16 months in prison. Moshe Carmel later published a best-selling book of letters from prison; Assir Ivri (Moshe Zlitzki-Carmel), *Me-Bein Ha-Chomot* (*From Within the Walls*), Hakibbutz Hameuchad, Ein Harod, 1942.

35. See Niv, op. cit., Vol. II; and for the Lehi point of view see Yaakov Bannai, *Hayalim Almonim* (*Lost Soldiers*), Tel Aviv, 1958 (Hebrew). For a valuable source for the history of Lehi, a collection of documents, see Lohamei Herut Israel, *Ktavim*, Vol. I, 1959; Vol. II, 1960, Tel Aviv.

36. See the joint statements of The Jewish Agency executive and National Council of 6 September 1939, 15 September 1940, 2 May 1941, 9 July 1941, 2 October 1941, 21 June 1942, 10 July 1942, 8 August 1942, 27 June 1943, and 27 October 1944; documents Nos. 228, 242, 246, 247, 247, 251, 252, 258, 259, 273, in Atiash Moshe (ed.), *Sefer Ha-Teudot Shel Ha-Vaad Ha-Leumi Be-Eretz Israel* (*The Documents of the National Council*), Jerusalem, 1963.

37. See Menachem Begin, *The Revolt*, W. H. Allen, London, 1951. The author was the commander of the *I.Z.L.* (since 1943) and later leader of the Herut party.

38. See Bauer, op. cit., pp. 271–83.

39. For detailed figures see a memorandum by Moshe Shertok (Sharett) to the Anglo-American Commission of Inquiry on Palestine of 28 March 1946, quoted in Sharett, *Be Sha'ar Ha-Umot* (*In the Gate of Nations*), Am Oved, Tel Aviv, 1958, pp. 45–53.

40. See Bauer, op. cit., pp. 117–19.

41. The decision of the Haganah's National Command of 15 May 1941, on the establishment of the Palmach, and its special 'Emergency Order' issued four days later, are quoted in *Sefer Ha-Palmach*, Vol. I, pp. 76–8; the background to the decision is described by Yigal Allon in *Sefer Ha-Palmach*, Vol. I, pp. 5–12. See also Avidar, op. cit., pp. 174–5; and Bauer, op. cit., pp. 125–30.

42. See David Hacohen, 'Me-Parshiot Ha'Shituf' ('From the Chapter of Cooperation') and Professor Y. Rattner, 'Kivrat Derech', in *Sefer Ha-Palmach*, Vol. I, pp. 79–82 and pp. 139–46; Bauer, op. cit., pp. 95–188.

43. See Allon in *Sefer Ha-Palmach*, Vol. I, pp. 23–39; and Bauer, op. cit., pp. 173–88.

44. Most revealing in this respect is the training schedule of the Palmach's squad commanders' course: of 493 hours of training no less than 81 were dedicated to 'The Independent Commander' and only 25 to 'The Commander in the Framework of the Platoon'. 120 hours were allocated to indoctrination and cultural activities. See 'The Training Schedule of the Squad Commanders Course in Dalya', in *Sefer Ha-Palmach*, Vol. I, p. 434. (The course commander was a future Chief of Staff, Haim Bar Lev.)

45. See *Sefer Ha-Palmach*, pp. 393–417.

46. For descriptions of the political conditions in Palestine in the mid-forties see Bernard Joseph, op. cit.; Jon Kimche, *Seven Fallen Pillars*, Secker & Warburg, London, 1950; Harry Sacher, *Israel: The Establishment of the State*, Weidenfeld & Nicolson, London, 1952; Christopher Sykes, *Cross Roads to Israel*, Collins, London, 1965; J. C. Hurewitz, *The Struggle for Palestine*, Norton, New York, 1950; David Horowitz, *State in a Making*, Knopf, New York, 1953; and David Ben Gurion, *Ba'-Ma'aracha* (*In the Struggle*), Mifleget Poalei Eeretz Israel, Vol. II, Tel Aviv, 1949. (This is a collection of Ben Gurion's speeches and articles which is a most valuable source for the Yishuv and the Zionist movement during the forties.)

47. See Bauer, op. cit., pp. 189–224.

48. For accounts of the operations of the Haganah against the British in 1946, see *Sefer Ha-Palmach*, Vol. I, pp. 529–676. See in Particular the Palmach Command's communiqué on the 'Night of the Bridges', pp. 650–52.

49. See Avidar, op. cit., pp. 212–29.

50. See Richard Crossman, *Palestine Mission*, London, 1947.

51. The Jewish preparations for war are described by Ben Gurion in his introduction to the official history of the War of Independence: the History branch of the Israeli Army, *Toldot Milchemet Ha-Komemiut* (*History of the War of Foundation*), Maarachot Publishing House, 1959, pp. 11–60; see also Avidar, op. cit., pp. 256–63.

52. See *Toldot Milchemet Ha-Kommemiut*, pp. 71–3, and Avidar, op. cit., pp. 264–5. For detailed figures see *Sefer Ha-Palmach*, Vol. I, pp. 860–62.

53. See *Toldot Milchemet Ha-Kommemiut*, pp. 72–4.

54. In 1944 the ratio between Palmach and Hish men in the course was about equal, although the Palmach was a much smaller force than the Hish. See Avidar, op. cit., p. 179.

55. See Avidar, op. cit., p. 266, and Ben Gurion in *Toldot Milchemet Ha-Kommemiut*, p. 26.

56. Avidar, op. cit., p. 266.

57. For the role of the Palmach Command in the War of Independence see Yitzhak Rabin, *Sefer Ha-Palmach*, pp. 734–6.

58. Both the I.Z.L. and Lehi agreed to disband before the official establishment of the State of Israel but I.Z.L. men joined the army in formations and not as individuals. Government policy towards the 'dissident organizations' during the 1948 War is stated by David Ben Gurion, *Medinat Israel Ha-Mithadeshet* (*The Restored State of Israel*), Am Oved, Tel Aviv, 1969, pp. 179–91, 281–5.

59. *Toldot Milhemet Ha-Kommemiut*, pp. 79–80.

60. For Israeli assessments of the implications of the British withdrawal see Jon and David Kimche, *Both Sides of The Hill*, Secker & Warburg, London, 1960, pp. 105–16; *Toldot Milhemet Ha-Kommemiut*, pp. 65–8 and Natanel Lorch, *The Edge of the Sword*, Putnam, New York, 1961, pp. 50–52. (Lieut.-Col. Lorch was the first official historian of the Israeli Army.)

61. See David Ben Gurion's introduction to the official history, *Toldot Milhemet Ha-Kommemiut*, pp. 11–60.

62. See Kimche, *Both Sides of the Hill*, Chaps. 2–4.

63. See the memoirs of the British Commander of the Arab Legion, Sir John Bagot Glubb, *A Soldier with the Arabs*, Hodder & Stoughton, 1967.

64. According to an Israeli estimate of the time, Egypt had 48 guns, 25–30 armoured cars, 10–20 tanks, and 21–5 aircraft; Iraq had 48 guns, 25–30 armoured cars and 20 aircraft; Syria had 24 guns, 36 armoured cars, 10–20 tanks and 14 aircraft; Jordan had 24 guns

and 45 armoured cars; and Lebanon had 8 guns and 9 armoured cars. See Israel Beer, *Be-Ma'agal Be'aiot Bitachon* (*In the Circle of Security Problems*), Am Oved, Tel Aviv, 1957, pp. 166–7.

65. The tactical problems of the battles are described in Shlomo Gazit, *Sefer Ha-Palmach*, Vol. II, pp. 40–43; see also the standing order of the Palmach Command for the protection of convoys, *Sefer Ha-Palmach*, Vol. II, pp. 43–5; and Menahem Russak in *Sefer Ha-Palmach*, Vol. II, pp. 99–106.

66. For the 'Battle of the Roads' as seen by the Commander of the *Harel* Brigade, see Yitzhak Rabin in *Ma'arachot*, No. 182, pp. 99–106.

67. The mass flight of the Arabs became a subject of political controversy almost immediately. In fact the attitude of the Jewish authorities varied according to the local military situation. In Haifa the Jewish Mayor requested the Arabs to remain; elsewhere, nearer the front lines, Israeli military authorities made no effort to persuade the Arabs to remain – and sometimes forced men to leave. See Rony Gabbai, *A Political Study of the Arab–Jewish Conflict: The Arab Refugee Problem*, E. Droz, Geneva, 1959.

68. For details, see Kimche, *Both Sides of the Hill*, pp. 119–24.

69. The battle for the Old City is described in Shmuel Bazak, *Be-Ir David U-Be-Shvi Ha-Legion* (*In Jerusalem and in the Legion's Jail*), Mass, Jerusalem, 1949.

70. The Etzion bloc was the scene of some of the most bitter fighting of the first part of the war, and a test case for the doctrine that no Jewish settlement, however isolated, was to be evacuated. See Don Horowitz, *Shana-Be-Sograim* (*Year in Brackets*), Sifriat Paolim, Merhavia, 1949 (Hebrew); and A. Trainin and U. Ofek, *Ma'oz Etzion* (*Fortress Etzion*), Ma'arachot Publishing House, Tel Aviv, 1950.

71. Ben Gurion, *Medinat Israel*, p. 106. Ben Gurion's figures are incomplete; they ignore the registered Him soldiers, headquarter troops and supply services.

72. Kimche, *Both Sides of the Hill*, p. 161; similar although not identical figures for the number of rifles, machine-guns, and mortars are given in Avidar, op. cit., p. 311.

73. For the formation of the 8th Brigade see Yeruham Cohen, *Le-Or Ha-Yom U-Be-Mahshach* (*In the Light of Day and in the Darkness*), Amikam, Tel Aviv, 1969, pp. 143–5. Major Cohen was a staff officer in the 8th Brigade and later Yigal Allon's aide-de-camp. For the formation of the 7th Brigade see Lieut.-Col.

Israel Beer, 'Kravot Latrun' ('The Battles of Latrun'), *Ma'ara-chot*, No. 96, pp. 31–5.

74. See Ben Gurion, *Medinat Israel*, p. 80; *Iton Rishmi* (Official Gazette), 1948, Appendix A, p. 9.

75. See I. Beer, *Ma'arachot*, No. 96, pp. 8–88.

76. For Ben Gurion's own account see Ben Gurion, *Medinat Israel*, pp. 179–91.

77. Ben Gurion, *Medinat Israel*, p. 139.

78. See I. Beer, *Ma'arachot*, No. 96, and Beni and Ra'anana, 'Sadot Ha-Derech' ('The Fields of the Way') in *Sefer Ha-Palmach*, Vol. II, pp. 508–11.

79. For contrasting views see Ben Gurion, *Medinat Israel*, pp. 270–80, and *Sefer Ha-Palmach*, pp. 985–6.

80. Ben Gurion, *Medinat Israel*, pp. 285–312; Lorch, op. cit., pp. 335–62; Yeruham Cohen, op. cit.

81. For the military and political aspects of operation Horev, see Cohen, op. cit., pp. 223–56; for the political background see also the memoirs of the U.S. Ambassador to Israel, James G. McDonald, *My Mission to Israel*, Simon & Schuster, New York, 1951.

CHAPTER 2   The Army of Independence

1. See Adam Shatkai, 'Soleley Ha-Atzma'ut Ba-Avir' ('The Founders of Independence in the Air'), in *Hel He-Avir* (the official journal of the Israeli Air Force), No. 45, July–Aug. 1958, pp. 54–5.

2. A characteristic example can be found in Yeruham Cohen's report of Yigal Allon's meeting with his brigade commanders after the failure of th eattack on Iraq el Manshie in the course of operation Yoav; see Cohen, op. cit., pp. 176–9.

3. Y. Allon in *Sefer Ha-Palmach*, Vol. II, p. 280.

4. Lorch, op. cit., p. 280.

5. ibid., p. 281.

6. ibid., p. 285.

7. ibid., p. 346.

8. ibid., pp. 179–80. For a more detailed account of the considerations which affected Allon's decision see Cohen, op. cit., pp. 171–80.

9. ibid., pp. 181–2; *Sefer Ha-Palmach*, Vol. II, pp. 629–39; *Toldot Milhemet Ha-Kommemiut*, pp. 308–10.

10. *Sefer Ha-Palmach*, Vol. II, pp. 315–17.
11. For an authoritative history of the Givati Brigade see Avraham Aafilon, *Hativat Givati Mul Ha-Polesh Ha-Mizri* (*The Givati Brigade Facing the Egyptian Invader*), 1963. For a less authoritative but lively description see Uri Avneri, *Be-Sdot Pleshet 1948* (*In the Fields of the Philistines*), Tverski, Tel Aviv, 1950.
12. See Y. Sadeh in *Sefer Ha-Palmach*, Vol. II, pp. 211–13.
13. See *Ma'arachot*, Nos. 72–3, May 1952, p. 27.
14. For Yigal Yadin's views on the implementation of the 'indirect approach' in the War of Independence see an appendix to the revised edition of Liddell Hart's *The Strategy of Indirect Approach*, Faber & Faber, London; Y. Rabin's analysis of the War of Independence in terms of the concept of the 'indirect approach' was published in *Ma'arachot*, No. 151, April 1963; see also Yadin's remarks reported in *Ma'arachot* No. 71, 1953, p. 11.
15. See Edward N. Luttwak, *Dictionary of Modern War*, Allen Lane, London, 1971, p. 115.
16. See B. H. Liddell Hart, *Encounter*, February 1968, p. 17.
17. See Israel Beer, 'Kravot Latrun', *Ma'arachot*, No. 96, November 1955.
18. For an account of the air operations in the War of Independence see Adam Shatkai, *Hel Avir*, Nos. 43–4, 45, 46, 1958. The article is an authoritative study of the evolution of the Israeli Air Force and its role in the war.
19. For an account of the naval operations in the War of Independence see Eliezer Tal, *Mivzaei Hel Ha-Yam Be-Milhemet Ha-Kommemiut* (*The Operation of the Navy in the War of Foundation*), Ma'arachot Publishing House, Tel Aviv, 1964.

CHAPTER 3   After the Armistice: A New Army

1. A study made in January 1948 showed that 88% of the privates and N.C.O.s interviewed had definitely decided not to remain in the army as regulars once the war was over; 3% were inclined to remain, and 9% said that they were considering the possibility of staying. A similar distribution was found among junior officers. The study was carried out by Professor Louis Guttman, the then Scientific Director of the Israel Institute of Applied Social Research.
2. See Y. Harkaby's article in *Ma'arachot*, No. 166, March 1965.
3. The general elections for the first Knesset took place on 25 Janu-

ary 1949. Mapai received 155,274 votes out of 415,260, while Mapam emerged as the second biggest party with 64,018 votes. See *Iton Rismi*, No. 49, 7 February 1949.

4. Y. Allon; for other expressions of this view see *Al Ha-Mishmar* (*Mapam*'s daily), 28 October 1948 (editorial); 2 November 1948 (editorial); Meir Yaari, 'Im Yesod Ha-Medina' ('With the Foundation of the State') in *Leahdut Ha'avoda* (Mapam's monthly), June 1948; Israel Galili, '*Ye'uda Shel Zva Ha-Haganah*' ('The Goal of the Defence Army'), also in *Leahdut Ha'avocha*.

5. Ben Gurion's 'Letter to a Palmach Soldier' was published in the daily paper of the General Federation of Labour, *Davar*, 29 October 1948. See also Ben Gurion, *Medinat Israel*, pp. 175–273.

6. See Ben Gurion's Introduction to *Toldot Milchemet Ha-Kommemiut*, pp. 27–9.

7. See Ben Gurion, *Medinat Israel*, pp. 264–7.

8. For an assessment of the work of the team, by General Laskov, see *Ma'arachot*, Nos. 191–2, 1968.

9. For the considerations that led to the adoption of the Israeli reserve system, see Yigal Allon, *Massach Shel Hol* (*A Curtain of Sand*) (3rd edn), Hakibbutz Hameuchad, Tel Aviv, 1959, pp. 35–51.

10. See *Ma'arachot*, Nos. 191–2, 1968.

11. Defence Service Law 1959 (consolidated version), *Sefer Ha-Chukim*, 24 September 1959, p. 289. This version consolidates the Defence Service Law with the many amendments adopted between 1949 and 1959. See also Appendix 1.

12. See Government of Israel, *Statistical Abstract of Israel*, Jerusalem, 1965.

13. Ben Gurion, *Medinat Israel*, p. 266.

14. Allon, *Massach Shel Hol*, pp. 276–7.

15. The echoes of this debate can still be traced in an article in *Ma'arachot* which discusses the experiences of the first decade of the 'military residence' in Haifa. The author was one of Yadin's critics who later changed his mind, and became the headmaster of the military residence. See Shmuel Aviad, 'Ha-Pnimiya Ha-Zvait' in *Ma'arachot*, No. 157, October 1962.

16. The functions of Poum were described by its first commander, Col. Aharon Rabinowitz-Yaariv (later Maj.-Gen. and Head of the Intelligence branch, G.H.Q.), in *Ma'arachot*, No. 96, November 1965; see also an article by Lieut.-Col. Z. Borovski in *Ma'arachot*, No. 109, October 1956, which gives details of the composition of

the subjects of study in Poum (15% the structure of I.D.F., 23% staff work, 40% theory of war, 11% military education, 7% general education, 9% sport).

17. See Laskov, *Ma'arachot* Nos. 191–2, 1968.

18. ibid.

19. ibid.

20. See Edward N. Luttwak, *Dictionary of Modern War*, Allen Lane, London, 1971, p. 115.

21. ibid., p. 94.

22. See Laskov, *Ma'arachot*, Nos. 191–2, 1968, p. 43.

23. Nadav Safran *et al.*, *From War to War*, Pegasus, New York, 1969, p. 157.

24. *Statistical Abstract of Israel*, 1965, p. 46.

CHAPTER 4 Decline and Revival

1. The concepts of 'basic security' and 'current security' (as seen by a former deputy Minister of Defence) are discussed in Shimon Peres, *Hashlav Ha-Ba* (*The Next Phase*), Am Hasefer, Tel Aviv, 1965, pp. 9–15.

2. For an analysis of the strategic implications of Israel's geography see Yigal Allon, *Massach Shel Hol* (*A Curtain of Sand*), Hakibbutz Hameuchad, Tel Aviv, 1959, pp. 52–82.

3. ibid., pp. 67–9, 253–9.

4. See S. Aronson and D. Horowitz, 'Hastrategia Shel Tagmul Mevukar' ('The Strategy of Controlled Retaliation'), in *Medinah U-Memshal* (*State and Government*), Vol. I, No. I, Summer 1971; see also Peres, *Hashlav Ha-Ba*, pp. 25–8.

5. See Uri Milstein, *Milchamot Hatzanhanim* (*The Wars of the Paratroopers*), Ramdor, Tel Aviv, 1968; Arieh Avnery, *Pshitot Ha-Tagmul* (*The Reprisal Attacks*), Sifriat Hamachon, Tel Aviv, 1966; and Dr Michael Bar Zohar and Eitan Haver, *Sefer Hatzanhanim* (*The Book of the Paratroopers*), Lewin-Epstein, Tel Aviv, 1969. All three books deal with the origins of the Israeli Army paratroopers and describe in detail the atmosphere in the Army during the early fifties including the effects of combat failures on the Army's morale. These three books are not always reliable but include much useful information. The role of the paratroopers in the early and mid-fifties and their operations are also described in the memoirs of one of their officers: Moshe Yanuka,

Me'Kibiya Ad Ha-Mitle (*From Kibiya to the Mitle*), Bitan, Tel Aviv, 1967.

6. See Bar Zohar and Haver, op. cit., p. 60.
7. Ben Gurion, *Medinat Israel*, Vol. I, p. 482.
8. See Bar Zohar and Haver, op. cit., p. 63.
9. The beginnings of Commando 101 are described in Avnery, op. cit.; Bar Zohar and Haver, op. cit.; Milstein, op. cit.; and Yanuka, op. cit.
10. For a vivid description of paratrooper training in 1954 by a distinguished officer, Gen. Mordechai Gur, then a young captain, see Col. M. Gur, 'Rashita Shel Plugah' ('The Beginnings of a Company'), *Ma'arachot*, No. 177, August 1966.
11. Bar Zohar and Haver, op. cit., pp. 89–90.
12. For descriptions of paratroopers' operations which exemplify Sharon's tactics see Uri Milstein, 'A Paratroopers' Raid' in Y. Allon, *The Making of the Israel Army*, Valentine Mitchell, London, 1970, pp. 242–323 (a translation from Milstein, op. cit., pp. 55–60); M. Dayan, *Diary of the Sinai Campaign 1956* Sphere Books, London, 1967, Chap. 3; and Col. M. Gur, 'Khan Yunis', *Ma'arachot*, No. 176, June 1966. The paratroopers' style of combat and leadership is described in M. Gur's articles in *Ma'arachot*, No. 172, January 1966 and No. 173, February 1966.
13. See Lieut.-Gen. Haim Laskov and Maj.-Gen. Meir Zorea, 'Ve-Haya Ki Yetz Le-Milchama' ('And When He will Go to War'), in *Ma'ariv*, 10 October 1965. In this most revealing article Lt.-Gen. Laskov (Dayan's successor as Chief of Staff) and General Zorea criticize Dayan's ideas on armour use in the planning of the Sinai Campaign; see also an analysis of the evolution of Israeli armour doctrine by Col. Dr Yuhuda Wallach in *Ma'arachot*, No. 197, 1969.
14. See an introduction by General Weizman (Commander of the Israel Air Force 1958–66) in Shiff, *Knafaim Me Al Le Suez* (*Wings over Suez*), Ot-Paz, Tel Aviv, 1970, pp. 12–13. See also the articles of the contributors to a debate on the role of the Air Force: 'Lohem' (Pseud.), in *Ma'arachot*, Nos. 72–3, May 1952; and M.S.L.T. (Pseud.) in *Ma'arachot*, No. 75, October 1952.
15. Shiff, op. cit., pp. 79–80.
16. Ben Gurion, *Medinat Israel*, pp. 205–6.
17. See Shiff, op. cit., pp. 88–9.
18. See an interview with Maj.-Gen. M. Hod in the Israel daily, *Ha-Yom*, 1 May 1968 (interviewer: M. Shai); and Shiff, op. cit., pp. 87–9, 94.

19. The need for multi-purpose aircraft is emphasized by General Weizman in his introduction to Shiff's book. See Shiff, op. cit., pp. 11–12.

20. The Air Force sponsored research by social scientists in order to improve its selection techniques. Some of the conclusions of one of these research projects were reported in M. Lissak and E. Yuchtman, 'Perah Ha-Tais: Kama Aspectim Shel Nituach Tafkid' ('The Air Force Cadet: Some Aspects of Role Analysis'), in *Megamot*, Vol. 13, No. 1–2, pp. 66–73.

21. See Peres, *David's Sling*, Weidenfeld & Nicolson, London, 1970, Chap. 3.

22. See Bar Zohar, op. cit., pp. 57–103; Evron, op. cit., pp. 15–44.

23. Dayan, *Diary of the Sinai Campaign*, p. 209.

24. ibid., p. 205.

25. See ibid., pp. 79–80, 105–6, 116; Shiff, op. cit., pp. 84–5; Evron, op. cit., pp. 126–9; Peres, *David's Sling*, Chap. 10; and Bar Zohar, op. cit., pp. 133–8.

26. Shabtai Teveth, *The Tanks of Tammuz*, Sphere Books, London, 1970; according to Y. Wallach there were two Cromwells and two Shermans. See Dr Wallach in *Ma'arachot*, No. 197, 1961, p. 15. The two sources probably refer to different stages of the War of Independence.

27. Teveth, op. cit., p. 49.

28. ibid., p. 51.

29. The connection between the availability of armour equipment and the development of operational doctrines is emphasized by Col. Dr Wallach in his study of the evolution of the Israeli armour doctrine. See *Ma'arachot*, No. 197, 1969, pp. 15–18.

30. For a first-hand account of the obstacles which the Israelis had to overcome in their efforts to purchase modern arms during the early and mid-fifties, see Shimon Peres, *David's Sling*, Chap. 3. As Director-General of the Israeli Ministry of Defence, Peres was in charge of negotiations for arms purchases in France during the mid-fifties. See also Michael Bar Zohar, *Gesher Al Ha-Yam Ha-Tichon* (*Bridge across the Mediterranean*), Am Ha-Sefer, Tel Aviv, 1964; Joseph Evron, *Be Yom Sagrir* (*The Day of the Pelting Rain*), Ot-Paz, Tel Aviv, 1968.

31. See Dr Wallach in *Ma'arachot*, No. 197, 1969, p. 16.

32. Teveth, op. cit., p. 51.

33. See Lieut.-Gen. Laskov and Maj.-Gen. Zohar on the armour debate in *Ma'ariv*, 10 October 1965.

34. This view was spelled out in an article signed 'Shirionai' ('An

Armour Man'), published in the first post-campaign issue of *Ma'arachot*, No. 194, January 1957, pp. 29–31; an explicit statement on the change of armour doctrine can be found in Maj.-Gen. (later Lieut.-Gen.) Bar Lev's article in *Ma'arachot*, No. 130, August 1960.

35. See Dayan, *Diary*, pp. 90–91; and Laskov and Zorea, *Ma'ariv*, 10 October 1965.

36. Moshe Sharret's ideas are analysed by M. Brecher, *The Foreign Policy System of Israel*, Oxford University Press, London.

37. For contrasting views on the 'Lavon Affair' and its background, see Ben Gurion, *Devarim Ke-Havayatam* (*Things as They are*), Am Ha-Sefer, Tel Aviv, 1965; Y. Ariely, *Ha-Knunia* (*The Conspiracy*), Kadima, Tel Aviv, 1965; Eliyahu Hasin and Don Horowitz, *Ha-Parasha* (*The Affair*), Am Ha-Sefer, Tel Aviv, 1961, pp. 9–32; and Amos Perlmutter, *The Military and Politics in Israel*, Cass, London, 1969.

38. See M. Bar-On, 'Ma'arachet Kadesh: Matarot Vehessegim' ('The Sinai Campaign: Goals and Achievement') in *Yediot Aharonot*, 29 October 1971 (Col. Bar-On was Dayan's aide-de-camp in 1956); see also Dayan's letter to Ben Gurion of 5 December quoted in Dayan, *Diary*, pp. 20–21.

39. See Ben Gurion's interview with Ze'ev Shiff in *Ha-Aretz*, 1 November 1968.

CHAPTER 5 The Sinai Campaign: Prelude and Aftermath

1. See Peres, *Ha-Shlav Ha-Ba*, p. 54; Dayan, *Diary*, Chap. 1 (in particular the Egyptian intelligence document quoted on pp. 53–4). For a comparison see E. L. M. Burns, *Between Jew and Arab*, Harrap, London, 1962, p. 89. General Burns, Chief of Staff of the United Nations Truce Supervision Organization, maintains that it was impossible to prove that Fedayeen activities were initiated by the Egyptians but his own account leaves little room for doubt that this was the case.

2. For an account of the operation by one of the participants, see Col. (later Gen.) M. Gur in *Ma'arachot*, No. 173, February 1956.

3. See Uri Ra'anan, *U.S.S.R. Arms and the Third World*, M.I.T. Press, Cambridge, Mass., 1969.

4. For an account of the operation see M. Gur in *Ma'arachot*, No. 176, June 1956.

5. See Milstein, op. cit., pp. 55–60.

6. See Moshe Dayan, *Diary*, pp. 16–17.
7. ibid., p. 59.
8. See an interview with Ben Gurion on the 12th anniversary of the Sinai Campaign in *Ha-Aretz*, 11 November 1968.
9. Dayan, *Diary*, p. 65.
10. ibid., p. 43.
11. ibid., p. 63.
12. See Col. M. Bar-On's article on the Sinai Campaign in *Yedioth Aharonot*, 10 October 1971.
13. See Dayan, *Diary*, Appendix 8.
14. ibid., p. 41.
15. See E. Talmi, *Milhamot Israel 1949–1959* (*The Wars of Israel 1949–1969*), Davar, Tel Aviv, 1969, p. 345.
16. Dayan, *Diary*, p. 81.
17. ibid.
18. Teveth, op. cit., p. 55; the same episode is also described in Aviezer Golan, *Ha-Mefakdim* (*The Commanders*), Moses, Tel Aviv, 1968, p. 60.
19. Dayan, *Diary*, p. 42.
20. Laskov, Zorea in *Ma'ariv*, 10 October 1965.
21. Brig.-Gen. S. L. A. Marshal, *Sinai Victory*, Morrow, New York, 1958.
22. See Dayan, *Diary*, Appendix 4.
23. ibid., pp. 412, 85.
24. ibid., pp. 412, 97.
25. Marshal, *Sinai Victory*, Chap. 16.
26. Laskov, Zorea, *Ma'ariv*, 10 October 1965.
27. ibid., p. 40.
28. Lieut.-Gen. Y. Rabin in *Ma'arachot*, No. 130, August 1960.
29. Dayan, *Diary*, p. 39.
30. See Don Horowitz, 'Flexible Responsiveness and Military Strategy', in *Policy Sciences*, Vol. I, 1970, pp. 191–205.

CHAPTER 6 From War to War: 1956–67

1. See President Nasser's letter to King Hussein of Jordan of 22 March 1961, and his speech on the sixth anniversary of the establishment of the U.A.R., *Al Ahram*, 23 February 1964. See also an address of the Israeli Army Chief of Staff, Lieut.-Gen. Zvi Zur, reported in *Ma'arachot*, No. 135, May 1961; and Prime Minister David Ben Gurion's Independence Day address to the Army reported in *Ma'arachot*, No. 151, April 1963.

2. This strategy was elaborated in President Nasser's address to the Legislative Council of the Gaza Strip, *Al Ahram*, 26 June 1962; and in Nasser's address to the Conference of Representatives of the Palestine Liberation Organization in Cairo on 31 May 1965, *Al Ahram*, 1 June 1965.
3. For Israeli estimates of the strength of the Arab armies, see Eliahu Levi (ed.), *This was Goliath*, published by the Israel Defence Forces, October 1967.
4. ibid.
5. For a study of the arms race as a whole see Safran, *From War to War*, Pegasus, New York, 1969.
6. See *This was Goliath*.
7. For example see Shimon Peres, *Ha-Shlav Ha-Ba* (*The Next Phase*), Am-Hasefer, Tel Aviv, 1965, pp. 113–19.
8. See, for example, Yigal Allon, *Massach Shel Hol* (*A Curtain of Sand*), Hakibbutz Hameuchad, Tel Aviv, 1959, pp. 194–7.
9. See Leonard Beaton, John Maddox, *The Spread of Nuclear Weapons*, London, 1962, Chap. 11.
10. See, for example, Shimon Peres, *Ha-Shlav Ha-Ba*, p. 123.
11. See Safran, op. cit., p. 158.
12. See Shimon Peres, *David's Sling*, 1970, Chap. 4.
13. Safran, op. cit., p. 443.
14. See Lieut.-Gen. Haim Laskov, in *Ma'arachot*, No. 132, December 1960; and Y. Allon, *Massach Shel Hol*, pp. 68–9.
15. This view was expressed by Allon in *Massach Shel Hol*, 1960, p. 61.
16. See for example Laskov's articles in *Ma'arachot*, No. 114, July 1958; No. 130, August 1960; No. 132, December 1960; No. 133, January 1961; No. 137, May 1961; Nos. 191–2, June 1968. *Ma'arachot Shirion* (The Israeli Armour Corps journal), No. 21, October 1970; *Ma'ariv*, 10 October 1965 (co-author Meir Zorea).
17. See Laskov in *Ma'arachot Shirion*, No. 21, October 1970, and *Ma'arachot*, No. 132, December 1960; and Yitzhak Rabin in *Ma'arachot*, No. 130, August 1960; also Dayan, *Diary*, p. 39.
18. See Don Horowitz, 'Flexible Responsiveness and Military Strategy', *Policy Sciences*, 1970, pp. 191–205.
19. Dayan, *Diary*, p. 39.
20. Golan, op. cit., p. 14.
21. An interview with Col. G. Arad on *Galei Zahal*, 20 January 1970.
22. Yehuda Emir, 'Bnei Kibbutzim Be-Zahal' ('The Children of the

Kibbutzim in Zahal', *Megamoth*, Vol. 15, Nos. 2–3, August 1967, pp. 250–58.

23. ibid.

24. See Col. Dr Yehuda Wallach's account of the development of Israel armour doctrine in *Ma'arachot*, No. 197, January 1969.

25. The debate was renewed after the 1967 War in a series of articles by a military commentator in one of Israel's leading dailies. See Benjamin Amidror in *Ha-Aretz*, November 1970.

26. Some of the scientific experiments conducted for the improvement of the selection procedures are referred to in M. Lissak and E. Yuchtman's article in *Megamoth*, Vol. 14, Nos. 1–2.

27. See Gen. Ezer Weizman's introduction to Shiff, *Knafaim Me Al Le Suez* (*Wings over Suez*), Libmann, Haifa, 1970, pp. 14–15.

28. On Ben Gurion's views during the planning stages of the campaign, see Yossef Evron, *Be Yom Sagrir*, Ot-Paz, Tel Aviv, 1968, pp. 22–42. (The book is based on the personal diary of Shimon Peres.)

29. Golan, op. cit., p. 28.

30. Shiff, op. cit., pp. 157–61.

31. See Dan Margalit, *Sheder Min Ha-Bait Ha-Lavan* (*Message from the White House*), Ot-Paz, Tel Aviv, 1971, p. 215.

32. See *Jerusalem Post*, July 1969.

33. Quoted in the Israeli daily *Davar*, 14 October 1958.

CHAPTER 7 War: 1967

1. See David Kimche, Dan Bawly, *The Sandstorm*, Secker & Warburg, London, 1968, Chap. 4.

2. See for example, Theodore Draper, *Israel and World Politics*, Viking, New York, 1968; Moshe Gilboa, *Shesh Shanim Shisha Yamim* (*Six Years, Six Days*) (revised edn), Am Oved, Tel Aviv, 1969; John Bagot Glubb, *The Middle East Crisis*, Hodder & Stoughton, London, 1967; Michael Howard and Robert Hunter, *Israel and the Arab World: The Crisis of 1967*, The Institute for Strategic Studies, London, 1967; Walter Laqueur, *The Road to Jerusalem*, Macmillan, New York, 1968; Eric Rouleau, Jean-Francis-Held, Jean et Simon Lacouture, *Israel et les Arabes, le 3e combat*, editions du Seuil, Paris, 1967; Shmuel Seguev, *La Guerre de Six Jours*, Calman-Lévy, Paris, 1967; C. Yost, 'The Middle East War: How it Began', *Foreign Affairs*, January 1968, pp. 304–20; Michael Bar Zohar, *Histoire Secrète de la Guerre d'Israel*, Fayard, Paris 1968; The Shiloah Centre for

Middle Eastern and African Studies, *Middle East Record*, Israel University Press, Jerusalem, 1971.

3. Lieut.-Gen. Rabin later stated that the war had started at the worst possible moment from the Israeli point of view. See Yitzhak Rabin, in *Ot*, No. 6, 3 June 1971.
4. An interview of Eitan Haver with Yeshayahu Gavish in *Yediot Aharonot*, 3 April 1970.
5. 'Press Release', The Institute for Strategic Studies, London, 6 June 1967.
6. Safran, op. cit., Appendix B, pp. 441–4.
7. Golan, op. cit., p. 139.
8. Safran, op. cit., p. 441.
9. Press Release, The Institute for Strategic Studies, London, 6 June 1967.
10. R. and W. Churchill, *The Six Day War*, Heinemann, London, 1967, p. 82.
11. Calculated on the basis of the Israeli publication, *This was Goliath*, Tel Aviv, 1967; compare *Middle East Record 1967*, The Shiloah Institute, p. 205; Safran, op. cit., pp. 319, 434–44.
12. Ibid.
13. Egyptian battle orders for air support to an attack on Elat were captured by Israel and published after the war. See Appendix 5 in Shimshon Yitzhaki, *Be-Einey Ha-Aravim* (*In Arab Eyes*), Ma'archot Publishing House, Tel Aviv, 1969, pp. 233, 235.
14. Calculated on the basis of Israeli estimates and other sources. See *This was Goliath; Middle East Record 1967*; Safran, op. cit., pp. 434–44; *Le Monde*, 22 June 1967.
15. See an interview with Prime Minister Eshkol in *Ma'ariv*, 4 October 1967.
16. See R. and W. Churchill, op. cit., p. 81.
17. Paraphrased from ibid., pp. 78–9.
18. ibid.
19. See Safran, op. cit., p. 322.
20. The figures were announced for the first time by Gen. Hod on *Kol Israel* (Radio Israel) on the early morning of 6 June 1967. Quoted in *Middle East Record 1967*, p. 214.
21. Gen. S. L. A. Marshall, C.B.S./T.V., 18 July, Boston Channel 5. Quoted in Safran, op. cit.
22. Safran, op. cit., p. 328. But this apparently refers to the air-to-air score in general. According to Hod as quoted by the Churchills, no Israeli aircraft were shot down in actual dogfights. See R. and W. Churchill, op. cit., p. 91.

23. See *Le Monde*, 7 June 1967.
24. Shiff, op. cit., p. 117.
25. See Lieut.-Col. E. Reiner on the battle of the Dotan Valley in *Ma'arachot*, Nos. 191–2, 1967.
26. Interview with General Gavish in *Yediot Ahranot*, 3 April 1970.
27. See Maj.-Gen. Sharon in press conference, 12 June 1967; I.D.F. Spokesman's Office, 'The Six Day War: Sinai Front', July 1967.
28. The decision to block the routes through which the Egyptian forces were retreating was made by Gavish on the second day of the war. See Golan, op. cit., p. 54.
29. See Lieut.-Col. A. Ayalon, *The Six Day War*, I.D.F. Spokesman, April 1968.
30. For accounts of Tal's breakthrough see Col. M. Pail's article in *Ma'arachot*, No. 193, and Maj. Avraham's article in *Ma'arachot*, No. 202.
31. See 'Mi-Bir Lahfan Ad La-Mitle' ('From Bir Lahfan to the Mitla'), in *Ma'arachot*, Nos. 185–6, 1967.
32. For accounts of the operations of Sharon's *Ugdah*, see M. Barkai's articles in *Ma'arachot*, Nos. 185–6, 1967; No. 187, 1967; No. 190, 1968.
33. See Col. M. Pail in *Ma'arachot*, No. 193, 1968.
34. ibid.
35. R. and W. Churchill, op. cit., p. 121.
36. Interview with General Gavish, *Yediot Aharonot*, 3 April 1970.
37. See Golan, op. cit., p. 54. Gavish himself referred to the decision in his interview, *Yediot Aharonot*, 3 April 1970.
38. B. H. Liddell Hart, 'Strategy of a War', *Encounter*, Vol., No. 2, February 1968, p. 17.
39. Kimche, Bawly, op. cit., p. 186.
40. For an account of the 'Granit Force' operations by its commander see Col. I. Granit, 'Koach Messima Meshurian', ('An Armoured Task Force'), in *Ma'arachot*, No. 202, 1968.
41. See an interview with Lieut.-Gen. Rabin on the fourth anniversary of the 1967 War, in *Ot*, 3 June 1971.
42. The circumstances in which Ben Ari's Harel Brigade was committed by Dayan himself to the Central Command are described in Gilboa, op. cit., p. 222.
43. See Col. M. Gur in Press Conference, I.D.F. Spokesman's Office, 'The Six Day War: Central Front', July 1967.
44. See Gilboa, op. cit., pp. 223–4; R. and W. Churchill, op. cit., pp. 127–8.

45. The most detailed account of the battle for Jerusalem in the 1967 War can be found in Moshe Nathan, *Ha-Milchama Al Yerushalayim (The War for Jerusalem)*, Ot-Paz, Tel Aviv, 1968.
46. General Uzi Narkiss in Press Conference, I.D.F. Spokesman's Office, 'The Six Day War: Central Front', July 1967.
47. Maj.-Gen. David Elazar in Press Conference, 16 June, I.D.F. Spokesman's Office, 'The Six Day War: Northern Front', Tel Aviv, August 1967.
48. Lt.-Col. Moshe, 'The Six Day War: Northern Front'.
49. Maj.-Gen. Elad Peled, 'The Six Day War: Northern Front'.
50. Col. Uri, 'The Six Day War: Northern Front'.
51. ibid.
52. See Col. Moshe's article in *Ma'arachot Shirion*, Nos. 18–19, June 1968; for a detailed account of the operations of Col. Moshe's brigade see Aviezer Golan, *Anshei Ha-Plada (Men of Steel)*, Ot-Paz, Tel Aviv, 1969.
53. Col. Uri, I.D.F. Spokesman's Office, 'The Six Day War: Northern Front'.
54. Col. M. Gur, I.D.F. Spokesman's Office, 'The Six Day War: Central Front'.
55. R. and W. Churchill, op. cit., p. 84.
56. Col. Uri Ben Ari, I.D.F. Spokesman's Office, 'The Six Day War: Central Front'.
57. Israel Ministry of Defence, *The Six Day War*, Tel Aviv, 1967, p. 120.
58. Kimche, Bawly, op. cit., Chap. 10.
59. See Col. Albert in Press Conference, I.D.F. Spokesman's Office, 'The Six Day War: Northern Front'. For a detailed account of battles on the Syrian front during the 1967 War see Yehezkel Hameiri, *Mishnei Evrei Ha-Rama (From Both Sides of the Plateau)*, Lewin-Epstein, Tel Aviv, 1970.
60. *Al Thawra*, Damascus, 11 June 1967 (edited by Safran, op. cit.).

CHAPTER 8 1967: An Overview

1. The figures of Israeli casualties are based on the I.D.F. announcement of 11 June 1967 (*Jerusalem Post*, 12 June 1967); the varying estimates of Arab casualties are cited in *Middle East Record 1967*, pp. 232–3.
2. For an Israeli assessment of Soviet intentions on the eve of the war, see *Ma'arachot*, No. 209, 1970, pp. 2–7.
3. See Safran, op. cit., p. 319.

4. For a report from Israeli sources on the meeting in the Pentagon at which American intelligence estimates were conveyed to Abba Eban, see Gilboa, op. cit., pp. 147–8.

5. For analyses of the coverage of the June 1967 crisis and war by the mass media, see: R. and W. Churchill, op. cit., pp. 219–41; Walter Laqueur, *The Road to War*, Penguin, London, 1969, pp. 207–53.

6. See, for example, Alastair Buchan in *Encounter*, Vol. 19, 2 August 1967.

7. This view was shared by Arab writers such as Dr Sadek el Athem and Constantin Zureik. For extracts from Arab analyses of the causes of the 1967 defeat see Y. Harkaby (ed.), *Lekah Ha-Aravim Me-Tvusatam (Lessons Drawn by the Arabs in the Wake of Defeat)*, Am Oved, Tel Aviv, 1969.

8. Y. Harkaby, 'Basic Factors of the Arab Collapse During the Six Day War', *Orbis*, Fall 1967, pp. 678–9.

9. ibid., p. 683.

10. See Don Horowitz, 'Flexible Responsiveness and Military Strategy', *Policy Sciences*, Vol. I, 1970, pp. 191–205.

11. See Harkaby, in *Orbis*, Fall 1967, pp. 687–8.

12. See Hasaneyn Haykal's articles in *Al Ahram*, 6 October 1967 and 13 October 1967.

13. See E. Rouleau *et al.*, op. cit., and the Lebanese daily *Muharir* of 15 September 1967: Haykal too speaks about attempts to conceal the news from those who should have been informed, *Al Ahram*, 6 October 1967.

14. The U.A.R. accepted the cease-fire resolution only on the evening of 8 September 1967. See *Middle East Record 1967*, pp. 238–9.

15. Maj.-Gen. Elad Peled in Press Conference, I.D.F. Spokesman's Office, 'The Six Day War: Northern Front', Tel Aviv, 1967.

16. Col. M. Gur in Press Conference, I.D.F. Spokesman's Office, 'The Six Day War: Central Front', Tel Aviv, 1967.

17. This view is presented in Haim Laskov's article on the lessons of the 1956 Sinai Campaign in *Ma'arachot Shirion*, 21 October 1970.

18. Gilboa, op. cit., p. 293.

19. Kimche, Bawly, op. cit., pp. 163–4.

20. See *Ma'arachot*, Nos. 185–6, 1967, pp. 56–68; Col. Meir Pail 'Shlosha Kravot Rafiah, 1949–1956–1967' ('Three Battles at Rafah'), in *Ma'arachot*, No. 193, 1968.

21. See an article by Col. Issachar (Shadmi) in *Ma'arachot Shirion*, Nos. 18–19, June 1968.

22. For a general account of the development of Israeli armour

doctrine see Col. Dr Yehuda Wallach in *Ma'arachot*, No. 497, 1958.
23. The critics' views were expressed in a series of articles by the military commentator Benjamin Amidror; see *Ha'aretz*, October 1970.
24. *Ma'ariv*, 8 May 1970.
25. Shiff, op. cit., pp. 87–8. Ben Gurion's sceptical attitude is referred to in General Weizman's introduction to Shiff's book, op. cit., pp. 12–13.

CHAPTER 9 *Zahal* in the Seventies

1. I.D.F. Spokesman's Office, 'The Six Day War: Southern Front', 1967.
2. The I.A.F. gained about 15 additional minutes of warning. See Brig.-Gen. Y. Raviv, 'Bitachon Israel' ('The Security of Israel') in *Ma'arachot*, No. 204, 1970, p. 4; and Shiff, op. cit., p. 101.
3. For reports on the scale of post-war Russian arms deliveries see *New York Times*, 25 June 1967; *The Times*, 27 June 1967; *Aviation Week*, 16 October 1967, 25 December 1967.
4. Y. Raviv in *Ma'arachot*, No. 204, p. 22; Shiff, op. cit., pp. 19–67, 179–227.
5. For an authoritative assessment of the 1967–1970 'War after The War' from an Israeli point of view, see Y. Raviv's article in *Ma'arachot*, No. 204, 1970, pp. 4–23.
6. I.D.F. Spokesman's Office, 'The Six Day War: Northern Front', 1967.
7. Ephraim Talmi, *Milhamot Israel 1949–1969* (*The Wars of Israel 1949–1969*), Davar, Tel Aviv, 1969, Vol. I, pp. 185–6.
8. For an analysis of the effects of the Karameh operation on the guerrillas see Ehud Ya'ari, *Fata'h*, Lewin-Epstein, Tel Aviv, 1970, pp. 229–42.
9. Michael Howard, Robert Hunter, *Israel and the Arab World: The Crisis of 1967*, The Institute for Strategic Studies, Adelphi Paper, London, October 1967, p. 43.
10. For an authoritative survey of Israeli policy in the occupied territories see Brig.-Gen. S. Gazit, 'Ha-Schtachim Ha-Moh-zakim' ('The Captured Territories'), in *Ma'arachot*, No. 204, 1970, pp. 25–39. (General Gazit is the coordinator of all Israeli activities in the occupied territories.)
11. For an official rationale of Israel's rejection of death penalty in the occupied territories see S. Gazit in *Ma'arachot*, No. 204, p. 37.

12. The fundamental causes are analysed in Ya'ari, op. cit., pp. 82–102.
13. See Katzin Bachir, 'Har Dov', in *Ma'arachot*, No. 212, 1971, pp. 2–8.
14. This order of priorities was laid down by Moshe Dayan in an address to students in Haifa on 3 March 1968. See Moshe Dayan, *Mapa Hadasha Yehasim Aherim* (*New Map, New Relations*), Shikmona, Tel Aviv, 1969, p. 86.
15. See Eli Landau, *Suez – Esh Al Hamain* (*Suez – Fire on the Water*), Ot-Paz, Tel Aviv, 1970, pp. 30–42.
16. See Kimche, Bawly, op. cit., p. 273.
17. The raid is described in detail in Landau, op. cit., pp. 102–5.
18. See Landau, op. cit., pp. 108–23.
19. See Y. Raviv, in *Ma'arachot*, No. 204, p. 12.
20. For a detailed description of the operation by the only military correspondent who accompanied the raiding force, see Landau, op. cit., pp. 179–202.
21. Radio Cairo, 31 March 1969.
22. Radio Cairo, 23 July 1969.
23. See *Ma'arachot*, No. 204, p. 11.
24. Shiff, op. cit., p. 427.
25. See *Ma'arachot*, No. 204, p. 22.
26. The circumstances in which the Israeli decision on the 'bombing in depth' campaign was made, and the arguments raised at the time for and against, are reported in Dan Margalit, *Sheder Me-Ha-Bait Ha-Lavan* (*Message from the White House*), Ot-Paz, Tel Aviv, 1971, pp. 35–50.
27. Interview by Amos Elon with Golda Meir in *Ha'aretz*, 24 July 1970.
28. See Margalit, op. cit., pp. 42–3, 56–7.
29. See Ben Gurion's talk with Army officers in November 1969, in *Medinat Israel Ha-Mehudeshet*, Vol. I, p. 537.
30. The different assessments of Israeli policy makers on the likelihood of a direct Russian intervention are reported in detail in Margalit, op. cit., pp. 51–67, 101–45.
31. See an interview with Dayan in *Ma'ariv*, 18 June 1971.
32. Israeli reluctance to repeat the experience of a direct clash with the Soviet forces was expressed by Dayan in an interview in *Ma'ariv*, 18 June 1971.
33. For an analysis of Israel's defence expenditure by a leading economist see Professor Michael Bruno in *Ma'ariv*, 22 October 1971.

Appendix 1

The Nahal

The Nahal, an acronym for Noar Halutzi Lohem (Pioneer Fighting Youth, is an independent corps with its own training base and inspectorate. Its creation in 1949 was one of the side-effects of the abolition of the Palmach in that the Nahal was intended to carry over some of the functions of the Palmach and its general ethos, but without its politics. The Palmach had drawn much of its manpower from the youth movements which were so important in the Yishuv's social life; split on party lines but all based on the same pioneering values, the youth movements demanded, and obtained, a niche in the new Army.

In the youth movements, boys and girls of the same age group form cohesive clusters (or *garinim* – nuclei) which are eventually intended to set up new agricultural settlements or join existing ones. In the decade prior to independence, land settlement had been a weapon in the Yishuv's political struggle and as such it was in part a military activity. The Palmach had catered to the special needs of the youth movements since their boys and girls could join by the group, as *garinim*, training, working and living together. Without the Palmach, however, conscript service in the Army threatened to undermine the youth movements by splitting the *garinim*, separating boys and girls and sending them to different units and bases. The conflict between the social cohesion of the *garinim* and the requirements of military efficiency was, and is, inescapable, but since the youth movements were politically powerful, they secured the formation of Nahal and its retention ever since.

Under the Nahal system, the *garinim* join the Army *en bloc* to receive their basic training, after which each *garin* is sent for agricultural training at a school maintained by the Nahal, or for on-the-job training in a frontier kibbutz. There the *garin* lives as an Army unit subject to military regulations, but its social life is its own. For a year the *garin* lives and works within a kibbutz, learning agricultural techniques and coping with the problems of collective life. Able-bodied boys are then sent for a short but intensive period of advanced military training, mostly as commandos, paratroopers or tank men. Some are also detached temporarily for N.C.O. or officer training. After this stage the *garin* finally reaches its goal, forming a new Nahal settlement or joining an existing one.

Nahal villages are established in areas which are too insecure for regular civilian settlement, along the borders and usually fairly remote from existing settlements. Their location is determined by the Nahal command in consultation with civilian authorities as well as with the kibbutz and moshav federations to which each *garin* is affiliated. Army and civilian authorities provide funds for land-reclamation, equipment, and feed stocks, as well as rather spartan creature comforts, while the federation to which the *garin* is affiliated provides technical aid. Army control (and money) continues until the settlement becomes self-supporting, and turns itself into a normal civilian kibbutz or moshav.

During the period of compulsory military service, Nahal members have to remain on their settlements (the only way of leaving the Nahal is to join some other branch of the Army), but once they complete their conscript term, Nahal members have the choice of staying with their now civilian *garin* or of leaving the collective. Many leave, but the map of Israel is dotted with villages established by Nahal, many of which have long since become ordinary civilian kibbutzim and moshavim, in areas made secure by the very existence of these population clusters. Some Nahal settlements need a steady flow of aid and drafts of new *garinim* for many years before they become self-supporting, and a *garin* (or parts of several) finally chooses to remain and develop the village; a few have been abandoned and some are kept alive with no hope of 'civilianization'.

There is a fine idealism about the 'Pioneer Fighting Youth' which still attracts many of the best youth of the country though only a minority remain on the settlements after their period of conscript service. But from a purely military point of view, the Nahal is not efficient. Though each *garin* releases some of its members (by collective decision) for officer training, these men must then return to serve with their *garin*, and a great deal of officer talent is therefore lost to the Army at large. Another problem is that the Nahal system cannot easily be squared with the prolonged training needed by modern mechanized forces. One can organize perfectly good paratroop companies out of Nahal members with a few months' training, but it is far more difficult to do the same with tank battalions. Though not as influential as they used to be, the youth movements still have enough power to protect the Nahal from the advocates of military efficiency, especially since the productive use of military man-power is an ideal vehicle for nation-building, and Nahal has become a major cultural export in Israel's aid programmes.

Appendix 2

The Defence Service Law and its Implementation

First enacted in 1949, repeatedly amended, consolidated in 1959 and amended further, the Defence Service Law forms the legal basis of military service in Israel.

Under the terms of the Law, all Israeli citizens and resident aliens, both male and female, are subject to conscription for a term of full-time regular service, subject to recall for one day per month thereafter, as well as for an annual period of reserve duty. The applicable age limits, and the duration of conscription of the annual recall, have been repeatedly changed since the Law was first enacted.

Conscription

Israelis are inducted into the Army at the age of 18, for a term of thirty-six months in the case of males, and twenty-four months in the case of females. Immigrants who reach the country before the age of twenty-nine if male, and twenty-six if female, are subject to the same terms of conscription. Persons beyond these age limits are still subject to conscription but for much shorter terms. At present, over-age females are not normally inducted while males serve for only a three–four week period of basic training.

Exemptions

Muslim and Christian Arabs are exempted from military service, though they may apply to join as volunteers; members of the Druze sect have been subject to compulsory military service ever since 1955, at the request of the then community leaders. Conscientious objectors are normally granted exemption and assigned to alternative civilian duties if their objection is proved to be ethical and unconditional. Political objection, contingent on Government policy, is not accorded recognition. Ultra-Orthodox males, i.e. full-time Yeshiva students and their teachers, are normally exempted from service under the discretionary powers given by the Law to the Minister of Defence. The minimum standards, both physical and educational, for admission into the Army are very low as compared to most modern armed forces. As a result, it is estimated that almost ninety per cent of those theoretically eligible are actually inducted, as against no more than fifty per cent in the case of most other conscript armies.

Standards of admission are higher in the case of females and the conditions of exemption are less restrictive. Religious females whose families (and themselves) object to the 'immodesty' of military service are normally exempted on proof of regular religious observance. In addition, females who are already married prior to induction are exempt from conscription. It is estimated that only about fifty per cent of all eligible females are in fact inducted into the Army.

Reserve Duties

Following completion of their conscript service, trained soldiers still deemed fit for military service are transferred to the reserves until the age of fifty-four (inclusive) in the case of males and thirty-eight in the case of females, though mothers and pregnant women are deleted from the rolls, and even childless female reservists are rarely recalled.

All reservists are liable for recall for one day each month or up to three consecutive days every three months. For male reservists up to the age of thirty-nine, and for childless females up to the age of thirty-four, the length of the annual recall is laid down at thirty-one days, with an additional seven days for officers and N.C.O.s. Beyond these age limits, service is reduced to fourteen days for privates and twenty-one days for officers and N.C.O.s. In practice, the reserve terms have varied over the years; since 1967 first-line reservists have frequently been recalled for longer periods, as much as sixty days per year. Even without counting these additional periods, ordered by the Minister of Defence under his discretionary powers, the cumulative military service of a male Israeli between the ages of twenty-two and fifty-five approximates the length of volunteer (professional) contract terms in most Western armies.

One provision of the Law has never been implemented: 'The first twelve months of the regular service ... after basic training [shall] be devoted mainly to agricultural training.' Inserted in the Law at the insistence of the pioneering wing of the Labour-Zionist parties, this provision was even then recognized to be unrealistic. The Minister of Defence was accordingly empowered to waive the requirement in the case of Air Force and Navy conscripts; in practice, ground force troops were also exempted, and the Law was subsequently amended to provide for a general discretionary exemption. Nevertheless, this is a provisional amendment which must be renewed annually by the Knesset, though it is only the Nahal corps (see Appendix I) that actually includes agricultural training in the term of conscript service.

Appendix 3

Israeli Prime Ministers and Ministers of Defence
Israeli Prime Ministers
David Ben Gurion: May 1948 – January 1954
Moshe Sharett: January 1954 – November 1955
David Ben Gurion: November 1955 – June 1963
Levi Eshkol: June 1963 – January 1969
Golda Meir: January 1969 – April 1974

Israeli Ministers of Defence
David Ben Gurion: (Prime Minister) May 1948 – January 1954
Pinchas Lavon: January 1954 – February 1955
David Ben Gurion: February 1955 – November 1955
David Ben Gurion: (Prime Minister) November 1955 – June 1963
Levi Eshkol: (Prime Minister) June 1963 – June 1967
Moshe Dayan: June 1967 – April 1974

Deputy Ministers of Defence
Shimon Peres: December 1959 – February 1965
Zvi Dinstein: January 1966 – June 1967

Israeli Army Ranks* (and corresponding British ranks)
Turai – Private
Turai Rishon – Lance-Corporal
Rav Turai – Corporal
Samal – Sergeant
Samal Rishon – Staff Sergeant
Rav Samal – Sergeant-Major
Rav Samal Rishon – Regimental Sergeant-Major
Segen Mishne – Second Lieutenant
Segen – Lieutenant
Seren – Captain
Rav Seren – Major

* The ranks of the Air Force and Navy are identical with those of the army.

Sgan Aluf – Lieutenant-Colonel
*Aluf Mishne** – Colonel
Tat Aluf† – Brigadier-General
Aluf – Major-General
Rav Aluf‡ – Lieutenant-General

Formations and Standard Ranks of Commanding Officers
(Ground Forces)
Kitah – Squad: *Rav Turai* (Corporal)
Machlakah – Platoon: *Segen* (Lieutenant)
Plugah – Company: *Seren* (Captain)
Gdud – Battalion: *Sgan Aluf* (Lieutenant-Colonel)
Hativa – Brigade: *Aluf Mishne* (Colonel)
Ugdah – Division or Divisional Force: *Tat Aluf* (Brigadier-General;
   post 1967) or *Aluf* (Major-General)

Commands and Forces H.Q.s
The Air Force H.Q.
The Navy H.Q.
The Northern Command
The Central Command§
The Southern Command

G.H.Q. Branches
A.G.M. – General Staff branch (replaced the Operations branch of
   the War of Independence)
A.G.A. – Quartermaster branch
A.K.A. – Manpower branch
A.M.N. – Intelligence branch (after 1955)
In the years 1948–51 there was also an Instruction branch; for a few
months in 1948 there was a Planning branch; in 1949–51 there was a
General Controller branch.

Israeli Chiefs of Staff¶	**Born**	
Ya'akov Dori	1899	1948–9
Yigal Yadin	1917	1949–52

   * The *Aluf Mishne* rank was introduced after the War of Independence.
   † The *Tat Aluf* rank was introduced after the 1967 war. Earlier the *Aluf*
rank was regarded as corresponding to Brigadier-General and the *Rav Aluf*
rank to a Major-General.
   ‡ The *Rav Aluf* rank is held only by the Chief of Staff.
   § The Central Command replaced the Central and Eastern Fronts of
1948–9. In the early fifties there was an additional Command responsible for
the national reserve known as the 8th Command.
   ¶ Some Chiefs of Staff had a deputy, others had not. The latter was
normally the Head of General Staff branch G.H.Q.

Israeli Chiefs of Staff	Born	
Mordechai Makleff	1920	1952–3
Moshe Dayan	1915	1953–8
Haim Laskov	1919	1958–60
Zvi Zur	1923	1960–63
Yitzhak Rabin	1922	1963–7
Haim Bar Lev	1924	1968–71
David Elazar	1925	1972–

Heads of General Staff (Operations) Branch G.H.Q. (A.G.M.)

Yigal Yadin	1948–9
Mordechai Makleff	1949–52
Moshe Dayan	1952–3
Yossef Avidar	1953–5
Haim Laskov	1955–6
Meir Amit	1956–8
Zvi Zur	1958
Meir Zorea	1958–9
Yitzhak Rabin	1959–63
Haim Bar Lev	1964–6
Ezer Weizman	1966–9
David Elazar	1969–71
Israel Tal	1972–

Heads of Manpower Branch (A.K.A.)

Moshe Zadok	1948–9
Shimon Maze	1949–52
Zvi Zur	1952–6
Gideon Schoken	1956–9
Aharon Doron	1959–63
Haim Ben David	1963–6
Shmuel Eyal	1966–9
Shlomo Lahat	1969–72
Herzel Shafir	1972–

Heads of Quartermaster Branch A.G.A.

Yossef Avidar	1948–9
Mordechai Green	1949–50
Ephraim Ben Artzi	1950–52
Zvi Ayalon	1952–4
Meir Ilan	1954–60
Moshe Goren	1960–64
Matityahu Peled	1964–9
Amos Horev	1969–

Heads of Instruction Branch or Department*

Instruction Branch

Eliyahu Ben Hur	1948
Haim Laskov	1948–51

Instruction Department

Yitzhak Rabin	1953–6
Haim Bar Lev	1956–7
Avraham Yoffe	1957–8
Meir Zorea	1958
Yossef Geva	1958–60
Zvi Zamir	1960–62
Yeshayahu Gavish	1962–5
Ariel Sharon	1966–9
Yitzhak Hoffi	1969–72
Shmuel Gonen	1972–

Heads of the Intelligence Branch (A.M.N.)†

Yehoshafat Harkaby	1955–9
Haim Herzog	1959–61
Meir Amit	1962–3
Aharon Ya'ariv	1964–72
Eliahu Zeira	1972–

Commanders of the Navy

Nachman Shulman	1948–9
Shlomo Shamir	1949–50
Mordechai Limon	1951–4
Shmuel Tankus	1955–60
Yohai Ben Nun	1960–66
Shlomo Erell	1966–8
Avraham Botzer	1968–72
Benyamin Telem	1972–

Commanders of the Israel Air Force

Aharon Remez	1948–50
Shlomo Shamir	1950–51
Haim Laskov	1951–3

* An Instruction branch G.H.Q. existed until 1951. Since 1953 the responsibility for instruction and the study of tactics and doctrines lies with the Instruction department of the General Staff branch. In recent years the head of the department has held the *Aluf* rank like his superior, the head of the General Staff branch.

† The Intelligence became an independent branch of the General Staff in 1955. Earlier it was a department of the General Staff branch.

Dan Tolkowsky	1953–8	
Ezer Weizman	1958–66	
Mordechai Hod	1966–	

C.O. Northern Command

Moshe Carmel	1948–9	
Yossef Avidar	1949–52	
Moshe Dayan	1952	
Haim Bar Lev (Acting C.O.)	1952–3	No C.O. was appointed; both were acting C.O.s while Chief of Staff at the Command
Assaf Simchoni (Acting C.O.)	1953–4	
Moshe Zadok	1954–6	
Yitzhak Rabin	1956–9	
Meir Zorea	1959–62	
Avraham Yoffe	1962–4	
David Elazar	1964–9	
Mordechai Gur	1969–72	
Yitzhak Hoffi	1972–	

C.O. Central (and Eastern) Command

Zvi Ayalon	1948–9	(Central Command)
Shlomo Shamir (concurrent)	1948–9	(Eastern Command)
Zvi Ayalon	1949–51	
Yossef Avidar	1952–3	
Zvi Ayalon	1954–6	
Zvi Zur	1956–8	
Meir Amit	1958–9	
Yossef Geva	1960–65	
Uzi Narkiss	1965–9	
Rehavam Ze'evi	1969–	

C.O. Southern Command

Yigal Allon	1948–9
Moshe Dayan	1949–51
Moshe Zadok	1951–4
Assaf Simchoni	1955–6
Haim Laskov	1956–8
Avraham Yoffe	1958–62
Zvi Zamir	1962–5
Yeshayahu Gavish	1965–9
Ariel Sharon	1969–

Commanders of the Armour Corps

Haim Laskov	1956
Uri Ben Ari	1956–7
Haim Bar Lev	1957–61
David Elazar	1961–4
Israel Tal	1964–9
Avraham Adan	1969–

Appendix 4

	1964–6; deputy Chief of Staff 1967; Chief of Staff 1968–71
Israel Barnea, b. 1908	Military Attaché in Moscow 1949–50; Chief Transport Officer, 1951–2
Ephraim Ben Artzi, b. 1910	Military Attaché in Washington 1948–50; head of Quartermaster branch 1950–2
Haim Ben David, b. 1915	Head of Manpower branch 1963–6
Michael Ben Gal, b. 1908	President of Military Court of Appeals 1958–63
Eliyahu Ben Hur, b. 1917	Head of Instruction branch 1948. (The Instruction branch was abolished after the war and incorporated into the General Staff branch)
Yohai Ben Nun, b. 1914	Commander of the Navy 1960–6
Avraham Botzer, b. 1929	Commander of the Navy 1968–72
Moshe Carmel, b. 1911	C.O. Northern Front (Command) 1948–9
Moshe Dayan, b. 1915	(*Rav Aluf*); C.O. Southern Command 1949–51; C.O. Northern Command 1952; head of General Staff branch 1952–3; Chief of Staff 1953–8; Minister of Defence 1967–1974
Ya'acov Dori, b. 1899	(*Rav Aluf*); Chief of Staff 1948–9
Aharon Doron, b. 1922	Head of Manpower branch 1959–63
David Elazar, b. 1925	(*Rav Aluf*); Commander of the Armour Corps 1961–4; C.O. Northern Command 1964–9; head of General Staff branch 1969–71; Chief of Staff 1972–4
Shlomo Erell, b. 1920	Commander of the Navy 1966–8
Dan Even, b. 1912	C.O. Eastern Front (Command) 1949. (The Eastern Front was later incorporated into the Central Command)
Shmuel Eyal, b. 1922	Head of Manpower branch 1966–9
Yeshayahu Gavish, b. 1925	Head of Instruction department in the General Staff branch 1962–5; C.O. Southern Command 1965–9
Yossef Geva, b. 1924	Head of Instruction department in the General Staff branch 1958–60; C.O. Central Command 1960–65; Military Attaché in Washington 1966–8
Moshe Goren, b. 1921	Head of Quartermaster branch 1960–64; Military Attaché in London 1964–6

Shlomo Goren, b. 1918 — Military Chief Rabbi 1948–72

Mordechai Green, b. 1919 — Head of Quartermaster branch 1949–50

Mordechai Gur, b. 1930 — C.O. Northern Command 1969–72

Yehoshafat Harkaby, b. 1921 — Head of Intelligence branch 1955–9

Haim Herzog, b. 1918 — Head of Intelligence branch 1959–61

Mordechai Hod, b. 1926 — Commander of the Air Force 1966–

Yitzhak Hoffi, b. 1927 — Head of Instruction department in the General Staff branch 1969–72

Amos Horev, b. 1924 — Chief Ordnance Officer 1965–6; head of Quartermaster branch 1969–73

Meir Ilan, b. 1918 — Head of Quartermaster branch 1954–60

Shlomo Lahat, b. 1927 — Commander of the Armoured Forces in Sinai 1969; head of Manpower branch 1969–72

Dan Lanner, b. 1923 — Commander of the Armoured Forces in Sinai 1970–

Haim Laskov, b. 1919 — (*Rav Aluf*); head of Instruction branch 1948–51. (The Branch was later incorporated into the General Staff branch); Air Force Commander 1951–3; deputy Chief of Staff and head of General Staff branch 1955–6; Commander of the Armour Corps 1956; C.O. Southern Command 1956–8; Chief of Staff 1958–60

Mordechai Limon, b. 1923 — Commander of the Navy 1951–4; Ministry of Defence representative in Paris 1962–9

Mordechai Makleff, b. 1920 — (*Rav Aluf*); deputy Chief of Staff and head of General Staff branch 1949–52; Chief of Staff 1952–3

David Marcus, b. 1901 — Commander of Jerusalem Front 1948 (a former colonel in the U.S. army, accidentally killed during the War of Independence at Abu Gosh near Jerusalem)

Shimon Maze, b. 1915 — Head of Manpower branch 1949–52

Uzi Narkiss, b. 1925 — Commander of the National Security College (for senior Government officials and Army officers) 1963–5; C.O. Central Command 1965–9

Elad Peled, b. 1927 — Commander of National Security College 1965–7; Ugdah Commander in 1967

Matityahu Peled, b. 1923 — Head of Quartermaster branch 1964–8

Yaakov Peri, b. 1915 — President of Military Court of Appeals 1963–9

Yitzhak Rabin, b. 1922 — (*Rav Aluf*); head of Instruction department in the General Staff branch 1953–6; C.O. Northern Command 1956–9; deputy Chief of Staff and head of General Staff branch 1959–63; Chief of Staff 1963–7

Yohanan Rattner, b. 1891 — Head of Planning branch 1948; Military Attaché in Moscow 1948–9

Aharon Remez, b. 1919 — Commander of the Air Force 1948–50

Yitzhak Sadeh, b. 1890 — Commander of the 8th Brigade 1948 (former Palmach Commander and a Chief of Staff of the *Haganah*)

Gideon Schoken, b. 1919 — Head of Manpower branch 1956–9

David Shaltiel, b. 1903 — Commander of the Jerusalem Front 1948; Military Attaché in Paris 1950–51

Shlomo Shamir, b. 1910 — C.O. Eastern Front (Command) 1948–9; Commander of the Navy 1949–50; Commander of the Air Force 1950–51

Ariel Sharon, b. 1928 — Commander of the Paratroopers 1954–6; head of Instruction department in the General Staff branch 1966–9; Ugdah Commander 1967; C.O. Southern Command 1969–73

Nachman Shulman, b. 1904 — Commander of the Navy 1948–9

Assaf Simchoni, b. 1922 — C.O. Southern Command 1955–6

Israel Tal, b. 1924 — Commander of the Armour Corps 1964–9; Ugdah Commander in 1967; head of the General Staff branch 1972–

Shmuel Tankus (Tene), b. 1914 — Commander of the Navy 1955–60

Dan Tolkowsky, b. 1921 — Commander of the Air Force 1953–8

Ezer Weizman, b. 1924 — Commander of the Air Force 1958–66; head of General Staff branch 1966–9

Aharon Ya'ariv, b. 1921	Head of Intelligence branch 1964–72
Yigal Yadin, b. 1917	(*Rav Aluf*); head of Operations in General Staff branch 1948–9; Chief of Staff 1949–52
Avraham Yoffe, b. 1914	Head of Instruction department in General Staff branch 1957–8; C.O. Southern Command 1958–62; C.O. Northern Command 1962–4; Ugdah Commander 1967
Moshe Zadok, b. 1906	Head of Manpower branch 1948–9; C.O. Southern Command 1951–4; C.O. Northern Command 1954–6; Staff Officer for Special Emergency Preparations 1956–7
Zvi Zamir, b. 1925	Head of Instruction department in General Staff branch 1960–2; C.O. Southern Command 1962–5; Military Attaché in London 1966–8
Rehavam Ze'evi, b. 1926	Assistant to head of General Staff Branch 1964–9; C.O. Central Command 1969
Eliahu Zeira, b. 1929	Military Attaché in Washington 1970; head of Intelligence branch 1972–
Meir Zorea, b. 1921	Head of General Staff branch 1958–9; C.O. Northern Command 1959–62
Zvi Zur, b. 1926	(*Rav Aluf*); head of Manpower branch 1952–6; C.O. Central Command 1956–8; deputy Chief of Staff and head of General Staff branch 1958; Chief of Staff 1960–63

Appendix 5

Extracts from *Education Processes in the Israel Defence Forces*
by Col. Mordechai Bar-On (Chief Education Officer, I.D.F.), published by the I.D.F., Tel Aviv, 1962

There has always been a consensus among the citizens of Israel to the
effect that the I.D.F. is one of the primary educational factors in the
country, which serves as a highly important agency for social development and as a melting pot for integration and immigrant absorption.

What is more, during all the years of the I.D.F.'s existence, it has
been highly evident that the larger part of the younger generation
joins the army willingly and usually full of positive expectations,
though they know full well that they must expect a hard and even
dangerous time, as far as living conditions and physical hardships are
concerned.

In a poll conducted by the I.D.F. amongst seventeen-year-old boys,
that is to say about a year before the draft, one of the questions asked
was whether they would be prepared to volunteer for the army if the
Compulsory Service Law should be abolished. Seventy per cent of the
boys answered in the affirmative, twenty per cent were doubtful and
only ten per cent answered in the negative. There is, of course, no
certainty whatsoever that the number of actual volunteers would be
anything like so large, but the poll certainly bears out that more than
three out of four boys regard military service as a positive factor from
their own personal viewpoint, and the two years which they are about
to spend in the army as a period which is likely to contribute, in one
way or another, to the progress of their maturity . . .

From the viewpoint of Israel as a modern Western society, many of
the immigrants from Islamic countries brought with them the general
educational and cultural backwardness of their countries of origin.* A

---

* This term expresses no value judgement, but records a relative fact:
backwardness is, in this case, measured from the viewpoint of the absorbing
society, which is essentially Western and modern.

situation arose in which definite correlations developed between the country of origin and the social standing of immigrants, deriving from their educational level (see table on p. 440). Moreover, statistics show that the problem tends, to some extent, to be inherited even by the second generation; although the gap has closed to a considerable extent, there are still signs of family deprivation even amongst native Israelis whose parents have come from Islamic countries.

The I.D.F., like any modern bureaucracy exposed day and night to public criticism, is extremely careful to pay attention to principles of achievement in the promotion of its soldiers and in their allocation to different duties. Moreover, as a machine dealing with the lives of human beings and with problems which might decide the fate of a nation, it is subject to a definite limit in its ability to distort the criteria of advancement and allocation of tasks in favour of considerations of social development. The establishment of a high correlation between the educational level and the degree of success in the army is inevitable . . .

Inevitably a situation develops where, after a year and a half of military service, we find that a considerable number of native Israelis or soldiers of Western origin have left the infantry companies because the army needs them for advanced professional or officer courses, while a fairly high percentage of soldiers who remain simple riflemen to the end of their service are of Islamic country origin (see table on p. 440). It can be seen from the table that a soldier is considered as a failure if he was dropped from service as a result of psychological, social or disciplinary maladjustment.

The soldiers are well aware of this situation and they could easily blame it on discrimination or unjustified preference for, or against, certain communities. However, as a matter of fact, such complaints are heard only rarely in the I.D.F.

We even have the evidence of a public commission of enquiry, which examined the situation of immigrants from North Africa in Israel, and saw fit to include the following passage in the report which it presented to the House of Representatives (Knesset):

We regard it as our duty to single out one institution which at all stages of our enquiry was mentioned exclusively in a favourable sense, namely the I.D.F. All those who have testified to discrimination have specifically pointed out that no discrimination and no favouritism has been found or felt in the I.D.F.*

The I.D.F. performs a range of additional non-military activities

* Report of the Commission of Enquiry on the Wadi Salib events, 1958.

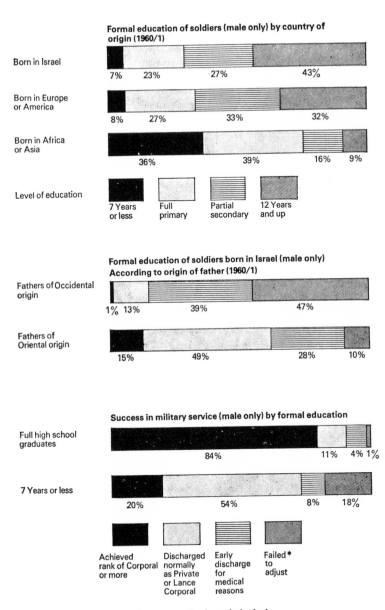

Formal education of soldiers (male only) by country of origin (1960/1)

Born in Israel
7% 23% 27% 43%

Born in Europe or America
8% 27% 33% 32%

Born in Africa or Asia
36% 39% 16% 9%

Level of education

7 Years or less — Full primary — Partial secondary — 12 Years and up

Formal education of soldiers born in Israel (male only) According to origin of father (1960/1)

Fathers of Occidental origin
1% 13% 39% 47%

Fathers of Oriental origin
15% 49% 28% 10%

Success in military service (male only) by formal education

Full high school graduates
84% 11% 4% 1%

7 Years or less
20% 54% 8% 18%

Achieved rank of Corporal or more — Discharged normally as Private or Lance Corporal — Early discharge for medical reasons — Failed* to adjust

*Soldiers dropped from service as a result of psychological or disciplinary maladjustment.

Fig 7

and functions in the course of its peace-time operations, not to mention such matters as assistance in flood disasters, retrieval of accident victims from inaccessible places and similar matters which are well known to many armies.

One further activity deserves particular mention, because it affects the general educational atmosphere in the I.D.F. and because it is symptomatic of the manner in which the I.D.F. envisages the extent of its responsibility in the educational field, namely, the service of girl soldiers in teaching assignments in border settlements.

All girls who graduate from teachers' seminaries enlist in the I.D.F. on completion of their studies. A number of them serve in teaching assignments within the army, in soldier schools. The others are given short periods of recruit training, and are then dispatched to the Ministry of Education and Culture for two years, and posted to ordinary primary schools in the border settlements, where it is difficult to find salaried teachers, and their whole army duties for those two years consist of teaching immigrant children. The army continues to maintain contact with them, to deal with their personal affairs and to exercise disciplinary supervision over them, while their functional activation as teachers is entrusted to the Ministry of Education.

The Ministry of Education needs more teachers for border settlements than there are graduates from seminaries, and moreover has started a widespread adult education project in the same border settlements. Therefore the I.D.F. provides, in addition to hundreds of qualified teachers, several hundreds of girls who have graduated from high school and volunteered for teaching assignments amongst the civilian population on the border, and these girls are also posted to the same settlements in the Negev and in Galilee, after taking short extension courses in adult education sponsored by the Ministry of Education . . .

In the first place it should be recalled that a large number of technical jobs in the I.D.F., including jobs that require a fairly long training period, are performed by draftees and not by regulars. This means that a considerable number of men have an opportunity for vocational training and for several years of experience on-the-job in a trade; the number of people who receive their vocational training in the army, or who at least consolidate their know-how by practical experience, is large in comparison with the range and scope of the economy. The army therefore is not at all a marginal factor in the training of vocational cadres, but is one of the main agents in that process.

The vocational training provided by the I.D.F. may be classified under three groups:

(a) Trades for which the training period is no more than a few months. Such trades are taught to soldiers even when they have had no previous contact with them. The short training period enables the army to derive benefit from the soldier's output for a comparatively long time after he has concluded his basic vocational training. Such boys learn the trade from the beginning, and also enjoy a long period of practical work in it.

(b) Trades with a long training period, but which are not specific to the army. For this purpose the army usually draws its tradesmen from boys who have been trained at civilian vocational schools, or as apprentices in the civilian industry. They are given short courses in which their know-how is adapted to the specific military equipment. These boys usually acquire in the army their experience in practical work, while the army, in turn, cooperates with the schools in order to adapt their curricula, to the maximum possible extent, to the needs of the army without affecting the civilian character of the school.

(c) Trades with a long training period which are specific to the army or for which the civilian industry and the civilian vocational training system do not provide sufficient candidates. For this purpose the I.D.F. maintains its own pre-military technical training system. There are special technical schools for the Air Force, the Signal Corps, the Navy, the Ordnance Corps and the Engineer Corps. These schools fill up year after year with thousands of boys of the age of sixteen or seventeen who stay there for a year or two and acquire specific vocational training and general education. Their years in national service will be applied to work in their trade...

What is more, part of the modern skills depend on basic orientations and on a type of manual ability and a certain trend of intelligence, which are developed in the child at an early age because of the prevailing occupation with certain games or with certain types of household equipment and the like. This fact causes certain adaptation difficulties, even in the second generation...*

* Some years ago, an interesting experiment was carried out in the I.D.F. It was found that recruits from Yemenite families failed in psycho-technical tests and mainly in the manipulation of mechanical tools. There were those that claimed that this involved an injustice and that the Yemenites should be subjected to special tests that would bring out their natural abilities such as threading beads or work requiring fast finger movements. When the experiment was made, the percentage of success of the Yemenites in the new tests rose as a matter of course, but success in the psycho-technical test proved no longer to be a basis for prediction of the youngster's ability to succeed in the service. It was found that the I.D.F. as a modern organization requires types of mechanical aptitude which relate to wheels and squares but not to beads and thin threads.

For many years there has existed an I.D.F. regulation requiring every soldier who in his youth has not completed primary school to spend three months out of his term of service in a school designated to complete his primary education. Studies in this school are highly intensive* and at their conclusion a certificate is issued which is recognized by the Ministry of Education, and which attests that its holder has completed elementary school. This certificate is in great demand, because it enables the soldier to apply for better jobs. Eighty-five per cent of the soldiers attending the school are new immigrants from the Islamic countries and another seven per cent are born Israelis whose parents came from Islamic countries.

The practice has always been to let the soldier acquire his elementary education during the last three months of his service, after he has first completed his Hebrew language studies in regional schools and in the course of the military service itself.

In the year 1963, it was decided to make an attempt to transfer the study course to the beginning of the service. This decision was based on the assumption that there is a correlation between the educational standard and the prospects of success in the I.D.F. and on the belief, based on this assumption, that additional education would improve the youngsters' chances to make progress and achieve success in the I.D.F.

In the years 1963 and 1964 a number of experiments were undertaken in teaching the young soldiers immediately after their enlistment, even before they completed their basic training. The course of these studies was followed up scientifically and the prospects of these soldiers' military success were checked by means of a control group. To the surprise of many, these experiments proved to be a failure in all respects.

Even at the end of the service, one can still discern the remains of a psychological defence mechanism which deters the soldier from studying. While at this stage there are many soldiers who come willingly to the school, there are not a few who fear that they will reveal their ignorance and educational shortcomings and that they may appear to the outside world as needing special treatment.

* School hours are 9 a day apart from extra curricular activities in different fields of art and culture. Classes consist of 10 pupils each, and each class has two teachers. Students can therefore be dealt with on an almost individual basis. The subjects taught are Hebrew, arithmetic, general history, Jewish history, geography, citizenship, Bible and basic science. The overall number of school hours is 600. Details may be found in the pamphlet 'Education in the I.D.F.', 1966.

Nevertheless, experience has shown that in the adult soldier, at the end of his term of service, this opposition, which is due to fear rather than indifference, can be overcome.

A completely different situation prevailed in the courses which were held at the beginning of the service. As a matter of fact, it proved extremely difficult to conduct a course in an orderly manner. Most soldiers demonstrated extreme opposition to the very idea of learning. Indifference proved to be the lesser evil, since its alternatives were interruptions, lack of discipline, offensive attitudes to the teachers and malicious interference during the lessons. It became necessary to send many soldiers to jail, and, until the end of the course, the cooperation of a considerable part of the pupils could not be secured. Motivation for studying was close to nil.

Still more surprising were the results of the comparative follow-up of the measure of success of the pupils during their military service. It was found that the groups of soldiers who had been taught in the Military Education School at the beginning of their service proved subsequently to be somewhat worse than the soldiers of the control group; in other words, amongst the ex-pupils there were more who deserted, went to jail, were discharged for inadaptability, dropped out from combat units, or displayed other indicators of failure in service, and fewer of them were promoted or distinguished themselves as soldiers in any manner.

The unfavourable difference was too small to be meaningful, and may perhaps be explained on the grounds that every soldier needs an initial period of living in hard conditions and under rigid discipline as is the case in basic training camps, in order to get into the groove and adjust his behaviour to the needs of military discipline. The fact that the students passed their first months of service in an easier and more liberal atmosphere than that which is maintained in camp, and that the first thing that greeted them every morning was not the fearsome moustache of the sergeant-major but the pleasant smile of the girl teacher, confused their expectations and created within them an antagonism during the period of basic training which came after their study period.

In any case we certainly may be justified in concluding that the additional portion of education given to these soldiers did not improve their chances of success in the service . . .

The success of the educated soldier is due to understanding, emotional balance, self-assurance and overall mental factors, which are acquired by way of slow assimilation during many years of learning at an early age. A concentrated dose of study given to the adult can be useful to him in many other respects. But it cannot qualitatively change the intellectual capacity of the individual, and certainly not his character and his deeper mentality, the more so if it is provided in such a short time, and against the psychological opposition of the soldier himself.

The interesting phenomenon which we shall have to analyse for our purpose is the enormous difference between the learning motivation of the soldier at the beginning of his service and that at the end of his term. The difference is so large that it cannot be explained only by the age difference or by the small amount of knowledge which the soldier acquires during his service by way of diffusion.

The only reasonable explanation is connected with the profound changes which military service makes in the soldier's inner self-assurance, in his willingness to try his strength again in different fields, in the way in which he looks upon himself, and upon his life, and in his orientations and thoughts towards the surrounding world . . .

With the advancement of the national education system, the I.D.F. has also started to raise the standards of education which it provides for soldiers. This year, for the first time, a number of courses for post-elementary education up to 10th grade level have been opened for draftees in addition to the high schools for regulars, which have existed already for a long time. This particularly stresses the development of the ability to form abstract conceptions, the study of English, a more thorough acquaintance with the natural sciences and a development of the pupil's ability to express himself. These courses also conclude with the issue of certificates which are recognized by the government and serve as a good entrance ticket for all kinds of advanced vocational courses or for places of employment which offer jobs in a higher income bracket.

The second project is connected with the intention to encourage social and intellectual advancement from amongst the deprived communities themselves, and the creation of an elite which in the future will be able to carry on the load of social development.

Every year a group of youngsters originating from the Islamic countries, who have completed the secondary school, are sent to a special one-year extension course within their terms of service and at the expense of the I.D.F. The purpose of this extension course is to enable them to be admitted to the university and to provide them with a better starting line so that they may satisfy academic requirements and conclude their studies successfully.

Follow up at Israeli universities shows that out of every hundred students who have received this encouraging education aid in the I.D.F., about ninety succeed in concluding their studies and achieving graduate rank, while no more than five would be able to do so without the special programme.

Index

morale, 83, 101, 103, 108, 162,
164; of Egyptian Army, 326; of
Israeli civilians, 224; of Israeli
pilots, 200
Moshavim, founded, 4
Mosquito aircraft, 124, 192
Mount Gilboa, 268
Mount Hermon: Israeli raid on,
312; recaptured by Israelis, 392–
4; seized by Syrians, 373, 378,
390
Mount of Olives, 262, 270
Mount Scopus, 212, 260, 262, 268,
270
Morocco, intervention in 1973
War, 390
Mufti of Jerusalem, 9
Mustang aircraft, 124, 155
Mystère aircraft, 124, 125, 154,
155, 194, 229; Mark IV, 218;
Mark IVA, 192, 197

Nablus, 9, 260, 265, 268
Nafah battle, 373–6, 388
Nahal, 96, 139, 202, 421–3
Nahalin raid, 112
Naj Hammadi raid, 318
Nakhl, 255
Narkiss, Uzi, 74, 335
Nasser, President, 48, 135, 138, 165
166, 205; refusal to accept UN
ceasefire, 1967, 287; repudiates
UN cease fire, 321; secret visit
to Moscow, 323; and Tiran
Straits blockade, 224
National Command, *see* Haganah
'National Home', 7, 16, 22
National Religious party, 80
National Water Carrier, *see*
Jordan River waters plan
Navy, 67, 132–3, 258, 296–7;
strategic role of, 395
Nazis, 10, 16, 19, 205
Negev desert, 2, 76, 222
Netzer, Moshe, 74
night fighting, preference for by
paratroops, 216; abandoned in

favour of mechanization, 370–
71
'Night of the Bridges', 22
Nodedet, 13
Noratlas aircraft, 330
Nord aircraft, 155
notrim, 13, 15, 17
Nuri-es-Said, 143
nuclear weaponry, 329–30, 361

Oded Brigade, 36, 43, 45
officer corps, Egyptian, 234
officer corps, Israeli, 69–70, 71,
83–8, 183, 184, 203, 223, 335–6;
age statistics, 182; in Armour
Corps, 370; educational standards
of, 182, 185, 335; General rank
list, 433–7; job rotation, 181–2,
183; as pressure group, 221;
quality of reserve, 181; reform
of training by Dayan, 117;
shortage of, 83–4, 102; training
courses for, 86–7, 88; two-
careers scheme, 118
Oil diplomacy, 342, 397
Okunev, Col.-Gen., and Egyptian
air defences, 323
'Open Bridges' policy, 305
Operations: Dani, 41, 42, 68;
Dekel, 42; Hiram, 48, 68;
Horev, 48, 50, 64, 67, 68, 72;
Nachshon, 31, 61, 62; Sabha, 117;
Uvdah, 52; Yiftah, 55, 56;
Yoav, 47–8, 58, 63, 67, 68
'optional control', 163, 172–4; *see
also* Laskov
Ordnance Corps, 178–9, 180, 329
Oriental Jewry, educational
standards of, 185, 186
Orthodox Jewry, 2
Osa missile boats, 395
Ottoman Empire, 6–7
Ouragan aircraft, 124, 125, 192,
197, 218, 229, 230

Palestine, British conquest of, 7;
British evacuation of, 27, 31

War of 1967—*cont.*
strike by IAF, 225–31; Syrian
front, 272–81; Tal's tactics employed, 292–6; Israelis unprepared for, 213
War of Attrition (1969–71), 218,
302, 303, 314–27, 327, 331, 332,
358; on Canal front, 314–15, 338,
344; Egyptian anti-aircraft
defences, 350; and manpower
problems, 334; declared by
Nasser, 321; territorial defence
re-thinking, 333
War of October 1973, 337–97;
Baluza-Ras Sudar road battles,
345, 347, 352; Bar Lev, Haim,
appointed to Command, 355,
378; 'Bar Lev Line', 338–9;
abandoned by Israelis, 344, 356
Egyptian Canal crossing, 338,
344–5, 348, 376; Israeli Canal
crossing, 378–87; Egyptian 3rd
Corps trapped, 387; Syrian
attack in Golan, 338, 348;
Israeli strategy, 355–7, 377
missile sites destroyed by Israelis,
385–6; Israeli advance into
Syria, 389–90; Syrian Army
defeat, 391; Israeli defences
defeated, 352, 363, 364, 373
War Game, 1952, 130
War Game, 1953, 130
Warsaw Ghetto, 41
Weizmann, Chaim, 69
Weizmann, Ezer, 69, 202;
Commander of Air Force, 123,
193, 194, 197, 298; insistence on
cannon in aircraft, 199
West Bank, 75, 265; base for Arab
attacks, 108, 308
West Germany: arms supplies to
Israel, 170–71; helicopter
supplies, 194
White Paper of 1939, 16
Wingate, Orde Charles, 14–16
World War I, 2, 295
World War II, 187, 291, 295

World Zionist Organization
(WZO), 8, 69

Ya'ariv, Aharon, 220, 336, 339
Yadin, Yigal, 31, 39, 59, 63, 64, 69,
102, 130, 131; organizes Army
Reserve system, 88; Chief of
Staff, 75, 76; resignation, 101–2,
130
Yad Mordechai kibbutz, 41
Yaffe, Shaul, 127
Yafo destroyer, 331
Yarmuk River, 279
Yemen War, 166–7, 170, 209, 222,
344
Yiftah Brigade, 73, 101
Yishuv, 4, 6, 7, 12; conflict with
British, 14; political elite of, 69;
and Haganah, 18–19; and
Histadrut, 44; hostility of Arabs
to, 5, 8, 9; internal competitive
trends in, 43; and IZL, 18–19
Yoffe, Avraham, 79, 156, 157, 233,
234, 237, 258; and 'indirect
approach', 248
Yom Kippur War, *see* War of
1973

Z-class destroyers, 132, 331
Zahal, 1, 2, 37; anti-militaristic
attitude, 206; armoured warfare
principles, 92–3; Brigade system,
89–91; defensive war, 302;
discipline, 80–83; education
department, 438–46; equipment
problems, 41, 147, 362; growth
problems, 42–3, 169; agent of
transformation of immigrants,
205; maintenance problems, 179,
190–91; manpower branch, 186;
see also Manpower; mobility,
289–90; and positional warfare,
warfare, 318; rank structures,
84, 237, 335–6; reorganization,
45, 47, 397; and society in
Israel, 202–8; supply systems,
174–5; support corps, 202, 292;